# ON THE SIDE OF TRUTH

# On the Side
## of Truth
### GEORGE N. SHUSTER
### An Evaluation with Readings

EDITED BY
**Vincent P. Lannie**

UNIVERSITY OF NOTRE DAME PRESS
NOTRE DAME                                    LONDON

**Library of Congress Cataloging in Publication Data**

Shuster, George Nauman, 1894-
  On the side of truth.

  1. Shuster, George Nauman, 1894-      I. Lannie,
Vincent P., ed. II. Title.
LD7251.N288S45  1974      378.1'12'0924  [B]
ISBN 0-268-00520-6          73-11564

Manufactured in the United States of America

*For*
*The Lights In My House*

*Joanne*
*and*
*Christian*

# Contents

# Foreword

How can one write adequately about another human being whom he loves? Poets have had the least trouble, because they were most often men writing about women, and poetry has stronger wings and higher flight than prose. I lose on both counts, because this is prose and George Shuster, if anything, is very much a man.

I suppose the first thing I can say about him is that in many ways he reminds me of my father and, since my father has been dead for more than a decade, I have more or less unconsciously looked upon George as a father. I'm sure that I merely join a veritable army in doing this. So many, young and old, have looked to him as a father that he must be forgiven if he very often speaks to all of us as a father, in the spiritual, intellectual, moral, as well as personal, sense. And we are all grateful for his love, his words, his kindly wisdom.

Another measure of my esteem for George Shuster is my conviction that if I were given one choice of a man who might, because of the whole thrust of his life and thought, be immediately ordained a priest, I would without hesitation choose George Shuster. I happen to esteem priesthood most highly, for what it is and what it does, in relation to the Person of Christ and His divine mission. It is in this context that, while he has always been a quintessential layman and an ideal husband and father, there is something essentially priestly about his relationship to others. George might well prefer to be praised in other words, but each of us must prefer the words that are best in our worlds, however imperfectly they may capture reality in another universe.

I am particularly indebted to George Shuster since he stepped in to help me at a time when he could have done many other more agreeable or simpler tasks—also more lucrative. He had just finished twenty years as President of Hunter College. He had many offers to do very enjoyable or otherwise very pleasant tasks all around the world. I asked him to return to where he had received his baccalaureate and master's degree in English thirty years ago.

He could have listened to Thomas Wolfe who said, "You can't go home again." But George did come home again, and I am happy to say that it was really home to him.

We had real problems. We wanted to balance off a great deal of science and engineering research with equally or more important research in the humanities and the social sciences—under the rubric of the Center for the Study of Man in Contemporary Society—of which George became the eminent Director.

George Shuster had hardly spent a year at the University before he became the confidant of young and older scholars alike. They all depended on him to bring to life (and financial support) areas long dead or at least moribund. With very little internal financial support from the University, George inspired and helped to be supported from outside many millions of dollars of humanistic and social science research. Almost single handedly, he initiated a wide range of research in Catholic education, Latin American and African Studies, demography, Soviet and Chinese Studies, and a whole host of other important academic fields of research. Overnight, we were rejuvenated.

All this happened during a time when Notre Dame passed from clerical to lay control. As a member of the new lay Board of Trustees, George helped give direction and purpose to the new Board. The enlightened fashion in which it operated was due in no small measure to his wise counsel.

I cannot adequately describe what it meant to have George Shuster as a personal assistant during these crucial years. I can only say that this very night on which I pen these lines we had a dinner honoring George Shuster, one of our Trustees, his wife, and family (some Notre Dame graduates and students) being our hosts.

At the conclusion of the dinner, I was handed a letter saying that our hosts wished to contribute a large amount of money to the University in honor of George Shuster. Even in his present retirement, George continues to help us.

I salute Professor Vincent Lannie for collecting George Shuster's writings in the areas of religion, politics, and education. These deserve to be read and pondered by those who cherish George Shuster's life and thought.

For myself, I still cherish the presence of George Shuster, as this very evening we talked and discussed and I was, as always, inspired. There will never be another George Shuster at Notre Dame, but while the true George and his lovely wife, Doris, are with us, we need no others. May the good Lord bless and keep them.

Theodore M. Hesburgh, C.S.C.
*President, University of Notre Dame*

# George N. Shuster:
# A Personal Glimpse

High on the eleventh floor of the University of Notre Dame's Memorial Library, George Shuster maintains a large but unpretentious office. From this citadel overlooking the campus, "the old man," as many of his university colleagues refer to him, retains an interest in the Center for the Study of Man in Contemporary Society. Now Director Emeritus, he still shares the vision that has geared the center to examine the multifaceted dimensions of man's role and destiny in a changing world and expanding universe. Still vigorous and alert at seventy-nine, he continues a lifetime habit of rising early and spending several hours at his desk before and after breakfast. Although his steps are slower than in the past, he spends afternoons in the office unless he is presenting a speech or attending a conference. A man of unalterable principle, Shuster is generous in interpersonal relations but tough as nails when convinced of a position. Yet his cherished belief that graciousness and courtesy are human virtues of the highest order has not left him—even when he bemoans their absence in contemporary society or is harassed by interviewers seeking information about his life.

Shuster lives with his wife of forty-nine years in a home filled with mementoes of a distinguished life. A charming conversationalist with strong views, Doris regards her husband as an intellectual who has always exhib-

Adapted from the article by Vincent P. Lannie in *Leaders in American Education,* Seventieth Yearbook of the National Society for the Study of Education, Part II (Chicago: University of Chicago Press, 1971), pp. 306-320.

1

ited a remarkable degree of courtesy, gentleness, and strength—qualities which attracted her to him fifty years ago when he was her professor. Doris has had her share of arguments with him, especially since she believes that occasional quarrels foster a successful marriage. In half serious and half humorous tones, she fumes because Shuster cannot zipper the back of her dresses and carelessly burns holes in the furniture with his infernal pipes. But she would not trade a day of her married life and would cherish another half century with her husband. Shuster is much too reserved to express deep feelings for his wife. Yet on one occasion he did pay tribute to "the light in my own house." He had just retired from Hunter College in New York City and had finished writing his recollections as president. In the last paragraph of *The Ground I Walked On,* Shuster, reminiscing about the bitter and the sweet he and his wife had experienced together, ends the book with these sentiments: "It is often said a wife is the shadow of her husband, or that a husband is the shadow of his wife. That is not true of us. We made one shadow, and for it I am in this place saying thanks."[1]

Shuster wrote his memoirs in the same year he retired from Hunter. He received several offers but accepted the Reverend Theodore Hesburgh's invitation to serve as the first lay assistant to the president of Notre Dame. He had been a Notre Dame undergraduate before World War I and returned as an English instructor after military service in Europe. He joined the staff of *Commonweal* magazine in 1924 and in time became its managing editor. During the Spanish Civil War he resigned from *Commonweal* rather than compromise his anti-Franco views. After completing a doctorate in literature at Columbia University, he received a fellowship which enabled him to visit Germany (though not for the first time) and witness the Nazi occupation of the land of his forefathers.

Shuster returned to New York on the eve of the outbreak of World War II. One day in 1939 he received a call from Carlton J. Hayes, noted Columbia historian, Catholic convert, and friend from *Commonweal* days, to attend a tea at his home. Unaware of the purpose of this invitation, Shuster arrived to find the chairman of the Board of Higher Education of New York City seated with his friend. Shuster was surprised when he was offered the presidency of Hunter College. In a city where religious affiliations are integrally related to political realities, it had been a tradition for

---

[1] George N. Shuster, *The Ground I Walked On* (New York: Farrar, Straus and Cudahy, 1961), p. 252. (See also University of Notre Dame Press, enlarged edition, 1969.)

Hunter's president to be a Catholic. The present incumbent had proved unsatisfactory and was retiring at the end of the year. Meetings with the Board and a faculty committee went well and both groups urged Shuster to accept the post. A prominent New York Catholic and a good friend, John Burke, president of B. Altman Company, urged him to consider the proposal since Shuster was a leading Catholic liberal who could function effectively with Catholics and non-Catholics alike. Because of the political influence of the "Power House" on Madison Avenue, the residence of the Archbishop of New York, Burke advised Shuster to seek an interview with the then Archbishop Francis Spellman "for the purpose of sniffing out what the climate might be." The meeting went well and the churchman promised not to interfere with any of Shuster's decisions at Hunter. Spellman did suggest that Shuster refrain from voicing opinions on controversial noneducational issues (he had done so regularly in his *Commonweal* editorials) advice which quickly "went through both ears without delay."[2] Overcoming doubts about his qualifications for an administrative office, and with the encouragement of his wife, Shuster accepted the position. Looking back on her husband's decision after thirty years, Doris believes he saw an opportunity to put Hunter on the academic map and to show non-Catholics that there were Catholics genuinely interested in American public education.

For twenty-one years Shuster presided over the destiny of Hunter College—a period that witnessed the end of the depression, World War II, the rise of the iron and bamboo curtains, and the spectre of McCarthyism. Hunter became an integral part of his life and he affectionately referred to it as "the greatest college community center to be found anywhere in the world."[3] Although abortive Communist attempts to penetrate faculty and student body caused him many a harried day, they never diminished his belief in academic freedom and the right of the faculty to pursue truth as they saw it.

As president of a municipal college, Shuster rubbed shoulders with leading New York politicians. He came to know three of the city's mayors quite well: Fiorello LaGuardia, "The Little Flower;" William O'Dwyer, whose "Celtic charm, presence, and a measure of the rarest kind of social tact" did not preclude benefacting old cronies who merited no help; and Robert Wagner, whose "remarkable urbanity" proved that "a gentleman's

[2] *Ibid.,* pp. 22-23.
[3] *Ibid.,* p. 138.

government can in some measure survive in New York." But it was the unpredictable and flamboyant LaGuardia who profoundly impressed Shuster. Relations between both men remained cordial even when a full measure of diplomacy was needed to keep them intact. Though his first meeting with LaGuardia found His Honor with sleeves rolled up eating frankfurters and potato salad, Shuster gradually penetrated the complexity and depth of the mayor's personality. If "there was something of the Cola di Rienzi in his blood" and the showman who loved to conduct an orchestra or to read the comics over the radio during a newspaper strike, he also possessed "a concern for humanity no social worker has ever equalled." "A compound of Garrison and taxi-driver, of cop and preacher, of dictator and humble servant," LaGuardia sometimes frightened Shuster and occasionally annoyed him with boorish antics. Yet he could not imagine "any man in City Hall" with whom association would have been a greater honor.[4]

On the academic side, Shuster formed a close association with Alvin Johnson, founder and first president of the New School of Social Research. Johnson and Shuster shared similar beliefs about the life of the mind and the spirit. Both men were intellectual mavericks and both men abhorred any brand of totalitarianism. Johnson's capacity for intellectual pioneering was manifested in the New School—a place "in which there was a surprise round every corner." From the outset he enthroned freedom as queen of the New School and welcomed any scholar who had not "tied himself to a totalitarian chariot wheel."[5] As a result, he threw open the doors of the institution to learned victims of totalitarianism and championed the conviction that a vibrant religious faith was the "supreme barrier" to the march of Nazism.

Shuster also entertained a distant respect for Nicholas Murray Butler, president of Columbia University. Butler was dean of American college presidents at the time, and detractors disparaged him as "Nicholas Miraculous" when he became more dogmatic with each passing year at Morningside Heights. But at last Butler's tenure came to an end and LaGuardia presented a citation honoring the educator, now old, blind, and feeble. A police band played the "Sidewalks of New York" outside Butler's home as he responded to the mayor's speech with tears in his tired eyes. Although many at Columbia cheered the end of the Butler era, Shuster felt that it would be "a generation or ten" before a man of his depth and magnetism

[4] *Ibid.*, pp. 7-21.
[5] *Ibid.*, pp. 140-142.

would grace the university campus. Butler's great "mistake had been," declares Shuster, "that he knew not when the time had come to go."[6] Shuster would not make the same mistake; he would leave Hunter before madatory retirement age.

During Shuster's tenure Hunter inaugurated its concert series and opera workshop—both of which enjoyed considerable success in succeeding years. Many famous artists performed in the college auditorium, and Shuster remembers each one of them on an individual basis: Lotte Lehmann, singing the "Ave Maria" to the point of exhaustion; Emmanuel Feuermann, a "cellist of incomparable depth and skill"; Vladimir Horowitz, "frail, reticent and tempestuous"; Ezio Pinza, whose "matchless voice had risen to song and encore until very late"; Bruno Walter, "the beloved of the Lord"; Artur Schnabel, who played "gloriously, though outwardly with what almost seemed Prussian precision"; Lily Pons, "delicate, exquisite and magical"; Elizabeth Schwartzkopf, "tranquil and reflective, unforgettably beautiful"; Renata Tibaldi, "who sang like a queen and had the graciousness of one"; Irmgard Seefried, "genial, earthy and ready to enjoy a gust of laughter"; Hilda Gueden, "tempestuous and sometimes malicious"; and Artur Rubenstein, "who surely merits whatever kind of halo Hunter College could place above his head." But two artists have remained especially close to Shuster: Regina Resnik graduated from Hunter; and Martina Arroyo came to the college from Hunter High School. Eventually both were acclaimed in the operatic world, and Shuster long beamed as an admiring surrogate father.[7]

In addition to expanding the fine arts, Shuster opened the doors of the college to talented refugees who had escaped the Nazi terror which brutalized Europe in the late 1930's and early 1940's. In a macabre way, Europe's loss was America's gain, since an assortment of intellectuals, Jew and Gentile, found their way to the safe shores of this country. On many an evening during those dark years, people overflowed the Hunter College auditorium to hear these exiles talk about contemporary tyranny and their scholarly and professional interests. The guest list was indeed impressive: Carlo Sforza and Max Ascoli from Italy; Thomas Mann, Heinrich Bruening, Manfred George, and Alfred Bassermann from Germany; Jacques and Raissa Maritain from France; Kurt von Schuschnigg from Austria; and countless others from eastern and central Europe. Anyone who espoused freedom

[6]*Ibid.*, pp. 41-43.
[7]*Ibid.*, pp. 175-184.

and opposed totalitarianism was welcomed at Hunter and entertained at the Shuster home in Connecticut.[8]

Partisan politics was forbidden on campus, though various groups were free to express views about civic matters. Occasionally this open-forum policy drew criticism from contending organizations. At such times Shuster, reared in midwestern LaFollette liberalism, would call attention to the words inscribed on the south wall of Hunter's building: "We are of different opinions at different hours, but we may always be said to be at heart on the side of truth."[9] Shuster had come across this passage in Emerson's *Conduct of Life,* and it remained an integral canon of his intellectual and moral creed.

American college presidents traditionally have engaged in public service. Shuster was no exception, having served on national commissions during and after World War II. With the outbreak of war in 1941, he sat as a member of New York's Enemy Alien Boards, which screened Germans, Italians, and Japanese who had been detained by the Federal Bureau of Investigation. Later the Department of Justice established appeal boards at various internment camps throughout the country. And although Shuster was a specialist in German affairs with a native command of the language, bureaucratic inefficiency assigned him to a camp for Japanese at Santa Fe, New Mexico!

After the war Shuster was appointed as deputy to John J. McCloy, United States high commissioner for Germany, "for the beautiful but presumably cantankerous state of Bavaria." As a leading American educator and Catholic who spoke fluent German and who had previously visited the area, his task was to aid in restoring this wartorn region and especially in reforming its educational system. One newspaper applauded the fact that the new commissioner was the president of a "famous college for hunters," hoping perhaps that he would lift the American ban on hunting rifles for Germans. Shuster was aware that Bavarian anti-semitism indicated a degree of superficiality of much of Bavaria's Catholic heritage. Yet he never indicted all Bavarian Catholics for participating in the Nazi "final solution" of the Jews and even insisted that not a few of them possessed the gift of distinguishing between "human frailty and inhuman malice." This last sentiment loomed important to Shuster as the American occupation attempted to democratize Germany along American models. Newspapers, communica-

8 *Ibid.,* pp. 142-170.
9 *Ibid.,* p. 58.

tion media, and schools were reformed; and organizations such as Parent Teacher Associations and civil liberties groups emerged as examples of a vibrant democratic life. No doubt these efforts introduced a kind of leaven. But Shuster contended that ultimately "the Bavarians would remain what they had always been, just as Virginians will perennially be Virginians. The Bavarian dearly loves freedom, but it is not our kind. He is tolerant of others because fundamentally he is tolerant of his own foibles." And unless some deeply profound changes affect Bavarian life, "he will go right on being a person who on the one hand piously makes a pilgrimage to some shrine like Andechs and on the other has a love affair at Fasching time."[10]

In another postwar assignment Shuster interviewed captured generals and Nazi officials to secure information for a future evaluation of wartime policies. He thought that the generals were a superior lot who should not have been put on trial for directing Hitler's war effort. "What can a soldier do but try to win the battles which the civilians make it necessary for him to fight?" questioned Shuster to the perplexing dilemma of public duty and private responsibility.[11] But for Nazi officialdom he had no such reservations. These were the vermin who implemented Hitler's inhuman cruelties throughout Europe—especially the destruction of six million Jews.

Shuster's most memorable conversations were with Hermann Goering over a period of several days. Imprisoned and certain to receive the death penalty at Nuremberg, Goering still impressed Shuster as an "extraordinary swashbuckler who had lost none of his verve or presence of mind" and who exercised a "curious fascination" over his guards and fellow prisoners. His lethargic responses to questions were usually accurate though some answers "were colored by his delight in playing a game of wits." But on one occasion Goering's mask of aplomb fell as he struggled for the right words. In this conversation Shuster theorized that had Hitler condemned the Japanese attack on the United States, there would not have been war between their countries and Germany would now not be in total defeat. There was a long moment of silence. Then Goering lifted his eyes from the ground, measured his interrogator intently, and responded, "If I believed that, Professor, I would go upstairs and commit suicide." Shuster smugly replied that prison precautions precluded any such possibility. "A man can take his life," Goering answered scornfully, "any time he wants to." These

[10] *Ibid.*, pp. 189-203.
[11] *Ibid.*, p. 226.

words etched deeply into Shuster's mind when some time later Goering kept his promise and cheated humanity's verdict with a vial of poison.[12]

Yet Shuster meditated not so much on these men who were prisoners of a diabolical ideal as upon the countless Germans who understood Hitler's intentions and surrendered their lives in opposition to them. Nevertheless, he can never forget the Nazi evil and the "human wolves" who screamed their fanatical glee as millions were fed to the ovens as sacrificial victims upon the altar of a warped genius.

During the 1940's Shuster participated on a Department of State committee to advise the government's newly organized cultural relations program. He spent long and arduous hours discussing various conceptions of cultural relations with Vice President Henry Wallace ("he ... invariably astonished me by seeming to be asleep and then suddenly proceeding to comment with great force and originality on the subject under discussion"), James T. Shotwell, James B. Conant, and Archibald MacLeish.[13] The time was not wasted since he felt that the work of this committee found fruition in the creation of UNESCO. He served on the American delegation to the conference which gave birth to this branch of the United Nations. There was great disagreement over the name of this organization, with the scientists demanding that "Science" be included in the title. All the delegates agreed that "Education" should be represented, while a significant number opted for "Culture" as well. In true consensus fashion all the options were included, and the United Nations Educational, Scientific and Cultural Organization came into existence.

Some associates discounted Shuster's association with an organization that would be of little value toward the improvement of world conditions. Certainly he experienced discouragement when it was used as a pawn in the cold war between East and West. But he remains committed to UNESCO as an effective educational instrument in improving the lot of the underdeveloped countries of the world. "I cannot imagine that any agency could plot for itself a larger task," concludes Shuster, "or one more likely to prove worthwhile if it were accomplished."[14]

Shuster experienced pangs of guilt because national and international responsibilities meant prolonged absences from Hunter. Yet he remains con-

[12] *Ibid.*, pp. 222-224.
[13] *Ibid.*, p.219
[14] *Ibid.*, pp. 238-245.

vinced that these excursions made him more cognizant of human needs than if he had remained in his presidential chair. But by 1961 he was tired, having been Hunter's president for over twenty years. Moreover, municipal partisan politics made it increasingly difficult for him to keep his sanity and often his integrity. Mindful of the painful consequences of Nicholas Murray Butler's overstay at Columbia years before, and with his wife's support, Shuster resigned from Hunter. He remained adamant in this decision, resisting the tempting offer to become chancellor of the municipal college system of New York City. Hunter would never lose his interest or his esteem, for "I remain deeply grateful for every year I was privileged to spend at Hunter."[15]

Though sometimes critical of the University of Notre Dame, Shuster's affection for his alma mater had never waned. Yet it was "in quite a dispassionate mood" that he accepted Father Hesburgh's invitation to attempt to develop an idea which the university and the Ford Foundation had spelled out as the Center for the Study of Man in Contemporary Society. It was to provide the core round which research in the humanities and social sciences would investigate man in the universe. Since Shuster wished to encourage religious studies, he was also instrumental in establishing the Institute for Advanced Religious Studies. Finally, as assistant to the president and as a member of Notre Dame's board of trustees, he shared in formulating decisions which thrust the university into the forefront of Catholic higher education.

The man of affairs represents only one part of Shuster's life. There is also the man of letters and contemplation who has expressed his thought and ideals in books, articles, and pamphlets. These two components have rarely been at odds, for the active man has really been a manifestation of the reflective man. A devoted Catholic who has not always fared well with the Church's leadership, he has written poignantly of his religious faith—the central force in his life—of literature, politics, and education. A political activist who has spent his life opposing totalitarianism, he has recorded vivid impressions of Nazism, Fascism, and Communism. An educator for most of his adult life, he has detailed—by no means systematically—a philosophy of education with special emphasis on Catholic education.

Shuster has remained a potent voice in American and international affairs for over forty years. He has made mistakes and he would be the first to admit them. But he may always be said to have been "on the side of truth."

[15] *Ibid.,* p. 50.

# I

# AN AUTOBIOGRAPHY

I was born in what still is one of the most charming small towns in Wisconsin, even though progress as understood during the early twentieth century destroyed some gracious structures and replaced them with hideous ones. Lancaster, when I appeared on the scene, was a county seat and therefore assured of a permanent complement of judges, lawyers, sheriffs, and similar dignitaries. The jail was, to be sure, usually occupied only by a couple of old soaks, who as they recovered from their hangovers stared gloomily through the grilled windows. Our asylum and "poor farm" just outside the city limits were more lugubrious institutions, and as youngsters our blood curdled at the news that somebody we knew had been sent off to one or the other. But above all, we were dominated by memories of the Civil War. Lancaster erected the first monument in memory of the boys in blue in the whole of the United States, and surprisingly this was and remains in its simple way very beautiful. Of course we likewise had our surviving heroes, intact or minus an arm or a leg. Because of what the area economy had been, namely a blend of lead mining and farming, our best families had come from the East or the South. We therefore had, though the temperature tumbled to twenty degrees below zero in winter, charming southern style houses with great french windows, as well as New England

George N. Shuster, "An Autobiography," in *Leaders in American Education,* Seventieth Yearbook of the National Society for the Study of Education, Part II (Chicago: University of Chicago Press, 1971), pp. 277-303.

13

colonials. Our own house was New York colonial, to which my father had added a long annex in no style whatever.*

Both of my grandfathers lived on farms, though this was more or less accidental. The one on my paternal side had come over because his father, a notary public, had been forced to leave Germany in a hurry by reason of what happened in 1848. It was a staunchly Catholic group, though by no means puritanical. My father was born as one of a sizable family in a stone house built in a picturesque little valley, and apparently there was plenty of singing and storytelling. My mother's parents had been lured from Pennsylvania by an adroit real estate man, who had given them a most alluring description of the farm on which they made a down payment. It turned out to be mostly woodland, with a relatively large log house and an orchard from peddling the products of which my grandfather paid his bills for quite some time. He was a Lutheran, but gave little or no attention to what this implied. His wife, however, was deeply religious. I still have her book of daily devotions; and if she lived up to what this advised she must have lived austerely indeed. But she appears to have been rather genial and to have sung innumerable German folk songs with considerable ability.

I was reared a Catholic and sent to the parochial school. My mother did not, however, transfer her allegiance from Lutheranism until years after she married. But until quite a bit later we saw little or nothing of our Lutheran relatives, who then proved to be very likable.

My most vivid boyhood memories have to do with a retired U.S. Navy captain, presumably Congregationalist, who built the replica of a battleship on his front lawn in which his two orphaned grandchildren and I played day in and out, sinking pirate vessels or enemy cruisers with little wooden replicas of cannons and doing similar deeds of valor. The captain had also rigged up a telescope in the attic of his house, with the help of which we could see the Mississippi twelve miles away, though there was only a small gap in its magnificent range of bluffs. I am afraid that these experiences, plus all the Civil War heroics, filled me with romantic dreams of martial valor, which virtue, if it be one, was markedly absent from my family tree.

*The pertinent dates follow. I was born on August 27, 1894, was admitted to Notre Dame in 1912 and awarded an A.B. three years later. After military service (1917-1919) I returned to Notre Dame as professor of English and later, chairman of the Department of English, earning an M.A. degree in 1920. During 1924 I joined the staff of the *Commonweal*, later becoming managing editor. Having left the *Commonweal*, I was a fellow of the Social Science Research Council from 1937 to 1939. Then I became acting president and, a year later, president of Hunter College (1939-1960). In 1961 I returned to Notre Dame as professor of English and assistant to the president.

As a matter of fact, I came later on within half a foot of embarking on a military career, but desisted for reasons which are of no special interest. The captain's estimable lady, settled by a strange quirk of fate in our town, was one of the earliest graduates of Smith College. When I was ten or so, she began giving me copies of *Harper's* which introduced me to a world of which I had never dreamed. I believe she rather enjoyed talking with me, because her husband was a dour man who never approved of entertaining anybody. In retrospect this seems a great pity for there were some people in the town who might have interested and entertained her.

There was a good deal of interreligious bickering in Lancaster, though the small Catholic minority normally ran for cover only when some itinerant ex-monk came to town and relit the fires of the Inquisition. It never bothered me very much, except that in school we were asked to pray for the poor Protestants who as a consequence of not having the true faith would all doubtless end up in hell. I was distressed about this, particularly because a very pretty little Methodist girl with long blond hair lived just down our street. Otherwise our prejudices were purely political. My mother was invariably greatly impressed by her favorite candidate for the presidency, but if after eight months in office he had not espoused her recipes for the improvement of the nation she referred to him at best with veiled contempt. My father and I became partisans of Robert La Follette, Sr., by reason of hearing him speak for two hours from the rear of a little whistle-stop train.

A few of the leading merchants in our town were later on revealed as German Jews. My father talked with them in their native language and held them in high esteem. It never occurred to us at the time to think of them as being Jewish, and if it had it would not have mattered in the least. Of course, I should have thought, yes, the Jews did crucify Christ, but Mr. Schneider and Mr. Blumenthal weren't there at the time. As for Negroes, my grandfather's farm was surrounded by a semicircle of farms which a Southern planter had bought for the slaves he freed. As a result, my mother was for some time the only white child in the one-room school she attended. She was treated like a princess; and all during my boyhood a former classmate or other used to drop in for a chat. And then there was Tom Greene, one of the freed slaves, in whose wagon I rode for days during summers, listening to yarns which I have long since wished I could remember.

Then for some reason or other I belatedly took an interest in my studies and was held to be a bright boy. My mother having been taken seriously ill, it was decided that I should go to a boarding preparatory school. No Catholic boy in our area had ever done that before, excepting one who had left to enter a seminary. The parish priest was therefore consulted and it was decided that I should go to St. Lawrence College, which was as like a seminary as could be managed. It turned out to be a Swiss preparatory school transplanted to the United States. The course of study would induce in a modern American lad feelings akin to despair. Bed and board were spartan, indeed, but the atmosphere was warm and human. There I met Father Corbinian, beyond any question the greatest teacher I have known. He taught German and Greek, and as a result I devoted myself to the tasks he assigned and the vistas he opened with all the enthusiasm I could muster. I read immense quantities of German literature, from Goethe at one end of the spectrum to Karl May on the other. But the farthest point I reached in Greek was a couple of Plato's *Dialogues* and one or two of the orations of Demosthenes.

The next stage in my development was Notre Dame, then called a university because by so doing it was easier to get a charter. Frankly, I chose to go there because it had a football team and therefore sounded less formidably academic than St. Lawrence College. One afternoon of practice convinced me that football was not for me. I was strong and wiry at the time, but no match for the replicas of Hercules who had been recruited. Soon, however, I found myself in great demand for totally other reasons. Because of the intensive work done in preparatory school, I was adjudged to have amassed credits well in excess of those demanded by Notre Dame for matriculation and therewith triumphantly became a sophomore. This fact must have been very impressive because I was besought by a professor of English to correct his freshman themes. A more dreadful assortment of scrawling attempts at prose cannot be imagined, but there was one boy who wrote so well that I sought him out. We remained friends until he died, though he never lived up to his promise. Not long thereafter the librarian looked me up and suggested that during certain hours I sit at the front desk of his establishment and dole out books. This proved to be the most desirable employment I have ever had. In those days of teaching by textbook, virtually no one disturbed my leisure. Owing largely to the efforts of two or three extraordinary men, the library was for its time far better than anyone could have expected.

I read widely and thus began my first personal intellectual adventure. The course offerings in psychology were perfunctory but on the library shelves were the books of James, Ladd, and other Americans, as well as those of the Germans on whom they had leaned. If I had thought at the time of an academic career, psychology would no doubt have been my chosen field. But—and this will probably show how isolated we were from the mainstream of university life—all the devotees of the liberal arts at Notre Dame at that time thought that the rainbow's end was a great career in journalism or creative writing. Some of us succeeded in a measure, though none won Pulitzer prizes. At any rate, James remained a strong influence on my intellectual life. Let me add that the two chores, neither of which I had asked for, netted enough to enable me to pay my way at Notre Dame. My parents were thereby enabled to send my sisters to college.

I majored in the classics, which were avoided by virtually all students except those belonging to the captive audience assembled by the seminary which trained priests for the Congregation of the Holy Cross, which governed the university. It was fortunate that I did, because Scheier, educated at Leyden in Holland, was an excellent if eccentric scholar. We ranged far, at a rapid rate, doing the whole of the *Odyssey* in one semester and nearly all of *Appolonius Rhodius* in another, ending later with the corpus of Greek drama, from Aeschylus to Aristophanes. The courses in Latin literature were more perfunctory, though we did some rather unusual readings. Then I discovered one day that I could read Plato in Greek with no more than cursory help from the dictionary. To me that seemed a feat as unusual as finding the North Pole.

The rest of my course of study was routine, excepting for the university's debating team, which demanded wide reading about some selected theme of current interest as well as writing and speaking skills. There were distinguished scientists on the campus, for example, Julius Nieuwland, who found out how to make artificial rubber, but to my great regret in later life I learned nothing of what they had to offer excepting for some work in general biology. There was a good course in early Greek philosophy, but all the others in this field were taught against the background of a series of textbooks thought to be neo-Scholastic in character. The references to Aquinas or Augustine were perfunctory. But my hours in the library brought me close to Newman, who with Plato no doubt steered my thinking in the way in which it was to go. I suppose, in essence, this meant that I came to believe that, although tradition and the conclusions at which it had arrived are important and even in some sense conclusive, emphasis must be placed on the discovery of new ideas and their development.

The Notre Dame of those days was provincial, rather lazy (only the engineering students seemed to work hard), not too inquisitive, and permeated by religious feeling. The old Latin Liturgy was rendered well, the Sunday sermons were usually good, and receiving the Sacraments was taken for granted. Nobody pushed compendia of dogma down our throats. Not a few students were disturbed by evolution, but this had no terrors for me because of Zahm's *Evolution and Dogma,* way ahead of its time. But I was uneasy about some trends in modernist theology and brooded over Winston Churchill's *Inside of the Cup,* which was both novel and tract. But for the most part these were passing moods. The university campus was beautiful, the atmosphere friendly, the rules normally circumventible. Nobody went home on weekends. The student body ate in common and the president was seated at the head table with some other campus dignitaries. No one had a car or even dreamed of owning one. There was a street car which clattered to and from South Bend, but most of our locomotion was done on foot, sometimes on walks many miles long. Good theater was brought to South Bend by companies on tour, an amiable practice to which TV called a halt, so that we could see Maude Adams, Julia Marlowe, and many another person of ability and fame. No doubt we boys, glued to our chairs in an era before that of picture magazines, could be completely bowled over by the beauty of an actress. There were also flourishing athletic programs, notably in football and baseball, though there was then only a small attendance on the part of the general public. In short, Notre Dame was what the people of the United States have forgotten there could be, namely, an academic community in which everybody knew everybody and in which friendships were fostered and communication made an art.

Leaving, I had some chance to learn the hardships of becoming a writer. I supplemented my earnings in various ways, some of them fairly lucrative and others not. Trying my hand at being a reporter, I found myself in various situations often boring and sometimes dangerous. Rejection slips in number went into the waste basket, there were some acceptances, and I wrote a novel, the only copy of which was lost by a publisher's reader. At the time I could have shot him, which treatment was being accorded by most of my novel's heroes to their human environment, but I have long since been grateful. Then I was mustered into military service.

Having been a captain in the Notre Dame cadet corps, remote from the realities of Verdun though that was, I could have had a commission virtually for the asking. But I could not bring myself to accept one. The war seemed to me unnecessary and the decision to enter it fallacious. On the other hand, it appeared to me completely obvious that I could not reconcile with my conscience not sharing the burden with others of my age. Why should I imagine that because of my superior education and presumably superior outlook I should burn up my draft card and let others do the grimy job? And so I entered military service as a private, was transferred to an intelligence unit because of my knowledge of the German language, and then found myself at the front as a member of a Franco-American group assigned to pick up enemy telephone and telegraph conversation. I was very lucky to emerge from the fighting a very much alive, though in many ways worn to a frazzle, sergeant first-class. From this vantage point in time I should like to salute my French comrades, now surely all passed on to the land of shadows and benediction. Whatever people have said latterly about the country of de Gaulle does not apply to them. They were soldiers, sometimes scoundrels after their fashion, but gentlemen. I would have walked confidently with any of them through a night of fire.

Then, because of my knowledge of German, there followed several months of service as an interpreter for an Intelligence colonel in occupied Germany. This was my first visit to the country the literature of which I had read so diligently. Since most of my days in the performance of this kind of duty were spent in the beautiful Moselle Valley (I was sent farther east upon occasion), I drank my fill of the landscape and what it meant. To some extent I fell in love with a girl, but she viewed me with indifference verging on contempt. I must add that none of this experience led me to change my mind in the least about the war.

I should now say something about my war experience because of its impact on my outlook on life. First of all, there was the discovery of France. We landed at Nantes after eleven stormy and most disagreeable days on the sea, our ship being escorted by a ring of destroyers bobbing up and down like corks in the agitated waters. Then because of the privileged character of our unit we went eastward in a third-class coach on a regular train. For a young man who then knew only the Middle West from Indianapolis to the Minnesota Iron Range, the historical character of the landscape through which we passed was breathtaking. We finally got off the train—how little needed is sleep when one is young—and were driven in a kind of bus to Langres, in the moonlight, over the drawbridge and through the great gate. this I knew was Caesar's city; and later on Christendom had built the huge hulk of the cathedral which now loomed up out of the dark in the golden shimmer of the night. Then we went up to the shattered front, first to Baccarat, where I slept on the front step of a half-ruined building, listening to the booming of guns still far away. Then further on to a louse- and rat-filled dugout north of Pexonne.

Our troops were very green, blunders were frequent and unavoidable. The Germans staged fairly extensive raids, lasting for hours. The roar of exploding shells, the heavy thuds of belching mortars, the smell of gas—all of this left the four of us on duty in the dugout in a state of superanxiety during a fifty-two hour attack. We were wearing masks, bayonets were on our rifles, and grenades were in our hands. But the storm passed us by, my first real wartime storm; and when we went up next morning to repair the lines on which our work depended, I came upon my first dead soldier, that is, one not in a casket or on a stretcher. He was a young French lad, not more than eighteen, with a love letter to his girl in the Loire country still in his pocket. My companion and I carried him back, cursing so vehemently that if the Lord God was listening He must have been shocked. Later on came Chateau Thierry and St. Mihiel, each with its rivers of blood. I was a veteran now, and like all veterans I do not talk about such things.

Finally, I was sitting in a room in Toul, to which some of us had come to serve as instructors, listening to the news on Morse code. And so I overheard the German request for an armistice. The first person I ran into outside, jubilant as I was over the news, happened to be a French machine gunner whom I had met on some segment of the front. "What shall I do now?" he asked gloomily. "I have been a machine gunner since before the day the war started, and there is nothing I know about except fighting." Years later I met him by accident, an old drunk, with the ribbons which are France's greatest tribute to valor faded on his shirt. I have concluded that this is the way in which I could sum up the war. But I must add that when it was all over, I found myself for the first time genuinely religious. Before that, I had lived up to all the rules and tried to believe what I was supposed to as a Catholic. Now I was personally religious, deeply so, but no longer a subservient soul. It seemed to me that I had found God across all the suffering I had seen. Many men I knew had lost every vestige of belief, and one could not blame them. Just what happened to me I cannot easily explain.

Since demobilization had to take a long time, the army decided that it ought to shunt its critical, restless, college-educated soldiers somewhere. And so one morning I found myself in Poitiers, enrolled in the old university of that city. What I knew of the French language I had picked up on the Vosges front. Our bereted companions in blue became good friends; and face to face with the problem of conversing I acquired a truly terrifying kind of French. I taught myself to read a little, while sitting in dugouts, by putting New Testaments in English and French side by side. And so I was not completely speechless when I came to Poitiers, a marvelous place in which to begin acquaintance with a France not torn by shot and shell. It was and still is a city the structures of which proceed from Roman to Romanesque, from Gothic to Renaissance. Every day I walked up the street along which Jeanne d'Arc had once ridden and passed the palace of Eleanor of Aquitaine. I grew very fond of the university and some of its professors, emerging finally with a *Certificat d'Aptitude,* which somewhat rashly announced to the world that I was prepared to teach French culture.

After I was mustered out, I could find no job to my liking and therefore responded affirmatively to an invitation to come to Notre Dame and teach English. This was attributable to some things I had written. I had no intention of staying, but at the end of my first year I made an important decision. A lucrative job offer had come in just the kind of journalism I liked, but I allowed the president of the university to talk me into staying. The Rev. James Burns, C.S.C., was by far the most creative and imaginative Catholic educator of his time, though he was then known primarily as a pioneer in the history of Catholic schools. He saw that if Notre Dame was to build a worthy institution of higher learning round the nuclei of quality it already possessed, notably in some of the natural sciences, it would be necessary to assemble a lay teaching staff having some semblance of academic stature. This in turn would require an endowment; and he took the first steps in the university's history to create one. It was a busy life I led at Notre Dame, teaching, helping to edit a local magazine, the *Ave Maria,* spending endless hours with students, and writing my first book. When Father Burns's tenure in office came to an end, I made, in 1924, two decisions which would affect the rest of my life. First, I married one of my summer school students, the beautiful and pert Doris Cunningham. Second, I decided to go to New York, find a job (I had saved some money, so that it was not of immediate importance), and study for the doctorate at Columbia. Fortunately, Ashley Thorndike, then chairman of the Department of English, had recommended my book to its publisher, and I could enter through the front door.

Then I made another fateful decision. The *Commonweal* had just been founded and I cast my lot with it. At first this seemed reconcilable with the quest for a doctorate and fortunately I did make considerable headway. It was hard, often grueling work, but it was fascinating. The *Commonweal* was a distinguished if perilous venture. Michael Williams and his friends who founded it were bent on proving that not all Catholics were priest-ridden or devotees of Tammany Hall. Therefore, it was to be edited and published by laymen and given as much of an ecumenical flavor as the circumstances permitted. This flavor was limited, to be sure. An Episcopalian served on our advisory board, and another was on the staff. The magazine was to be as like the *New Republic* as possible, though serving Catholic interests primarily. From the beginning it had an interested group of non-Catholic readers. But though its "snob appeal" was obvious enough to be resented by not a few, the magazine was quite liberal in tone and temper. Two fellowships were sandwiched in by me for study in Germany, and as a result I wrote three books, the second of which was the first eyewitness account of what was going on there after Hitler's seizure of power. This and its predecessor were favorably received and I acquired a reputation as a commentator on German affairs. I had rather thought that all this was forgotten, but to my surprise young delvers have now ferreted much of it out. I left the *Commonweal* in 1937, primarily because of the unpopularity resulting from my advocacy of neutrality toward Franco, exiting with a magnificent two-year fellowship for study abroad, generously sponsored by Carlton Hayes and Lindsay Rogers of Columbia.

Summarizing very briefly the impact of European experiences on my intellectual formation, I would say that the first important change in my outlook was caused by the discovery of French literature and thought, which had played only a small part in my earlier education Now I came to know, in addition to poets and novelists (my master's degree thesis was a study of Huysmans), Montaigne, Fénélon, and Pascal, with the last of whom I still sense great affinity of spirit, though he was far more Jansenistic than I ever cared to be and hostile to the Jesuits, whose history I greatly admire. France likewise made something of a medievalist of me by reason of Chartres, Bourges, and Paris's Notre Dame, to mention only a few of the cathedrals.

Still, it was always Germany which interested me most. In addition to the associations growing out of variegated studies of the political and social situation, I saw a good deal of German university life and came to know writers and artists. The heart of any university of my acquaintance was of course the *institut,* presided over by one or more professors. Here, research was carried on with unflagging zeal with the help of assistants who often toiled like slaves chained to Roman galleys. From among these the explorers (*Forscher*) of the future would be selected. It seemed to me a rigorous system which we Americans could imitate but seldom manage to duplicate. Meanwhile the German university's student body as a whole moved along rather haphazardly through a series of lectures, seminars, and examinations, often quite impersonal and mechanical. The liveliest institution in Berlin during pre-Nazi times was the *Hochschule fuer Politik,* in which political and social problems were discussed from a variety of points of view, liberal, radical, and conservative. I could not spend more than a month there, but that provided a most rewarding experience. German theology was then noted for meticulous exegesis and tireless historical delving. But there were among Catholic scholars some original thinkers and impressive lecturers, Guardini, Adam, and Lippert among them, who came to occupy places in my scheme of things beside Friedrich von Huegel, who had meant so much to me during my *Commonweal* days.

Fortunately, all this did not entirely wean me away from pursuing the doctorate later on to be awarded by Columbia University, my gratitude to and affection for which have never waned. It taught me what a great university is like and what scholarship truly is. During the fellowship periods abroad I had managed a number of weeks at the British Museum and the Bodleian filling in gaps in the research done for *A History of the English Ode from Milton to Keats,* which promises to be the most enduring of my books. Through this I acquired a key to the academic door, at a time when reopening the journalistic one did not seem alluring. Indeed, the field of comparative literature then being relatively untilled, the road ahead seemed promising. Then to my complete amazement I found myself being talked to by members of New York City's Board of Higher Education and members of the faculty of Hunter College. Then came an offer of appointment to the presidency of the college with which I was to be identified for more than twenty years. I hesitated a long while, first, because of the obvious fact that I knew nothing about being a president, and then because of the intergroup conflict in which members of the faculty were embroiled. It was John Burke, son of old Eli, president of Altman's and one of New York's most prominent Catholic laymen, who more than anyone else induced me to risk trying it out. To be sure, the position also provided a platform as a commentator on totalitarianism, and as things worked out I put that visibility to good use.

When I took office in 1939, Hunter was a college for women, waiting for the completion of its new multistoried building on Park Avenue and meanwhile cramming seven thousand fully matriculated students into buildings on its Bronx campus and into various structures downtown. New York was still wallowing in the Great Depression, which I have called the Great Disaster. Many of the girls came from very poor families and would indeed in many instances not have thought of higher education if they could have found jobs. Indeed, quite a sizable number could not find them even after graduation. As for the faculty, it was struggling to come to grips with the democratic reorganization which had been decreed by the board of higher education. Virtually everything was to be entrusted to committees of the faculty; and it certainly looked for a time as if such feathers as had been left on the presidential skin were to be plucked to the best of everyone's ability. We also had a rather small but potentially noisy group of left-wing students organized as the American Student Union, the counterpart of which was the then Communist-dominated teachers' union. This last bears no relationship whatever to the teachers' union currently active in New York. The municipal colleges were supposed to be populated by Communists, which surmisal of course added not a whit to their reputations. As a matter of fact, the Catholic portion of the Hunter student body made it "the largest Catholic college for women," as we sometimes pointed out half facetiously and half in earnest. If there could have been anything these young ladies did not possess, it was sympathetic sentiment about communism.

But in a relatively short time much that was good and experimentally useful in the democratic procedures had been retained and the rest discarded. The true structure of the college emerged. What had been a teacher training institution some forty years earlier became a college of liberal arts, which of course continued to prepare teachers for their careers of service but did not permit them to major in education. There were two demonstration schools under its auspices, one housing children of nursery and elementary school age, the other a high school the pupils in which were selected in accordance with their ability.

The faculty was, to be sure, in part masculine, and this portion was by no means lacking in distinction. Nevertheless, the high academic quality of Hunter was largely attributable to its "learned lady" professors, whom at that time only institutions which were professedly colleges for women would employ. There were eminent, sometimes even internationally respected, scholars in English, in other languages and literatures, history, the social sciences and, indeed, one or another of the natural sciences. In due time we built up a very distinguished art department, too, and strengthened our work in music. In some areas of inquiry, notably the humanities, the Hunter faculty ranked very high among the academic institutions of the United States in the number and quality of its scholarly publications. We had an amiable custom of honoring the author of a scholarly volume with a luncheon to which he or she could invite friends from other colleges and universities. One by-product of this was unsought advertising of Hunter's virtues.

Not a few of these women had done their undergraduate work at Hunter and, never having married, dedicated themselves to the college with greater enthusiasm than is shown by many mothers to their children. We all lived in a deep or moderating depression during the ten years after 1939. Budgets were pared down, promotions were hard to come by, teaching loads were inordinately heavy. And yet some of our faculty developed innovative instructional programs or dedicated themselves to student leadership. It was also a source of satisfaction to me personally that we were dealing for the most part with poor youngsters, some of them almost desperately poor. A coat stolen from a student locker room could cause a family tragedy. Often enough a girl would faint because of not having enough to eat. To be sure, we had wealthy girls too, who refused to go to the exclusive private colleges their mothers had attended. In many respects our students were insulated and often tightly homebound. I knew young women from Brooklyn who had never seen the Hudson River, let alone what lay beyond it. We therefore arranged for no end of field trips, notably those organized by our geographers, and so got to places far remote from New York City. On the whole, exceptions having been duly noted, the moral climate was one of surprising innocence. You can therefore imagine the furor in the offices of the deans of students when some girls reported that they had been queried by a stranger about their sex lives. If the interviewer believed everything he was told, he was definitely a misguided social scientist. All this occurred during the research phase of the Kinsey report.

Some of our students came from families enamored of the radical Left, while the backgrounds of others were decidedly conservative. The Left often made a good deal of noise, while the Right retreated into its bastions of indignation. The faculty was overwhelmingly conservative but would allow no deviation from its predominatingly liberal views. It resented the fact that the American Student Union was active on the premises, but any attempt to curb or suppress it would have created a wall of opposition that would have been defended by the majority. I have sometimes been accused of having been "soft on the Communists." But, quite apart from the fact that I grew up in Wisconsin with a Farmer-Labor–LaFollette climate about me, I very soon concluded that administration opposition to student extremism is futile and that the only way of redressing the balance is to create a strong liberal-conservative student movement. This we succeeded in doing, with magnificent assistance from Eleanor Roosevelt.

Insofar as the academic program was concerned, I was persuaded during my first years in office that education in the strict liberal arts sense was not adequate. Girls had to bring to the labor market after graduation some skill which would enable them to find employment, at least until such time as the demand for teachers grew larger. I had to use all my persuasive powers to introduce courses in typewriting and stenography, offered at first without credit. These courses I called a "vocational inlay." Of course I nevertheless subscribed to the ideals of Phi Beta Kappa, to which nearly all the distinguished members of the Hunter faculty belonged. During all my years at Hunter I taught a course at the request of my colleagues, first in comparative literature and then in modern German government and politics. We also had a sheaf of honor societies, each cherished by its initiates. I have tried in vain to recall how many of these invited me to honorary membership, as of course they would have any other president. Let me add that I came to the college deeply prejudiced against sororities. But I must candidly say that without these, life on the Hunter campus at that time would have been far less satisfactory than it was. Members of the Hunter faculty established the first truly interracial sorority, having a charter of its own. It collapsed when what we then called Negro students no longer wished to belong to it.

Everybody will understand that not a few of our students entered with chips on their shoulders. They would have preferred to go to some private alma mater having a campus and a more savory social reputation. But after a while, in spite of subways and the social atmospheres of their homes, they helped to create a climate of quite singular friendliness. If I passed a student without being greeted with a smile, I knew that she was a freshman. When anyone asks me whether a "day college" can have a sense of cordial solidarity, I look at him with astonishment. To be sure, it soon became apparent that anyone who tried to run that kind of show was bound not to lead a leisurely life. There were dances, games, teas, and whatever else a feminine constituency could dream up. But a still far greater occupational hazard was attending innumerable meetings of the Board of Higher Education and its various committees. Not that the board was a disagreeable body—quite the contrary. Not a few of its members became my close friends. But they sometimes seemed to suffer from a really puritanical sense of their responsibilities and to want to take a picture of every leaf on the educational bush.

The war years brought great changes. To begin with, our enrollment dropped for the first time, due to a congeries of circumstances. There was a trough in the birth rate. Many young women could find lucrative employment. Others married soldier boys before they left for the wars. And so we were not too gravely affected when the Navy commandeered the whole of the Bronx campus in order to make provision for the training of WAVES. Downtown there was a great flurry of patriotic activities, particularly in the form of dances and receptions to which service men were invited without it being at all clear which kind of hero would show up. Some affairs were urbane and successful, even leading to correspondence and in subsequent years to matrimony. But there were comical situations, too. One evening I looked in on one of the many dances to which I was invited only to find that in the center of the room there was a solid phalanx of sailors who just wouldn't be pried apart. I spent a busy hour shaking hands with individual seamen and introducing them to girls. Even so, they were in sum total the unhappiest group of terpsichoreans on record. They had been rounded up and ordered to attend.

I do not wish to give the impression that everything at Hunter was charming and played to soft music. It certainly was not. During the early depression-ridden years some members of the faculty loathed the unwashed and often quite foreign young women they taught. And some of these in turn were so unhappy at home that the bitterness never rubbed off. Not a few had been thrust out of a foreign language environment and had little if any idea of how they could overcome their handicaps. Others had sordid, unhappy love affairs which left scars on their personalities. At the time, we could afford practically no professional counseling other than that provided for strictly academic affairs. The assistance we offered was made possible by able volunteers, some of whom far overstepped the boundaries of what could legitimately be expected of persons from whom all this was a labor of love.

After the war was over, affluence began to heat up the frigid atmosphere of depression-time New York. When the UN Security Council finally ended its ill-starred and bizarre occupancy of the Bronx campus, that part of Hunter became coeducational. This created new problems. Many of the first young men to enter had not been admitted to other municipal colleges and were genuinely averse to invading what had been a feminine precinct.

Gradually this hurdle was surmounted, too. One reason was a first-rate athletic program for men, supervised by a professor the college was very fortunate to acquire. Another reason was that the service fraternities, organized in New York high schools from among former Scouts of both sexes, exercised leadership of a kind I had not imagined could exist. As a result, uptown and downtown we breathed in fresh air.

We boldly changed the climate of what had been known as the Evening Session and which soon took on the luster of the title, School of General Studies. This had been frequented for the most part by young people who did not qualify for matriculation. It was a sort of institution akin to that which would later on be established as a community college, though the teachers had no pension or tenure rights and were for a long time scandalously underpaid. Even for their sakes we could not close down this part of our activity because most of them would have had no employment whatsoever. The other municipal college presidents and I tried in every possible way to improve the situation and at long last were in some measure successful. But the tragedies which occurred when an instructor reached retirement age and had subsequently to try to exist on welfare doles were dire indeed. When one remembers the resistance of a great part of our people to social security, which at long last mitigated some of this distress, one is sorry to remember how callous a republic like ours could have been.

As I have said, the climate changed and nothing was affected more than that which was known as the School of General Studies. Hunter being where it was, on Park Avenue, we threw the doors wide open to educational activities of many kinds. Groups could ask for the use of rooms or even of halls where these were free. There were all sorts of goings-on— classes taught under the auspices of labor unions, Negro choral groups, instruction for amateur silversmiths (astonishingly successful, this). Hunter began its now quite famous concert series and organized an opera workshop. As I have already indicated, the warm spirit of Eleanor Roosevelt hovered over the campus during all the years I was there. She came again and again and again, asking no emolument whatever, always attracting everybody who could get into the hall. With the help of friends we had purchased the old Sara Delano Roosevelt house for use by student social and religious groups. I am sure Mrs. Roosevelt was much happier being with our students than she had ever been in that house.

We also professionalized our offerings to some extent, first by establishing a collegiate nursing program at the request of the city, which badly needed it, and second by creating the privately financed Graduate School of Social Work. Both, I may gratefully say, have flourished ever since. Meanwhile, in view of the very great need for teachers in the schools of New York City and its environs, the State provided funds for the development of a training program extending over the first year of graduate study. On the basis of this, there was rather hastily erected the Graduate School of the City University of New York, which has since survived any number of growing pains. This belongs, however, to an era after my time.

Meanwhile, my family lived in a pleasant old house on Shippan Point, which juts into the Connecticut Sound just east of Stamford. We were fated to have only one child of our own, our son Robert, who, in addition to other enterprises, now manages one of New York's numerous art galleries. But we filled the house with other people's children—Felicity, Jennifer, Inge, Bruce, and Ali. Other young people stayed there, too; and sometimes we bedded down more than a dozen, for it was a roomy house. I commuted regularly from New York, which often meant that on rainy or starry nights the Sound splashed on my ears at an hour near midnight. Of course I had sometimes to stay in the city; and when the periods of government service began in earnest I was obliged to be away for lengths of time. Inevitably the house grew emptier and emptier, as the young people got married or embarked on careers. There were also almost always grown guests, ranging all the way from Heinrich Bruening to Van Wyck Brooks. My wife managed none the less to become deeply involved in the affairs of Stamford as well as those of New York. We lived for twenty-three years in that house; and when we finally turned the keys over to another owner, so many memories were left behind that it almost seemed as if they would suffice for eternity. But we left sorrows behind us, too, some of them great ones, for which I learned to be thankful, because I think it is only through suffering that one can gain insight into the true meaning of the human pilgrimage. As a good though now forgotten poet wrote,

> Sweet sorrow, play a grateful part,
> Break me the marble of my heart.

I come now to an aspect of higher educational administration which has always astonished Europeans, who know nothing of our identification of the academic presidency with relative permanence. This is involvement in government service and in civic as well as scholarly organizations. Once I tried to justify this by saying that if a president could not be seen off the campus, he could not be seen on it either. But, though there is truth in this statement, the fact is that during the war and its aftermath it would have been impossible not to do what one was asked if it was at all within the area of one's competence. Refuse I did, of course, upon occasion; and, though I accepted more than a dozen assignments they did not add up in terms of time or importance to those taken on by men like James Conant or Henry Wriston. It should be added, perhaps, that being a municipal college president was irreconcilable with political activity. We simply had to make every effort to get along with any city or state administration.

My first two assignments were not overly time-consuming. The Committee Advisory to the Department of State on Cultural Affairs was established in 1942 as part of the good-neighbor policy toward Latin America. This was already "cold war" in a sense, since both the United States and Great Britain deemed it expedient to offset Nazi propaganda in the countries to the south of us. Cultural affairs in any but a random sense were then novel and so the committee was able to establish guidelines which to a greater or lesser degree have been followed ever since. Many of its members, James Conant and James T. Shotwell among them, I had known previously, but others, in particular Vice-President Henry Wallace and G. Howland Shaw, then assistant secretary of state, were new acquaintances. Mr. Shaw was not only one of our best experts in the field of Islam but also a man with a deep, broad concern for underprivileged youth. The committee was disbanded when the Office of War Information was established because it was unwilling to consider itself a propaganda organization. The other assignment was to membership on a commission assembled by the Council on Foreign Relations shortly after the entry of the United States into the Second World War to consider the form which the peace in Europe might take once the fighting was over. The commission met regularly, its guests being representatives of governments in exile, or in such cases as those of Germany and Austria, distinguished men who had been compelled to leave their countries. It was an excellent commission, though unfortunately nothing came of its work because of the astonishing concessions made to the Soviet Union as the war came to a close.

My next involvements became increasingly time-consuming. Sitting on an Enemy Alien Board to consider whether detained Germans, Italians, and Japanese should be released, paroled, or confined may not seem particularly impressive in retrospect, but it meant many nights and days either in New York or Santa Fe, New Mexico. Fortunately, I was young enough then to take this pretty well in stride and show up at Hunter not too dazed by all the late hours. My family, to be sure, often saw very little of me. The value of my personal experience, however, seemed to me great. For the first time I met Japanese, some of them simple folk, cooks especially, while others were merchants or students. Then I spent the summer of 1945 in Europe as chairman of a group formed by Secretary Robert Patterson to interview captured erstwhile foes, from Hermann Goering and Franz von Papen to the generals who had fought on the eastern front. I believe we did manage to collect information which would not have been available otherwise, and this was duly deposited for the benefit of whomever cared to look at it. At any rate, I picked up my study of Germany again, at least to some extent, for after 1934 I had been unable to get a German visa. All of us on the commission likewise saw the havoc wrought by the war, which had taken so great a toll that one hardly dared dream that restoration would be possible. Who could have imagined then that twenty-three years after the defeat the currency of the West German Federal Republic would have become the strongest in the world?

Then came the founding of Unesco. I served on the U.S. delegations to the London and Paris conferences which established the organization, later on took the chairmanship of the U.S. National Commission at the request of John Foster Dulles, and finally became the representative of the government of the United States on the Unesco Executive Board. The London conference drafted the constitution, opening with the since famous preamble urging that the "defenses of the peace" must be erected in the minds of men. We were then, in 1945, strongly under the influence of the dread war which had just ended and which was attributable to the evil genius of Adolf Hitler. Could not education, if dedicated to the cause of understanding, greatly help to insure that the peoples of the world would henceforth take recourse to peaceful means of settling disputes? This hope was also dominant throughout the Paris Conference (1946), which perhaps assembled the most brilliant body of scholars, writers, journalists, and representatives of the educational systems of many countries ever to come together up to that time. But when the moment came to develop leadership for the organization, the post of director general went by default to Julian Huxley. There was an informal but at the time binding agreement that if Unesco headquarters were established in Paris, the director general should not be French; and of course the Germans, Austrians, Spanish, and Japanese nations were not represented. Although cordially invited to do so, the Russians sent no delegation. As for the United States, it put forward no candidate seriously and publicly, though had it done so, he could easily have been elected.

The British really had two candidates but the Labour government's Ministry of Education strongly supported Mr. Huxley, and he was chosen in spite of grave doubts as to his ability to manage the enterprise. Then he began to circulate a pamphlet bound in green which set out to prove that his version of an ultra neo-Darwinian and humanistic faith ought to be adopted as official Unesco doctrine. This aroused violent opposition on the part of church groups of all kinds, especially in the United States. The State Department, to which this part of our cultural foreign policy was assigned, went to great pains to tell the citizenry that it had not the slightest interest in supporting Mr. Huxley's theological proposals.

Unesco thus came into being under two great handicaps. It had been created on the assumption that the Soviet Union would subscribe to the constitution and take its place among the nations. Stalin had not the slight-est intention of doing so and meanwhile proceeded to fasten his grip on the European satellite countries which had so thoughtlessly been turned over to Communist domination. Years later the Soviet Union did join the organization but for some time used the position it thus acquired to keep up a continuing and sometimes raucous political drumfire. The second handicap was that after Mr. Huxley's fiasco it was impossible to establish any generally acceptable Unesco philosophy of education. And so, after many good and bad starts, the organization gradually became what it now is—a genuinely necessary and effective international educational service agency. I believe that it has in many ways proved that if it did not exist it would have to be created. To be sure, it has suffered by reason of the declining prestige of the UN itself and from budgetary stringencies. But, like some of the other subsidiary organizations, it has given a good account of its stewardship. The amount of time required for service as U.S. Repre-sentative became so large that I was compelled to resign from the post in 1962.

My major departure from college routine grew directly out of my Ger-man interests and I shall confess that I accepted appointment in 1950 as land commissioner for Bavaria (or, more realistically, as John J. McCloy's deputy for that country) with reluctance. But there was no way out of doing so, especially since the Board of Higher Education was greatly im-pressed by the glory which this assignment would presumably bring to the municipal colleges. And so, excepting for some decisions which had to be made via long distance, I was away from Hunter for the better part of two years. But of all such assignments I have accepted this was by all odds the most interesting and rewarding. I am probably the only American who can say that he has visited almost every city and town in Bavaria. This was because the High Commission had field offices all over the beautiful coun-try and it was part of my assignment to visit as many of them as possible. Here I shall make only a very brief comment on education. I had several times been requested by General Clay to accept the post of director of education in his military government. But, despite my sincere admiration for him, I repeated that I would do so only if that post were separated from military government. In 1950, when the State Department took over, we looked back on the history of a dogged attempt to remodel German education according to the American pattern. Only so, it was thought, could the virus of nazism be exterminated. Textbooks were to be rewritten, coeducational high schools were to take the place of the *gymnasia,* and teaching about the evils of nazism was prescribed. Much of this the Ger-mans stoutly resisted, though some beneficial changes did occur, especially in the teaching of history and political science. Of course, the effort was

greatly lamed by the fact that the British and the French did not do in
their zones what we were trying to do in ours. Now the time had come to
propose cooperation with the Germans, and this led eventually to a broad
program of exchange of students and professors, as well as to the establishment of institutes of American studies. We assisted worthy innovative efforts whenever we were invited to do so. But the old order of educational
reform by fiat had to be abandoned.

I have been often asked to express an opinion about which persons
during my long career have seemed to me especially impressive. All attempts to do something like this are probably rather meaningless enterprises because one does not manage to take advantage of all the opportunities provided to know important people. Thus, I could no doubt have
become very well acquainted with General deGaulle if a number of things
had not intervened. Let me nevertheless present my catalog of the distinguished personages I have known. As heads of states, I would nominate
Harry Truman and Konrad Adenauer. There was little in the earlier record
of either to indicate that he would master the problems which confronted
him with such consummate skill. It was not my good fortune to meet
Winston Churchill more than casually. If I say that John Foster Dulles was
perhaps the most eminent diplomat of my time, please do not misunder-
stand what I mean. He and to a greater degree General MacArthur pursued
a policy to which I did not subscribe. But at least the policy had an
objective and was not a vague nebulous something without substance. I
have also greatly admired Dean Rusk. Among authors I have known, I
probably would choose Thornton Wilder and Thomas Mann. In the field of
education it would seem to me necessary to choose Nicholas Murray Butler
and Robert Hutchins, if only because they challenged existing ideas of
what education was all about. And if you ask me about senators, I would
give the accolade to John Sherman Cooper, liberal Republican from Kentucky, and to Hubert Humphrey. This is all I shall say except that I believe
that Henry Luce and Iphigene Sulzberger, for a long while the guiding
spirit of the *New York Times,* were the most illustrious publishers I have
known, with Alfred Knopf leading the procession in a different category.

The last years of my presidency were troubled because the Fineberg Law,
enacted by the state of New York and approved by all the courts, compelled
the Board of Higher Education to take disciplinary action against members of
the faculty who belonged to the Communist party. There was certainly little
reason why I should have entertained deep affection for many such members,
nor did I have any responsibility other than to furnish such evidence, pro or
contra, as the college records contained. Some of our faculty had long since
overtly cut off relations with the party with which they had been affiliated
for a short period of time during the turbulent thirties. A very few, however,

had permitted a Communist noose to be knotted round their throats. There was a good deal of faculty and student sympathy with these colleagues and teachers, largely because it looked as if our proud record in defense of academic freedom was being tarnished. Few knew as I did how stupidly some of the accused had behaved. Meanwhile I was subjected to a great deal of abuse off the campus for having said that instead of being investigated by him, the universities should investigate Joe McCarthy. Still I received a great many compliments, especially from faculty men and women in the Middle West, so that the balance was more than even.

I retired from the presidency of Hunter in 1960, after more than twenty years in office, before I would have been obliged to simply because I was very tired and because the ever increasing involvements in the total municipal college administration appeared to be turning my life into something I no longer found rewarding. Many of my associates were kind enough to regret my decision; such regrets might not have endured a longer tenure. The convocation marking my departure was quite a glorious affair. Henry Heald delivered the obituary address, and the erstwhile enemies, Cardinal Spellman and Eleanor Roosevelt, were seated on the stage, he in the resplendent robes of his office and she in her Oxford cap and gown. Thus the twenty-one years at Hunter came to a close.

It had not seemed to me that anyone would be likely to request my services and I looked forward to little more than some writing and lecturing while continuing my service on Unesco's Executive Board. But almost in the twinkling of an eye there was a spate of interesting job opportunities. I decided to cast my lot with Father Hesburgh at Notre Dame and see if a distinguished Catholic university could be created there. The gamble, in view of his leadership, was worth taking. Many of my friends doubted that anything significant would come of it, and indeed some of my former colleagues at Hunter were quite distressed by reason of their assumption that I had preferred going to Notre Dame instead of lasting out my years with them. It seems to me that the decision I made was very much the right one. It is true that whether Father Hesburgh, despite his truly remarkable gifts, can manage to achieve excellence is still open to question. The sportswriters of the nation have long since had their idea of Notre Dame; and whether any president, however able, can weave his way to academic distinction between football and basketball is still an open question.

But I have been on the campus long enough to know that a new idea of how a Catholic university can emerge into fellowship with the other great universities of the United States is being formulated. Notre Dame was a small institution when I first knew it and extremely fortunate to have a kernel from which distinction could be evolved. This was satisfactorily enough a natural science kernel. John Zahm, friend of Theodore Roosevelt and his companion in explorations of the Amazon River, was a very great geographer as well as a brilliant student of evolution. Julius Nieuwland discovered among other things how to make artificial rubber. There were others. Around this somewhat mysteriously organized nucleus, would it be possible to build a university eminent also in the social sciences and the humanities? This was the question to which at Notre Dame I have devoted such energies as have been given to me, and I think the answer is affirmative. That is, it will be if the university can enlist the enduring enthusiastic dedication of its best young faculty members. This is going to be difficult because of the strong and indeed sometimes bitter competition for scholars of quality, at any age. If Father Hesburgh and his associates can hold their own in this arena, the future seems most promising. Of course Notre Dame is already strongly committed to freedom and the ecumenical spirit. This commitment it will have to strengthen and I have no doubt that it will. At any rate, I am grateful for the opportunity I have had to participate in what is both a hope and an achievement.

# II

# ON RELIGION

"I may as well say here," wrote Shuster in a self-portrait in 1948, "that religion has persistently been to me an affair of persons. The chain of logic, which for some is almost the chain of being, weaves no magic spell for me."[1] As a youngster growing up in a devout home, he attended Mass, memorized the catechism, received the sacraments, and served as an altar boy. It was neither priests nor nuns who exerted the formative influence on him, but rather his father, whose principal fault was an unwieldy Celtic imagination of the southern German variety. Neither learned, nor pietistic, nor worldly wise, he was a "serene and humble Christian" who "possessed an instinct for religious conduct which was as rare as it was beautiful." When his father died, the young boy became convinced that "I should never meet a better Christian." At preparatory school his Greek and German teacher served as an "exemplary humanist" who "took the narrowness out of religion" and opened up its spiritual and intellectual dimensions. While at Notre Dame he wrestled with the perennial problem of evil in a world created by the Supreme Good. If man constantly aspired to the Infinite Being, why was religion "so powerless to transform even its most meticulous practitioners?" Despite these probing questions, he never doubted that God created the universe and rested his belief in God's existence upon the conviction that

[1] George N. Shuster, "George N. Shuster," in Louis Finkelstein (ed.), *American Spiritual Autobiographies* (New York: Harper and Brothers, 1948), p. 26.

"the conscious individual soul must have a Substratum, just as natural reality derives from Nature." Yet he graduated from college as "a brooding and gawky oaf"—still perplexed by the question of good and evil.[2]

It was as a young soldier in the bloody battle of Chateau-Thierry in World War I that Shuster first glimpsed an insight into this dilemma. The battlefield was a sea of mangled corpses and the Marne River sobbed its crimson water on either shore in endless flow. Late one afternoon the sun shone over the valley until it seemed "a cup of sacrificial fire." Immediately the impressionable young man recalled to mind Christ's promise that the chalice of His blood was shed for all mankind. "And for the first time I seemed to grasp the meaning of the Christian sacrifice, which is not apart from humanity but with it, tragically with it, young as the Prophets were and yet old, immemorial, as is the deep aspiration of the race for holiness that can blot out sin." At this point in his life, reflects Shuster, regardless of psychological explanations, he had "some inkling of what it means, in terms of pain and glory, to be a Christian."[3]

Other soldiers despaired of God. Shuster found the fullness of God and became a new man. For the rest of his life he would manifest this new faith in "a deep interest in the life of the Church." Not simply the narrow, institutionalized Church, but an expansive and resurrected view of Christianity which was not always understood or appreciated in pre-ecumenical days. He so cherished this religious experience that he felt it incumbent "to give to others some impression of what riches had come to me." This was an important reason why he joined the staff of *Commonweal*—a modest journal with an ambitious desire "to help Catholics feel intellectually at home in America."[4]

It is not surprising, therefore, that Shuster's first book in a religious vein, published in 1927, three years after joining *Commonweal,* was entitled *The Catholic Spirit in America.*[5] Its pages reveal the frustrations that existed in an era when Catholic intellectuals were beginning to portray the Church's contributions to the national culture and when American Catholics increasingly resented a second-class citizenship that had hounded them from colonial days and especially since the nineteenth-century waves of immigration. The 1920's were not unlike the 1960's in that there existed a rebellion against

---

[2] *Ibid., p. 31.*
[3] *Ibid.,* p. 32.
[4] *Ibid.,* p. 34.
[5] George N. Shuster, *The Catholic Spirit in America* (New York: Dial Press, 1927.)

established moral standards and a type of backlash typified by a resurgent Ku Klux Klan. There emerged a challenge and a spirit of confrontation which produced the Al Smith presidential candidacy, an anti-Catholic crusade against him, and books such as *The Catholic Spirit in America*. Neither polemical nor apologetical, it was written to document several of Shuster's long held convictions: that the American Catholic tradition differed from the Protestant national spirit; that Catholics were loyal Americans; and that Catholics were not bound to choose between allegiance to church or state.

Shuster concedes that America is basically a Protestant country whose roots go back to Reformation Christianity. Although there is no longer a union of church and state in the United States, the Protestant tradition has long permeated all facets of American life from public education to hotel reading matter. The Catholic Church, on the other hand, with its hierarchical structure and ecclesiastical norms, has long been viewed as a threat to this heritage. Catholics who came to this country found themselves at odds with the entrenched Protestant majority and were forced to the lower rungs of the social and economic ladder. Shuster reviews the Catholic immigrants' struggle to preserve their religious faith (and for many their ethnic identity) in a hostile environment.

Such historical elements, among many, combined to shape the spirit of American Catholicism. The English-Protestant character of American society hampered the immigrant-Catholic participation in the intellectual growth and life of the country. This caused many Catholics to appear intellectually inferior, and this complex further withdrew them from the mainstream of American life. "The handicaps which the foreigner brought with him have greatly impeded the work of the Church, although something may be said for them as sources of loyalty; *but those acquired by reason of social conditions in the United States have caused nine-tenths of the ill-feeling against the Church.*"[6] In citing hostility of rural America to a largely urban Catholicism, Shuster criticizes the nineteenth-century Church leadership which fostered religious and ethnic ghettoism in the cities in order to increase religious observation and minimize religious defection. While lamenting the absence of Catholic contribution to American culture, Shuster attributes this deficiency to a "siege mentality" which afforded little time for anything but physical labor and the preservation of the faith against an unresponsive majority.

Shuster's forays into history enabled him to deal more effectively with the contemporary issues of the day: Catholic allegiance to democratic principles;

[6] *Ibid.*, p. 6.

public versus parochial schools; the candidacy of Al Smith; and the Mexican persecution of the Catholic Church. He commented upon each of these questions and made predictions about the future of the Church in America. He realized the need for a religious renewal, but he did not contemplate the *aggiornamento* of the 1960's. He envisioned the day when external religion would more deeply influence the daily lives of Americans; a time, for example, when chapels would be installed in business establishments and even in apartment houses. Inter-denominational ecumenism would arise, not from an increase of individual good will and doctrinal unity, but from the realization that both the Catholic and Protestant communities have changed a great deal from Reformation days. Both sides needed to take a fresh look at each other in the spirit of reconciliation and mutual charity. Shuster may have missed the mark in details, but he was focusing in the right direction with hopes that now seem commonplace.

The mystical and speculative side of Shuster's religious commitment is evident in his translation of two German volumes into English. In an editorial note to Siegfried Behn's *The Eternal Magnet* (1929), Shuster recalls the satisfaction of first reading this book in German and his desire to translate it for American audiences.[7] Pessimistic in tone, the book laments the increasing barbarity of modern warfare and society's inconsistent approach to it. While people expressed concern over the dum-dum bullet, declares Behn, they freely accepted the use of flame throwers which caused more destruction and a more anguished death. In view of the atrocities that occurred in his country less than a decade later, Behn's intuitions were obviously well justified. With regard to human comprehension of reality, he denied that speculation could lead to a complete understanding of the truth. On the contrary, one must always arrive at that point where faith in the insolvable is absolutely necessary. Such a conviction no doubt found a responsive chord in the American translator.

Several years later Shuster continued his interest in the mystical by translating Peter Lippert's *Job the Man Speaks with God* (1936), a poetical volume with overtones of *The Imitation of Christ* in its mode of expression.[8] It seems to have been a wonderful book for meditation with a great sense of mankind's suffering. Perhaps its German author, like Behn and Shuster,

[7] Siegfried Behn, *The Eternal Magnet* (New York: Devin-Adair Company, 1929.)

[8] Peter Lippert, *Job the Man Speaks with God* (New York: Longmans, Green and Company, 1936.)

sensed the terrible political currents swirling inexorably around him. Shuster's anguish over developments in Nazi Germany may have been why he chose to translate the book. Certainly he feared the mounting wave of evil sweeping across Germany. Lippert's poetical expression of the purpose of his book made a profound impression upon Shuster:

> This book does not relate the personal confessions of any human being. 'The man Job' who in it speaks with God, is man of all ages—man struggling for the quest of God, praying in anguish, unable to cease looking for God because God is the passion of his being. . ,. As he reflects he grows more and more uncertain; when he strives he always loses courage; and yet he cannot help reflecting and striving.
>
> But when now and then he has found the word of Love, this invariably becomes his final word. . . . When Job no longer tries to talk and to argue, when he is no longer good for anything save loving and trusting, then he has solved the riddle of God—in so far as human beings can. Then is the man Job become wise.[9]

No doubt that Shuster has long been impressed with such thoughts. When he wrote his spiritual autobiography years later, he expressed similar sentiments. He believed that a broadside of divine love could stagger the heart of man into dispelling the "grossness of the world." Santayana believed that this could never come to pass, but Shuster prayed that he was wrong. "Love is the weapon, yes. But hope is no man's land. One must have faith that it is good to be there."[10]

Mysticism is but one part of Shuster's religious nature. He has always regarded religion primarily as an "affair of persons"—its influence on people and their influence on others. As a result, he has written about several prominent Catholic churchmen for whom he has had great respect and admiration. Shuster admired Pius XI whom he had personally known, and several of his tributes present a positive assessment of the pontiff's work. He alludes to the pope's great love for all things human, his attraction to non-Catholics, and his rise from northern Italian peasant stock—qualities, it may be said in retrospect, which made Pope John XXIII so lovable and accessible some twenty years later. Now Pius XI is all but forgotten. One wonders about the perspective of history and whether, even in Shuster's time, the pope was truly an innovative spirit in the Church. Yet both men saw the evils of their time, particularly in Hitler's Germany, and so their insights are those of men of that era.

[9] *Ibid.*, pp. v-vi.
[10] "George N. Shuster," p. 37.

During the "cold war" Shuster wrote *In Silence I Speak* (1956), an account of the tribulations of the unhappy Cardinal Mindszenty—now a living relic of that semi-distant and militant struggle between Catholicism and Communism behind the iron curtain.[11] In the preface Shuster notes that "modern totalitarianism has been in a constant state of movement and evolution, so that any comment on its phases may well seem of transitory significance."[12] And so it was with this book. It had scarcely appeared in bookstores when the Hungarian revolution took place, with the colossal statue of Stalin in Budapest toppled to the ground, Mindszenty himself spirited from prison to the American embassy for protection, and the Soviet restoration of "order" throughout Hungary—all within an incredibly short period of time.

Shuster's third clerical portrait was that of the late Albert Cardinal Meyer of Chicago (1964). This pamphlet was one of a series of brief biographies to be published on ecclesiastics who influenced the Second Vatican Council. Shuster had long known Meyer and considered him "every inch a prince of the Church, handsome, quiet, dignified." Although such qualities do not guarantee an effective churchman, Shuster presented a positive picture of Meyer at the Council—a man preaching moderation while insisting on the indispensable need for reform and renewal in the Church. Meyer was a scholar as well as a competent administrator and a humble priest. In fact, there was in him, declares Shuster, "a readiness to meet other men and women without prejudice, and a certain genuine earnestness which is rooted in the remembrance of pioneer days and of the touching fidelity of older generations to what in their not infrequent poverty and simple circumstances they considered a treasure beyond price, namely, their belief that in Christ there is salvation."[13] One cannot help observing how much of the Shuster personality and value system can be found in this portrayal. Both were midwesterners, both valued tradition and manliness, both were intellectually gifted, both treasured their religious faith, and both were humble men.

During the 1930's Shuster expressed concern for the fate of religion under totalitarian regimes in Germany, Italy, and Spain. As editor of *Commonweal* Shuster was upset when Pope Pius XI signed a concordat in 1933 with Nazi Germany. Two years later he wrote *Like A Mighty Army: Hitler Versus*

[11] George N. Shuster, *In Silence I Speak* (New York: Farrar, Straus and Cudahy, 1956.)

[12] *Ibid.*, p. vii.

[13] George N. Shuster, *Albert Gregory Cardinal Meyer* (University of Notre Dame: University of Notre Dame Press, 1964), pp. 7, 45.

*Established Religion* (1935), which equated Nazism as a competing and antithetical religion against Western religion.[14] It had already proclaimed enmity against Judaism and was beginning to manifest hostility to Protestantism and Catholicism. Judaism suffered more in the long run because of Nazism's warped racial views, but Christianity was denigrated as a weak and impotent faith that would eventually wither away. Toward the end of the book Shuster presents a striking observation that could give rise to even greater discussion in a world that has progressed nearly forty years since its publication. He sees the problem as a sexual and materialistic one, and in a way predicts the sexual revolution of the 1960's, which has been both a symptom and a blossoming of forces set in motion by twentieth century scientific and social developments.

> Since prophylactic medicine has altered the consequences of sexual intercourse, and since nomadic habits have undermined the ideal of home stability, the old Christian ideal of the married state appears to be narrow and unsatisfying. ... If we are candid we shall admit that most of the so-called fundamental challenges to the Church have their origin in sexual desire. ... When one weighs all this carefully, one comes within an inch of thinking that the religion of the future will be the concern of a few who have withdrawn from the world; and that the masses will turn to the Church only occasionally when ... the choice confronting everyone is old Huysman's choice between the mouth of a pistol and the foot of the Cross.[15]

In a more optimistic tone, however, he points out that the religion of no-religion generally fails to function and that in time the human spirit yearns to return to more substantial religious beliefs. "If for a few years the Church can be loyal to itself, preferring a thousand sacrifices to one compromise," concludes Shuster in traditional Augustinian thought, "there will be a resurrection of belief such as has not been witnessed in many hundreds of years."[16]

After World War II Shuster's anxiety shifted to the fear of religion in European Communist countries. His investigations resulted in the publication of *Religion Behind the Iron Curtain* (1954), a book that examines the strengths and weaknesses of both church and state.[17] His picture of East

[14] George N. Shuster, *Like A Mighty Army: Hitler Versus Established Religion* (New York: D. Appleton Century Company, 1935.)

[15] *Ibid.*, pp. 279-280.

[16] *Ibid.*, p. 281.

[17] George N. Shuster, *Religion Behind the Iron Curtain* (New York: Macmillan Company, 1954.)

Germany represents it as one of the more lenient of Communist states insofar as travel and religious freedom were concerned (though this state of affairs changed after a subsequent uprising). Throughout the book Shuster points out the excesses and shortcomings of church and state. Such a stand is not always popular, especially when objectivity is labelled cowardness, when lack of extremism is interpreted as not taking a stand, and when the wisdom of saying "not to decide is to decide" is twisted into a philosophy of absolutes. The times were dark and perilous, voiced Shuster in weary tones, but "one must believe and hope that so much agony of body and spirit will constitute the great tribulation from out of whose womb humanity will be reborn through the mercy of God."[18]

[18]*Ibid.*, p. xxi.

# Spiritual Autobiography

A boy reared in a family like mine would have been singularly dull-witted if he had failed to perceive that religion was all around like a suit of clothes or the things in a room. Our Wisconsin town was steeped in doctrine and precept. On Sundays it dutifully went to a surprising variety of churches, and then laboriously spent the rest of the day doing nothing. My grandfather, a not too faithful Lutheran, attended services only when he felt like it—a wholly unpredictable state of mind. The rest of the family, being Catholic, were out of bed at the crack of the Sabbath dawn. Generally I served Mass, mumbling the Latin responses in a curiously fascinating but quite non-erudite style which has embedded itself in my memory. And of course I learned the catechism, taking special pride in the glibness with which I could name the seven corporal works of mercy and the seven capital sins.

The town was overwhelmingly committed to the Protestant faith, though there was a good deal of Catholic folklore in that region, which Marquette had explored and which Father Stephen Mazzuchelli had served as an architect and an educator. Some rather intelligent Jews had come in with the German migration of the forties, but there was no synagogue. If there had been, we should scarce have noticed it. I never heard of anti-Semitism until after I left college. But as a result of some polemic extravaganzas of the eighties, Catholic and Protestant eyed each other askance. Occasionally, in my day, an ex-nun, or even a spurious ex-monk, arrived to speak in a hall normally dedicated to fiddlers and square dancing; and for some mornings thereafter we Catholic children would sneak up back alleys in order to get to school without bloody noses. This did no great harm, being a lesson in the truth that one must be prepared to suffer for what one believes. On the other hand, Providence favored us by sending one of the earliest graduates of an Eastern college for women—I think it was Smith—to dwell in our midst. She was a formidable but warmhearted and well-read person who used to give me, already then serious in spite of an addiction to variegated deviltry, copies of *Harper's* and the *Atlantic* when she had finished reading them, and who held all prejudice in such abhorrence that I considered her a sort of Congregational saint. It may be, as was rumored, that she was not too easy for her husband to manage. But in her mansion in eternity she must know that she gave a little Catholic lad who came to play with her grandchildren unforgettable proof that courtesy is the only liberal view worth discussing.

Because this paper is inevitably a confession, I may as well say here that religion has persistently been to me an affair of persons. The chain of logic, which for some is almost the chain of being, weaves no magic spell for me. I respected my teachers not for what they said but for what they were. And therewith such intellectual living as I did in my early youth was largely concerned with impressions of good and evil in action. I recall, as if it were yesterday, the earnestness with which I prepared for my first Holy Communion. Perhaps what I then experienced was not so much belief as a kind of awe akin to fear. Our teachers were experts in the infinite forms of Divine punishment which might be inflicted on bad boys guilty of such crimes as falling asleep during the sermon or pulling a girl's braids in catechism class. No doubt I was most influenced, quite unconsciously, by my father. He was by no means a learned man, and his principal weakness, which could be exasperating as well as amusing, was the result of one of those Celtic imaginations sometimes found in South Germans. This led him to embellish his narrative of every occurrence with incidents having no foundation in fact. But he was a serene and humble Christian, never clerical or anti-clerical, neither pietistic nor worldly-wise. He possessed an instinct for religious conduct which was as rare as it was beautiful. I remember that our parish once had an unworthy priest. My father refused to accompany the unctuous committee of parishioners which went to report sundry goings-on to the Bishop. Instead, on the day of reckoning, he carried the offender's bags to the station (we had neither cars nor taxis in those days) without saying so much as one word; and I am sure this gesture of reverence for the office, combined with a silent rebuke to its incumbent, did the distraught young cleric a world of good. My father was not a saint, nor was he, like his favorite uncle, a self-taught scholar, but when he was dead I looked at his weary old face and was sure that I should never meet a better Christian.

Naturally I had my first glimpses of evil. Such experiences are of a family, perhaps, with temptation, but they are of a very different cast of feature. Nothing in life is more cruel than is the revelation of sexual grossness to young children, and yet nothing is more commonplace. Living as we then did close to nature, there was for us no mystery about generation. But the discovery of lust without modesty or reverence, or worse still of sadism in the young human animal, was so revolting that I have never since been able to forget that man is capable of evil which is worse than brutality because it is corruption. Perhaps it is strange that, in this mood, I should still have thought that the love of woman was a good thing. But despite all my subsequent reverence for the celibacy of the saints, I did not dream of it for myself. Instead I was driven by my revulsion to idealize womanhood, so that it was only much later that I realized how infamously vile the mind of woman can sometimes be. This was further testimony, had it been needed, that human betterment without continuous inner sanctification is an illusion.

When I was thirteen, my mother was taken seriously ill and I was bundled off to a boarding school known as St. Lawrence College. It was an American replica of a Swiss *gymnasium,* conducted by Capuchins who for the most part had come from abroad. The majority of the students were poor boys, many of them past twenty, who planned to study for the priesthood. Everything about the institution was Spartan except its mind. We arose so early that I still shudder to think of it (one whole winter month we dressed by the light of Halley's comet), washed in icy water, went to Mass to which innumerable prayers were adjoined, and proceeded to the refectory for a breakfast that was the product of chance and the vilest cook in history. I believe I must have been the most homesick boy who ever lived. Yet the hearts of our masters were as warm as the dormitories in which we slept were cold.

Then I was introduced to the greatest teacher I have met. His subjects were Greek and German, about neither of which I knew anything except what a dreary freshman year had taught me. Father Corbinian had learned at Munich how to be an exemplary humanist. But he was far more than that. Seen in one way he was as childlike as Brother Juniper, but he had a singularly creative and uninhibited mind. He could have written a hymn to Brother Shakespeare even as his great precursor had indited a hymn to the sun. For him and for the pleasure of sharing what he had to say about Plato and Sophocles, Goethe and Schiller, I studied his languages so hard that when I left the school I wrote better German than I did English. Father Corbinian gave my mind a permanent direction because he took the narrowness out of religion. Perhaps I might not have managed without him. Later on Gilson would say that Jerusalem and Athens have been made one in the Catholic tradition. For my Capuchin friend, both cities were, it may be said, suburbs of Christianity; and we never had the feeling that it was necessary to change our intellectual clothes when we visited them. Nor did he keep us locked up in antiquity. He was surprisingly aware of contemporary intellectual developments, so that we followed even then what has become known as the Catholic renaissance in European letters. It goes without saying that under such teachers we studied neither in order to study nor for profit. We believed that culture was only the underside of fortitude and honor.

By way of contrast my college days, though happy and reasonably carefree, were, from the religious point of view, troubled. Personal awareness of modern critical attitudes came to me strangely enough through a novel— Winston Churchill's forgotten *Inside of the Cup*. Of course I had read or heard of many of the standard forms of dissent to our position, and the Capuchins had even discussed with us, calmly and reasonably, the issues at stake in the Modernist debate. But I had never known a living, breathing dissenter, so that the hero of Churchill's somewhat wordy novel, questioning as he did the orthodox views of the Episcopal Church, was for me a fascinating and frankly appalling substitute for reality. None of the Scripture critics or church historians I have since met in the flesh have seemed to me half so formidable. In addition, we were caught up in the business about evolution. I shall confess that I have never been able to understand why such a fuss was made about Darwinism. Yet trouble there was in plenty, and several of my friends decided that since we human beings had been stamped in the same mint as the ape we were expendable only across the counters of this life. My own wrestling was with a quite different problem. Man, his relationship to the chimpanzee notwithstanding, had aspirations to a higher form of being. Why, then, was religion so powerless to transform even its most meticulous practitioners? Monks did pretty well about suppressing sexual desire, but were often as mean and spiteful as wrangling sea gulls. Catholic and Protestant alike appeared to enjoy being intellectually opaque, and to covet a similitude to the Pharisees of the Gospel. In short, were we not deluding ourselves when we said that we could alter the psyche of man?

To report these things is to indicate that my view of life, with all its limitations, was taking shape. No doubt I was to some extent the creature of environment. The best teaching at Notre Dame (save in Latin and Greek, which Scheier expounded eccentrically but magnificently) was in the social sciences, in which the reading we did was broad and pertinent. I became a little of a radical and thought Herbert Croly God's best gift to America. But at the same time I pessimistically reminded myself that if religious discipline could do so little to change human nature, there was small likelihood that more superficial treatments would help a great deal. It was what people did to their innermost selves that counted, and it seemed improbable that they would ever do more than barely enough to keep out of jail.

I was ineradicably persuaded that there exists a deep cleavage between the human spirit and the world of nature. Plato when first read with rapture appealed to me as a kindred soul and a great master of the logic born of insight, rather than the logic of humdrum evidence. While I did not doubt that visible creation must have had a Creator, my belief in God was based upon the conviction that the conscious individual soul must have a Substratum, just as natural reality derives from Nature. This soul is, above all, conscious of a *telos,* a purpose, which is to seek and find the Good. It yearns to do so, even as an animal desires to propagate its kind. Since it was, in my opinion, wholly evident that the mind of man was independent of brute creation, Darwinism seemed to me only an interesting account of the probable derivation of the human body from higher forms of animal life. Later on I found confirmation for my views in the writings of Cardinal Newman, Max Scheler, Maine de Biran, Friedrich Von Huegel, and, above all, Saint Augustine. Perhaps I should add that Neo-Platonism meanwhile seemed to me unadulterated stargazing. On the other hand, I read a good deal of St. Thomas, and came to have some dim awareness of his significance. But—and I am saying this in order to be honest, and not because I am in any sense content with myself—I should not be willing to exchange one of the Epistles of St. Paul for the whole of the *Summa.*

All this does not mean that I left college with a stable religious philosophy. To all who remember the days of their youth, it will suffice to indicate that I was a brooding and gawky oaf. My trouble was in part (as it still is) that my doctrine and my nature were of different dimensions. I loved to feast my eyes on beautiful things, and I could not control a riotous imagination. What was wrong with me was curiously like what had once been wrong with Luther: I did not doubt that the business of the soul was the imperturbable quest of the Good, but I felt that this business was wholly beyond my powers. Nevertheless I am afraid that Luther would have been shocked by some of my predilections. I mooned over Sherwood Anderson, sighed over the early Yeats, and sat up nights with *Jean-Christophe.* Those who studied the dust above every battle might have discovered, with the help of an extremely powerful microscope, the special molecule I happened to be. I was, of course, as far removed as possible from all anti-clericalism, and continued to entertain a great deal of regard for many priests. Yet I felt certain that those I liked best were wholly incapable of understanding my point of view. I was in some acute danger of becoming a person who put a nickel's worth of conformity into the ecclesiastical slot of a Sunday and then went off on a private picnic for the rest of the week.

Then, after sundry vicissitudes, came the First World War. There is no need to describe what this ordeal meant. Military service was for me a sore trial because, while I did not believe that the cause for which we had taken up arms was worth my life or that of any other young American, I felt strongly that the country had the right to exact a full measure of devotion. We may pass over these forgotten agonies, which were those of a generation. But it was, perhaps, by reason of my wartime experience that I really found out what the Church is. One major event I have described previously in another place, and shall allude to briefly here though I know it will not mean to others what it means to me. The Battle of Chateau-Thierry had just been fought. Bloody corpses still bobbed up and down in the waters of the Marne, even as the wheat field ripened on the slopes. This place, where so many young bodies had been beaten into stiff stillness, did not seem to me so much horrible as indescribably tragic. Late one afternoon the sun flooded the valley, filling the oval with golden light till it seemed a cup of sacrificial fire. There came to mind the words of the Gospel and of the Liturgy: "This is the chalice of my blood, of the New and eternal Testament, shed for you and for many." And for the first time I seemed to grasp the meaning of the Christian sacrifice, which is not apart from humanity but with it, tragically with it, young as the Prophets were and yet old, immemorial, as is the deep aspiration of the race for holiness that can blot out sin. Perhaps the psychologist will say that everything I had learned and been now came to my rescue in an hour of emotional exhaustion. But I was not then tired or weak. I had now some inkling of what it means, in terms of pain and glory, to be a Christian.

It is true that the Church attracted me because so much of what we saw about us in Europe was ancient and beautiful. I shall never forget coming into Chartres a little before dawn, to see the miraculous spires of the cathedral against the grey sky; or observing Palm Sunday in the old Church of St. Radegonde at Poitiers, with the light coming through the matchless Romanesque window above the high altar; or hearing Mass in what for me is still the most impressive Gothic room I have seen, the Cathedral of Metz. The knowledge that generations of men had cared so deeply for the Catholic faith that they made for it so many shrines of matchless loveliness, was singularly comforting; and in my admiration of what I saw there may well have been some admixture of wholly improper personal pride, compensating subtly and no doubt unfortunately for years of living as a member of a cramped minority. But at least I did not succumb to the disease of thinking that religion was esthetic; and I have never been able to understand those who profess to believe that Catholicism is beautifully woven emotional tapestry. It is true that the great art and music of the Church can quite take one's breath away. Yet they are always things man has made for religion. They are hardly even symbols for the kind of man religion has sometimes made. What now held me in thrall was the significant order with which the Church endows life. Of necessity this order awakens fierce opposition. Why, for example, the outsider will inquire, should the Pope—and what feelings the mention of his name can arouse—decree that a man shall keep one wife until death? No simple answer to that question can be found, even now when easy divorce has made a farcical enterprise of marriage. It seems to me, however, that the most important point was well expressed by Chesterton: "Two times two may be four, but two times one are not two but two thousand times one. That is why the world will always return to monogamy." The values are here seen to be not those of quantitative enjoyment—for indeed there could be no denying that a man who took unto himself a fresh and comely wife when he tired, as is probably inevitable, of his helpmeet, would be acting shrewdly in terms of indulgence merely—or, on the other hand not purely, thinly idealistic either. The marriage sacrament is designed, as Chesterton well sees, to give a new dimension to quantity. It is not good for man to be alone. But he can have comradeship only if he will create it. Sublimation is the sole thoroughfare which leads to the infinite, even in the realm of human variety.

Perhaps no other aspect of the Catholic life impressed me so deeply, however, as did the arrangement of the liturgical year. It is impossible to suggest, in a few words, how admirably religious tradition has created a pattern of the seasons which is consonant not only with the life of man but also, one may say reverently, with the eternal Divine activity in so far as that has been made known to us. The Church moves from Advent into the time of the Epiphany, from the Lenten days into the period of the reign of the Holy Spirit. Liturgical prayer blends the Testaments, and associates the saints with Sacrifice. There is here room for everything—the harvest of fruits and the harvest of souls in preparation for immortality, the feasts of joy and the days on which the sins of men are remembered. It is no more possible to exhaust the endless riches of the liturgy than it is to think to a conclusion the architecture of light, color, and form which make up the cycle of nature's change from spring to wintertime. Here are penitence and thanksgiving, human restraint and the frenzy—for it is this word which sainted mystics have always used—of the Divine affection for the created soul.

Returning from service abroad, I had a deep interest in the life of the Church; and this was augmented when I went back to Notre Dame in order to teach English. For nearly four precious years I profited by the intimate friendship of a priest in whose soul integrity, courage, and spiritual discernment were remarkably combined—Father Daniel Hudson, in his youth a convert from right out of the heart of New England Brahminism and in his old age a rarely beautiful spirit, like his own favorite Henry Suso. Thus I could truly feel that I had been fortunate, and be grateful. And since gratitude imposes an obligation, I could not well avoid trying to give to others some impression of what riches had come to me. That is the reason why I joined the staff of the *Commonweal*. This paper was a modest, but as I now realize, very ambitious effort to help Catholics feel intellectually at home in America.

I may say, to anyone who inquires into such things, that it would be difficult for a man who has gone the way I have gone not to have become aware of at least a few of the major problems which a modern Catholic must of necessity encounter. In my time the gulf which separates the educated American Catholic from his fellow-men in this country, at least, has widened rather than narrowed; and it is probable that something comparable has happened in other lands as well. The reason why this is so—and you will note that I am discounting some recent debating—is the ever-increasing secularization of the environment in which we live. It often seems to me that the dinner parties to which one is invited were never so gay and brilliant as they are now. But the people who come to them are interested in what concerns a man like me most deeply only as one might be fascinated by an old book or an ancient mariner. This society does not seem to realize that it is quite as absorbed in purely contemporary becoming as a devotee of a crystal ball might be in that curious object. It is healthy, in the valetudinarian sense; has a place for food and an hour for sex; changes its husbands and wives seemingly without reflection, because it has not time to look backward or forward; and believes it has found wonderful new drugs for social malformations just as it has discovered penicillin and will soon have a cure for cancer. Sometimes people will inquire courteously into the state of the Catholic mind. And one then has a feeling that this is set aside half unconsciously as a kind of last resort. If nothing else works, maybe we can always go back to the church. But there are so many other things that might work, and some favorite author is sure to be expounding a new one.

Sometimes I find it quite agonizing to observe the disintegration of an era with a sense of absolute powerlessness to do anything about it. The fact that one may be attacked, vilified, slandered, and abused meanwhile, is then almost a relief. There are so many matters of which a Catholic is believed to be ignorant—science, the higher criticism, psychology, democracy, economics. Yet it is not so much unawareness of which one is found guilty, but rather a chronic disposition to be out of date. Recently I tried to make a little conversation by regretting that the old Franconian city of Wuerzburg, a baroque jewel if there ever was one, had been so nearly destroyed. My companion stared at me uncomprehendingly. "One of the advantages of modern war," he declared firmly, "is that it makes room for Le Corbusier." And I suppose that one good thing about the fading out of the Christian Gospel must be, for such minds, that it has made room for Marx, who in turn is already out of date, even if the doctrine to follow his is still awaiting a publisher. The fact that the Gosepl is, as Newman made us see it, a continuously unfolding panorama of insight, and that the wisest word ever spoken of faith is that it can move even mountains, is apparently the least well realized of possibilities.

Therefore it is like balm to discover those Jews and Protestants in whom religious conviction still abides. Perhaps I may be permitted to say this, by way of conclusion, so that the religious convictions which I take with me into the approaching final period of my life may be more apparent than they might otherwise be. One of the reasons why Von Huegel is so great a writer is because he makes it marvelously evident that although mental prayer is the highest devotion, the forms of petition which a great religious community creates are rich not merely because of what is objectively in them, as word or statement, but also because of that which they can evoke from those who reverently use them. And so it seems to me far less important to note that Jew and Protestant and Catholic hold some beliefs in common than to observe that they are under the spell of the same hallowed forms of prayer. It is at once an august mystery and a curious fact that the *Sanctus,* which in the Mass precedes the Canon, is an old Hebrew expression of reverence for God. When a Protestant who has made holiness the business of his life reads the words of a Psalm he may well be drawing from it vastly more of goodness and glory than do I. And it has sometimes occurred to me that if the synagogue should adopt for its part the words of the Lord's Prayer it would be building between itself and the Christian Church a bridge like no other of which one can conceive.

At any rate such hope as one can entertain for the fate of our society springs, I think, from its perpetual commemoration, in humility and petition, of its possible destiny which is holiness, the *sanctificatio cordis* of which Paul spoke; and the specter of its doom which now stands at the gate, a figure more terrifying than even some beast of apocalyptic vision, is the final symbol of the deep disquiet which assent to unholiness breeds. I shall confess that, these things being so, there is reason to fear for the future of man. Yet it is evident that sometime there would be no future for him on this planet anyway. Where he may go from here, is always the fateful question. The Church says that its community is timeless. Some of it is militant, some suffering, some victorious. Enlisting for the quest of that victory seems to me worth the price of the discipline, the discomfort that is in one's members, the fighting on so many fronts. I should for my part not be able to find elsewhere a cause that did not seem tawdry by comparison.

Meanwhile I may grouse and mutter when some spiritual brass hat makes a fool of himself. There are times when I am absent on leave, or without leave. It is bitter, too, to discover that some other private in the ranks has a good deal more of courage and stamina than I possess. Or difficult to keep the curl off my lips when some squad is in a dither or goes on a wild goose chase. But I know always that this is the militia of God who have been given the mighty weapon of Love. *Magna res est amor,* à Kempis says. Yes, there is nothing so staggering as is the broadside of divine affection which might move through the pitiable heart of man against the grossness of the world Santayana says resignedly that it never will. I pray every day that he may be wrong—pray in spite of my own natural addiction to pessimism. Love is the weapon, yes. But hope is no man's land. One must have faith that it is good to be there.

# The Catholic Spirit in America

What was the Catholic share in the civilization fostered by the Anglo-American settlers? To some extent this question is crucial for our present purpose, because of the assumption, prevalent among those who are anxious to create an American caste, that the actual labor of building up these United States was uniquely a Protestant affair. I have made it sufficiently clear, I hope, that this book is not an attempt to steal from the Puritan or anybody else the credit to which he is legitimately entitled. On the other hand it is only reasonable to expect that the public ear will be quite as eager to welcome the narrative of what English Catholic pioneers and their successors managed to accomplish. This narrative may profitably be divided into two parts, the first of which relates to colonization that was solidly and frankly Catholic, the second of which has to do with the Catholic share in the American renaissance, particularly in New England.

Everybody knows that during the spring of 1634 Leonard Calvert, representing his brother the Lord Baltimore, landed with a group of Catholic colonists and began the settlement of St. Mary's, Maryland. The government was firmly established in 1636; and from then until 1649, every governor was made to swear "that he would not, by himself or another, directly or indirectly, trouble, molest or discountenance, any person professing to believe in Jesus Christ, for or in respect of religion; that he would make no difference of person, in conferring offices, favors or rewards, for or in respect

From *The Catholic Spirit in America* by George N. Shuster (New York: Dial Press, 1927), pp. 85-120.

of religion, but merely as they should be found faithful and well-deserving, and endued with moral virtues and abilities; that his aim should be public unity, and that if any person or officer should molest any person, professing to believe in Jesus Christ, on account of his religion, he would protect the person molested and punish the offender."

It was the first manifesto of the principle of tolerance in America. No one believing in Jesus Christ (and in those days not to believe in Him was to place oneself outside the pale of society) was to be persecuted or penalized for adhering to some specific creed or none. To some extent Lord Baltimore may have been governed by prudence in announcing this singularly liberal policy; but there is plenty of evidence to show that he and the men who followed him had been convinced by the trend of events in England that mutual forbearance alone promised peace and advancement in the domain of religion. He went even farther, and by insisting firmly upon absolute separation between Church and State in Maryland shocked more than a little the good Jesuits of the colony, who had been prepared for such a doctrine neither by the custom of states nor by the rules of canon and civil law. And so the Calverts became, more than a century prior to the Virginia Bill of Rights, sponsors and supporters of a principle which has now become so firmly embedded in American life that most of us accept it as casually as we do the rising of the sun.

What followed is not pleasant history, and a mere reference to it will suffice here. During 1649 a band of Puritans, forced to leave Virginia because of their incompatibility with the Established Church, were given a grant of land at Annapolis. No sooner had they settled than they refused to abide by the agreement made prior to their coming—a promise to take the oath of allegiance to the Maryland government. Their reasons were characteristic. The word "royal" occurred in the text of the oath, and also some allusion to the Roman Catholic religion. For a while they were placated by certain changes made to humor them, but by 1651 they had become so certain of Cromwell's triumph that they refused to elect delegates to the colonial Assembly. Two years later they addressed a petition to Richard Bennett and William Claiborne, Cromwellian commissioners for the colonies of Maryland and Virginia, complaining of a state of affairs under which they were obliged to swear "absolute subjection to a government where the ministers of state are bound by oath to countenance and defend the Roman Popish religion." Thereupon the commissioners arrived with armed forces and, in 1654, convened a legislature which deprived Catholics of "protection" under the law. The rest of the story is largely the record of a struggle which ended, under William and Mary, with the setting up of the Established Church in Maryland, to which the contumacious Puritans were obliged to pay tribute. Thus began and ended the first episode in the history of American tolerance—an episode which more than faintly suggests a parallel with some developments in our own time.

The Catholic stock which Lord Baltimore had planted in Maryland lived on and increased. Charles Carroll—who added "of Carrollton" to his signature at the bottom of the Declaration of Independence so that British wrath might not mistake its man—came of it. Later on it participated in the great migration westward, settling in Kentucky about 1785 and going from there to other places. The history of this great journey has never been satisfactorily written, but one can trace it to some extent by the remains which testify to its individuality. At Bardstown, amidst farm lands that were certainly not remarkably productive, the Marylanders built a little city which soon became the seat of a bishopric and the center to which various religious orders came. They preserved the best virtues of their stock and created the one typically English Catholic culture in the United States. No men have had a better right to the title "American," and none have ever taken greater pride in it.

The Spaldings are, perhaps, the best and most typical representatives of this variety of Catholic culture. Archbishop Martin J. Spalding and his nephew, Archbishop John Lancaster Spalding, were prelates who combined the vision of two advances—that of the Church and that of the nation— throughout their lives. As a theologian, historian and director of ecclesiastical affairs, the first restored to the old see of Baltimore the ideals of the sturdy folk who had first made Maryland possible. He also typified for Europe the American churchman that was to be—loyal, generous, public-spirited, not querulous. His nephew, renowned of course for much purely religious work, was also the first outstanding intellectual voice of Catholics in this country. Dealing intelligently and helpfully with the social problems which made their appearance soon after the close of the Civil War—labor, education, democratic culture—he combined age-old principles with an understanding of the here and now. We still relish his courteous, lapidary literary style; the justness of his vision; and the quality of his citizenship which, bred to the traditions of which the United States may justly be proud, was also, every inch, a Catholic citizenship.

If these are representative instances of the development of which pioneer Catholic stock proved capable,—and they are by no means isolated instances— the coming over of staunch American Protestants to the Church is no less colorful and significant a proof that the religion institutionalized in Europe during centuries did not spoil or slaughter souls in the New World. I have no brief to offer for the convert. It is entirely apart from my purpose here to uphold the reasonableness of his step, or to defend him against accusations of improper motivation. The men and women who in New England (and to a considerable extent elsewhere) voluntarily entered the Catholic society may have been hopelessly misguided, so far as I am here concerned. All I claim is this: their conversion, far from weakening the Americanism to which they had a clear title by reason of birth, breeding and spiritual heritage, strengthened their desire to serve the nation, to defend and develop the principles to which it had been officially pledged, and to give of themselves that others might live more abundantly. In a word, they did not attain to the full stature of their Americanism until they joined the Church.

The very origins of Catholicism in New England are associated with the willingness of certain eminent convert families to make great sacrifices for it. But although beginnings are always something, and immigration—chiefly Irish—had swelled the number of Catholics resident in the United States to a number which John Gilmary Shea estimated as having been 1,726,470 in the year 1850, it was a formidable step which the New Englander of the Emersonian period took when he entered the Church. Many came, nevertheless; and among them were two whom later epochs naturally regard as especially typical. Orestes Brownson was certainly one of the most inquisitive and relentlessly intellectual men of his time, vehemently given to constructive change though that was. Successively a Presbyterian, a Universalist, an Owenite, a Unitarian minister, a Saint-Simonian pamphleteer, a follower of Matthew Arnold's "new dispensation" and a spiritist, he had some right to believe that he had looked for the things of the soul in about every place where it was thought they might be hidden. His final acceptance of Catholicism was an act for the sincerity of which he gave testimony during many penitential days. It was not easy in those times to be the lay theologian, editor, critic and pamphleteer which Brownson was during many years; and I believe that the change from a spiritual world in which there had been the glorious bustle of Concord thinking and Brook Farm experimenting to the narrow little universe of a timid and provincial Catholicism often bruised his soul. Nevertheless he stood his ground to the end, setting an example of fortitude that deserves a fame it has never received, and incidentally stating his political creed—*The American Republic*—with a subtlety and breadth truly remarkable.

Orestes Brownson justified his faith in the Church and his confidence in the nation. His friend Isaac Hecker attempted a grandiose synthesis of the two. Perhaps the dream was too magnificent; at any rate Hecker, graduating from Brook Farm into a Catholic religious community, nursed in his heart a program of action which generations have not sufficed to carry out beyond the initial stages. Time and time again he was rudely beaten by his own idealistic temperament, by the failure of others to understand, and by the tremendous enmity of the age itself. And yet, though there are written estimates of Father Hecker which talk of him with niggardly cynicism, it is hard to understand how any American can fail to be deeply stirred by the work Isaac Hecker laid out for himself and the spirit in which he undertook it. His hope was to draw out from the increasingly large body of American Catholics such a treasure of creative intelligence and artistic feeling, such a blossoming of spiritual insight and charity, that the nation round about would catch fire in a salutary way. He was clear-sighted enough to see that the New England renaissance was not going to be the saving contagious flame; and though his own hope was also not realized, a thousand times more of its effect is today concretely visible than there is of inherited Bostonian idealism. From nothing did the man suffer more than from certain hasty, misguided accusations of "Americanism," and of nothing was he more conscious than of the quality of his citizenship.

It may well be noted that neither of these two men—or the many notable others who, like Elizabeth Seton, moved in the same spiritual direction—were ·at all of the type which rushes to Catholic cathedrals for aesthetic satisfaction. They were logical, truth-seeking, workaday, dogmatic people. There was a brief era, notable particularly in California, when love of ecclesiastical beauty drew some poets into the Church. But for the most part American aesthetes, though they can tell you all about the "charm" of Catholic ritual and, like some contemporary refined Hebraic souls, can make you as sick of their adjectives as ever you get of too much incense, have resolutely avoided taking the fatal step. The lovers of beauty in New England's great day sincerely admired Catholic things and sometimes—as in the cases of Longfellow and even Lowell—spoke intelligently about them. But the men and women who went the whole and often tragic distance were earnest folk intent upon accepting truth when they believed it had been offered them and devoted likewise to the nobler purposes of their country.

And yet this movement towards the Church in the "great epoch" was not a dour thing comprised of syllogisms but vibrant and vital, characterized not a little by the "romantic" fervor which then was moving round the earth. The influence of Cardinal Newman upon it, for instance, is difficult to overestimate. His attempt to awaken Oxford roused and modified many an American Anglican heart. It also fortified numerous souls newly become Catholic. So often does one come across it—in John Banister Tabb and James Kent Stone, for instance—that one is forced to believe an important part of the history of the Oxford Movement still remains to be written. This fact is noted here as further evidence that the Americans who accepted the Catholic idea were neither esoteric nor sterile, but truly alive. And if they were thoroughly convinced that the faith gained in bitter combat might prove a beneficent force in the renaissance of their country, it was at least partly because they had really grown up with that country and learned to know what it was.

I cannot ·refrain from ending these brief remarks about men who were essentially of American stuff, despite all flighty assertion to the contrary, with some reference to the figure who adorns most enlightened dithyrambs about our quality and destiny as a people. Walt Whitman has become, for many, the apotheosis of democracy, because he happened to be a barbarian! No conception could, of course, more pitilessly travesty him. Essentially the man was not even tentatively wild; in his heart he was tame, with that mammoth tameness which is sentimental, tearful and unsteady. Had he been a four-square savage, he would have swallowed beauty without losing his presence of mind; had he been a soldier he would have saluted Lincoln with a silent quatrain, as Tabb saluted Damien; had he been something of a pioneer, he would hardly have applauded himself. Walt Whitman, both as moralist and poet, was the creature of that ultimate refinement which we call leisure. He was prodigal with the stars because he had never been obliged to walk with the stars in their orbits. But it is quite true that he was tall enough to reach the stars—a circumstance which Americans generally have neither understood nor forgiven.

We have neither understood nor forgiven because the man was not one of us. America has been a giant swarm of immigrants thumbing vast spaces for a page on which to scrawl:—an uprooted swarm hunting multitudinous hives, carrying the hastily sorted baggage of lost cities, and marked with a simplicity that on the one hand was greed and on the other an earnest spiritual fidelity. It is no wonder that our fathers were stripped clean and made to look at loveliness as something not to be clutched, while they stalked the buffalo as they stalked each other—excepting when they made an inventory of those holiest and most wise of platitudes, which we call traditions. And certainly it is no wonder that Walt understood them not at all—Walt half asleep by the sea, rifling the cargoes of the great romantics and guzzling the wine of Shelley like a new god Pan. He was the maker of a bacchanalian threnody. His was a stave in the song Europe had been giddy with since the days of Rousseau.

The United States was destined to become the immigrant's work-shop. The Catholic Church was destined to become the immigrant's church. During the course of this astounding, quite unparalleled adventure, the issue narrowed into a query: Could the Church in caring for the immigrant spiritually, cooperate with the nation which was necessarily intent upon improving him civically? If this question could not be answered affirmatively—and there have been numerous occasions when some persons hastened to answer it in the negative—then Catholicism had really entered a country where it did not belong. In our present day and age, however, the nature of the correct reply has become so clear that the "No's" combine a great deal of caution with more than a relative indifference to history. Of course it is not yet altogether clear. Let us admit cheerfully that we are still not in a position to know how the final balance sheet of the immigration epoch will look, and that the Church in America has still to surmount many of the handicaps which this epoch imposed upon it.

Immigration is always more than a change of position. Normally it means going from a crowded space into an empty space—from a world crammed so tight that all kinds of rules are needed to render movement safe and even possible, into a world where one can walk arms akimbo without brushing against a soul. In the second place, there are reasons why the immigrant goes. Perhaps economic or social conditions have made life intolerable, as is likely to be the case when destructive wars, revolutions or industrial changes have occurred. Again, a group of persons may find themselves *non gratae* for some reason or other, and so practically forced to seek a living elsewhere. Finally, there may exist a desire to migrate, dependent upon any one of a dozen motives ranging from lofty idealism to a gross confidence that there will be more to eat for less work. At any rate immigration is not all of one piece, although it always implies trading a routine to which one has grown accustomed for newer and relatively freer conditions.

The circumstances thus hastily sketched profoundly influenced the settlement of the United States and therefore also the work of the Church. Customs which had prevailed in European homelands were abandoned in the new world, often at a serious loss of moral and social safeguards. More important, however, is the fact that the country absorbed so many who were penniless, who possessed the culture that goes with destitution, and who were interested first of all in improving their fortunes. These men and women proved easy marks for rapacious employers, both as bond-servants and later on as factory slaves. Our contemporary social order bears many a scar that had in its origin in this process of brutalization; and it is certainly (let us note in passing) a blessing for the white race that negro slavery saved it from the degradation of old-fashioned plantation drudgery. Finally, though we were fortunate in getting settlers who virtually exiled themselves for treasured ideals (and we got them from Germany, Poland and Ireland as well as from England), we also took in crowds of degenerate wretches whom old world governments were glad to get off their hands. In a word, the impact of immigration upon American institutions was really so heavy that they were often in danger of collapse.

When Washington arrived in New York to take the inaugural oath, the Catholic Church was certainly not prepared to meet the demands that would soon be placed upon it. It constituted a sorry and timid minority. Although the first Amendment to the federal constitution went far towards guaranteeing freedom of religious worship, many of the states recognized established churches in accordance with the practice of British law, and some specifically pointed a finger of reproof at Roman Catholics. Owing to the watchfulness of

Mr. John Jay, New York state required its subjects to "abjure" foreign priests and potentates, even in matters ecclesiastical. Groups of the faithful kept on existing, of course, but there is no doubt that thousands were lost in every state through lack of priests. Mr. Michael O'Brien, the tireless scribe of the American Irish Historical Society, estimates that a heavy percentage of those whom later genealogists would patriotically label "Scotch-Irish," Presbyterian wise, were scions of old families whose orthodoxy might have been vouched for by St. Columba himself. Rome, of course, knew very little about the infant United States, and even if it had the French Revolution and other matters were quite enough to absorb its attention.

Nor is this everything. Such ecclesiastics and laymen as were on the scene had lost practically all idea of ecclesiastical organization and discipline. They were not only without bishops but feared that acquiring one or two might be the signal for a massacre as well as an uncomfortable financial burden. Moreover the flame of democratic ardor which rose high during the "Citizen Genêt" days blazed furiously under more than one biretta and trustee cloak. A cynical spectator might well have fancied that the Catholic Church was bent on proving itself a useless nuisance. But in 1790 Father John Carroll, a singularly holy, humble and tactful man whom non-Catholics can form a better idea of if they think of Bishop Asbury, was consecrated first bishop of the American Church. His story is that of a bitter, heart-rending struggle for unity, but it is the story of constructive work. At its close there stood, unmistakable and clear, the word "Beginning."

The tide came and the Church proved fortunate in two respects. First, the major groups of Catholic immigrants were poor, often illiterate and sometimes very coarse, but they were people accustomed to making sacrifices for their convictions. Upon the heroic loyalty of Irish, German and French peasants, the Catholic structure could be reared as upon rock. It is not my purpose to eulogize these folk, among whom my own ancestors were. But it may be said of them that they were the sap of Europe, brave, spirited, unspoiled people whom no builder of empire would have turned away. Nine tenths of what the Church has accomplished in the United States is due to them—a tribute which shows clearly enough for all to see the democratic character of American Catholic growth. Secondly, there was soon no dearth of idealistic priests and religious, some of whom were princes, nobles and scholars in their home countries, to take up the work of direction. It can safely be said that no other class of immigrants drew after them so many of Europe's best as did the Catholics. More than one French seigneur and Austrian count labored in the wilderness as a missionary of the Church, riding cheerfully on farm wagons, breasting storms and snows, sitting past midnight at the death-beds of the poor.

After them came religious communities, men and women, often destined to find that their foundations here were to be made possible by Protestant generosity. One cannot say too often that if there is any phase of American life which reveals the fine nobility of our civic purpose, it is the long list of benefactions by those outside the church to convents and monasteries. These in turn brought something of old-world culture and of Christian charity. People unfamiliar with the subject often think of the "monastic life" as a single definite thing designed for a single, definite purpose. There are certain common characteristics; but the various foundations have each a very real individuality of tradition and tendency. Not a single one has ever been barred from the United States, and so the religious development of Catholics here gained a richness of quality and a diversity that match the complexity of our general national civilization. If this circumstance has sometimes created problems (as all contrasts do), one cannot doubt that the present stability and vitality of American Catholicism are largely due to irrigation by an unimpeded current of monasticism.

Gradually but steadily the immigrant population produced its own priesthood and hierarchy. The principle that a native clergy must be developed in every new country as speedily as possible had not been enunciated by Rome in the early nineteenth century as firmly as it has since been, but undoubtedly the whole weight of Catholic tradition was in support of that principle. It is interesting to remember that even Benjamin Franklin thought Catholics here would be best served by placing them under the jurisdiction of a foreign hierarchy. Sometimes certain groups of Catholics have agreed with him. But the Holy See has resolutely decided against all these, and may now be justly proud of the compactly organized and on the whole admirably motivated clergy which has almost entirely grown out of Americanized immigrant races. How peculiar it is that those who still conceive of the Popes as foreign "potentates" never stop to consider the illogical action of these "alien rulers" in seeing to it that the Church here become entirely native in complexion, bound by nothing whatever excepting spiritual allegiance! In all truth, the patriot ought to be proud of Catholicism because it is a genuine American institution. It is the work of people who have helped to build cities and to develop farms—who have even done their part in making good government subsist amongst us.

In the year 1927 Catholics are conscious that a share of the religious socialization of the immigrant has been achieved, as far as they are concerned. Tens of thousands were, no doubt, lost during the era of settlement; but very likely most of these were people to whom spiritual belief was merely a convention not worth much effort to retain. Few have been lost because of incompatibility between their citizenship and their religion—a very few, scandalized, perhaps, by unworthy leaders or disgusted by a certain cheapness of thought which has now and then characterized groups of Catholics lacking in charity or intelligence. But after all allowances have been made, Catholic experience during the era of immigration is a triumphant proof that the task of civil and religious socialization has been able to proceed without any duality whatever. The major portion of the conflicts which have arisen are, as we shall see, the result of circumstances quite non-religious in character.

The social status of the Catholic immigrant was often very low. It may be said without unkindness that the fine qualities of the Irish did not always compensate for that illiterate mentality which had been forced upon them during hundreds of years of political serfdom. You cannot beat and starve a people in the manner which Elizabeth's generals, Cromwell's soldiers and others thought eminently fitting where the Irish were concerned, without robbing them of their hunger for these dignities of culture which are largely the result of a consciousness of tradition. Similarly the German peasant, the toil-roughened Pole and the woefully primitive Italian would probably not have been apt pupils at Mr. Bronson Alcott's transcendental school. In the matter of disciplined intelligence as well as in the lesser sphere of social graces the run of English settlers had what may be termed a flying start. It may be added that unlike the better class of Jews, the Catholic immigrants did not always hanker immediately for the things they were without.

In the second place, conscious as he necessarily had to be that the racial and cultural complexion of America was English, the immigrant tended, individually and collectively, to adhere to his own racial tradition. This, precisely because it was modern, was often bound up with intense nationalistic feeling. Although the Irish began very early to take an active part in United States politics, they were really unified only by that melancholy consciousness of "unhappy Erin" which some of their great leaders kept vigorously alive. The Germans clung to their language, their partly vernacular liturgy, and quite generally to their sense of racial solidarity. Other immigrant groups acted similarly. To some extent these actions were inevitable, and to an even greater extent they were profitable, for the reason that they introduced important and attractive variations into the English monotone. But unfortunately no tradition can flourish in an alien atmosphere. That "provincialism" which characterizes all the Shanghais and Honolulus of the world settled upon immigrant conservatism here. Irish America, for instance, has had absolutely no part in the whole "Celtic renaissance," never getting farther intellectually than the outlook of Davis and Moore. And although the German Catholic press has been served by a number of first-rate men, it was never able to do more than cling to the skirts of intellectual and spiritual advancement in the mother country.

Moreover, there were reasons inherent in immigrant life in America for attributing a certain inferiority to Catholics. New England got its laborers and servants from among the Irish. When Emerson addressed some words of counsel to the "American young man," he recommended an interest in the uplifting of the negro, the Irishman and the Catholic. Hawthorne's descriptions of Irish life under incipient New England industrial conditions are so graphic that I cannot refrain from quoting an apt passage. An entry into the note-books for July 15th, 1837, records: "Went with B——— yesterday to visit several Irish shanties, endeavoring to find out who had stolen some rails of a fence. At the first door at which we knocked (a shanty with an earthen mound heaped up against the wall, two or three feet thick) the inmates were not up, though it was past eight o'clock. At last a middle-aged woman showed herself, half dressed, and completing her toilet. Threats were made of tearing down her house; for she is a lady of very indifferent morals and sells rum. Few of these people are connected with the mill-dam,—or, at least, many are not so, but have intruded themselves into the vacant huts which were occupied by the mill-dam people last year. In two or three places hereabouts there is quite a village of these dwellings, with a clay and board chimney, or oftener an old barrel, smoked and charred with the fire. One of the little hamlets stands on both sides of a deep dell, wooded and bush-grown, with a vista, as it were, into the heart of a wood in one direction, and to the broad, sunny river on the other. At two doors we saw very pretty and modest-looking young women,—one with a child in her arms. Indeed, they all have innumerable little children; and they are invariably in good health, though always dirty of face."

A later immigrant population was submerged under the rising wave of industrialism. Italians, Poles, Hungarians, Austrians, who in their home land had been simple villagers, became factory hands, keepers of tiny, fly-infested shops, venders, and finally bootleggers. Such conditions are not those which a benevolent well-wisher of the human race would recommend. They cannot be fully guaranteed to produce a moronic population, but their general tendency is undoubtedly in that direction. Social workers have cited so many examples that it is really useless for me to labor the point. And yet on the whole the chief complaints entertained by native Americans against the industrialized immigrant have not been based on statistics showing a wholesale moral collapse. Generally the argument has stressed about the same matters as Hawthorne's report did:—poverty, uninhabitable and slovenly houses, markedly alien habits, plenty of children and no maids, a certain clannishness. More particularly it has stressed the Tammany Halls which in almost every large city have capitalized the political ambitions and—though that is not now true of Tammany Hall itself—the political venality of the everlasting East or West Side. After all, in the business of civic corruption so much depends upon the name and appearance of one's club!

Regarding all of these matters, one fact needs to be emphasized. The handicaps which the foreigner brought with him have greatly impeded the work of the Church, although something may be said for them as sources of loyalty; *but those acquired by reason of social conditions in the United States have caused nine tenths of the ill-feeling against that Church.* Agitation against the Catholic has to a large extent been agitation against a class of people considered undesirable for other than religious reasons. The truth of this statement will become more apparent if we stop to consider what happens when a new district is opened to industrial production. Prior to the coming of the factory, the mine or the mill, there may have been a quiet town, populated by persons in easy circumstances between whom there existed a bond created by education, racial and social similarity, and perhaps the Protestant faith. Very likely a trim little church sheltered a congregation reasonably attentive to the remarks of the rector, and conscious at all events of the eminent respectability of being a pew holder. Now a heterogeneous population, bearing all the ear-marks Hawthorne so carefully noted and guilty of varied strangenesses of language and custom, begins to creep into the more antiquated houses. These prove inadequate, and a series of tents, shanties and crudely constructed dwellings gradually filter through all but the most exclusive streets. With these things come factory smoke, gaudy cinemas, replicas of Coney Island, secret sources of illicit liquor—in short, all the usual adornments of the factory town.

What follows? Well, two things. First, the Chamber of Commerce begins to whoop up a boom. Normally that means pressure on the City Council—more taxes for boulevards and parks, catering to the "foreign element" that can vote or at least does, and abolition of cherished property restrictions. Secondly, the trim little church and its congregation are submerged under an attack of untidiness and indifference. Generally the church finally surrenders to a good price for its real-estate, but anyhow the congregation moves out to more exclusive quarters, taking with it an intense resentment of the new order and what is presumed to have caused it. Seldom will a good American rise in wrath and condemn industry for the havoc wrought. Industry is business, and as such is reverenced by the Anglo-Saxon mind. But the working people—the foreigners, the Catholics! These obtrude themselves. everywhere, make matters worse by erecting atrocious but invariably huge churches, and end by running the municipal government to suit themselves— or those who know how to organize them.

I honestly believe that most American suspicion of Catholics from the point of view of the constitutional ideal of government is due to what has happened in large cities like New York and Chicago. The ward and its cabal, the party boss, and graft-riddled police force, the nepotistic judiciary—all these are laid to politicians who are, as a matter of fact, often men with names having something like a Catholic ring. A serious study of the situation would, of course, reveal the complete innocence of the Church. It is precisely because the Catholic clergy has so scrupulously refrained from indulging in civic or political instruction—precisely because it has issued no edicts against concrete governmental immorality—that the ignorance and supineness of certain large groups of Catholic voters is so complete. Of course the more notorious worthies are Catholics only in name. But apart from all such details, the fact remains that almost all agitation against the Church in large cities is not based on resentment of Catholic doctrine or religious belief but upon political and social conduct which has proved galling. The same thing is true, naturally enough, about the Jews and Protestant foreigners. But for some queer reason nobody seems to realize that there are innumerable Protestant foreigners, or to notice that a good share of city riff-raff come from families with an American pedigree as long as Jesse James's. It is possibly an oversight!

During recent years the honors for anti-Romanism have gone to the Ku Klux Klan. Having seen something of the methods and leadership of this highly commercial organization, I really do not think it has been or will be capable of doing any great injury to the Catholic cause, provided ecclesiastical buildings are adequately insured. But the phenomenon to which it bears witness—the phenomenon of the readiness of millions of hard-working, upright rural citizens to contribute money and wear uniforms in order that a number of individuals, usually disreputable and never distinguished, might glut their mean ambitions—is truly startling. One cannot get rid of the thing with an angry snort, because it is big and human enough to merit earnest attention. What has the Catholic done to merit this irate anathema? Here once again, I believe, we are confronted with a situation that has little or nothing to do with the Church, but which is an outgrowth of immigrant conditions.

The people who support the Klan are the people who abhor the city—abhor its sudden usurpation of economic and social power, the impression it gives of moral degradation, and the smell it leaves in the nostrils. Add to that a certain distaste deeply rooted in mankind though it is extremely difficult to explain—the distaste fomented by the mixing of races. This exists almost everywhere, but is perhaps most acute in the United States because of the problem created by the presence of the negro. Now all this is the work of the foreigner, thinks the rustic sage. The foreigner is the Catholic, and therefore! Rural anti-Romanism is based on instinct, not on intelligence, but somehow one admires it more for being so. There is an appalling rural problem in these United States, which is only very secondarily economic in character. The root is rather the fact that life has ebbed from the country, has followed the high tension wires of urban existence, and has returned in the shape of corrupt politics, naked chorus girls, poodle dogs, salacious books and the grosser offenses of the stock exchange. No wonder there is resentment. The country may not be any better, but it occupies the critic's seat.

Blaming all this on the Catholic Church (and, of course, on the Jews and the negroes) is really very funny. One may reasonably suppose that Broadway would be several thousand shades brighter and the moral complexion of the whole city as many shades darker if Catholicism lost its restraining grip on millions of people. But we shall be frank and admit that a certain portion of rural resentment *is* the Church's fault. Catholic concentration in certain large cities is not altogether a matter of chance. It was deliberately promoted by a number of well-meaning but short-sighted leaders who supposed that only group solidarity could preserve the faith. They overestimated the difficulties of rural ministry, and they really believed that antipathy to Catholics was essentially religious rather than social in character. As a matter of fact, a contemporary statistician (the Reverend J. Elliott Ross) has shown that where Catholic life has been established outside large cities, it has borne fruit more vigorously—judging by outward signs—than it has under industrial conditions. If more immigrants of fifty years ago had gone to the land, if their families had increased to the extent customary in the country, the Church would not be identified today with the city as against agriculture, its numerical strength would perhaps be greater and more evenly distributed, and contact would have dispelled the myriad gross illusions that exist about the "religion of the Popes."

Looking over the whole scene, one sees that the coming of the immigrant was an extremely perilous though inevitable adventure. To the Catholic Church fell a large share of the work of ministering to the spiritual needs of the new population. This work taxed its resources to the utmost. It faced conditions it was powerless to alter, met with numerous rebuffs, but succeeded in enkindling loyalty and enthusiasm upon the heels of which prosperity followed. To the nation at large, the immigrant was often a troublesome figure, although the blame for most of what is attributed to him really belongs to a system of industrial exploitation which was not modified until the establishment of organized labor and the spread of a new spirit among employers and financiers. The incessant clash between the old settler and the newcomer frequently led to convenient abuse of the Catholic Church, erroneously but nevertheless gloriously identified with the immigrant. The Church often suffered heavy losses of prestige and of that good will which instills optimism and so makes toil seem easier. In return that Church generously contributed to the national welfare, going out of its way to encourage loyalty to the United States among its members and performing deeds of mercy calculated to alleviate untold misery and to forestall wholesale immorality.

The Catholic record during the nation's wars is not and cannot be challenged. Every conflict has found the "Romanist" immigrant ready to take his part and even more. Similarly the Church has so resolutely opposed communistic movements that it may almost be said to have jeopardized its reputation as the sponsor of social action. The greatest civic service it has rendered, however, is the moral influence it has exerted over families and individuals. Although the "Thou shalt nots" it has thundered have done much, its most genuine achievement has been the promotion of positive good. Dealing with fallible, imperfect men, convinced that man is imperfect and fallible, it has proposed, day in and day out, nothing less than the Eight Beatitudes. One does not know where the nation could look for better or more exalted rules of conduct.

What of culture? One cannot conceive of either a nation or of the Kingdom of God without the twin elements of beauty and reason. These are the distinguishing characteristics of man, and we believe Christ had them in mind when He spoke of the coming of the Sacred Spirit. To them every specifically Catholic civilization has been faithful, so that even those to whom the assumptions of the Christian faith are chimerical reverence the harmony, the aspiration, of those best expressions of the European spirit which have been fittingly termed "memorials of the blessed." There is a strict, Diana-like beauty which belongs to logic and mathematical investigation; there is a softer loveliness, having more both of the senses and of mystical contemplativeness. Sons of the Church have joined the two in philosophic poems, in grave, full-blown minsters, and most particularly in the liturgy. Round about this central religious art of all Catholic ages, speculation and logic have flourished, lesser poets have sung of human adventure, and artisans have managed to be both busy and creative.

One would, of course, look in vain for achievement of this sort in the United States. Catholics have not even done what might reasonably have been expected of them to foster letters, speculation and the arts. There are some painters among them, but there has been only one John La Farge, who got few ecclesiastical commissions despite the magnificent possibilities of his stained glass. There have been Catholic poets, but all would have starved much sooner if they had depended upon the cheques and discrimination of their confreres. There has been a Catholic press, but barring notable efforts here and there in the periodical field, one characterizes this succinctly by saying that it knew only two moments of genuine vitality—one an Irish moment, when the passionate outcry of the Celtic cause rang true; the other a German moment, in which there was struck something like a note of sincere enthusiasm for a rich old culture. One may say in extenuation that the pressure of America's industrial revolution lay heavily upon Catholics. They were poor and weary, they had little time.

And yet this is not altogether an honest excuse. I cannot help thinking that the Catholic Church stripped bare, which one confronts in this country, is the outcome of martial conditions imposed by environment. It is the result of sacrificing much to gain more. During the hundred and fifty years of American Independence, the Catholic task has been to keep the faith alive—to build up a steadfast society of practicing members, and to defend itself against constant abuse. Necessarily the character of all primarily religious thinking became apologetic. We listened to a never-ending series of arguments about every detail of a complex creed, and our children were prepared for life by committing to memory a summary of dogmas called the catechism and by being exhorted to conform. The tenor of popular Catholic pedagogy became almost entirely logical and intellectual. Indeed, the priests were thought of as essentially "authorities," whose business it was to "know," and the layman was an adjunct individual obliged to "believe." This was certainly not an ideal state of affairs: based upon an incorrect theory of pedagogy, it created conditions not normal to full-grown spiritual life.

The leisurely, wise Old World Church had created a better system of popular education—the liturgy. In this marvelous, symmetrical blending of dogma and mystical insight, of sacrifice and prayer, charity and intelligence, there is fully expressed a faith which when reduced to intellectual outlines however correct always seems a little bleak and acrid. And about all this, like the glow which rests upon a perfect landscape, there lies a sacred glory, a loveliness, which transcends every other literary work of man. If those who have been deeply offended by some acrimonious phrase of Catholic apologetic, possibly with a result that they have kept angrily aloof from Catholic things ever since, would only read the texts of the *Missa Solemnis* or the *Missa pro Defunctis* over which Bach and Bruckner pondered! They could hardly fail to realize, then, that the love of God verily fills to the brim the faith that had lived on from the tomb of the Apostles. I have read the Mass for Good Friday many and many a time, but never without being profoundly moved by the vision of an earth there re-created by charity and goodness—an earth upon which Christ's death would have blossomed into that abundant life He so greatly desired. All this, of course, must be *believed,* not toyed with in a mere aesthetic mood. It is only as truth that it is really beautiful, but so it is beautiful beyond comparison.

Someday we shall restore liturgy to its place as the rhythm and the meaning of Catholic life; and having done that, we shall see rise round the chancel once again the myriad carven forms of man's aspiration, and shall hear the wonderful ecstasy of Heaven even in our profane songs. Liturgy is community religion; art is community intuition. Neither can flourish in cramped quarters, and Catholics even today live in something like an armed camp. It must be admitted, however, that any departure from a semi-military discipline is dangerous for all forms of society. Here Imperial Rome is as pertinent an example as the Church under the Renaissance Popes. If the strictures which have hemmed in American Catholics (and of these there are many besides the one I have named) involve a loss of creative freedom, they have nevertheless aided in making the basic task of religious socialization a success. One can safely say as much—for the past. Today it is already apparent, however, that something more must be attempted. A state of siege, accepted too long as a normal condition, destroys morale; and besides it is apparent that Catholicism in general is everywhere experiencing an awakening of its creative and intellectual force. One cannot doubt that unless it supports the numerous cultural essays which characterize it as present in America, its grip on men will relax and its service to the nation remain a mere fraction of what might have been.

In this connection it is profitable to note a peculiar historical phenomenon. The various United States frontiers all produced their books and bibelots, their magazines and literary cenacles. Cincinnati had the honor of being publisher to John Keats. There were budding novelists galore in all the pioneer states. But although Catholics were often numerically strong in the West and Middle-West, they contributed nothing of their own to the current literary and artistic production. Moreover, they remained practically without influence upon those who were doing things. Although James Hall, the greatest of early Middle-Western editors, defended Catholics against their critics, he went bankrupt as a result. The prevailing atmosphere was contentious and hostile. Father Stephen Theodore Badin, whose *Real Principles of Roman Catholics* was followed by an endless series of similar defenses, was during the major portion of his life an Indian missionary. It is significant that his one literary venture had to be an apologetic battle with chimeras and absurdities. So rare was literary talent among Catholics that when the weekly *Ave Maria* was begun at Notre Dame, Indiana, about 1875, its issues were made up almost entirely of translations from the French.

The contrast between this state of affairs and Puritan New England is highly remarkable. There, as we have seen, there existed a really notable interest in Catholic affairs and more than occasionally in the Catholic religion. This was not in any manner attributable to numerical and social influence—indeed, the "servant class" standard was anything excepting an inducement. What then was the cause? The only answer I can find is that the renaissance in New England was the adventure of educated men, who approached history and thought with some degree of scientific curiosity, who knew how to travel, and who were not altogether hidebound by prepossessions. This answer is substantiated by subsequent history. The Catholic tradition has never been refused a hearing in America wherever men existed who were really scholarly and interested in spiritual exploration. A "hearing" is, of course, hardly the proper word. There were lamentably few Catholics to contribute to the conversation; and for the most part, cultural concern with the Church in this country has been the result of patient personal investigation.

# The Life of Pope Pius XI

When Pope Pius XI died on the morning of February 10, 1939, one of the most extraordinary periods in the history of the Catholic Church and of human society came to a point of rest. Yet what are seventeen years in the long chronicle of that great religious institution of which he was the earthly ruler? Two hundred and sixty Popes had preceded him. Some of them had witnessed still more tragic and unsettled times. The first Pope Pius had lived during the persecutions of ancient Rome. The seventh had been Napoleon's prisoner. The ninth had been forced to surrender Rome to the legions of Garibaldi. To be a good Pope, one must possess the courage to see the world and its history as they are. Pius XI was unflinching and without illusions.

Desio, the town in which he was born on May 31, 1857, is just a little place about ten miles from Milan on the road to beautiful Lake Como. One can see the mountains in the distance; and even today there is not much else to look at in Desio, except a memorial to the town's most illustrious scion, Pope Pius. He was the fourth son of Francisco Ratti, and was christened Ambroglio Damiano Achille. The family were simple people, though they could trace their healthy lineage far back into the Middle Ages. Achille, as he was called, studied in the neighboring city of Monza, and then entered the Milan Seminary. He was ordained a priest in 1879, and spent some additional years of study in the Eternal City. Then he returned to the Milan Seminary as a professor.

From *Pope Pius XI and American Public Opinion,* edited by Robert J. Cuddihy and George N. Shuster (New York: Funk & Wagnalls Co., 1939), pp. 15-38. Reprinted by permission of the publisher.

Milan has a famous library, rich in Christian antiquities, called the Ambrosiana in memory of Saint Ambrose, the city's greatest bishop and one of the Church's most illustrious scholars. In 1907 Father Ratti was named Prefect of this institution, and so could indulge to the full his yearning for scholarship and his interest in the progress of intellectual culture. During that same year he published one of the more important of his essays in research— an edition of the "Atlantic Code" of Leonardo da Vinci. He was a careful and tireless worker, who is said to have had three writing desks, each piled high with materials concerning a special subject. The restoration of ancient manuscripts was often confided to him, and some of his work in this field was done for the J. P. Morgan collection. Nevertheless he was no mere book-worm. Trips to France and England gave him an insight into the life of other countries; and in Milan he organized a famous catechism class for chimney sweeps, gaining in this and other ways a firsthand knowledge of social conditions in the largest industrial city of Italy.

The appointment as Prefect of the Ambrosiana brought with it the rank of Domestic Prelate, one of the grades of the monsignorial dignity. Then he was transferred to the Vatican Library in 1911, and appointed a Canon of St. Peter's. Three years later he was placed in charge of this magnificent collection, for which he was destined to do so much in later years. Americans are justly proud of the fact that the modern equipment installed in this age-old Library come from the United States. But in 1914 the task was one of attempting to put some kind of order into a chaos of books and manuscripts. Monsignor Ratti confidently expected to devote his life to that task and to scholarly interests associated with it. One of his better known "intellectual holidays" came in 1914, when he traveled to Oxford and delivered a Latin address in honor of the 400th anniversary of the birth of Roger Bacon, mediaeval friar and scientist.

During these years Father Ratti had also been able to follow an avocation which at one time made him more famous than all his other labors. He was an expert mountain climber, who not merely wrote on the subject but scaled peaks along routes no one else had gone. During the summer of 1889, he and a companion made the first Italian ascent of Monte Rosa from the eastern side; and in the next year he and his good friend Father Luigi Graselli discovered a new route by which one could climb Mount Blanc on Italian soil. Father Graselli died in 1912, and the next year also proved to be Monsignor Ratti's last in the mountains. Concerning these he once wrote: "While one contemplates the immensity and beauty of the scenes which unfold themselves as one looks from the sublime summits of the Alps, the soul soars upward to God, the author and master of nature." His essays on mountaineering were collected and published in 1923.

When the World War broke out, Pope Pius X died grieving by reason of the things he saw would come upon mankind. His successor, Pope Benedict XV, was one of the greatest rulers the Catholic Church has ever had.

Few sovereigns have so perfectly blended kindliness with devotion to the well-being of all mankind, and infinite tact with great resolution of purpose. He steadfastly refused to take sides in the conflict, reserving all his energies to serve the cause of peace. So great an influence became his that virtually every people recognized anew the moral authority of the Vatican. When the conflict ended and reconstruction was about to begin, there was great need of dependable emissaries to reorganize the Church in troubled regions.

Nowhere were conditions more disturbed and chaotic than in Eastern Europe. A new Poland was about to result from many peace treaties, and the Baltic states—Lithuania and the others—had been severed from Russia. Early in 1918—that is, before the War ended and while the German army still occupied the greater portion of Eastern Europe—Monsignor Ratti was sent to Warsaw as Apostolic Visitator. The appointment called him away from his beloved Vatican Library with such startling suddenness that at first he doubted the news as well as his own fitness. Pope Benedict had chosen well. The newly appointed Visitator was first of all familiar with the German language, to perfect his knowledge of which he had translated difficult books. In addition he was very well read in Eastern European history, and cherished those dreams of Church Reunion to which he would turn with great zeal during his Pontificate.

Yet if he had foreseen all the difficulties that would cross his path, Monsignor Ratti might well have drawn back. National and class hatred was at the boiling point throughout the region. Monsignor Ratti was still able to deal with Kerensky concerning the appointment of a bishop to the See of Minsk. Soon, however, the Bolshevist Revolution had triumphed, the Germans had been defeated, and a new world was emerging. On June 6, 1919, Monsignor Ratti became Papal Nuncio to Poland, thus restoring a tie with the Holy See that had been abruptly broken off in 1792, when Poland was divided. The situation was complex and grave. Having won a long and seemingly hopeless struggle for freedom, the Poles were now eager to include within the boundaries of their new state all territories that had at any time been ruled over by Polish kings. The first consequence was a war with Russia, which the Vatican attempted in vain to prevent. In a little while disaster was imminent. Red armies were marching on Moscow, and the end of Poland seemed at hand. But General Weygand, a French commander of genius, succeeded in organizing resistance and routing the Russians.

Monsignor Ratti remained at his post during the time of peril, offering fervent prayer for peace. Not long afterward, Germans and Poles clashed over the Silesian question. How much of this territory, which formed the south-eastern portion of Germany, was to become Polish? The Allied Powers decided upon a plebiscite. Almost immediately the clergy on both sides began to participate in an active campaign, which was often more military than political. Monsignor Ratti thereupon went to the disputed region and urged all the clergy to maintain a neutral attitude. The Vatican itself intervened, bidding every priest to remain silent. But passions were so strong that the order could not always be enforced.

On December 2, 1920, the Papal Nuncio returned to Rome. The following year, he was consecrated Cardinal Archbishop of Milan. Doubtless he expected to remain at this post for many years. Pope Benedict was a comparatively young man, and no one anticipated his sudden death. But he was stricken with pneumonia, which at first seemed not to threaten his life; and yet the illness took a decided turn for the worse, and on January 22, 1922, the Pope died. The Conclave which followed was of short duration. Cardinal Ratti was chosen on the fourteenth ballot, the date of election being February 6, 1922. His name had seldom been mentioned in the press, but in inner ecclesiastical circles he had been a favored candidate.

The new Pope then surprised all Italy by breaking with a tradition which his three predecessors had established. On the day of his coronation, he walked out upon the central balcony of St. Peter's, gave his blessing, and explained, "Pius is a name meaning peace, and I shall bear it for that reason." Ever since the taking of Rome by Italian nationalists in 1870, the Popes had not been seen outside the Vatican buildings, as a sign of protest against the usurpation of the temporal power of the Holy See. Pope Pius broke with this precedent and thus indicated that he was willing to cooperate in every way possible with the Italian State. In his first Encyclical Letter, dated December 23, 1922, he nevertheless reaffirmed the just claims of the Popes to their temporal possessions.

This Encyclical was an ardent plea for peace. It seemed, however, that Italy was not minded to respond. The first months of Pope Pius's reign were marked by growing hostility between the Fascists and other political groups. There had been numerous disorders under his predecessor's reign—attempts by Socialists to take over industrial plants, street battles between Blackshirts and adherents of the new Popular Party (which had organized Catholics independently of, though with the permission of, the Vatican), and opposition to the authority of the state. Then on October 29, 1922, Mussolini ordered his cohorts to march on Rome; and they met with no opposition from the army or the police. Those were anxious days. An anti-clerical group inside the Fascist Party continued to war on Catholics, whether clerical or lay. On the other hand, Mussolini himself made overtures that breathed a real desire to make peace with the Church. He averred in particular that he was a "Catholic" and that it seemed to him impossible to make Catholicism an Italian state religion.

During the months that followed, the Church had much to deplore. Armed bands of Fascists arbitrarily gratified their lust for power. A climax was reached when Don Minzoni, one of the most beloved of Italian priests, was ambushed at Argenta and slain. Such actions naturally aroused a great deal of indignation. Nevertheless the authorities of the Church also noted with pleasure that in several respects the new Fascist rulers were an improvement over the older "Liberals." For example, the value of religious instruction in the schools was officially proclaimed, and the right of the Church to determine who the teachers were to be was conceded. Pope Pius himself dealt with the situation in an address to the Secret Consistory on March 24, 1923. He praised all that was just in the new order of things, but reproved with great frankness and energy the evils which a revolutionary dictatorship had brought to Italy.

It is impossible to describe here in any detail the development of the Church in Italy under the Fascist regime. We must content ourselves with noting that there existed a Fascist Party group which was violently anti-clerical, and a group which desired amity with the Church. Undoubtedly the second had the support of the monarchy, the army and the diplomatic corps. In like manner there was a group of Catholic churchmen who felt that peace with the Fascisti was obtainable, and a group which disapproved of compromise. The Holy Father himself adopted the attitude which had characterized him during his period of service as Nuncio to Poland. He counseled priests to abstain from political activity, thus virtually forcing the leaders of the Popular Party to resign.

Instead more and more reliance was placed upon "Catholic Action," which the Holy Father had first proposed in his Encyclical Letter of December 23, 1922. Originally this was intended to supply a kind of framework inside which the clergy and the laity could join hands in the work of the Christian apostolate. New rights and privileges were conferred upon the layman, who was said to "share in the priesthood." But under the new conditions prevailing in Italy, "Catholic Action Clubs" began to assume a quasi-political character. They supported actions calculated to assure defense of the Church's rights, and to provide as much organized protest as possible to hostile government decrees. One result of this trend was that outside Italy many assumed that "Catholic Action" was to supplant all other forms of corporate Catholic activity. This impression persisted until 1937, when three further Encyclical Letters, dealing with Communism and with conditions in Germany and Mexico, made it clear that other established forms of Catholic organization were likewise endorsed.

Then in 1929 Pope Pius reached one of the most important decisions of his Pontificate. The Lateran Treaties, signed on February 11, 1929, settled the "Roman Question" in a manner that aroused the admiration of diplomats and historians. There were three separate agreements. In the first all territories that once belonged to the Papal States were ceded to Italy, except a small area including the Vatican buildings proper and the adjacent park. This domain was called "Vatican City" and accorded all the rights of an independent realm. For its part, the Italian government solemnly acknowledged the independent sovereignty of the Holy See, and declared that Catholicism was the "sole state religion" of Italy. The second agreement stipulated that 1,750,000,00 lire were to be paid the Vatican as indemnity for the surrendered territory. The third agreement was designed to prepare the way for a "Concordat." It was a formal statement of the rights which Church and State conceded to each. Highly important concessions to Catholic principles in educational and marriage legislation were made. Of course these Treaties were criticized by men in several camps. But it is apparent that if the Italian government really meant to live up to the promises made, the outlook for religious peace in Italy was very bright.

It is probable that intentions on both sides were of the best. But political attitudes are fluid things, especially when times are as troubled as they have recently been. The four years which followed the signing of the Lateran Treaties were ruffled by four conflicts, all of which were tentatively glossed over by recourse to compromise. They had to do with education, the organization of Catholic youth, the freedom of Catholic Action, and the failure of the government to respect the Church's wishes in the matter of marriage legislation. Not a few of the Pope's Encyclical Letters were kept out of the Italian press; others were ridiculed. In one instance copies intended for publication in foreign countries had to be smuggled out of Italy in advance.

Meanwhile storm clouds had massed on many another horizon. At first the outlook for a moderately satisfactory agreement with the Bolshevist regime in Russia had not seemed hopeless. In order to relieve the famine which then raged in the Volga basin, the Papacy had organized relief work on a large scale. But during 1923, Archbishop Cieplak and other churchmen were imprisoned, brought to trial, and sentenced to death or life imprisonment by judges who disregarded completely the norms of justice. The Vatican thereupon broke off negotiations for an exchange of diplomatic representatives; and ever since the Church has been committed to an unwavering crusade against Communism. Though it seemed at one time that Stalin might make concessions to religion and thus mitigate the opposition of Rome, nothing came of those hopes.

The doctrines of Lenin and Trotski engaged the Pope's attention in countries other than Russia. When the struggle between Church and State in Mexico was resumed under the Presidency of General Plutarcho Calles, the

Vatican did not think the underlying difficulties were essentially different from what they had been during any phase of the "Mexican Revolution." Pope Pius urged Catholics to abstain from all violence. But though a measure of peace was restored, largely as a result of the diplomatic intervention of Mr. Dwight L. Morrow, conditions improved very little. Gradually it came to be taken for granted that the forces which had committed Russia to godlessness were at work in Mexico also. Despite ceaseless efforts to sponsor conciliation, the Catholic population continued to suffer and the educational, charitable and religious work of the Church was hampered. In 1937 Pope Pius wrote an Encyclical Letter urging Mexican Catholics to renewed effort.

With the rise of Hitlerism in Germany, the Communist question became even more important than it had previously been. Did not the Nazis profess to be the defenders of civilization against the Bolshevist tide? In spite of grave misgivings, the Vatican attempted to meet the new German government half way. A Concordat which seemed to assure the continuance of Catholic educational and charitable work on a fair basis was signed during 1933. But the ink was hardly dry when violations of the most important clauses were reported. As the years went on, it became clear that Hitler would not rest until he had completely subordinated the Church to the German State. During March, 1937, an Encyclical Letter written in the German language was distributed to priests and read from all the pulpits of Germany. This action did not bring about any improvement in the position of the Church. Indeed, the plight of Catholics became so desperate that to all but a very few Catholics throughout the world it became apparent that "Brown Bolshevism" was even worse than "Red Bolshevism."

Meanwhile the Rome-Berlin "axis" had come into being. Mussolini traveled through Germany. He assented to the annexation of Austria, and did not act in an effective manner to secure the release from prison of Dr. Kurt von Schuschnigg, former Austrian Chancellor, who was bound to the Vatican by especially intimate ties. When Hitler came to Rome, no meeting between him and the Pope was arranged. Instead the Holy Father protested against the coming of one whose sign was a cross hostile to the Cross of Christ. He also issued instructions forbidding the teaching of racist doctrines in any Catholic institution. The answer came from Mussolini, who decreed race laws for Italy. This action was widely looked upon as a retaliation against the Vatican. Nothing remained for the Pope to do except to protest against the new Italian legislation. Almost the last act of his life was to arrange for a convocation of Italian bishops, for the purpose of denouncing the race laws.

The struggle of the Church against Communism and National Socialism became especially tragic when civil war broke out in Spain. A "Popular Front" government was elected in 1936, and some of its radical supporters immediately began to make a scapegoat of the Church. On the other hand,

Nazi sympathizers and propagandists had also obtained a foothold in the country. When General Franco revolted and entered Spain with troops brought from Morocco with Italian aid, Leftist radicals started a "reign of terror" during the course of which thousands of priests and religious were slain. Churches and convents were looted and burned. Pope Pius at first hoped that "moderate elements" would triumph over extremists, and that the savage civil war could be ended before irreparable damage had been done. But it soon became evident that the future of the Church in Spain could be assured only if the radical Leftists were defeated, and that on neither side was there a disposition to seek anything but a smashing victory. The Vatican strove constantly to restrain the Insurgents from committing excesses, but it abstained from any other action likely to aid the Loyalists. Victims of the war besieged the Pontiff with petitions it was not in his power to grant. But his conduct was always that of a saintly lover of peace who permitted no word of hatred to cross his lips.

Ardent devotion to peace was from the beginning characteristic of this great Pope. He had dedicated his reign to the ideal of "the peace of Christ in the kingdom of Christ"; and he once prayed that God might scatter the nations that wished for war. During the crisis which settled upon Europe when Germany threatened the sovereignty of Czechoslovakia in 1938, he delivered a radio address to the world in which he offered what remained of his life to God as a willing sacrifice to avert the horrors of war from the peoples of the earth. His voice trembled with emotion as he spoke, and all who listened came away moved. It was partly in appreciation of this idealism that Prime Minister Neville Chamberlain paid a significant visit to the Vatican while in Rome for conferences with Mussolini.

Pope Pius did not only attempt to ward off evil from human society. He also outlined a program of action designed to promote the good. He wrote Encyclicals on family life, social reform, and education, in which the teachings of the Church were applied to modern circumstances. The most widely noticed of these documents was *Quadragesimo Anno*—"After Forty Years"— which proposed a corporative economic society divorced from all totalitarian or dictatorial tendencies. It defended the rights of labor against unjust aggression, and attacked the selfishness of plutocratic control. The abiding value of this great new charter of human rights is not lessened by the fact that some have sought, for selfish ends, to misinterpret it or rob it of its true meaning.

There is much else of absorbing interest in the chronicle of this Pope's relations with governments and his efforts to wrestle with the problems of modern society. He wrote thirty Encyclical Letters on a great variety of subjects; and though each drew from reports prepared by specialists in the particular subject under discussion, the actual composition was the Pope's own work. On everything he said and did he left the imprint of his mind and of his unmistakable style. He was destined to find that few of the projects on which he had set store could be realized in this stormy and revolutionist world. The times were filled with distress and evil. Nevertheless there was much that gave him encouragement—the sincere affection and loyalty of millions of Catholics, the esteem of those not of "the household of the faith," and the consciousness that he was the advocate of a peace which in the end would be accorded to all men of good will.

Perhaps the future will remember Pope Pius for things which at present seem less sensational than diplomatic activities or proclamations on world problems. He was first of all interested in the life of the Church and of course influenced it profoundly. One memorable fact is the large number of canonizations and beatifications which have marked his reign. He raised to the honor of sainthood Jeanne d'Arc, Thomas More, John Fisher, and Robert Bellarmine—surely as noble a galaxy of the servants of heroic virtue as any time has proposed for emulation. He honored in like manner the Jesuit martyrs—Isaac Jogues and the others—who suffered death at the hands of the Iroquois; and he beatified the first American woman so signaled out—Mother Mary Cabrini. Thirteen illustrious names were added to the roster of holiness during the year 1933—the Holy Year—alone. There can be no doubt that in the future his reign will be looked upon as a time of unusual spiritual fortitude. Thousands of martyrs died as witnesses to the faith in many lands.

Then, too, few Popes have appointed so many Cardinals and Bishops. On December 16, 1935, twenty new prelates were added to the College of Cardinals. Occasionally he made a quite personal choice. When he returned from Poland, he stopped in Vienna, which was then in the throes of political change. At the railroad station he was advised to spend the night at a quiet monastery in a by-street. There he met a simple priest with whom he conversed at great length. Once he had become Pope he remembered that excellent priest—now one of the glories of the Catholic hierarchy of Europe—and made him a Cardinal. Comparable to this was his insistence that a native priesthood in missionary countries deserved to have native bishops. These had often been discussed, but it was not the practice actually to choose them. Pope Pius named twenty-six in China, Japan, and other countries.

The supra-national character of the Church was always self-evident to him. That is why he looked forward so hopefully to the building of the Vatican Radio Station, which would permit Rome to address the world. Though nationalistic rivalry and other problems prevented it from rendering the service that had been planned, it did make possible a great number of broadcasts. When he gave his blessing over the radio, it is no exaggeration to say that millions throughout the world knelt to receive it. All other means of communication were similarly enlisted in the service of religion. He endorsed the use of airplanes and motor-boats in the mission field; sent Papal Legates over land and sea to International Eucharistic Congresses and other gatherings; and changed the legislation governing the election of Popes to permit attendance by Cardinals in every part of the world. He authorized the use of the automobile in the Vatican establishment. Perhaps the most significant of all his manifold scientific interests were these: the creation of a Papal Academy of Sciences, and the Mission Museum. The second houses a collection of the greatest interest and value.

Historians will be concerned in particular with the effect of those great documents in which he sought to influence and guide the minds of his flock. The Catholic Church looks back upon a long line of illustrious teachers, whom it speaks of as "doctors" and "fathers." One thinks it not incorrect to say that Pope Pius will rank with them. The present essay is not a theological treatise, and yet it cannot leave altogether unnoticed an aspect of the Pontiff's achievement which he himself would have considered more important than all else. We shall, therefore, call attention to certain basic teachings concerning the Christian religion and its bearing on the individual, the family and the structure of society.

The ideal of Christ the King is as old as the Church, but was restated in modern terms in the Encyclical which bears the title *Quas primas.* When publication of this great paper was first announced in 1925, not a few took alarm, believing on the basis of early garbled reports that Pope Pius was about to proclaim the right of the Catholic Church to rule in a temporal sense over the whole world. The text was cabled to the American press, which was somewhat taken aback when its editors found out that a deep and difficult theological document was before them. Pope Pius had revived teaching concerning the living presence of Christ in the Church, and therewith of course in the visible world, which had been formulated many centuries ago by St. Paul, St. Augustine, and St. Thomas Aquinas. He then also instituted a feast-day of Christ the King; and the great truth celebrated on that day, and indeed throughout the year, has deeply impressed itself not on Catholics merely but upon numerous believing Protestants as well. Sometimes also the faithful have more openly manifested their willingness to proclaim Christ the ruler of their hearts and their ambitions. Thus in Mexico the cry, *Viva Cristo Rey!,* was the slogan of Catholic resistance to a government committed to suppression of religious freedom.

Individual well-being and the spiritual recipes for attaining to it form the theme of several important Encyclicals. Years ago an American thinker published a book which urged all to practise the ancient habit of retreat from the world in order to meditate. Just as it is necessary for the city-dweller to go back annually to nature during some weeks of vacation, so (he held) is it expedient for the mind's sake to dwell awhile in silence. Pope Pius believed that religion could take deep root in man's heart only if the individual would retreat periodically from the busy world; and so he recommended the regular practice of those "spiritual exercises" which the great Loyola once designed for himself and his followers. He also proposed for imitation the similar practice of St. Francis de Sales and of St. Francis of Assisi. In so far as the priesthood was concerned, he relied particularly upon the fostering of right methods of training. With this he dealt in the Encyclical, *Studiorum Ducem,* which has to do primarily with the example set by St. Thomas Aquinas, the great medieval teacher of theology and philosophy. Later on the Pope issued regulations designed to improve and strengthen the educational system adopted in Catholic institutions which instruct the clergy.

The family was an object of constant solicitude. He was profoundly distressed by prevalent symptoms of moral decay, and likewise by the pressure of economic disorder on the home. A widely read Encyclical, *Casti Connubii,* set forth anew the Christian ideal of marriage. It also discussed such moot questions as sterilization, eugenics and birth control. Pope Pius insisted that resort to artificial methods of family limitation was immoral, though he was no less insistent that fathers and mothers could not be expected to live normal lives unless society provided the means for obtaining a decent livelihood. Later on, of course, the condemnation of sterilization became a grave issue when the German government, committed to the race laws advocated by National Socialism, proceeded to make sterilization an official practice. Pope Pius also insisted, in another Encyclical on education, that parents have the right to determine the manner in which their children are to be educated. Yet this right cannot absolve Catholic parents of the duty to insist upon a religious eudcation. For a child is not properly trained unless as much attention is paid to the soul as to the body and the mind.

Papal teaching on human society—especially the economic organization of that society—is as old as the institution of the Roman See, but it has latterly become of crucial importance owing to the emergence of totally new forces and conditions. Pope Pius was troubled especially by two facts: the deepening of class hatred, and the growing indifference of both extremes to any kind of moral principle. The ideal everyone seeks is, of course, social peace; and yet there can be no such peace as long as the aim on both sides is to dominate illegally. If the Communist seeks to create a social order inside which labor alone shall have the right to speak, or if the predatory capitalist attempts to wrest unto himself control of the resources which are the very life blood of men—then the sole result to be expected is the drying up of the sources from which the prosperity of men arises. That greed, whether of the right or the left, is the basic reason why the world in which we live is so appallingly incompatible with the scientific progress made by inventors and discoverers is a fact which Pope Pius never tired of stressing. And he saw that the first cause of that greed was widespread indifference to religious values and to the teaching of the Prince of Peace.

When read in their entirety these documents constitute a system of Catholic ethics for the new age. Those of differing creeds may question some of the conclusions arrived at, nor is every Papal statement an infallible utterance. But doubtless no one who reads through what Pope Pius wrote will question the high sincerity of his motives, or the noble idealism of his proposals. A whole literature has grown up round about his Encyclicals, and not the least valuable part of it bears the signature of men who clung to other faiths. This is a truly remarkable fact, testifying as hardly anything else could so effectively that the Papacy is a moral force which, when welded to the person of a great man, is without a rival anywhere.

Being a scholar and churchman who succeeded by dint of assiduity and determination to shirk no duty of his office, Pope Pius left behind no fund of anecdote such as surrounds the memory of the two preceding Pontiffs of the same name. He was not given to making witty retorts, or to cultivating personal friendships during leisure hours. There remains instead the remembrance of the deep, almost old-fashioned courtesy of his mind. All that is human interested him. Many a visitor to the Vatican was welcomed not because he represented political forces having an important bearing upon the work of the Church, but because his knowledge of an absorbing subject could add to the store of information which Pope Pius amassed during a lifetime and then placed at the disposal of all Christendom. He was extraordinarily well-read and unusually alert. Yet the work of the priesthood remained his chief concern, and to it all else was subordinated.

He had always been respected and admired by his own flock and by religious leaders of all creeds. But genuine personal affection came with the illness which beset him in 1936. Then age and incessant toil combined to weaken his magnificent constitution, and it was soon realized that the malady from which he suffered could find no permanent remedy in this life. He did not succumb to illness, however. Some had thought that he would never be able to walk again; others fancied that he should have to delegate the duties of his office to others. He surprised them all by rallying and demonstrating his splendid courage. Time and time again he met the most trying situations with calmness and determination, as when he refused to permit the downfall of Austria to affect the resolution of the Catholic Church to oppose what is false in Nazi teaching. In those days of upheaval he proved that he was a tower of strength, and a great shepherd of his people. No one ever clung so devotedly to the ideal of peace, but to him that ideal meant neither weakness nor surrender.

The world was touched and stirred, as it has been by no other phenomenon of recent history. It applauded the "old man of the Vatican" with a fervor marred by no qualifications or queries. And when at last the angel of death would not be gainsaid, and when men had sorrowingly to realize that a majestic voice would speak to them no more, the veneration accorded him was no formal courtesy but a deep profession of gratitude. To those who had borne the burden of a conflict against forces of evil and retrogression, his support had seemed that which alone made life bearable; and it was their gratefulness which eddied round his death bed like clouds of unseen incense, and their prayer which ushered his parting soul into the mansion eternally prepared for it. Before he died he made a remark that will forever be identified with his memory—"There is so much to do!" By that he gave encouragement to all who had loved or followed him. He assured them that work for righteousness' sake is worth doing—that despite all the seeming failure of justice in an unjust world, the truth is mighty and shall prevail. He is therefore enshrined in millions of hearts as a light and a guide, whose personal infirmity only threw into relief the staunch permanence of his resolve.

Perhaps one may venture to sum up in a few words the inner significance of his apostolate. Pope Pius had wished primarily to free the work of the Church from inhibitions that were the legacy of the past. His policy, therefore, was to bridge the gulf between Catholicism and Italy which was the legacy of 1870, and which to a large extent also kept the Church aloof from other peoples and movements. He sought also to liberate the clergy from commitments to political policies or forms of government, so that old and non-essential cleavages among Catholics might cease to be. Still more impressive was his desire to keep laity and clergy together—to dispel the notion that the priesthood was a thing utterly apart from normal life, in which the layman had no share. To him the Church knew no boundaries of race or nation. He infused into missionary activity a new vigor by conferring equality of status upon the young Church in Asia and Africa. Finally he made every possible effort to show that the faith of Christ does not stand apart from endeavors to better the conditions under which men and women live. In short, he flung the doors of the Sanctuary wide open; and it was not his fault but his tragedy that the invitation so often went unheeded.

For what he most desired was fated not to be. His Pontificate was not an era of peace but a time of deepening shadows at the edge of which conflict, more devastating than any humanity had known, waited for its endorsement as—in words once set down by Adolf Hitler—that which gives those who are destined to rule the earth their opportunity. The seventeen years were years of war, of persecution, of ruthless change and almost endless sorrow. A tide of refugees flung themselves at the barriers erected by peoples still remaining free. And in not a few countries the Church itself returned to the Catacombs. The aged Pontiff who rose from a bed of illness to stand at the helm of the vessel once confided to Peter the Apostle had no comforting vision of a tranquil haven soon to be reached. About him there was storm and a heavy sea. But one thinks his heart enshrined a great calm—the peace which God alone can give, which is the restfulness of the knowledge that eternity is triumphant over time.

# The Harrowing of the Cardinal

... Cardinal Mindszenty first came into quasi-political prominence by being thrown into prison by Hungarian Nazis during the fall of 1944. He was at the time Bishop of Veszprém. The narrative which follows, for which I am indebted to Lajos Hajdu-Nemeth, illustrates very well the situation in which Catholics found themselves. The Bishop had been carted off to a concentration camp at Sopronköhida, a place in the Western part of the country, together with a number of priests. He was termed "a dangerous enemy of the government." Since the roster of prisoners was constantly growing while the Russians were steadily advancing westward, the Bishop was confined under strict guard in a neighboring nunnery. Yet it was possible for Hajdu-Nemeth, then in the army, to arrange a private interview with the Bishop—with the connivance of the jailers in charge—and to plan a dramatic abduction of the episcopal captive. A military identity card, complete with a photograph, was prepared for "Joseph Szendi, corporal, honorably discharged." Civilian clothes as well as a horse and buggy were provided. Then almost in the twinkling of an eye the military front collapsed, the prison guards fled, and the inmates were left to fend for themselves. From such episodes one can glean what camaraderie there existed among Catholics, and how much steadfastness and loyalty they felt towards one another. Yet these were family virtues. Catholics were not masters of the nation's destiny. They were seemingly always apart, and often in the opposition.

With such matters the Cardinal had constantly to reckon, even as he did
with the traditions which were so deeply rooted in Hungarian intellectual soil.
Cardinal Mindszenty could not, for example, think of the past without
conjuring to mind the Hungarian bishop who almost single-handed had
brought about a rebirth of religion in his country and beyond that had greatly
influenced religious developments throughout Europe. Ottokar Prohaszka
might seem to some a spiritual Romanticist, even as Cardinal Newman (whom
he in many ways resembles) has been called a victim of the demon of the
absolute. Yet it is very obvious that he was a rarely gifted, saintly man whose
own constant quest for holiness made him aware of the difficulties others
have with weakness and sin. Bishop Prohaszka's father, a Sudeten German
officer in the armies of the Emperor Francis Joseph, met the daughter of an
Hungarian baker at a decorous reception and fell in love with her. She was a
slip of a thing and he a man of forty. But in the true style of yester-year
romance he surrendered his commission, took a humdrum civilian post,
married the girl and lived happily ever after. Their brilliant son studied for the
priesthood in Rome and elsewhere and then began the mission which in a
short lifetime profoundly altered European spiritual history.

Round about him was a clergy which was on the whole sound but
intellectually inert. Its members were, by and large, content with their official
status; and when modern thought or newer industrial conditions carried
intellectuals and people away from old moorings, they shrugged their shoulders and went off to play chess unless, indeed, their amusements were upon
occasion less innocent. Prohaszka carried on his mission of reform and
enlightenment with quite unparalleled regard for individuals and equally great
concern for the multitude. His pastoral and homiletic gifts were most unusual, and yet he found time not merely to familiarize himself with new trends in
scientific thought but also to master whatever was being said constructively
by Catholics about social problems. He visited the United States and predicted that there the problem of right relationships between capital and labor
would first be soundly solved. The revolutionary encyclical letter of Pope Leo
XIII on labor, entitled *Rerum Novarum,* was presented to the Hungarian
people in his own vigorous translation. Still he was no onesided devotee of
economics and political science. Though he could vie with the best of men in
urging people to perform their civic duties, his most popular book remained
the *Meditations on the Gospels,* which were translated into many languages
and are still widely read. That such a leader was destined to have enemies is
self-evident. But he also made a host of friends and disciples. To no other
man of his time did the Hungarian intelligentsia, Protestant or indeed those
without firm religious commitments, pay so marked a tribute of homage.
When he died in 1927 Catholic Hungary was prepared as it certainly would
not otherwise have been to meet the challenges which would soon assail it
from every quarter.

Prohaszka had come to Esztergom as a young priest, in his soul the zest he had imbibed from the Jesuits while studying in Rome; and though he was never permitted by his superiors to join the Society, he retained a spiritual kinship with the zealous and yet remarkably realistic men whom Loyola and his successors had drawn to themselves from the East of Europe—Stanislas Kotska and Casimir Sarvievius among them. His diary, a document characterized by fits and starts only, indicates that he walked among the columns of the basilica "by day or on moonlit nights," meditating. "Like Samson I stood under the magnificent pillars, not to bring them down but to derive strength from their glory," one reads. "All I have in me that has proved in a measure fruitful in this life and this dirty world comes from there." And of course there were many who did not approve of the charity which he harbored almost extravagantly for the poor, or of the flame of spiritual regeneration which burned in him, or of the uses to which he put his gift for oratory, or, above all, of his wrestling bouts with modern thought and new social conditions. They were by no means to be found only among the free-thinkers of the capital city, for whom the Catholic faith was a creed outworn, but also among his clerical colleagues. And these finally managed, long after Prohaszka had been raised to his episcopal See, to secure in Rome the condemnation of three of his pamphlets, so that they could coat his name with the tar of Modernism. Yet though this wounded him, he accepted it too as one of the penances to which he had grown accustomed.

And so when the boy Joseph Pehm [he had changed his name after the ordeal at the hands of the Nazis] had grown to manhood and become first Bishop of Veszprém and then Cardinal Mindszenty, Archbishop of Esztergom, he was the principal actor on a religious stage whose backdrop was not merely the more than two million acres of land, the edifices and structures, the Church organization (there were three archbishoprics and eight bishoprics to minister to a Catholic population of more than seven million souls), but also that of a fire that had been kept burning and kindled anew in many places and hearts. It was still glowing after 1945. During April of 1947 the twentieth anniversary of Bishop Prohaszka's death was observed and many thousands of people went despite all the difficulties of the time to the church built in honor of his memory at Szekesfehervar, which had been his See. The delegations also included large numbers of workers from the industrial suburbs of Budapest. Angrily the Communists responded with attacks on his teaching; and on the night of April 26th, an obscure leftwing poet escorted a handful of followers to Karolyi park and dragged the bronze statue of the Bishop from its pedestal. The head was severed from the figure by the fall, as if some dark symbolic rite were being enacted.

The news spread through Budapest like a clap of doom, and on the morning after a huge crowd came to the park, bringing flowers. They placed the severed head on the pedestal. All the bloom of the year engulfed it in a torrent of color and fragrance. And it was notable that among those who survived to participate in what seemed a second burial were many who did not belong to the Catholic Church. For they too had come to look upon Prohaszka as their own—as the luminous apostle of Christian doctrine, sentiment and faith, uncompromising and yet not narrow. One can only surmise that when Cardinal Mindszenty went in his turn to the park and saw what was being enacted there he sensed the beauty and the terror of his heritage in a manner different from what was possible among the pillars of Esztergom. There the past lay sometimes rigid, in clusters of crystals, but here in Karolyi Park it swept into the present, even as the ocean surf rises up after a hurricane and drowns the green of lawns and gardens.

Yes, the Cardinal must have thought of his luminous precursor, not in terms of whether his native gifts were lesser or equal, but certainly, sadly, as a soldier who faces defeat may think of one who stood always on the brink of victory. In many ways he himself was like the great Bishop of Szekesfehervar. His spirit, too, surged forward in quest of magnanimity. He prayed God for the grace to be an apostle of virtue and fidelity, endowed with all the electric fervor of the Hungarian race. Yet he was also in many respects quite different. We shall see from what manner of folk he sprang and how he was reared. Now perhaps it will help to say that whereas Prohaszka constantly looked to the future, there was embedded in Mindszenty's soul a deep respect for the pageant of the past. This he would attempt to revive over and over again, so that his people might take heart in recollection.

It was sometimes said by those of the clergy who did not gladly follow his leadership that he could not profess to be a truly educated man, and they were wont to compare him with his immediate predecessor in the See of Esztergom, Cardinal Justinian Séredi, learned Benedictine who had shared in a notable way in the reform, under the leadership of Pope Pius XI, of the canon law—the *Corpus Juris Canonici*. Moreover, Cardinal Mindszenty was reticent by nature with those whom he had not known for a long time, and this trait of his character was no doubt intensified by his experiences under the Nazis and their supporters. What wonder then that more talkative prelates found this intense man from the West a bit trying? It was impossible to doubt his integrity, his complete selflessness and his ardent zeal. But was he the diplomat suited to the New Order after 1945? Had he sufficiently emancipated himself from "reactionary" tendencies? And did he possess the wisdom which, embracing dove and serpent, training and experience alone could provide?

The situation which resulted in 1945 from the occupation of the country by Russian troops was very complicated. By reason of the dastardly things which had been done under the short-lived government of Béla Kun after the first World War, the nation was overwhelmingly opposed to Communist rule. Perhaps the leaders of the Socialists, strongly entrenched in the industrial suburbs, were even more negative than the bourgeoisie. On the other hand, because of the long years of the Horthy Regency and the period of Nazi domination, Hungary also lacked adequate familiarity with democratic institutions.

Finally there was the fact that after the second World War Hungary was governed by an Inter-Allied Control Commission. It was true enough that the occupying troops were Russians, and that their primitive lusts sorely tried the population. These soldiers considered no woman sacred, and their attitude towards such private property as they coveted was that of the lawfulness of immediate acquisition. The number of "incidents" was legion, and one of them brought about the death of the distinguished, broad-visioned and yet aristocratic bishop of the beautiful little city of Györ, Monsignor Vilmos Apor, who went to his death under a hail of bullets when he endeavored to protect a number of women who had sought refuge from the invading soldiery in the cellar of his palace. Efforts were, however, made by Russian officers to curb their troops; and if one placed store by the official pronouncements it seemed as if, once the pro-Nazis had been eliminated, the fury of the Russians curbed, and the hold of feudalism broken, things might perhaps become better rather than worse.

At any rate, many younger Catholic intellectuals in Hungary were persuaded that participation with the new political order was eminently desirable. To them the creation of a Christian Democratic Party seemed impossible although the aging Cardinal Séredi had advocated it; and their reasoning was strengthened by the fact that the Russians were angrily opposed to any such idea. It was decided that common cause would be made with the Small Landholders Party, traditionally a group which was "liberal" in the European sense. Today no one can assert that the die could have been cast more effectively.

On the one hand, there were those who insisted (as had Monsignor Ludwig Kaas during 1933 in Germany) that the ordeal to be faced was bound to be so dire that organized religion could fulfill its mission only by withdrawing from public life and concentrating on the quite private care of souls. On the other hand there were others who were persuaded that working together in amity with the "New Order" was to be commended because only by doing so could the various sins and omissions of the past be absolved. The intermediary position was occupied by men who felt that the Catholic mission in the world was most likely to succeed in the new Hungary if one did not insist too strongly on religious solidarity but emphasized instead one's comradeship with all those who, while they desired the reform of society, were nevertheless ready to do what they could to prevent the nation from being placed at the mercy of the Communist ideology. Among these last were the Jesuits who had expended heroic energy on building the peasant youth organization known as *Kalot,* the solidly knit membership of which numbered more than 200,000. The result was that Catholics formed a common front with the Small Landholders Party, a section of which held views concerning the separation of Church and State, especially in the area of education, that were quite different from those subscribed to by Catholics.

The elections held in November 1945 resulted in an overwhelming victory for the Small Landholders. Nevertheless Catholics, led by the somewhat impetuous Fathers Ladislas Banass and Stefan Balog, found themselves in a coalition government in which the badly defeated Communists and the other parties allied with them obtained three of the six ministries, including the absolutely vital Ministry of the Interior. This Ministry controlled the political as well as the ordinary police forces. The concession was made, of course, because the Occupying Powers insisted upon it. It was to prove a mortal wound in the side of the Republic.

No doubt it is possible to see matters more clearly today than anyone could at that time. Only later on was the skill of Mátyas Rákosi, chief of the Hungarian Communists, in seizing power through intrigue and double-crossing to be clearly revealed. We shall see in detail in what manner this gifted and sinister antagonist of the Cardinal succeeded in winning an overwhelming victory. In 1945 he was, however, very conciliatory and even upon occasion ingratiating.

It was perhaps only natural that while Cardinal Mindszenty held his peace and abstained from all attempts to chart a political course, Fathers Banass and Balog went very far in "reaching an understanding" with the Communists. While he was still Bishop of Veszprém, the Cardinal had deemed the activities of Father Balog in particular highly injudicious; and he admitted to friends that he had tried to steer this often impetuous priest away from the political arena. Father Banass, who was soon to be appointed to the See of Veszprém, for a time urged the faithful to establish good relations with the Communists, set what he termed an "example" by maintaining close ties with the Minister of the Interior, attended conferences sponsored by the Party, and even after he became a bishop was known to interrupt Confirmation tours in order to pay his respects to local Communist functionaries. As a result his picture appeared frequently in the Communist illustrated weeklies, accompanied by eulogistic captions.

The consequence was that many who had hesitated to curry favor with the Extreme Left were encouraged to do so, while those who had committed themselves to the opposition felt even more isolated. It was not easy to make oneself a target for the political police when churchmen in high office were breaking bread with ruthless Communist leaders. These things are not written here in reproof. In Germany several Bishops had also endeavored, during the early period of Hitler's rule, to establish friendly relations with prominent Nazis. One of them even permitted himself to be named by the Fuehrer to the Reichstag, and another upon occasion saluted in the approved Nazi style. Such actions do not constitute religious treason. They grow out of a one-sided, often irrational belief that the work of the Church is wholly autonomous and that as a result anything calculated to help that work along is legitimate or even desirable. Yet obviously a priesthood one part of which restored to such actions while the other part did not was in the mind of the informed public a sorely divided priesthood; and in a situation which could perhaps be mastered only if there was absolute solidarity, such divergent views and attitudes paved the way for disaster.

Cardinal Mindszenty was not, however, a man to hold his peace for long. He was named to the See of Esztergom on October 2, 1945; and it was plain for everyone to see that in changing his name to one reflecting the character of the people from whom he sprang he had symbolized his fidelity to the principles by which his life had always been guided. During the following January he delivered an address on the Feast of St. Margaret, daughter of King Béla IV who had become a holy Dominican nun and who was after her death designated the patroness of penitence, an address with which he may be said to have inaugurated that policy of resistance to Communism which he propagated unflinchingly until the time of his arrest. Since what he said electrified all of Hungary and threw down the gauntlet to Rákosi, some sentences from it should be called to mind.

> After a year of bitter suffering, Hungary finally saw the Tartars depart. They did not leave lightheartedly, for they had never had so much freedom or enjoyed so pleasant a life. . . . But they went back because the Great Khan had died. . . . History teaches us that all things on this earth are transitory, even as were the achievements of Genghis Khan, Napoleon and Hitler. Through such men God sends the scourge of many sufferings to the world. When the bony hand of death touches such men, the peoples and the nations breathe once more.

The effect of these words, veiled though they still might be, was immediate and unmistakable. A huge Communist parade was organized in Budapest, charging sedition and demanding the Cardinal's head. It was indeed to be expected that utterances like these, which greatly stirred the common people, should impress the Russians with the fact that conquering the Church in Hungary was not going to be a matter of waiting for the ripe fruit to tumble into the basket.

Reconstructing the picture as it was shortly after the close of the War is possible only with the help of motion pictures taken at the time; and fortunately we possess them in considerable number, though they are of varying value. First there are official films made for the most part by the Russians or under their direction. Second there are Catholic films, prepared by amateurs, often surreptitiously. Of central importance are two visual expressions which at the time made a profound mark on the popular imagination. The first is that of the battle for Budapest, fought out step by step between the attacking Russians and the defending German and Hungarian garrison, ordered by Hitler to hold the city until relief came. From house to house the struggle proceeded, reducing many parts of the metropolis to shambles; and as one studies the record of this sanguinary and destructive contest, from the picture chronicle taken on both sides, it becomes clear that this was for the Russians a memorable victory the fruits of which they would not easily surrender. The second impression is that created by the coming in of American Relief, which was distributed almost entirely in the western parts of the country through the great Catholic welfare organization—the Caritas—with the help of American officials. Priests, nuns and their lay assistants went everywhere, doling out food and clothing to children and adults in every city. In these pictures one sees bishops as well as the Cardinal eating with their famished flocks. Small wonder that this action revived among Hungarians sentiments of association with and admiration for the United States, which had grown increasingly strong over a period of years.

No peace treaty having as yet been signed, Hungary was under the control of the Inter-Allied Commission, although the military occupation as such was entrusted to the Russian army. Safety from the marauding soldiery could not be assured, but the hope that the Commission would not accede to the abrogation of fundamental civil rights was very strong, however illusory it was destined to prove to have been. Every act demonstrating American charitable interest in the welfare of the Hungarian people was accepted as proof of the resolute intention of the United States not to permit the establishment of political and economic slavery.

Nobody had any way of knowing how momentously roseate the views then prevalent in the Western world were concerning Stalin and Russian policy. For were there not all manner of folk who were committed to whatever was most progressive? And was not this "whatever" as a matter of fact Communism, which was all on the side of the working class? At any rate, the premise from which the Cardinal and those who supported him reasoned was, in so far as concern with the things of this world happened to be involved, that an America which had proved itself so merciful would also not be dissuaded from its mission of justice. To be sure, only a few succumbed to the illusion that a vast liberating army would soon be on the march. What nearly everybody believed was that the United States would not agree to letting the Russians have their way in Hungary. It was an idealistic position, if you insist, or at least one not based on a pessimistic evaluation of all the factors involved and it is not very strange that there should have been Hungarian "realists" as well, who argued that since the Russians had the power in their hands and seemed unlikely to relinquish it the prudent thing to do was to see what sort of an arrangement one could work out with them. Yet this "realism" in turn, when it was not merely an almost apocalyptic acceptance of martyrdom, was plausible only if one assumed that the Russians would somehow turn out to be not the Russians. And so in the end, as we shall see, the question would become this. Was there any way in which moral and spiritual resistance could prevent complete absorption into the Communist world, or had Hungary been led into a kind of quicksand from which escape was impossible?

One's response was likely to depend upon a number of circumstances, some quite personal, others the results of reading or environment. Thus, for example, younger Catholics, among the clergy and the laity alike, were often likely to believe that the older and therefore more experienced political leaders in their group were old-fashioned and therefore given to surmise that the time had come to make a clean break with the past. The ardor and "fresh, vigorous methods" of youth were advocated. Of course the more intellectual one was the more certain one usually became of the rightness of the position outlined. In such times bishops in particular are likely to seem rigid, unnecessarily conservative and cautious; and so some of them will be tempted to agree and in sheer self-defense to place themselves more or less resolutely at the disposition of the reformers. This is all the more natural because in representative Catholic organizations, whether liturgical, educational or social, a conflict is always in progress between those who cling to older ways and those who long to set off in new directions This is a healthy tug of war and prevents monotonous conformity. It is true, however, that in politics a totally different situation prevails. Statesmanship requires ability, of course, but it is uniquely the product of experience. Its goal is always advantageous compromise; and it takes a long time before a human being has learned to assess all the factors involved, to make a tenable concrete proposal, and to carry the day. Of democratic states one may say in particular that while in any instance "nine old men" may be too many, two or three are indispensable. The most dependable men now in the United States Senate, as in the British House of Commons, were not born yesterday.

Yet though these things must be borne in mind as one attempts to reconstruct the background against which the Cardinal's challenge to Rákosi was delivered, it is even more necessary to determine what the mood of the Hungarian people was, once the war was over. Naturally one cannot divine that mood in all its ramifications. But clearly here was a sorely beleaguered folk, harassed by day and night, sometimes digging its way out of ruins and again patiently straightening out fields over which great armies had passed. Almost everywhere there was manifest a very moving loyalty to the Church and to religious traditions.

No sooner, for example, had the mighty battle for Budapest ended than the accustomed feasts and processions were resumed, just as they were in Austria and South Germany. In the streets of once beautiful Munich, old Michael Cardinal Faulhaber led a bedraggled but steadfast Corpus Christi procession through the ominous debris. In Budapest the devastation was likewise great, though perhaps less ghastly and awesome, but there had been no twenty years during which public manifestations of religious belief had been forbidden. And so the people came out into city streets, as they did also in country fields and in villages, with banners and music, to honor the Virgin Mary or St. Stephen. They went on pilgrimages, or knelt for benediction at the four altars in the open air which grace every Corpus Christi Day.

There was at first nothing whatever, not the slightest trace, of political manifestation in all this activity. One can see all manner of folk in the religious films made at the time. The girls in peasant costume are bashful as their pictures are taken; and men with long mustaches primp themselves for the camera. It was all eternal folklore come to life anew, moving in the shadow of eternity but wearing all the lineaments of time. And of course it is easy to surmise that for those who wanted things to be not what they had always been but radically different and made according to their plans carefully drawn after the blueprints of Lenin and Stalin, there was present here what they called "conservatism" and "reaction" in all their nakedness.

It was in the midst of this constantly shifting but also unshiftingly constant scene created by popular Catholic belief and sentiment that Cardinal Mindszenty set up his pulpit. That he should have gone out to them rather than have stood waiting until they came to hear him at Esztergom was for this village peasant the most natural thing in the world. He could speak to his people with robust eloquence and sincerity, often with a sharp wit. Not one who graced well academic assemblages, he was also not the man to dissect a problem neatly and put it together again while you watched. Nor as he stood before his audience in the scarlet robes of his office did he coat his words with velvet or see to it that he was made up for television. But he was wonderfully able to talk to the people he knew in a way they respected and understood. The inflections he used were their inflections, and when he gestured his hands moved as did theirs.

It is quite illuminating, as it is often indescribably moving, to see him in the motion pictures which were surreptitiously taken of him in action at that time. As the struggle went on his face grew very grave, and sometimes as he sat back he was fearfully weary. And when at the bitter end he no longer believed that victory was possible and could only ask himself whether he had merited the grace of martyrdom, something came over his features that must have been on Thomas à Becket's, or that I have myself seen on the countenance of the great German priest and foe of the Nazis, Count von Galen, Cardinal Archbishop of Muenster. Perhaps the most singular fact in his. history is that he carried on so much of the struggle alone. Other good bishops, other eloquent priests, there were, Catholic and Protestant. But in all their words there was no resonance remotely comparable to his.

The core and also the climax of his effort followed a fateful decision to dedicate a whole year, beginning in 1947 and continuing into 1948, to Mary the Mother of God. This same year had also been previously dedicated by the Communists to the commemoration of the revolutionary year of 1848, which had ended with Kossuth's failure to win Hungarian independence, to the exile of many of the nation's best, and to the execution at the behest of the Austro-Hungarian Empire of hundreds of others. Thus there was present at the outset a sharp, clear conflict between the propagandistic purposes of Rákosi and those which the Cardinal had in mind. How this dramatic decision ripened in his soul is not clear, though its origin was doubtless the impression which had been made on him by the Marian Year in Canada, which he had attended. Men who have known him very intimately insist that he hoped only to prepare his people interiorly for the suffering and oppression which were to be meted out to them. And indeed for one whose zeal for the integrity of the religious spirit flamed so brightly, and in whose memory the example of all the saints of his country had been etched with something more powerful and enduring than any acid, no other motive was required. Others have felt that he hoped, through a great public manifestation of the true sentiment of the nation, to halt the progress of Communism and to influence as much as possible the nature of the Peace Treaty soon to be signed. It would, I think have been strange if such considerations had not also been in his mind. May he not have been praying with his people for two miracles—the one bringing some mitigation of their social and political fate, and the other ushering in an age of penitence and endurance during which no one would falter on the long, hard road to eternity?

At any rate, what followed was a wholly unprecedented effort to stop the wheels of history in the name of Christ. From the very beginning the Cardinal seemed, to many inside the Church as well as to those outside it, to have thrown all caution to the winds. He inaugurated the Marian Year on the Feast of the Assumption with a sermon preached in the presence of all the country's bishops. It established the pattern to which he would adhere. While the mood evoked was one of profound religious fervor, a battle cry was raised against the moral outrages from which the nation suffered—the treatment accorded to minorities, the abrogation of basic liberties, the usurpation of the rights of the Church. As the months passed, he drove himself to the uttermost limits of endurance in order to repeat these accusations. To shrine after shrine he journeyed and the crowds that came were enormous. In ancient Györ, where the image of the "Irish Madonna" is revered, there were 100,000 pilgrims in the audience. Comparable numbers appeared at Maria Remete, at Eger and on the ruins which now dominate Budapest. On Corpus Christi Day in the capital city, 600,000 marched in the procession. He traveled to small towns as well, and even to places in the east where the majority of those who listened were not of his faith.

At first the Communists looked on and restricted their attacks to what was said in the press. But the glint in Rákosi's eyes grew hard. On January 10, 1948, he addressed the Communist Party organization and subjected the Cardinal to a very bitter attack which for all its venom was astutely phrased. Agreement between Church and State was desirable, he said, but it was impossible to arrive at because the leaders of the Church were aggressively hostile to the government. The reasons for this antagonism were declared to be threefold. The Church was opposed to land reform, to the government's economic plan, and to peace.

A month later the indomitable Cardinal replied. Addressing an audience gathered in St. Stephen's Academy, Budapest, he concerned himself primarily with the Catholic attitude towards peace. He used quotations from the Papal Encyclicals in such a way that implicit in almost every word he uttered was criticism of the Communist position. Rákosi responded by ordering the suppression of all printed copies of the address. After that, observances of the Marian Year were made contingent upon approval by the Government. Whenever the Cardinal spoke, it was to an audience surrounded by the police. Finally on June 13, a large throng of the faithful gathered at a shrine erected in Budapest in honor of Our Lady of Fatima. When the crowd responded to a "planted" cheer for the Cardinal, it was attacked by the police and dispersed. Many persons present were arrested, and some were shipped off to forced labor camps.

Similar repressive measures were adopted thenceforth, so that the year of devotion ended under savage attack. On November 18, the Cardinal wrote a defense of the Marian Year. He used these memorable words:

> Two of my predecessors [in the See of Esztergom] were killed in action, two were robbed of all their possessions, one was taken prisoner and deported, one was assassinated. The greatest of them all went into exile. Karoly Ambrus visited and nursed those stricken by the plague and himself died of the disease.
>
> But of all my predecessors none was as lacking of support as am I. So systematic and adroit a net of untruthful propaganda—of lies disproved a hundred times and nevertheless repeated a hundred times more—was never spun round the heads of any of my seventy-eight precursors in office. I

stand for God, the Church, and Hungary. This responsibility has been placed on me as a result of the fate which has been meted out to our nation, now standing alone, an orphan among the peoples. When what is happening to me is compared with the suffering of my country, it is seen to be of trifling significance.

No answer, then, had been given to his plea for freedom save an implacable "NO." In a little while he would go, in dutiful imitation of his Master, to his Gethsemane. Talking to many who heard him, who was so earnest and without fear, one gathers that the hope he evoked in their breasts, without perhaps overtly suggesting it, was that the Christian peoples of the world would, without firing a shot, through the irresistible impact of their commitment to liberty and justice, send the Russians packing home. It may well be that the Cardinal, so like them in mood and conviction, for a time really thought so, too. And who shall say what the outcome of Western intransigence might have been? But he did not flinch when it became clear that no such easy form of redemption was at hand. Then he committed himself and his flock to the unrestricted service of the Church, even as the people of the Vendée had been consecrated to that same allegiance during the most frenzied days of the French Revolution.

# Albert Gregory Cardinal Meyer

The purpose here is to offer in outline the portrait of a Council Father, and so we shall attempt first of all to see in what manner the Cardinal dealt with the great issues which Pope John XXIII brought into the center of world discussion. These are, perhaps, five in number: (1) the corporate *worship* of God in the Church, centering round the Eucharistic feast; (2) the sources from which those who share in that worship derive their *knowledge* of the sacred mysteries, through the contemplation of which their faith is fed; (3) the manner in which we are to conceive of the *Christian community*—that is, whether it is restricted to those in union with the See of Peter or whether it is to embrace, in faith, hope and love, all those for whom the Son of Man is truly also the Son of God; (4) the character of the community of *mankind*, elected to be made up of the children of God, regardless of race or social status; (5) and finally, the grant of *freedom* of religious choice without which the rights of the conscience cannot be secured. To be sure, the Council was concerned with other matters, too, such as the special character of the apostolate of the laity and the principle of hierarchical collegiality. Doubtless still more will be discussed and all will be important. We shall consider one or two such issues.

### Liturgy and Word of God

It would be strange, indeed, if Cardinal Meyer, seminary professor and rector, did not attribute basic importance to the liturgy; and, indeed, as

From *Albert Gregory Cardinal Meyer* by George N. Shuster (Notre Dame: University of Notre Dame Press, 1964), pp. 26-45.

Bishop of Superior he devoted the *Program of Instructions* for the ecclesiastical year 1950-1951 to "The Sacred Liturgy of the Church." The exposition is learned, reverential. Nevertheless, it would be interesting to compare the views he held at that time with those he himself expounded at Vatican Council II.

"The Latin language has a special place," he wrote then, because it is a "symbol and bond of unity, giving worthy expression to the mysteries of the Faith, and to the marks of the true Church." Nevertheless, he recalled history: "Liturgical languages vary. Our Lord spoke Aramaic, as did the Apostles; soon the more universal language of Greek came into liturgical use ... with the spread of the Faith to the Roman Empire, Latin, which was originally the simple language of the country districts, came more and more into use." But the symbolic value of Latin should not lead anyone to doubt that Catholics who use Oriental or other languages are therefore of lesser value. "The Church," wrote the Bishop of Superior, "has no desire to force the Eastern Catholics to change their rite or liturgy. Eastern Catholics should not be called Uniates, as this term has come to have an insulting meaning; neither should we regard these Eastern Catholics as inferior, or refer to their customs as peculiar."

The Bible as a source from which the faith of the Church is fed was the subject of a clergy conference held in Chicago during February 1961. It was entitled "The New Catholic Approach to the Interpretation of Sacred Scripture," and was addressed by scholars of eminence. The occasion provided the Cardinal with an excellent opportunity to state his views and at least in some measure to summarize the discussion which had taken place at the Council. "We are witnessing," he said, "a remarkable and even exciting revival of biblical studies." This, he thought, was due on the one hand to "the rapid development and coming to maturity of those sciences which contribute so much to our understanding of the scriptures, such as studies in the original texts and languages, archaeology and history, and sound literary criticism," and on the other hand to "divinely guided encouragement from the Church."

He took comfort in the fact that not only had Catholic scholars taken rank with the best in each of these fields, but that "their efforts had an obvious effect on the general trend of biblical studies." They had meanwhile learned much by reason of the discoveries made by others. But—he was quick to add—the Church has always borne in mind that the purpose of scripture reading and study is not scientific. She has, the Cardinal said, "never looked upon the scriptures as a collection of ancient literature to be read as one might the Egyptian Book of the Dead or the documents from Mari and Ungarit. She is and always has been thoroughly conscious of the divine origin of the scriptures, of their supernatural character and their eminently spiritual purpose."

And so, speaking against the background of a paper written by Cardinal Bea, he offered some admonition to his clergy: "We must give the scholars time and freedom to make their advances, mindful that we cannot solve all problems now. Scholars in their work must be particularly careful not to treat the problem of the historical aspects of Sacred Scriptures with arguments that are not sufficiently solid. Popular writers must be most careful not to give the public immature and insufficiently documented theories. In the words of Cardinal Alfrink, the exegete on his part is not to use the liberty granted by [the Encyclical] *Divino Afflante Spiritu* in such a manner as to create difficulties for his brethren in their faith."

Later on in this address Cardinal Meyer came back to the same point: "Finally, we must constantly keep in mind the principle inculcated anew by Pope John that the work done on scripture must be done with a pastoral intent, having before one's eyes the good of souls, since this is the reason why God gave us the Sacred Scriptures. Even the scholar is not exempt from this important consideration, which *a fortiori* applies to the popularizer and the priest in the pastoral ministry or the teacher in the seminary and other schools." In other words, catechetical instruction or religious journalism should not anticipate the finding of scholars but rather follow them.

Pope John had said, "Therefore, beloved sons, onward, *in nomine Domini!*" But there are no doubt among these "beloved sons" not a few who, intoxicated not a little by the fact that obsolete caveats, which instead of buttressing orthodoxy made orthodoxy for many of the educated difficult to retain, now stood ready to espouse almost anything new just because it was new. Simpler folk of the Church of God, reared in a simpler time, might be as scandalized by seeing matters of old heritage and revered teaching being carted off by the critics to the incinerator, as an old mother might be, watching a daughter throw out of the house keepsakes identified with beloved ones.

## *Unity and Freedom*

The nature of the Christian community, as distinguishable from any of its currently demarcated segments, is of course the concern of ecumenism. Ecumenism has—it need hardly be said—a long history, some of it identified with St. Francis de Sales, the patron of the seminary over which Cardinal Meyer once presided, and some of it also with the University of Louvain and its one-time rector, Désiré Joseph Cardinal Mercier. But the realities with which it is concerned were never so vividly grasped by Christians as they have been since the persecution of Christian and Jew by modern totalitarian dictators. Awareness of the fact that Protestant and Catholic had faced martyrdom side by side with equal fortitude, because the glory of Christ would not dim before their eyes, made it forever impossible to consider ancient animosities as any longer truly pertinent.

Cardinal Meyer has spoken and written often on this subject. But since it may well be that his most significant treatment of the problem was an address to the Ministers' Week and Triennial Convention, which met at the Chicago Theological Seminary during January 1964, it will be presented here at some length. The address was entitled, "Notes on Some Catholic Approaches to Ecumenism," and began by quoting the very moving words addressed by Pope Paul VI to the observers present at the second session of Vatican Council II. These surely possess historic importance and it is evident that they made a profound impression on the Cardinal. The Pope said: "If we are in any way to blame for that separation [namely, that between Christians during and before the Reformation period], we humbly beg God's forgiveness and ask pardon, too, of our brethren who feel themselves to have been injured by us. For our part, we willingly forgive the injuries which the Catholic Church has suffered, and forget the grief endured during the long years of heresy and schism."

In this spirit, the Cardinal observed: "The unity we seek is not just any kind of unity, but the very unity which Christ prayed for—which he compares to the mysterious unity which exists between Himself and His Father—a unity of truth, of life, of power and of love. As such we see it as a visible union, yet not a mere natural unity of a single organization produced by human organizing ability—like a corporate merger or a political alliance. It is also something more than a unity merely of brotherhood and friendliness, such as we find in many organizations for religious tolerance and cooperation. It is even something more than a genuine Christian love and hope for mutual salvation. What is sought is a genuine unity in faith, since only on this firm foundation can charity and hope really abide in permanence."

The Cardinal did not minimize the difficulties which would be encountered in the quest. "Obviously," he said, "this marvelous union can only be the work of the Holy Spirit, since the Church is made up of sinful human beings filled with contradictory tendencies, with selfishness and blindness. In its human side, the Church is indeed liable to disruptive tendencies." There was little evidence of easy compromise in a later passage of the address: "It has been well said that the aim of the ecumenical dialogue is, in the first place, understanding the position of the other side and having our own doctrine understood by them. This is no easy task, but takes a great deal of effort and sympathy. From such understanding we can discover—speaking for us Catholics—how our own positions have suffered from long centuries of over (or under) emphasis. From such understanding we shall learn how our own Catholic theology must be purified and expanded through richer and deeper insights."

There followed a statement which is of significance also for the fifth of the great issues which Pope John XXIII spurred the Council to consider. Doubtless no other American prelate could have made it with greater authority. Cardinal Meyer said: "Yet underlying all these socioreligious tensions is the number one question for Americans. The most persistent critical suggestion for theological clarification that preoccupies Americans of all religious persuasions, and of no persuasion, is that of religious liberty. I believe, therefore, that both Protestant and Catholic ecumenists are convinced that the ecumenical movement cannot be securely founded until a clear statement on the subject of religious liberty is fully developed. We are looking for, and confidently hoping to receive, from Vatican Council II the further development of what is already contained in the encyclical letter of Pope John XXIII, *Pacem in terris*. This says: 'Every human being has the right to honor God according to the dictates of an upright conscience and the right to profess his religion privately and publicly.'

"The text of the fifth chapter on ecumenism, on religious liberty, prepared for the consideration of the Council Fathers, actually never came up for detailed discussion. In retrospect, I think we can say that it was just as well that it did not, since there was not sufficient time to do it justice. In looking forward to its discussion in the next session, we know that the text can be perfected. The basic proposition is already present, however, for it asserts that every man who follows his conscience in religious matters has a natural right to true and authentic religious liberty. The Church, of course, does not admit that any man is free to obey or disregard God's will as he chooses. The suggested text, however, recognizes that a man can do God's will only as he knows it. Even though his conscience be in error, if it is his sincere conscience, formed after earnest effort to find the truth, it represents God's will to him and he must follow it."

From this the Cardinal drew several practical conclusions among which the following is certainly one of the most important: "It seems to me that here, also, we have the principles to determine the goal of the ecumenical dialogue, and the related question of conversion. Conversion must be the result of every man's earnest effort to find the truth, and to form his conscience in accordance with this finding. I do not see why, therefore, there should be any opposition between the dialogue which aims primarily at understanding, and the continuing mission of the Church 'to preach the Gospel to every creature.' The purpose of the dialogue is not to win arguments but to achieve understanding. The work of conversion is the result of God's grace."

## Christian Realism: The Complex City

What of the community of mankind? In all the official and many of the unofficial statements made by Cardinal Meyer since he became a bishop there has been a constant insistence on what he has called "Christian Realism." This may be taken to mean that although each human being who sees life in the light of Christian teaching knows of his eternal destiny, which is the sight of God, he is always a man with weaknesses and obligations, rights and opportunities, to realize for himself and others. The Cardinal tried earnestly to form priests and people in this spirit. But inevitably his own thought would develop not in terms of basic principle but in the realization of what such principle implies for the realities of the given culture.

Nothing in the greatest encyclicals to have been published during this period—*Humani Generis, Mater et Magistra* and *Pacem in terris*—is more eloquently presented than is the idea of a community of men, each a person and therefore entitled to both justice and charity. As the Cardinal moved from the relatively simple social order of Superior, Wisconsin, to the complex city in which all the problems of a pluralistic society are presented in their full contemporary dimensions, he had to gird himself for the struggle. The Negro had long since been a citizen of Chicago and often enough a belea guered and despised citizen. Interracial conflict had upon occasion erupted into bloody violence, there was opposition to Negro competition in the ranks of labor, and of course the housing available to the "black man" was carefully segregated from that of the "white man."

Nor in a city so largely populated by ethnic groups, each proudly and stubbornly nurturing its identity, was there then an open society even in the Church. Older Catholic Negroes sometimes recall how, having newly arrived in Chicago, they would enter a church for mass on Sunday, only to feel a tap on the shoulder and a peremptory summons to go elsewhere. It was probably not until Bishop Bernard J. Sheil started a ferment in Catholic youth organizations that any serious attention was paid to the duty of treating the Negro as a fellow Christian. But in general the root problem was not ill will but ignorance. *Church and Society,* an exposition of Catholic social thought edited by Father Joseph N. Moody in 1953, does not mention "Race" in its index.

## A City Half Negro

Cardinal Meyer's first public statement on this perplexing question was an expression of his views before the President's Commission on Civil Rights on May 6, 1959. During the previous November the Bishops of the United States had issued a joint statement urging that "responsible and sober-minded Americans of all religious faiths, in all areas of our land, seize the mantle of leadership from the agitator and the racist." Reminding the Commission that the "separate but equal" doctrine which had brought the reconstruction period to a close "could not even serve a century," the Cardinal noted that "in effect, a new Emancipation Proclamation has been promulgated." Would another period of "experiment and failure" have to pass before this could be put into effect? He compared the influx of Negroes into Chicago with emigration from Europe during an earlier period, and stressed the hope that the Negro likewise would acquire the training needed to "occupy positions requiring high skill, professional knowledge and great responsibility." But the meat of his statement consisted of two questions and an answer: "Has this new and rapidly increasing Negro middle class been able to choose its place of residence as the children of our European immigrants were able to do? Does the fully competent Negro person have the option alluded to above? Unfortunately, the only honest answer we can give it, at best, is a qualified no."

The month of September 1960 was marked by a clergy conference on "The Catholic Church and the Negro in the Archdiocese of Chicago." Inevitably pastors were sorely troubled. Negro in-migration was inducing white Catholics to move to suburbia, so that once flourishing congregations were decimated. Whence were the revenues to come for the maintenance of churches and schools? Nor did the average pastor, accustomed to dealing with a flock which while often sinful could be counted upon to revere the essentials of the Catholic faith, have many illusions about his potential success as a missionary to the Negro. The clergy conference minced no words. An expert reported that even if in-migration were to cease, the higher population increase rate among Negroes would make Chicago in the foreseeable future a Negro city. "There is little doubt," he said, "that Chicago will be half Negro—geographically and population-wise—within twenty years."

The Cardinal did not refuse to accept the implications of this startling change. He said simply that it implies "certain important considerations." The clergy generally would have to learn more about the Negro people. Careful attention would have to be paid to parishes in changing neighborhoods. "It would appear," he said, "that two things are of paramount importance in this situation: on the one hand to avoid any spirit of 'defeat,' and on the other to develop a parish program which is apostolic. Plainly, as has been pointed out here today, the changing parish must become a 'mission-center.' " But if and when Negroes came into the Church, what then? The answer he gave to this question antedated the integration order of the year following: "The virtue of justice requires that we assume the mantle of leadership to insure that all our Catholics of the Negro race are integrated into the complete life of the Church. This obviously means that every Catholic child of the Negro race, whether his parents be Catholic or not, has as free access to our schools as any other Catholic child on all the levels of our academic training, elementary and secondary as well as the higher levels." Nor were the schools the only resources on which the mission to the Negro could rely. "We are thinking," the Cardinal said, "of accepted and wholehearted membership in the entire life of the parish, in our fraternal and parish organizations, in our hospitals, in the life of the community—without distinctions or restrictions based solely on the accidental facts of race or color, or for that matter, national backgrounds."

This was of course vigorous language, and it was doubtless too much to expect that all the clergy would endorse it with enthusiasm. Some as a matter of fact did not. But it would manifestly have been ridiculous to advocate what the hour plainly called for, namely a great missionary effort among the Negroes, while at the same time maintaining that their souls were somehow different from other souls and must therefore be assigned to special spatial and social dimensions. But of course grave, unresolved problems remain. Cardinal Meyer recognized from the outset that the mission to the Negro could not be a Catholic effort alone, and that even if it were successful beyond his or anyone else's hopes the solution of the social problems which in-migration brought with it must remain a community responsibility. The culmination of his efforts to bring about an intergroup program of action was undoubtedly the National Conference on Religion and Race, held in Chicago during January 1963. It is not too much to say that without his interest this meeting could not have achieved the success which so manifestly attended it.

His own address, which was a staunch refusal to approve of extremist approaches to the problem, was primarily an effort to look honestly at what he termed "two particularly urgent, massive questions." These were the training of Negro youth for careers, and "the vexed question of residential segregation, with all its implications in the field of home life, family morals, and community peace and friendship." It was necessary, he said, to face up to the fact that Negro young people were dropping out of school at an alarming rate. What was to be their future? "Is there more that we can do, as religious leaders," he asked, "to end unfair job discrimination based on race, religion, national origin? Have we done all we could even within our own institutions to open up employment opportunities to qualified minority group personnel, to go out of our way to create incentive for those who need it most?"

Concerning residential segregation he said: "Are we to continue to see fear and panic seize the white community in areas facing racial change? . . . Or can the forces of religion be used more effectively to prepare for change, to help community organizations which grow, not from fear, but from pride and stewardship over property, as well as from the spirit of neighborliness and openness to all who maintain community standards? At the same time, can religion help more effectively to establish the spirit and practice of open occupancy for an entire metropolitan area such as our own?"

One of the by-products of these sincere efforts was an event which could hardly have taken place prior to the era of ecumenism. The Second Methodist Conference on Human Relations, convened in Chicago during August 1963, included Cardinal Meyer among the recipients of civil rights awards. His address of acceptance was religiously motivated and delivered with sincerity and candor. "The indispensable foundation and beginning for restoring the relations of the human family in truth, in justice, in love and in freedom is," he said, "found in the relations between human beings. From that basis we can proceed to those other relationships between citizens and their respective political communities, between political communities themselves, and between these and the world community."

## *Experimental Parishes; TWO*

Being the spiritual head of a large archdiocese is never only a matter of making pronouncements. It involves hard, often troubling decisions about people and the tasks to be assigned to them, experimentation and venturesome participation. Chicago now has its "experimental" parishes, notably St. Agatha's, but of these the Cardinal is reluctant to speak, professing the view that there is no point in talking about an experiment until one has seen whether it is successful. Likewise he has entertained certain doubts about the wisdom of members of religious orders who think of abandoning their institutional service in order to embark on "apostolic" activities of a relatively undefined character.

During the close of 1960, the Archdiocese became involved in the most hardhitting and controversial of efforts to improve the lot of the Negro in Chicago or any other place, for that matter. This was the creation of The Woodlawn Organization, since familiarly known as TWO. It was the brainchild of Saul Alinsky, down-to-earth, University of Chicago-trained sociologist who once spearheaded the highly successful Behind the Stockyards Movement. The core of Alinsky's doctrine is that nothing on earth can help people unless they are effectively mobilized to help themselves; and the thorn in the side of the flesh of his opponents on the South Side of Chicago is that he has not only mobilized them, but has proved that through mobilization they can do themselves a great deal of good. But TWO and its supporting Industrial Areas Foundation, which is a somewhat flamboyant name for Alinsky's office, frankly take risks. In the interest of getting somewhere they influence people but do not always make friends.

On March 3, 1961, readers of the University of Chicago *Maroon* found an article (which two Chicago dailies had refused to publish) indicating that TWO and Alinsky had received approximately $100,000 from the "Chicago Catholic bishop" and the National Conference of Catholic Charities. Just what kinds of irate public opinion this item was supposed to stir up remains a mystery, but the fact was soon evident enough that the University was trying to shove out the adjacent Negro population of Woodlawn and buy up the property. This was of course all right except that there was no place for the population to go. The community was therefore shoving back and this the University liked not a whit. At any rate the archdiocese, solidly committed to the principle that helping the Negro to help himself made common sense, was knee deep in a kind of infighting which it could face only with a head bloody but unbowed.

Whether the archdiocese would have embarked on the venture if it had known in advance what the communiqués from the Woodlawn battlefront would say is a moot question.

But these developments have not caused a break in the relations between the archdiocese and the University of Chicago. The Cardinal has not only provided for unusually well qualified leadership for the Newman Club there, but has supported the work done in the Sociology of Religion with rare insight and understanding, even as he has the study of population problems.

The world community is of course much larger than Chicago or the United States. Vocal public opinion in the Middle West sometimes seems more isolationist than elsewhere, but the groundswell supporting the development of international law and efforts to promote economic and social development is nevertheless strong. The archdiocese has taken seriously its share of the task assigned to American Catholics to support the mission to Latin America, and under the leadership of Monsignor William Quinn has actually been in the forefront. Some indication of the attitude of Cardinal Meyer is provided by his sermon given at the dedication exercises for the Notre Dame Memorial Library (May 7, 1964). This sermon had for its text words from St. John's epistle, "Beloved, if God so loved us, we also ought to love one another."

He said in part: "And even more, it is a healing love in times not healthy that sends college students and graduates in the thousands into far places to work, with no thought of privilege or gain, in urban slums and destitute places throughout the world. Thus they plant hope and courage among men and women who have seen little enough of love. And among themselves these student workers form communities that transcend religious differences and make it possible for them to work together in the name of Christ. There is taking place everywhere a continuous coming-together of the community of scholars, on many campuses, in all countries, and among countries, so that hopefully we may say that the light of the Eternal Word becomes steadily brighter."

## *No Hothouse Plants*

This note of optimism, which Cardinal Meyer has caught from the torch kindled by Pope John XXIII, has characterized his work in education. Few churchmen have dedicated so many schools or participated in such a number of conferences devoted to the cause of the training of youth. He himself thinks that perhaps the address opening the 54th annual convention of the National Catholic Educational Association comes close to summarizing his views on the subject most effectively. It will suffice to quote from the Cardinal's pastoral letter for the holy season of Lent, 1962: "Still, in the sheltered environment of the home it is possible to raise a child who is actually a hothouse plant, unable to withstand the bitter blasts of vulgarity and temptation to be met with soon and often outside the home. A certain vigor and courage, a certain prudence and foresight, are needed to meet these challenges successfully."

In short, the education of youth is never automatically productive of good results, and never a process which depends exclusively on environment. Even in the seminary the outcome may upon occasion be failure. Nevertheless Catholic schools are worth all the effort expended because their purpose is to train "witnesses to Christ."

The intellect also gives testimony. It is a vital part of the total human endowment, to be taken as seriously as any other. Speaking at Bellarmine College, the Cardinal said, "If we accept the divine pedagogy of nature, we do so also through the conviction that piety never dispenses with technique or a knowledge of the facts. If we accept the divine pedagogy of our intellect, we do so through the conviction that science or art or philosophy can be ways of serving God, and can be good ways of serving God only if we strive to become good scientists, good philosophers, or good artists." His view of the matter seems to resemble that of François Mauriac, the French novelist, who urged the Christian artist to purify the source, so that what flows from it will be pure.

Of necessity every diocesan authority in the United States is concerned with the Catholic school system almost more than with anything else. That of Chicago is particularly large. It reflects in a quite sobering way the combined dedication of the clergy, the religious and the laity. Sometimes those who serve it will be tempted to suppose that because it has cost so much not in terms of money only but of human sacrifice as well, criticism is almost equivalent to treason. Cardinal Meyer has, however, not shied away from scrutiny. He and his Superintendent of Schools have alike been aware of problems and needs. When the University of Notre Dame launched its Study of Catholic Education, it was the Cardinal who placed a protecting hand over it. "We have nothing to fear from the truth," he said, "and can indeed learn from it."

### A Cardinal of the Middle West

It is on this note that any consideration of the work of Cardinal Meyer as a Father of the Council may profitably close. One of his biographers—unfortunately none has so far provided more than a short sketch—considers it fitting that his coat of arms should bear the motto *Adveniat regnum tuum,* which means, Thy Kingdom come. Perhaps it would be equally appropriate to repeat the words of Pope John, "Onward, *in nomine Domini!*" Certainly no one can go about Catholic Chicago without being immensely heartened. Thus the work of the volunteer movement of CALM, tutoring disadvantaged children in the inner city—Negroes, Puerto Ricans and Appalachian whites—is a tribute to the enthusiasm of youth and beyond that to its acceptance of hard work.

And yet also it is impossible to shirk the knowledge of much that is starkly adverse to a Catholic conception of society. There is, for instance, the great number of children born out of wedlock and destined to grow up in squalor, and on a much larger scale a manifest deterioration of morals, particularly among youth. Above all, perhaps, there is a general dearth of readiness to listen to that social counsel which is the gift of the papacy and of the Council.

Therefore one may rejoice that the Archdiocese of Chicago has a Cardinal who has neither underestimated the qualities of his flock nor easily attributed to them virtues they do not possess. His Lenten pastoral letters make hard-hitting comments. We may quote from that of 1960: "The charity of a convinced Christian spirit demands of us that we can and do appreciate the personal qualities of men and women who differ from us in religious conviction, whether we regard their natural qualifications or even the qualities which they manifest in the exercise of their own religious beliefs.... Undoubtedly the lives of many non-Catholics offer an inspiration to Catholics by their zeal and their spirit of self-sacrifice. Beyond doubt, also, there are many differing from us whose subjective sentiments are more pleasing to God than are the interior dispositions of many Catholics in their attendance at mass or other forms of Catholic worship. It must be from no sense of pharisaic pride or smug self-satisfaction that we assert holiness as a mark of the Catholic Church. ...

"On the other hand, the convinced Christian spirit will rightly glory in the evident principles of sanctity taught and upheld by the Church and in the fruitfulness which her history demonstrates these principles to have had. No one who is not sectarian in his thinking can deny how glorious is the panorama of Catholic holiness, ranging from the most glorious colors to almost imperceptible tints. How is it, then, it may be asked, that there are so many Catholics who are far from being saints? The real answer is to be seen in the teaching of Our Lord about the Church. The kingdom on this earth is compared to a net gathering together all manner of fish, and to a field containing wheat and cockle."

Many may not have thought that ecumenical discussion would get round to frankness of this kind. But certainly frankness is needed, too. It is pointless—indeed, it would be almost frivolous—to try to compare the princes of the American Church or make a brief for the relative superiority of any one. The two cardinals on the eastern seaboard, noted for personal kindness and great munificence, remind one not a little of Parkman's comment on the death of Jesuit Pére de Noüe at the hands of the Indians: "Thus, in an act of kindness and charity, died the first martyr of the Canadian mission." If either of them were to die thus, he would think he had been blest.

The two cardinals of the Middle West have been more concerned with the magisterium of the Church and its responsibilities in the time in which we live. They differ in temperament and point of view. But surely our country is fortunate in being represented at home and abroad by such men. Perhaps— one says this tentatively and with no desire to strike a clever judgment—it may be said that Cardinal Meyer's personality has been formed not only by scholarship assiduously pursued but also by what the Middle West uniquely has to offer: a readiness to meet other men and women without prejudice, and a certain genuine earnestness which is rooted in the remembrance of pioneer days and of the touching fidelity of older generations to what in their not infrequent poverty and simple circumstance they considered a treasure beyond price, namely their belief that in Christ there is salvation.

# Hitlerism
# and Organized Religion

## I

. . . What is the religion of National Socialism? The answer is by no means simple. Germany just after the War was a country in which one could distinguish five important attitudes toward religious belief. The Catholic Church, Lutheranism and Jewry were substantial institutionalized creeds; and though absolute unity did not prevail among the adherents to any one of the three, it was still relatively easy to define all. A fourth group comprised the neo-Pantheists, of whom there were several kinds concurring in nothing except the rightness of an impulse to believe in some form of World-Soul rather than in the Christian or Jewish God. The Marxists and the so-called Materialists spoke reverently of "Nature"; the primitivists preached allegiance to the ethical ideals symbolized by pagan deities; and the Wagnerians, or similar fellowships, were obscurely theosophic. Finally the fifth group was merely negative. It could not decide what to call the void where God had previously been, but the assumption that there was a void seemed to it imperative and entrancing.

We may digress for a moment to note that for various reasons the purely negative group was smaller in Germany than in many other countries. A tendency to seek earthly and sensual pleasures was evident here as elsewhere, but one seemed to notice a greater desire to keep alive at least a few sprigs of

From *Like a Mighty Army: Hitler Versus Established Religion* by George N. Shuster (New York: D. Appleton Century Co., 1935), pp. 3-7; 16-45. Reprinted by permission of Hawthorn Books Inc.

idealism. The legacy of long and serious religious debating could not be squandered easily. Successful modern German literature almost invariably propounds a spiritual problem; and it is not a coincidence that the great modern skeptical poets Rilke and George differed in everything except their insistence upon mystical faith. Moreover, the suffering and tragedy which came with a lost war made necessary some form of constant effort to sublimate the here-and-now. Though that war inflicted heavy losses on the institutionalized creeds, it encouraged the rise of many pseudo-faiths, a number of which even manifested considerable missionary fervor. For the most part they possessed an inlay of ethical conviction—sometimes, indeed, there was nothing substantial about them excepting an ethical conviction.

The first thing to note about the religion of Hitlerism is that it seems the common denominator of all these attitudes. Observe der Fuehrer personally. A Catholic? He has openly professed to be one, though he has subscribed to the orthodoxy of Rome neither in theory nor in practice. The genuine tie appears to be a natural fondness for some aspects of Catholic ritual and discipline—clouds of incense, the priestly function, hierarchical organization. A Lutheran? It is true that Hitler has shied away from the essence of the Reformation, which may be said to consist in perpetual reading of the Bible to the accompaniment of perpetual tears of contrition, but the nationalistic-ethical drift of his spiritualism is apparent and important. A pantheist? The deepest cravings of Hitler the Prophet are unquestionably for a God interpreted theosophically; and the fact that the daemon of his movement can only be some kind of emanation from the concept of World-Soul will become more apparent as we proceed. A negator, finally? Yes, this too; for the Hitler acrobatic with ethical principle must inevitably lead (does, in fact, already lead) to a denial, even though this denial is never formally conceded.

To define and explain these things is not easy. The reader of *Mein Kampf* will be impressed by the esteem in which Hitler professes to hold the churches. He says clearly that the "statesman" must avoid every kind of hostility to established religions; and while he denounces priests who engage in political conflict, he is sure that the state can survive only if it supports the priest as a spiritual leader and teacher. Hitler himself seems in many respects a fiery Christian moralistic pamphleteer. Denouncing prostitution, attacking the scurrility and obscenity of the theater, and advocating a healthy family life, he sounds like the very ally for whom the clergy pray. And when he deplores the century-old strife between Protestants and Catholics, he appears to be expressing the deepest longing of irenically minded Germans.

On the other hand, it was clear to lucid observers from the beginning that underneath these concessions and distinctions there lay what from the orthodox point of view is a dangerous heresy, and what more generally is a new religion. Statements by German Catholic and Protestant leaders during 1931 and 1932 stressed at least a part of this truth. The Hitler creed reposes upon this dogma: *in the beginning God created a race.* To this cardinal truth the German people must be converted if the national health, not to mention the national triumph to be hoped for, is earnestly desired. The second dogma is of equal importance with the first and reads: *the antithesis of race is the Jew.* To demonstrate this truth is the main purpose of *Mein Kampf,* which would never have been written if its author had not yearned to produce an anti-Semitic document of major proportions. The third dogma is a corollary of the second and may be stated thus: *Christ, being He whom the Jew rejected and the German acknowledged, is a moral and religious teacher of eminence provided He is thought of as the Teutonic race has thought of Him.*

It seems to be undeniable that these are the principal conclusions to which Hitler arrives in his writings and addresses. What, then, are the implications? First, the ethics of "race" must be suggested by self-assertiveness by and for the group. There are no principles, there are no aspirations, which hold good for humanity as a whole, excepting in so far as the rules which must be followed to make one race-group strong in combat can probably also be adopted by other race-groups. Second, a Manichean distinction between good and evil is introduced into human history. One portion of mankind can be "saved" through the application of biological and disciplinary measures; the other portion is irretrievably "lost." That this philosophy is entirely earthbound, goes without saying. The supernatural enters National Socialist thinking only as an addendum. Third, the God who creates a world in which race is the essential reality cannot be the God of the Jewish-Christian dispensation. It is true that the Hebrews were a chosen people, but only because the "revelation" had been entrusted to them; and Christian teaching holds that when they forgot this fact and imagined themselves destined to political leadership also, the significance of the Messianic coming escaped them. It is at all events clear that the Jewish-Christian God cannot be approached solely through the Nordic-German race. . . .

The Nazi movement was essentially an old soldier campaign which profited by the deep fissure that separated the German worker and the German middle-class. If this fissure had not been so perilously wide, National Socialism would have been limited to making an appeal for the army and navy—a program which would have been doomed to perpetual failure. But, things being what they were, it could construct an ideology complex enough to have in it something for everybody and yet, fundamentally, dependent in every part upon the issue of anti-Semitism. What, asked this ideology, was the simplest method of extricating Germany from the web of disaster? To look to other countries as the causes of the defeat, and therewith as also the sources from which help might eventually come? To cultivate good-will throughout the world in order to regain slowly that which ill-will had taken away? Not at all, said the Nazis. The simplest way out was to declare that the Germans themselves were responsible for all the evil suffered, and that conversely they alone could bring about the improvement hoped for. They had lost the War by refusing to fight it out. They had lost the peace by weakly paying reparations, accepting a form of government which guaranteed inferiority by reason of the cost of its social soft-heartedness, and believing that the world would respect an appeal to any arbiter save the sword.

But how explain why the Germans had done these things? Had Nietzsche been right, after all—did Germany wince under the curse of inferiority, weakness and supine materialism? Nazi theory read Nietzsche in the way it wished to read him, by simply identifying "weakness" with "Semitic tradition," which perforce includes Christianity. But to the masses it said merely that deep-rooted German instincts about the Jew were perfectly right. This Jew it was who had created Marxism and Bolshevism; who had undermined the nation's moral fiber with lascivious literature and a theater which led to the brothel; who had attacked maliciously the honor of the German soldier; who had sold the Fatherland for the price stipulated by international bankers; who had throttled industry by charging too much for capital; who had first engineered the inflation and then profited by it; and who was the ruthless foe of ethical and religious traditions by which the German people had lived.

This talk was inconsistent, wrong, wilfully prejudiced, wild, absurd—anything you like. But the remarkable thing about it happened to be that the German burgher ate it up. It provided him with a target easier and safer to aim at than France or a recalcitrant business cycle. Here was a devil who could be exorcised at practically no cost. Those terrible and unforgettable Nazi mass meetings of 1930, when gutter rats in brown uniforms roused mobs to frenzy with baseless attacks upon the Jew, were phenomena which still seem to me ghastlier than anything experienced during the War. All these hysterical, hypnotized people closed their eyes and saw—some Jew. In other words, they narrowed their vision to one hated object, exactly as an adept concentrates on a crystal, and transferred all their hates or dreams of vengeance to that. In the United States of yore, there were men and women who beheld the root of all evil in a bottle of rum; but theirs was a comparatively harmless delusion, circumscribed by a society and age in which even hate had an inlay of altruism. There never has been anything like this German phenomenon. It was a madman's perfect alibi!

How much of all this the Nazi demagogues themselves believed is a question difficult to answer. Concerned as they were with gunning for the *Semitic principle*—for the ancient tradition which enshrines the ethical and esthetic experience of the Jew—they may really have thought they saw the monstrous things which they described to the populace. Perhaps, on the other hand, they merely uttered gibberish, in accordance with Hitler's maxim that the mob is too stupid to grasp anything but nonsense. At any rate, no sooner had the party come to power than it began slowly and systematically to expound and enforce the theory of biological anti-Semitism and to attack those aspects of Christianity which were deemed to be of Jewish origin.

## II

It will be the purpose of subsequent chapters to show how this exposition and enforcement were accomplished. Now we must revert to the two fundamental doctrines of the Hitler creed, and study the man who did more than any other person to establish them. This man is Alfred Rosenberg. For a long while it was not altogether clear that Rosenberg really deserved to be called the "master mind" of National Socialism. To many it seemed that Hitler was personally committed to little excepting a desire to rule Germany and to promote the triumph of the military idea. Now we know, as a result of what has happened and of what individuals familiar with Nazi secrets have divulged, that the intellectual domination of Rosenberg has long been a fact. The strength of this man is due to the circumstance that he is something of a thinker—his writings systematize the intellectual confusion which now reigns in Germany, and he personally has the gift of remaining behind the scenes, much as certain great Catholic theologians have exerted lasting influence on the Church though their names were hardly known to the public. Latterly, however, he has not shrunk by any means from the glare of footlights.

No other member of the supreme Nazi council seems anywhere near as young as Rosenberg. Goering looks like a veteran police sergeant, with a passion for uniforms; Goebbels is a copy-writer grizzled with years of service under the 100 watt bulbs of a newspaper sanctum. But Rosenberg well-nigh appears to be a mature graduate student and—barring his worst moments— talks like one. His fanaticism is outwardly repressed, and his addresses breathe a desire to be judicious. Yet in essence this man is positively everything that used to be called a "dangerous radical."

Born in Reval, Russia, in 1893, Rosenberg was a university student in Russia when the War ended. He then fled to Munich, where he sought to make a living as an architect and a writer; and fortune smiled upon him when, during 1921, he became the editor of the *Völkischer Beobachter,* previously an anti-Semitic scandal-sheet. His earlier writings were elaborations of theories which would later on become Hitlerite doctrines. Thus he published a brochure about the Protocols of the Elders of Zion (1923); a lengthy essay which set out to prove that speculative capitalism and revolutionary Marxism were secretly allied (1924); and a panegyric which lauded Houston Stewart Chamberlain as the "founder of a new and glorious German future" (1927). It was he who first let it dawn upon Hitler that the unity of the Fatherland could not be achieved until all Germans had subscribed to a single *Weltan-schauung;* and it was likewise he who suggested that converts to the new dogmas could be made by thousands, granted that the right methods of catechetic were employed. Though Hitler himself never publicly identified himself with all the teachings of Rosenberg, the fact that both men were in substantial agreement was an open secret as early as 1923. If one takes the trouble to skim through the *Beobachter* and the *N.S. Monatshefte,* of which Rosenberg became editor in 1931, it will become evident that when Rosenberg was entrusted during 1934 "with supervision of the whole educational policy of the Party and affiliated organizations in so far as spiritual and philosophical matters are concerned," there was being realized a wish long aged in the Hitler wood. To deny that the two men are intellectually one and the same is pure obscurantism, naively willing to ignore the part which political expediency had always played in the development of der Fuehrer.

The chief Rosenberg doctrines are fully set forth in *Der Mythus des 20. Jahrhunderts,* a mammoth treatise published in 1930 and made "obligatory reading" for Nazis in 1934. This treatise is a memorable attempt to give National Socialism a religious and philosophic content; and while it would be mistaken to infer that the highest leaders of the Party subscribe to everything the book says, there is no doubt that all consider it an official document binding in the main on orthodox Nazis. How describe such a work? Essentially it is an elaboration of the maxim, "Werde was du bist" (become what you are), the "are" being taken to mean fellowship in the dominant German race. Man is the distillation of his ancestry; and God, conceived of idealistically, is He who steadily reveals Himself in the ancestor-man sequence. Since a culture requires an Absolute and is characterized by what it accepts as an Absolute, says Rosenberg, German civilization will become great if it incorporates the God whom it is capable of evoking.

What, then, is the German spiritual record? The Teutonic soul, according to Rosenberg, has found expression in two series of documents. First come the sagas and myths which enshrine love of heroism and addiction to the manly, martial virtues. In this literature Siegfried stands revealed as the true German saint, exemplifying the ethical standards and spiritual aspirations of which the Nordic soul is capable. If one compares the "cattle trader" morality of the Old Testament, in which the race of Jewish hagglers has mirrored its innermost mind, with Teutonic myth, it becomes apparent not only that the two are incompatible but also that the Old Testament is utterly unworthy of the German's attention. The second set of documents are the writings of various medieval mystics, notably Master Eckhart. Rosenberg's fantastic interpretation of the maxims of this brilliant Christian thinker enables him to conclude that Eckhart was a bad precursor of Nietzsche, who considered "freedom" the highest good of the soul provided only that it was regulated by "honor." In other words, Eckhart is an incorporation of the same beatitudes as characterized Siegfried, though he transferred them to the domain of philosophy and religion. For the moment we need not be concerned with the palpable amateurishness of this thesis. It will suffice to note that Rosenberg follows a well-known bevy of historic theorists who held that a chasm between Rome and Germany had existed during the whole of the Middle Ages, that the "mystics" are evidence of how deep that chasm was, and that the eventual logical consequence of their position was the Lutheran upheaval. Rosenberg correlates these theories—often at the expense of vitiating them—with the creed of Nordic race superiority. He concludes that both "myth" and "mystic" demonstrate that the German has his own way of discovering and manifesting God.

It follows, therefore, that Christianity has in several important ways deflected the Teutonic soul from its natural, predestined course. If one studies the problem carefully, says Rosenberg, one can distinguish in Christian tradition some things which are beneficial and reconcilable with the Nordic spirit, and other things which are baneful and incompatible. Good are certain ethical teachings of Jesus: His courage and freedom in interpreting the law; His dissatisfaction with Jewish cruelty and literalness; and His conception of union with the Divine. The evil in Christianity springs in the main from two sources: acceptance by the churches of the Old Testament, which Rosenberg despises flatly as a "jerusalemitic" hodge-podge of no value and which he repudiates so completely that the author of the Psalms is said by him to be the peer of "that scoundrel, Heinrich Heine"; and, secondly, the assimilation by the Catholic Church of "Asiatic" and "African" traditions and customs. He would, as a consequence, suppress the Old Testament altogether, and delete from the New whatever is not compatible with the outlook of a "modern European."

These conclusions will interest us later on, in so far as they affect the Christian Churches. We shall now ask: what is it exactly that Rosenberg is trying to do? The answer is that he desires to stamp out, through use of National Socialist power, every vestige of the Semitic tradition—that is, to repudiate not merely Jewry as that exists in our time, but also everything that Jewry has meant in the past and has contributed to western civilization. This is, he declares, the unavoidable task of those who would secure for the German people a religion in consonance with their aspirations to a position of military and economic leadership among European peoples. The Reich must be converted to a creed in the light of which it can press on to victory. Jewish leadership is, of course, held responsible for tendencies rooted deeply in modern history. Without it capitalism and Marxism, pacifism and Bolshevism, would never have affected the life of mankind. Yet, if one examines these more closely, they stand revealed as the necessary consequences of tendencies created by Christianity, *Écrasez l'infâme!*

All this could be debated with academic calm if Rosenberg were only an individual crank or preacher. He is, however, less an innovator than a compiler of doctrines which were partly in the air and partly in print. The groups which have held similar views are in the main three: first, the extremists of the *Völkische Bewegung,* among whom some early adherents to the Youth Movement were counted; second, the Tannenberg Union, presided over by General Erich Ludendorff, who organized it in 1924 and 1925 as a means of promoting the ideas of his wife, Mathilda; and the German Faith movement, the principal sponsors of which are Count von Reventlow, Professor Wilhelm Hauer and Professor Ernst Bergman. It is unfortunately impossible to describe these significant groups in anything like adequately piquant detail.

The *Völkische Bewegung* was a vague something in which a score of nationalistic points of view converged. The name was applied immediately after the War to a number of scattered patriotic groups which struggled to keep alive the spirit and traditions of the Imperial army; and quite naturally it made an appeal to those intransigent Protestants who had felt all along that the Papacy as a diplomatic power was hostile to Germany. One of the earliest pamphlets circulated in behalf of Hitler contains these words: "Please do contribute something to the Hitler movement, for it is a strictly Protestant endeavor. Though we have at present a number of Catholic leaders, they are there merely for the sake of appearances." This small but belligerent wing of the Lutheran Church had been convinced that the plea for peace submitted to the powers in 1917 by Pope Benedict XV was a ruse designed to undermine the morale of the German people and so to insure the triumph of the Allied cause. Numerous teachers and some professors belonged to the *Völkische Bewegung,* and it was to a great extent their authority which reinculcated in young Germany a strictly one-sided view of history as well as a fondness for ultra-nationalist writers like Langbehn and Lagarde. These last, who emphasized the doctrine that the German soul was governed by laws all its own, were the mediators through whom post-War patriotic sentiment regained contact with the "heroic idealists" of a century previous, notably the philosopher Fichte and the pedagogue Jahn.

General Ludendorff's Tannenberg Union was, as has been said, designed to provide a sounding-board for the pantheistic-patriotic extravaganzas which Frau Mathilda deduced largely from a crystal and a library of scatterbrained rosicrucian and theosophic books. Those who take the trouble to read her *Soul of Man* and her *Redemption through Jesus Christ* (she wrote a great deal more) will find that numerous passages in the Rosenberg treatises appear to have been transcribed from them. Yet this is not necessarily plagiarism. I consider Frau Ludendorff an extraordinarily typical representative of the chaotic mentality induced in many Germans by the especial feminine suffering incident to the War. A large number of semi-educated women ran utterly amuck in a welter of fancies they imagined were derived from Indian, Greek and Teutonic sources. Garbled versions of books like Rhode's *Psyche* leaped from brain to brain. Germany was also dotted with ladies who supposed they had been granted private revelations from on high, or at least from the stratosphere. Frau Ludendorff's vision was lurid with theosophic thought, anti-Semitic impulses and fears of the Jesuits, whom she termed "black men." All this attracted a gratifying number of male devotees. It is not altogether improbable, for example, that the S.S. (organized to be Hitler's pretorian guard) were uniformed in black so as to provide a satisfactory antidote to the Jesuit menace. During 1925, General Ludendorff himself issued a Tannenberg Union manifesto which can be described as a laconic and rugged digest of the principal points in Rosenberg's magnum opus. Republican Germany, however, did not take very eagerly to the *Soul of Man* and kindred illuminations. The Tannenberg Union was declared illegal; and it was not until 1935 and the occasion of Ludendorff's seventieth birthday that the society received full official recognition.

By comparison the German Faith movement has a long and definite historical background. As constituted, the organization dates, it is true, from a convention held in Eisenach during 1933. But fundamentally the profession of allegiance to "the religious heritage of the German people, the creative spiritual energies of which have flourished for a thousand years and are now a vital force in human life"—words taken from a resolution adopted at Eisenach—is nothing but the credo of young Friedrich Schlegel and his co-partners in the early Romantic movement. The late eighteenth century was pregnant with this idea. Something like it was often in the mind of the great Herder, whose quest for the German soul (which he ferreted out in a hundred domains) was at bottom a desire to establish a Teutonic theology. Perhaps also, the éthical objectives of post-Kantian philosophy, from Fichte to Hegel, were merely loftier versions of ends deemed desirable by the "creative spiritual energies" of the German soul. During the nineteenth century secularist idealism was combated on the one hand by the Christian ferment latent in Romanticism and on the other hand by the rise of positivistic rationalism which of sheer necessity implied a return to Kant. Would it eventually triumph nevertheless?

When German philosophy again laid the primary emphasis on "vitalism," immediately before and after the War, it virtually provided a guarantee that any fresh outburst of fanatical nationalist enthusiasm would dress itself in Romantic rainment copied by adroit tailors from models of the Napoleonic era. The fires which had burned on German patriotic altars during the Wars of Liberation would reappear again at post-War shrines. Nazi theorists like Bäumler and Rosenberg had only to imbue the old concepts with the intoxicating hates of the populace in order to be assured of a wide hearing. The irrational was declared superior to the rational by the leading authorities; and so it is probably not surprising that the "instincts" of blood and race should be voted wholly credible sources of truth. What were the "values" to be gained from ratiocination but the tawdry baubles of a "liberalistic" epoch? The new German civilization was to derive its confidence from the "deep wells of life." Accordingly, we may note in passing, there were no limits to the strain to which Nazis would subject the creative fancy. Those who did not balk at the major premises—that is, that Germans were capable of everything good, and Jews capable of everything bad—found it relatively easy to believe that the rule established by Hitler would last a thousand, or even thirty thousand, years, that the arts must be refashioned and the sciences rewritten (as witness the promulgation of a new astronomy by an ardent soul who claimed to have received the key to his discovery from Hitler himself), and that the intuitions of even a minor party official were nuggets of sacred ore mined in the very bowels of truth.

Nor can one penetrate to the core of the matter unless one has tried to wrestle with the problem of sex as posited by German vitalists. Walther Darré (now German Minister of Agriculture) says that the marriageability of men is to be judged by their achievement, while that of women is to be estimated by their conformity to the standards of the Nordic race. This conception is to be met with in various forms throughout Nazi thought. General Ludendorff holds that men are born to be soldiers, while women exist for the purpose of becoming mothers. The most eloquent of sermons was preached by Hitler against prostitution, and he observed that the only dependable remedy for it was early marriage between persons determined to rear a family. It must not be assumed—as is quite frequently done—that all these declarations are actuated merely by a desire to increase the number of recruits. And while it is true that the "old soldier" in the National Socialist cannot feel that the feminine sex has any business trying to play a part in politics or higher education, the Nazi attitude toward women is not determined either by the wish to fill all available positions with men. Nowhere else in modern Germany do philosophic and religious points of view count for so much as in this realm of masculine-feminine relations.

The "vitalistic" German is anxious to sense a nearness to nature, "the mother of all religions." For him the word nature does not stand for a ruthless process of selection, as the result of which man gradually evolved from a monkey, a fish or a bird. He is convinced rather that the "soul" immanent in the cosmos found in the human being its first satisfying expression. In the beginning, many believe, man was a unity of two sexes, and only gradually was there a separation into the two component parts now known as "male" and "female." If so much is assumed, the yearning of one sex for the other can be explained—a yearning which is not merely the instinct for purposive copulation, such as governs the animals, but a desire for "unity" in which each finds self-satisfaction. Civilization undermines this bliss by altering either man or woman. Dr. Magnus Hirschfeld, the Jewish psychiatrist previously referred to, held that marriage was the art of discerning the traits which both sexes share in common. Nazi "vitalists," however, believe that true mating can repose only on a foundation of differences recognized and jubilantly emphasized. When the male is a warrior and the female a homemaker, there exists between the two that tension which "nature" wishes and human happiness requires. To be sure, the warrior need not actually be at war. It is sufficient that he live *as if* a battle were always imminent.

A warrior husband seeks to beget warrior sons. No weaklings for him! *Mein Kampf* is prodigal, for instance, of denunciations of the intellectual, whose muscles soften while his theories improve. The pro-creative and educational objective of Nazidom is a youth without physical tares. That there are forces at work which prevent the attainment of that objective is a fact needing no extensive proof. But analysis reveals that the principal sources of deterioration are three in number: sexual vice, the fruit of which is that syphilis which Hitler has so roundly denounced; intellectualism and all its fruits, among which are indifference to physical training, celibacy and pacifism; and the permission to marry which is accorded weaklings by a too indulgent society. Accordingly a doctrine of happiness which starts with a "vital" sex life must necessarily combat these three fountains of evil.

Suppose now that one can identify all these baneful things with a definite, historic group ideology. What if the Jewish conception of the sex relationship is found to be radically different from the Germanic view? Or suppose further that the evils enumerated spring from a sinister plot which a Jewry bent on wiping out European man has concocted in secret. It will then follow that the first step toward sanitation must be an effort to dig up Jewry by the roots. Only then will further measures—war on prostitution, sterilization of the unfit, the grant of subsidies to racially pure couples who wish to marry, the fostering of illegitimate offspring born to Aryan couples (all of which are now provided for by laws passed under Hitler's dictation) lead to measurable success. I do not think it necessary to refute these baseless anti-Semitic charges. Jewry in several countries has been badly infected with materialism, as a drift toward almost absolute race suicide makes manifest; but this deterioration is obviously the result of emancipation, which happened to take place at a time when Europe as a whole was succumbing to the bourgeois-positivist mirage, and not the consequent deduction either from a "plot" or

from the austere Semitic code of sex morality. More worthy of note is the
fact that Nazi hatred for the Jew is largely rooted in sex attitudes. Almost all
the National-Socialist journals were originally "extras" filled to the brim with
juicy bits of Semitic scandal, more or less authentic. And it was by selling the
legend of the "dirtiness" of the Jew that scores of Nazi publicists earned their
reputations.

When Rosenberg's books are read with all this in mind they will take on, I
think, a new meaning. His "vitalism" is deeply rooted in what is termed the
"Germanic view of sex." Religion (or *Weltanschauung*) is properly that which
gives the relation between warrior husband and home-making wife its deepest
significance. It is true, of course, that Christianity exalts purity and condemns
sexual sin. But for Rosenberg sin does not exist, and against the theological
doctrine that it does he directs some of his most violent attacks. There is no
room in his philosophy for the "misdeeds of the fathers," which exact
penitence and mercy of the individual and society. Whereas the Christian
Church sees in the heritors of sexual or other disease poor wretches with
whom the community must bear patiently because they are immolated for
offenses against the Divine law, a Rosenberg Germany must ruthlessly stamp
them out. They are microbes which infect the body politic. They are a species
of worm which eats the substance of the state. They are, above all, a
demonstration of what human passion really and truly is. But the thumb of
the German pretorian is turned down—only the healthy Aryan male and his
eugenically chosen spouse can be suffered to live.

### III

To return to the German Faith Movement. Practically regarded, the effort
to establish a religion consonant with the principles advocated by Rosenberg
has been given no direct support by Hitler. That political genius is no stickler
for theological detail. Granted that the Jew is wiped out, the authority of the
"Nazi regiment" acknowledged everywhere, and military zeal inculcated even
in the Hausfrau, der Fuehrer is by and large content. But under the glare of
Nazi fanaticism many varieties of religious fruit begin to ripen. Of these the
German Faith Movement is the most important, but it can be seen in better
perspective if approached gradually, through the out-buildings occupied by
other sects.

During 1917, Professor Adolf Bartels joined a group of friends who were
interested in giving Protestant Evangelical Christianity a more "Germanic"
tinge. The Professor was a literary critic and historian who taught that
everything of value in a culture is the product of national feeling. His services
to the idea of *Heimatkunst* were praised by teachers in a number of countries;
and so when he helped organize the "German Church," the news was given a

modest measure of international circulation. Later on the skill of a fervent organizer, Dr. Joachim Niedlich, brought the "German Church" to the attention of important groups in the Fatherland. He was able to enlist temporarily the coöperation of various patriotic societies, notably the Stahlhelm, but most of them soon withdrew. At bottom the movement reposed on ideas voiced long before by Herder, who had asserted that while Christianity was a universal religion, "each people had received it in its own way," so that German Christianity was after all different from Italian Christianity. The "German Church" proposed that Christ should be conceived of as a hero, with Faustian characteristics aplenty; that the affinity between Him and the traditional German heroes and mystics ought to be stressed; and that, finally, His image could be discerned clearly in Luther, Frederick the Great, Moltke and Hindenburg. The movement had become avowedly anti-Semitic as early as 1922. Its advocates appealed to Marcion, looked upon by orthodox Christian theologians as the foremost heretic of the first centuries, as the champion of resistance to the Jewish element in the early Church. Teachers were its most ardent supporters; and it is probable that the movement is more consonant with the personal convictions of Hitler than is any other of the new creeds.

The relative moderateness of Bartels has its proper counterpart in the views of Hermann Wirth, as confused, interesting and gullible a soul as ever lived. Born in Holland and educated in philology by German professors, Wirth eventually discovered the source of all culture in Atlantis, the mythical land which is supposed to be buried some miles east of Charleston, S.C. It was from this center, inhabited by Aryans, that true religious insight came, to be vitiated later on by the Orient. The man of Atlantis believed in God-Father, the "world spirit," and in His "Son," who is the physical and ethical "order" of the universe. This strong and simple faith was perverted by oriental embroidery, primarily because the East lacked the racial substance which alone permits a culture to survive. Eventually Jesus appeared, an Aryan of genius who was able to work His way through the frippery of Judaism to the sound verity of the true Nordic faith. The essence of His teaching is that man carries the awareness of God about with him, in his own heart. During 1933, Wirth emerged as a lecturer on these and kindred topics. He claimed at that time to have discovered records proving that the religious beliefs of primitive Germany were in fact the same as those of Atlantis; and on the basis of this evidence he erected an ideology in which Wotan and other ancient deities figured as spiritual exemplars. Wirth's findings were decimated by critical scholarship, which voted them so much nonsense. But the good doctor was nothing daunted.

We shall hurry past many another interesting sage to the German Faith Movement, which is of genuine political and religious importance. Perhaps the easiest mode of access to it is through the unusually able propagandist, Count Ernst von Reventlow. The controversial skill of this pamphleteer was acquired during many years. Prior to the War he was a specialist in naval affairs, and then for a time functioned as one of the brightest Pan-German luminaries; but Von Reventlow was too individualistic even for a group so much to his liking, and severed his connection in order to embark on a career in conservative journalism, which soon touted him as an authority on agrarian questions. During the War he launched a bitter attack on Judaism and Freemasonry, to which he attributed most of the blame for Germany's defeat. It was in vain that the editor of the *Deutsche Tageszeitung,* for which the Count then toiled, stressed the fact that he himself was a Mason. The indefatigable debater then resigned and entered politics. Soon he was active as an apostle of religious and cultural reaction. When Hitler (whom he had supported with reservations) came to power, Von Reventlow's weekly *Reichswart,* which he had issued since 1924, soon became the most widely read of the "new religion" journals.

The program of the *Reichswart* was a two-sided one. It directed a steady and vigorous critical fire upon Reichsbischof Ludwig Mueller's endeavors to browbeat all Lutherans into German Christian uniformity, and did much to undermine Nazi confidence in this method of enforcing a liaison between Protestantism and National Socialism. On the other hand, it kept up a persistent demand for governmental recognition of the German Faith Movement as a church equal in status to the Catholic and Lutheran establishments and therewith entitled to a share of the ecclesiastical taxes. So adroit was the appeal that prominent Nazis—for example, Hitler's deputy, Rudolf Hess— supported Reventlow's demands in public long before the German Faith Movement had any large following.

That the Movement flourishes is obvious; but anything like a precise description of what it is remains unobtainable. During the summer of 1933, a convention assembled at Eisenach under the presidency of Professor Wilhelm Hauer requested Chancellor Hitler to grant official status to a faith rooted in the "creative religious energy" which the German people had manifested "during a thousand years." More concretely the convention was a prelude to the federation of various groups which, during the previous decade or longer, had sought to make Lutheranism a mystical-patriotic rather than a dogmatic religion. Perhaps there were a dozen organizations in the merger, but the bond between them is so precarious that it is impossible to tell which give more than nominal assent to the German Faith Movement program. Nevertheless the organizers have displayed a very great deal of energy, and several reliable German observers assure me that the zeal displayed virtually assures the Movement of a large following. So far little binds the faithful together excepting an oath of membership which excludes all of Jewish or colored blood, and all who belong or have belonged either to a secret society or to the Jesuit order. The last two motives for blackballing applicants seems a bit odd until one remembers that the Movement bears considerable affinity to Rosicrucianism, which (say stanch German historians of the mystical persuasion) was ruined by Masons and Jesuit spies.

The theology of this new movement is arranged in tiers. Men like Arthur Dinter, a writer and politician governed by Semitic and Roman phobias, comprise the lowest stratum, which is actuated by hatred of the foreigner. The second layer is represented chiefly by Professor Ernst Bergman, author of a "catechism" for the instruction of those who profess the German Faith. Probably his most important pronouncement is: "I believe in the God of the German Religion, who is operative in nature, in the supreme human spirit, and in the power of His people. And in Germany, which is creating a new humanity." Exactly what Bergmann means to say *positively* is almost impossible to determine. He says that God is "a moral concept which we read into the eternal energy of nature," but declares in the next breath that humanity is not Divine (though it is the point at which Divinity gushes forth) and that there is no essential difference between psychical and physical being. As a whole it is a theory which cannot be approached save through the history of German idealism and its contacts with natural science—a route which cannot be followed here.

It is far easier to understand what Bergmann says *negatively,* in attacking the Christian idea of God as professed by Protestants and Catholics. The idea of a "mediatory priesthood" is repudiated, and with it of course every contact between the German soul and Roman missionary effort. For of necessity, says Bergmann, such a priesthood posits the existence of God in a realm beyond this world, whereas all knowledge men have is of realities within this world. We know that the soul of a people is formed by the sum-total of its experience, and therefore the German God must be found in the sum-total of German experience. But to this the Christian God is a mere addendum, if only for the reason that "He permitted Versailles." The time has come to get rid of Him. Bergmann proposes a "German National Church" to which every German, Catholic as well as Protestant, will belong. Concerning this he is quite shockingly frank. Christ, he says for example, is the "Good Shepherd"; but the word "shepherd" today means "Breeder," and is applicable only to those who help breed good Germans! If Boniface had not triumphed, he remarks in the same book, *Die Deutsche Nationalkirche,* Germany would today probably include most of European Russia. Of Catholics he would demand a break with the Papacy, and the discontinuation of celibacy and auricular confession. Protestants, he thinks, would offer little effective resistance to a National Church officially proclaimed.

The highest tier is occupied by Professor Jakob Wilhelm Hauer, professor

of comparative religion, who has played an active rôle in some phases of the
Youth Movement. Returning to Germany after the War from missionary work
in India, he brought with him the idea that religion is a name given to the
residue of certain fundamental experiences: of the unity of man and nature;
of guilt and atonement; of awe in the presence of another personality; and of
introspective contemplation. This "feeling" is all there properly is to "religion," and the Christian confessions have sinned against the German people
by trying to substitute for it belief in an alien, objective Revelation. The
future must belong to those who "worship" in the genuine German tradition.
Hauer's analysis of that tradition is interesting. He proceeds from the old
German and Nordic religions through the medieval mystics (in consonance
here with Bergmann) to such assorted personalities as Paracelsus, Boehme,
Lessing, Frederick the Great, Kant, Fichte, Goethe and Lagarde. One is
doubtless safe in feeling that Hauer's doctrine is basically an effort to rescue
the liberal theology of the late nineteenth century by giving it a patriotic
content. It is our old friend the "religion of humanity" which appears here in
a new uniform: the "religion of German humanity." But Hauer is neither an
opportunist nor a fanatic. Unlike almost every other leader of the movement,
he is of the lineage of the great German modernists and not a blend of upstart
and crank.

Naturally the effort to popularize the movement could not be limited to
theoretical pronouncements, all of which would have sailed right over the
solid Nazi head. Painstakingly "congregations" were organized in various
places, generally through "public demonstrations" having a recognizable Nazi
flavor. A liturgy was arranged for Easter and Christmas. The first has become
the "Feast of Ostara," or of the sunrise in the east; the second has given way
to the "Feast of the Winter Solstice" which is celebrated in the woods before
the equivalent of a huge yulelog. Similarly the Christian sacraments of
baptism, confirmation and matrimony have given way to appropriate German
Faith ceremonies. An enterprising publisher has already produced a hymnal
offering substitutes for favorite old songs. Perhaps the most interesting
melody is a new version of "Silent Night," in which the refrain,

  *Christus der Retter is da,** and so forth,
becomes,
  *Deutscher, lausch' und wach' auf,*† and so forth.

Doubtless the most impressive of the new "sacraments" is the *Jugend-
weihe,* which takes the place of Confirmation. The community meets to
celebrate the fact that its young bloods have attained the age of manhood and
are now in a position to mate and bear arms. In some cases, say eye-witnesses,

*"Christ the Redeemer is here."
†"German, listen and wake up."

a conscious effort is made to revive the spirit of the "initiation" customary among savage tribes. More attention has been paid, however, to rendering the heathen wedding ceremony a thing for good Germans to gape at in wonder. The *Reichwart* has described several such marriages. At one, which took place in Leipzig during December, 1934, the bride and bridegroom met in a room where a vessel containing fire was placed on a pedestal covered with red damask, against a background of three pine trees. After the "fire symbolism" had been enjoyed by everyone, the newly married couple partook of bread and water. The bread indicates that man is the provider; the water refers to the "soothing drink which woman draws from the depths of her being, which is always close to mother earth." Another such wedding was honored by an address by Baldur von Shirach, official leader of German youth. After the "mouth-organ had played festively," he said in part: "Why do I stand here today? In order that I may tell you, in the name of the entire youth of our people, how greatly we rejoice that you have found your way to one another. Today the State blesses your union, and is glad that you have founded a comradeship which will give you strength and courage and belief to endure throughout the long future the heavy struggle which will be shared by all our people." The bridegroom was Youth Leader Deinert; the celebrant was the man entrusted by Hitler with the job of training Germany's young people. The German Faith Movement may rightly claim a decent amount of progress.

To date the greatest single triumph was, however, the publication of the *Deutscher Bauernkalender für 1935*. This "Calendar for German Farmers, 1935" was published by the Ministry of Agriculture, and breathed so much of the spirit of Rosenberg and Bergmann that the Government could hardly quell the subsequent excitement. All the time-honored names suddenly appeared in heathenish garb. Christmas was associated with Baldur and Jul; Easter was designated with less originality as the "Feast of Ostara." But the altering of Good Friday gave the most scandal: "Silent Friday," said the calendar. "In memory of the 4,500 Saxons brutally murdered by Charlemagne, and of the nine million other assassinated, tortured or burned fighters for justice, heroes of conscience, heretics and witches," The rest of the text reveled in insults flung at institutional Christianity. Shortly after publication, the calendar was disavowed by prominent Nazis.

It may be added that while Reventlow, Bergmann and their associates pride themselves on being orthodox National Socialists, they have quite generally refrained from bedecking the all-highest Adolf with the mantle of prophetic authority. This has, however, been done by not a few others, notably Dr. Reinhold Krause. Originally a leader of the "German Christian" movement headed by Reichsbischof Mueller . . ., Dr. Krause startled Germany on November 13, 1933, with a speech in which he championed the views of Rosenberg while clinging to a somewhat more orthodox point of view. He expressed himself as uncompromisingly anti-Catholic, and alleged that the "Church of the Middle Ages" had dug a yawning chasm between "God and the German man"; he declared that as soon as the Hitlerite maxim, "one folk and one leader" had been established in the political realm the time would be ripe to institute "one God and one Church," in the same spirit as that which had actuated Martin Luther; he demanded a purging of the New Testament from all "superstitions" and made short shrift of the "theology of the Rabbi Paul": and asserted finally that "our church must allow no persons of Jewish blood to enter it," since the religious task of the future *must* be to free the "heroic mission of Jesus" from the cobwebs in which racial perversion and theology have enmeshed it. When this speech proved very shocking to the orthodox Lutheran conscience, Dr. Krause seceded and formed the "German Folk Church." The principal requirement for admission seems to be ability to raise an initiation fee of fifty pfennigs. But the Krause religion, though interesting as a symptom, will soon die out as a corporate enterprise.

Viewed as a whole, these attempts to build a creed of nationalism have a common denominator, though their primary characteristic is incurable sectarianism. Even the most ambitious are held together only by opposition to the hitherto established orthodoxies, since the differences between one new prophet and another are too vast to be bridged even by a common ecstatic patriotism. German idealism has always been a solvent, not an annealing, agent. Now, as a hundred and more years ago, it combines an appeal to primitive racial instinct with a hankering after "modernistic" solutions of the problems of religious history. The new creeds are therefore ineradicably esoteric and philosophic. Each claims to possess the secret recipe according to which a genuinely German religious community can be established. But each turns out to be a reflection of the hopelessly romantic individualism of the nineteenth century, unable to steer by any compass save the principle of spiritual evolution or to muster any energy except that of a governmental power more or less sympathetic. If Hitlerism were rash enough to bestow especial benediction upon some one group, it might enforce a large measure of verbal allegiance to that. The rival doctors would, however, by no means be reconciled to the fortunate favorite. This one would, in fact, become the most unpopular thing in a Germany where little if anything is truly popular. . . .

# Religion
# Behind the Iron Curtain

The provinces of Eastern Germany which at present constitute the Russian Zone of Occupation no doubt afford the most advantageous point of departure for an inquiry into religious life behind the Iron Curtain. Not a little is known about conditions prevailing there; and for a variety of reasons the Soviet authorities have on the whole laid down policies which are in some respects more moderate than are those in force elsewhere. The beleaguered island of Berlin remains, to an even greater extent than Vienna, a point of exodus and ingress between West and East. It should be borne in mind that the Zone is merely the torso of prewar eastern Germany. The great agricultural regions of East Prussia, Pomerania, and Silesia were detached from Germany in 1945. Of the five remaining states, Brandenburg, Saxony, and Thuringia are the most important, and are in part highly industrialized.

When the Russian armies first marched in, ruthless violence was the order of the day. Some idea of the lawlessness which prevailed is given by the fact that more than half the Catholic clergy in the area were put to death in varying ways, and that the losses suffered by the Protestant clergy were also great. Gradually order was restored under a puppet German government to which at first all political parties were contributors. Soon, however, the Unity Party in which Socialists and Communists were merged gained complete control. Sizable police forces were created, and recruits were sought in both the East and the West. Economic conditions have on the whole remained primitive. Food resources have never been adequate, and in years of poor harvests (for example, 1952, when early frosts spoiled a large part of the potato crop) the plight of the population has been dire indeed. As a matter of fact, widespread famine would have decimated the population had it not been for relief shipments of foodstuffs from the West. The great religious eleemosynary organizations have siphoned more than a third of all supplies from outside Germany into the Eastern Zone; and in addition giving by West Germans has continued on a notable scale. Industrial production by nationalized mines and factories has, however, steadily increased, though wages are low and the working groups disgruntled.

The Constitution under which the East German government presumably functions is so similar to the basic written law elsewhere in the Russian sphere of influence that the provisions which govern religious activity will serve to illustrate rather well what the over-all juridical framework is. The exercise of religious beliefs shall not (we read) be curtailed. This is in accordance with the Soviet contention that full religious liberty is guaranteed by the Soviet Constitution. Church and State are declared wholly separate, so that the independence of religious organizations is formally recognized. To be sure, this recognition is subject to the whimsical impulses as well as to the over-all political strategy of the Communists. When parents give their consent, religious instruction may be imparted to children under fourteen years of age. After that age they are presumed to be their own masters, so that they themselves must decide whether they desire any additional religious indoctrination. The Constitution further provides that anyone who wishes to withdraw from the Church shall be able to do so without incurring any social stigma. A number of specific prohibitions are also included in the fundamental law; but these are quite like the caveats established by the Nazis. Thus any action by a religious association which is deemed to be in violation of the principles of the Constitution, or which may be interpreted as having a partisan political character, is subject to censure and punishment. It is likewise unlawful to impose an obligation to attend religious services—an obligation which the German *Wehrmacht* had traditionally made a part of military training. Private or parochial schools were forbidden, although until recently it was possible to send children residing in East Berlin to religious schools situated in the Western part of the city. Finally, no one can be made subject to a demand that he manifest a religious faith in public.

So much for the law. The pro-Soviet Unity Party has, however, its own code of conduct in so far as religion is concerned, resembling in this respect Communist parties in power elsewhere. A good deal of experience with this code has been accumulated, and religious leaders have commented on various aspects of it. The cardinal principle is that while open, full-scale onslaughts on religion are to be avoided, Communists must do everything in their power to spread the Gospel of dialectical materialism. A highly significant practical corollary is that since service to the Russian state is the major business of Communist parties, everything possible must be done to form a group of "democratic" or "patriotic" clergymen, so that after they have been wholly won over they can be appointed to positions of power and influence within the Church, thus curbing or if need be liquidating the "reactionary" and "imperialistic" clergy. This is the standard method of infiltrating religious organizations. Lay people, too, are subjected to the same pressures. If a number of them can be found who are willing to form a "progressive movement" designed to demonstrate that true religion is wholly in favor of the Communist system, the seeds of disunion can be planted. Some who join such groups are dupes, others are subject to intimidation for reasons ranging all the way from fear of public exposure of some weakness to dread of losing a position. In Eastern Germany there are also quite a number of truly religious persons who feel that the Church should disassociate itself from all worldly affairs, and avoid either support of or opposition to the civil govern-ment. For all such governments are, in their view, purely mundane and therefore evil—or at least necessary evils. The "neutralists," as they are familiarly called, are above all anxious to avoid any commitment which would align the Church with military effort and therefore with potential war. Such persons are not pro-Russian, but they are likely to be anti-Western.

Two statements by Communists prominent in the Unity Party may be cited as typical of the views prevailing in such circles. During January, 1950, a prominent Thuringian leader, speaking for internal Party consumption, stated frankly:

> We Marxists-Leninists are aware of the fact that religion is merely the opium of the people. We will always maintain this Communist principle, but the situation requires that we deal with the problem as such as diplomatically as possible. It may sound strange, but it is true that we must protect religion even while we are keeping a close watch on the clergy. Should any one among them become dangerous to us, he must be removed. Every district chairman must report priests to us who seem to be reactionary, so that the necessary further steps can be taken by the Land Board.

During June, 1949, the same policy had been formulated more bluntly at a meeting of officials responsible for the security of the East German State:

> Since the Church in the Greater German Republic [the official Commu-nist label for the government of the Russian Zone] is beginning to allow itself to be exploited as a trumpet by the Western Imperialists, we must see to it that these comedians of Heaven lose all interest in such activities. Enough room is still available in our camps for additional labor companies

composed of these black brethren. Physical work will persuade them once and for all to quit inciting against us the people who are still gullible enough to listen to them.

To date, however, neither the Lutheran Church, to which the great majority of Germans in the Russian Zone of Occupation belong, nor the Catholic Church has felt the full impact of the threats implied in such utterances. It may be added that, although the whole of Eastern Germany north of Silesia has long been strongly Protestant, displaced persons from the territories taken over by Poland have for the first time raised the number of Catholics in Thuringia, Anhalt, and Mecklenburg to more than 10 per cent. The initial step taken by the Communist-dominated government was to establish an Office for Religious Affairs. This is a part of standard Russian procedure, but in East Germany the agency, strikingly like the bureaus created by the Nazis for the regulation of religious affairs, ostensibly had for its primary purpose the consideration of complaints voiced by responsible ecclesiastical leaders. Some such protests were formulated in a letter addressed, on April 23, 1950, by Bishop Otto Dibelius to the Lutheran clergy and faithful. He listed as the principal objects of concern: the teaching of a materialistic philosophy of life as a substitute for religion in the schools and youth organizations; the pressure methods used to weaken the consciences of Church members; and the refusal of legal counsel to persons brought to trial on charges of opposition to the government. It soon became obvious, however, that the real task assigned to the Office for Religious Affairs was to recruit clergymen willing to serve the Communist State and to support any propagandistic efforts which it considered particularly worth while. The recruits were approvingly labeled "national," "patriotic," or "democratic," in accordance with the estimated local popularity of any such adjective. Those who remained aloof or critical were of course called "reactionary" or "imperialist." Wherever and whenever the number of recruits became sizable, the fortunes of the "reactionaries" declined. These were attacked in the official press, and their views were grossly misrepresented. Eventually some of them were brought to trial on charges of having succumbed to the lures of Wall Street, and upon occasion sentenced for espionage activities.

Still another phenomenon is worthy of note. Normally the Communists will treat with special consideration the representatives of a religious minority, particularly one which has suffered at the hands of the majority group. The purpose is to elicit a statement that all is well with the minority, which can be used propagandistically as evidence that only the larger "reactionary" Church is indulging in unwarranted criticism and opposition. Fortunately relations between Lutherans and Catholics in eastern Germany had improved very remarkably during the Nazi period, as a result of hardship and persecution both groups suffered. The younger clergy in particular had shared moving and harrowing experiences. Accordingly the Catholic minority was proof against party blandishments.

Oddly enough, therefore, the full weight of Communist opposition fell on Jehovah's Witnesses, a sect which has long had a following in Eastern Europe and so was well known in some sections of the expellee population. The Witnesses had also been a target for Nazi hostility, and many hundreds of them perished in Dachau and other concentration camps. During 1950, the Communists banned the sect in eastern Germany, on the ground that it was a branch of the American "espionage system," even though specially favorable treatment had been accorded to it in Poland. It is believed that by the close of the year nearly eight hundred Witnesses were serving terms in prisons and labor camps, and that life sentences had been imposed on thirteen of its principal advocates.

It has been surmised that all this happened because some prominent German Communists profess to be masters of "astrological science," and indeed several had been initiated into the recondite subject by no less a master than Rudolf Hess. Jehovah's Witnesses believe that the end of the world is rapidly approaching, on the basis of their deductions from Holy Writ, and therefore indulge in prophecies concerning the impending demise of our world, due to human sin and frailty. Communism believes in prophecy, too, but holds that the sole reliable form of soothsaying is that outlined by Marxist philosophy as a corollary of "natural science." This "science" enabled Stalin to predict the future of human society with complete accuracy. Communist literature is therefore rich in attacks on "bourgeois" and "mystical" soothsayers, and in equally savory eulogies of Stalin as a social-scientific fortune teller. But Jehovah's Witnesses, confident that the Word of God had been vouchsafed to them, are incorrigible. No "patriots" or "democrats" have been reported from their ranks.

Thus far the major denominations have fared less badly; but heavy blows have been struck at their influence. Many of them have fallen in the field of education. All private schools have been closed; only the unified educational system survives, and religious instruction is no longer a part of the normal academic curriculum. Recently most of the kindergartens have been placed under the control of the state. In order to understand how revolutionary these various actions are, one must call to mind certain interesting facts about German social history. Traditionally German schools provided for religious instruction, regardless of whether they were organized in accordance with the denominational affiliations of the pupils or were attended jointly by Catholic, Protestant, and other children. Even Socialist and Communist parents, who themselves seldom if ever entered a church, often insisted that their children receive religious instruction, either because they deemed it ethically beneficial or because they wanted their youngsters to profit by whatever modicum of prestige might later result from Church membership. In Germany prior to 1933, it was hardly possible to persuade even Communist parents to leave their young children in nurseries not supervised by Catholic or Protestant religious. I myself have seen workingmen in the "red" districts of Berlin greet the nuns to whom they entrusted their little ones with a clenched fist and a hearty smile. Moreover, eastern Germany had a number of excellent private schools which were conducted under Protestant auspices; and one or another of them was held in as high esteem as Eton or Andover. I think that it is not an exaggeration to say that Count Schwerin von Krosigk remained in Hitler's Cabinet, to which the Conservatives named him in 1933, solely because membership in it enabled him to save the school of which he was a director.

Today education is exclusively the business of the state, and the materialistic philosophy is taught—even as the tenets of Nazism were a few years ago—in all courses bearing on contemporary life. Marxist indoctrination is insisted upon at all levels, from the elementary school to the university. There is a great wealth of evidence on the subject, all indicating that (as one would expect) efforts to counteract it are out of the question. Yet it does not follow that the results are by any means what the Communist leaders desire. There is, to be sure, a complex and sometimes fantastically lavish plan for winning over youth. It involves on the one hand setting up at regular intervals grandiose youth rallies, such as the one staged annually in Berlin during the Pentecostal season, and on the other appointing very young people to important offices—so that boys of eighteen have served as mayors of cities. Literature of all kinds is made available in the quantity desired. A German can buy for the equivalent of about one dollar two fat volumes of the works of Lenin bound in full morocco. All this does unquestionably generate a great deal of intellectual and emotional fog, but no one of my acquaintance who knows eastern Germany thinks that the Communists have as yet succeeded in winning over German youth. If one bears in mind how many Communists have long lived there the reports are all the more astonishing.

Just as 1953 was drawing to a close Marianne and Egon Erwin Mueller, in behalf of the students of the Free University of Berlin and of West German student organizations generally, published an absorbing if harrowing analysis of the academic situation in the Russian Zone, on the basis of reports supplied by all the major universities and technical institutes in East Germany. This indicated how thoroughly the subordination of instruction to political purpose has been fostered. The right to determine the methods and the content of instruction has been taken from the professorate; the election of students to office in student councils and similar organizations is under rigid Party control; the admission of students is now almost everywhere determined by examinations given in political orthodoxy; and the academic institutions themselves have taken on the character of strictly regulated barracks, in which even recreational activities are decreed. The book (". . . *stürmt die Festung Wissenschaft*") reveals also how courageous and tenacious the opposition has been. A roster of hundreds of names of persons arrested, tried, and often imprisoned for activities looked upon with disfavor by the regime will give even the casual reader some insight into how costly and bitter the struggle was.

It may be observed at this point that a vital part of the Communist propaganda effort in this region is currying favor with former Nazis. Much of the effort is of long standing; but it was the Soviet note of March 10, 1952, to the Western Powers on German unification, that gave official confirmation of its existence. The note proposed that Germany be evacuated by all the Powers within a year, that the State then created be permitted to create a national army of its own, and that all former German soldiers and all erstwhile members of the Nazi Party receive full rights and privileges. The pertinent section of this document reads:

> All former members of the German Army, including officers and generals, except those who are serving sentences imposed by the courts for the commission of crimes, shall be accorded civil and political rights on a par with all other German citizens so that they may participate in the building of a peace-loving, democratic Germany.

Apparently the practice of welcoming them into the police forces and other branches of the East German civil service is already well established.

At any rate, the lot of the Christian clergy is a difficult one, exacting exemplary heroism. Intellectually they are isolated, because more and more of East Germany's well trained professional men have sought refuge in the West. They are under constant pressure to sponsor causes in which their Communist masters are particularly interested—the Stockholm peace petition, the abolition of the atom bomb, the return to the United States of every American soldier. On the other hand, they and the Christian Church they serve are continuously and vigorously attacked for indulging in "political activities," which include criticism of the wholly secularist educational system and of the materialistic philosophy. Their financial resources have been curtailed, though not so drastically as elsewhere. They may receive financial gifts from the West, even if the rate of exchange offered by the banks is so catastrophically bad that the money is virtually wasted. After 1949 clergymen were dropped from the category of intellectuals, and so could not claim the somewhat ameliorated rations made available to this group. Moreover, the number of pastors and curates is far smaller than that needed; and many now stationed in the Russian Zone have been overworked to the point of exhaustion. Hundreds of thousands of expellees have come from regions which were once German, and it is only too obvious that many believers of both confessions are not ministered unto. Inevitably there have also been some unavoidable transfers of specially endangered clerics to the West; but such shifts are fewer than might have been anticipated. In summary, one may end with an estimate made during the year 1950 that some nine hundred Lutheran parishes were without pastors, and that there was dire need of at least two hundred fifty Catholic priests.

Theoretically there is no dearth of theological faculties serving the Protestant churches, because formal action to close them in the six major universities of the Zone has not been taken. However, the requirement of political indoctrination is now rigidly enforced, so that it is out of the question to expect the training of a well instructed or devoted clergy in such institutions. The aim has been therefore to educate young men and women in the West and then somehow to arrange for their admission into the Russian Zone. This has grown steadily more difficult, not merely because of opposition from the Communist Government but also because of the candidates' need for unusual heroism and ability to adapt themselves to a course of training which alone will equip them for their almost superhuman tasks. Most of these young people come from escapee backgrounds, and are therefore in a sense preparing to go back to their places of origin. One cannot talk with them without feeling almost overawed in their presence. Yet they are usually quite simple and matter-of-fact. If there was a cloud of glory somewhere about them, they concealed it admirably. The Lutheran Church is permitting trained deacons to act temporarily as pastors, and has permitted laymen to preach while exercising their normal callings. One may say without hesitation that many of these lay people are devoted and exemplary. Both Lutherans and Catholics have also found it necessary to recruit catechists in order to provide religious instruction for children after school hours. The training given is hard and modern in every sense of the term.

Catholic and Protestant welfare agencies have not been suppressed, though there exists an official Government welfare agency. The Inner Mission and the Evangelisches Hilfswerk are Protestant; Caritas is Catholic. Through these are channeled most of the donations received from the West. This freedom is in marked contrast with the situation in Czechoslovakia and Hungary, not to mention Albania and the Balkan countries. Hospitals, homes for orphaned or sick children, and refuges for the aged and the crippled are still conducted under religious auspices, though there has been some curtailment of the training afforded to nurses and social workers at such institutions. No doubt this relative freedom has been strengthened by the poverty and dissatisfaction of the German worker in the Zone, who must contend not only with deteriorating standards of living but also with the abolition of all the freedoms implicit in collective bargaining, which his trade unions had won for him over a period of generations.

It has also proved possible to conserve some religious youth organizations, even if these may now be only local in character. Government-sponsored activities alone are sanctioned on a Zone-wide basis. Societies formed to rally university students still carry on their work. In so far as the press is concerned, Protestants are considerably better off than Catholics. There are a Lutheran press service, a newspaper (*Die Kirche*), and a number of local weeklies published in small editions. Catholics, however, have not been able to secure permission to set up a publishing house or to import printed matter from the West. Such reading materials as they distribute are more or less covertly smuggled into the Zone. Some cultural activities are likewise carried on under religious auspices, but these are overshadowed by the program of the government-sponsored Kulturbund, which at times receives lavish support.

Very noteworthy is the fact that the Lutheran Church has managed to arrange for periodic synodal conferences, attended by leaders from every part of the Eastern Zone. That which convened in East Berlin during April, 1950, was inspiring and impressive, but was overshadowed by the Kirchentag in the same place a year later. This was undoubtedly one of the most significant events in recent German spiritual history. More than a hundred thousand persons attended; and the wise, frank, and deeply Christian discussion profoundly moved persons from the West who were fortunate enough to participate. In all probability, no event of the postwar era has been more indicative of what religious faith can mean to sorely tried men and women. Some observers believe that it is in Eastern Germany, under constant threat of persecution, that the Christian Church has grown genuinely strong. It is unquestionably true that contact with the elite fashioned there on the anvil of ordeal is a humbling and strangely strengthening experience that makes one wonder whether the mantle of Western prosperity hides comparable religious treasure.

Nevertheless it is realistic to conclude that organized religion has lost some ground in the Eastern Zone even though the core may be sounder. The fact that so much influence was recovered, despite prewar weakness and the inroads of Nazism, is truly extraordinary; but the young had received very little sound training, and so, when the Communists insulated many of them against even conventional religious instruction, it was only natural that many should at least pay lip service to the Communist cause. Nor have efforts to recruit "patriotic" and "democratic" clergymen been wholly unavailing. Some Catholic priests and Protestant pastors alike have professed to see no reason why an agreement could not be reached between a socially oriented Christianity and Communism. The official propaganda, stressing peace and anti-imperialism, also made at least a temporary impression; and of course it has not been too difficult for some who once were Nazis, despite their clerical garb, to persuade themselves that Stalin is only a *Führer* in a somewhat unusual disguise.

What is the greatest impediment to the open profession of religious principles in Eastern Germany? No doubt it is the Communist system of justice. Whereas one can only tentatively evaluate the practice of the courts in the satellite countries proper, the relative freedom in Eastern Germany makes it possible to observe rather closely the course of legal procedure there. Basically the system is not very different from that established by the Nazis. Once it has been laid down as a principle that "the healthy feelings of the people" have priority over codified legislation, and once it has been made self-evident that the welfare of the community takes precedence over the rights of the individual, it is easy for a judge to hand down any decision which his political superiors desire. And while the Communists pay less attention than the Nazis to "healthy feelings" their addiction to the welfare of the State is no less ardent and complete. One case may be adduced here by way of illustration. On January 5, 1950, three young men were arrested because they had painted the word *Freiheit* (freedom) on house walls. Two of them had also passed round some pamphlets of Western origin, picked up during a trip to Berlin. The lower court found all three guilty and imposed sentences of three months in jail. But when the prosecutor appealed the case to a higher court the verdicts were revised to read ten years, five years, and two years respectively.

It was argued, and the court agreed, that these young men sought to create in the minds of East Germans the impression that they were not free. "This," said the court, "is gossip which in the most serious possible manner endangers the peace of the German people." For was it not true that the laboring masses of Eastern Germany had freed themselves from the enslaving chains of the lords of finance and industry? Indeed, the court went on to declare, one of the pamphlets which the defendants had circulated urged the population to resist the Communist occupation authorities. Because the ultimate consequence of taking such hate-mongering documents at their face value could only be a new war, the principal defendant, a boy of eighteen—was clearly guilty of having attempted to incite the nation to armed conflict. Of special interest is the sentence imposed upon the third defendant, aged twenty-two. He had not wished to distribute the pamphlets but had permitted himself to be talked into doing so once only. After that he had refused. Nevertheless he was sentenced to two years in prison because in the court's opinion he, as a member of the FDJ (the Communist youth organization, Freie deutsche Jugend), should have known better.

Under such a system of justice, which considers even the mildest form of propaganda against the government to be an action "inciting to war" or "undermining the peace," it is extremely dangerous to indulge in any form of criticism. On May 9, 1951, the Minister of Justice of the Eastern Zone issued a proclamation which reads in part as follows:

> The fascist tyrants who ruled over Germany threw tens of thousands of honest anti-fascists into prisons, houses of correction, and concentration camps. It was enough to have been a member of or an official in the labor movement to make one a victim of persecution, maltreatment and loss of freedom. We refer to these victims of Fascism with the term "political prisoners."
>
> Today no one is arrested because of his opinions. Anyone who attacks our anti-fascist democratic order, or who hampers the building up of our peace industry, commits a punishable offense and is penalized because of his criminal actions. Prisoners of this character are therefore to be called not "political prisoners" but just plain criminals. It is as a consequence forbidden to refer to them as "political prisoners." If in an individual case some more accurate description is desired, one should employ a concrete term, such as for example "criminal in accordance with Article 8 of the Constitution," "criminal in accordance with Article 6," etc.

Add to all this the characters of many persons entrusted with the administration of justice, and the maintenance of national security. The Investigating Committee of Freedom-Loving Lawyers in the Soviet Zone (Untersuchungsausschuss der freiheitlichen Juristen der Sowjetzone) has published a series of short biographies, in many cases fully documented, which reveal with startling clarity what kind of person has been recruited for the bench in the Russian Zone. Thus Bernhard Bechler, a Nazi who was for some time Minister of the Interior in the State of Brandenburg and was later Chief Inspector of the People's Police, had been assigned to the Eastern Front during the war, and was captured by the Russians. Soon thereafter he joined the Moscow-sponsored National Committee for a Free Germany, and was utilized in broadcasts to Germany. His wife, also an ardent Nazi, was thereupon visited by a stranger who told her of having listened to her husband's speeches. She took this as an insult, denounced the man to the police, and refused to ask clemency for him. As a result she was interned first by the Americans and then by the Russians. Meanwhile Bechler decided to marry his secretary, and persuaded the court to declare his wife dead, even though it was well known in which camp she was being detained. She was released unexpectedly during 1948 and returned home to see her children. Bechler managed to have her arrested once more, and this time the death sentence was imposed. To his great annoyance, however, the penalty was commuted to life imprisonment. Evidently some one higher up was playing grim jokes on the Chief Inspector!

It is no wonder that under such a system of jurisprudence security and freedom should seem very frail and unpredictable. Countless thousands of refugees have come into the Western Zone through the "open door" of Berlin, and others have crossed the frontiers to the south and west, taxing all the resources of the reception agencies.

Conditions in the Russian Zone have been relatively so tolerable, despite all that has been or could be adduced to make evident the callous tyranny which prevails, that many people, churchmen as well as men of affairs, argue that everything possible must be done to dissuade the Communists from adopting more ruthless policies and thus duplicating the situation which exists in Czechoslovakia. This point of view is not restricted to the "neutralists." It is held that the Church should scrupulously refrain from taking sides in the great debate between East and West, and even avoid being drawn into the discussion of Germany's own future. The exponents of this policy would do everything, even at the constant risk of martyrdom, to preach the Gospel of Christ. Some may dismiss the reasoning as fatuous, but it seems to me that it is tenable, at least for the very few who can live in the spirit of pre-Apocalyptic Christianity even during Apocalyptic times.

Would it be possible for the great majority of both the clergy and the laity to preach and practice the Christian faith without at the same time making concessions to the Communist philosophy? Nowhere else under the Russian tyranny has it been possible to do so. If it is difficult enough in the Western world to live as a Christian without making concessions to the all-pervading secularism, what must happen when the dictator is able to curb the apologist for the Scriptures by suppressing his independence? Nevertheless, if one responds to these questions pessimistically, the practical course to be taken by the Church is far from clear. Were the impression given that the Christian conscience favored the use of force in order to end the terror of Communist rule, the enemy would pillory it for having fomented war with all its unspeakable consequences. On the other hand, supine and hopeless conformity with the decrees of the Kremlin and its henchmen could result only in the gradual desiccation of orthodoxy. Of course it is true that Christianity can always survive in the Catacombs; but as it does so it will cry out in anguish, and sometimes (as we know from history) it will be anguish that those who hearken cannot distinguish from despair.

It is at this point that the great decision as to whether only the remaining free areas of the world can be protected only by effecting a coalition between the NATO Powers and Western Germany can be seen in the right perspective. Would such an alliance automatically seal the fate of Eastern Germany and at the same time render hopeless the situation of West Berlin, so brave and imperiled an island in the sea of Communism? Anyone who has seen with his own eyes the infinitely moving antitotalitarian crowds of that drab but still pulsing city, or who knows how many of them bear on their bodies and their souls not merely the scars of Hitlerism gone mad but also the deep and bitter wounds inflicted by the Cromwellian fanaticism of the East, knows that West Berlin has become the vital symbol of all the values for which men and women have lived and died on the soil of Europe; and the loss of it cannot for an instant be contemplated because the darkness which would ensue after the putting out of that fire would be contagious. It is not easy to refute the reasoning of persons who on such grounds have opposed the entry of Western Germany into a military alliance, for they have on their side all who plead in the East that the little of liberty they still possess be not taken away from them. Nevertheless I think that it was incumbent upon us, in view of the extremely ominous threat which lies upon our time—in which mighty and insignificant events alike are pushing us all forward to ultimate dramatic decisions the results of which only Infinite Wisdom can foresee—to make the choice for weal or woe in favor of bastions that can be defended, even as in battle outposts are endangered reluctantly. I say these things with a heavy heart, not knowing whether they be right or wrong, merely hoping that they may be right.

At any rate, the drawing up of an agreement between the NATO Powers and Western Germany and its discussion in the Bonn Parliament aroused fears that Communist policy would be altered. To some extent it was. A "strip of no man's land" was created along the borders of the Zone, and in various ways freedom of movement was curtailed. At the same time efforts were redoubled to make the youth organizations effective instruments of Communist propaganda. Loyalty tests for admission to the institutions of higher learning were administered with increased rigor, and forms of military drill were introduced for both boys and girls. Target practice in particular was ordained. But it appeared that Russia still hoped that a settlement of the crucial German problem that served its own best interests could be reached, and therefore preferred diplomatic and propagandistic maneuvers to drastic suppression. Open conflict over religious matters was therefore avoided, even though the noose around the throat of the Church was tightened.

This period of waiting with bated breath was marked by three assemblies of dramatic interest and importance. The world watched anxiously to see how the Russians would react to them. The first was the Lutheran World Federation meeting in Hanover, the See of Bishop Lilje, no doubt one of the ablest theologians and churchmen of our time. Many thousands of clerics and laymen, young and old, gathered in the heavily bombed city to discuss the challenge to the Christian conscience presented by the time in which we all live. There was not much allusion to political questions, although Bishop Berggrav of Norway, once a doughty antagonist of Nazism, declared firmly that it was the Church's duty to condemn vigorously the injustices of which governments are guilty. The Soviet Zone authorities had withdrawn their offer to make interzonal passes available in number, but did finally permit eight persons to attend.

Subsequently another great Protestant conference met in Berlin. And finally, during August, the Catholic Day brought together in the same city a crowd estimated at more than 200,000 persons, half of whom came from the East. The government did not hamper the travel of this mighty throng, although an earlier offer to make excursion tickets available was canceled. Here again, political topics were avoided, even if the newly appointed and very able Bishop of Berlin, Monsignor Wilhelm Weiskamm, assured the audience that "God also lives in a land where there are said to be no more crosses"—an allusion to government orders which had removed crucifixes from classrooms. These gatherings were major topics of conversation in all parts of Germany.

More controversial was an exchange of views between Bishop Otto Dibelius and the East German government. The Bishop addressed a Pastoral Letter to the faithful after permission to travel in the eastern part of his diocese had been refused to him. This document was an eloquent plea for pastoral unity, far more outspoken than anything he had previously uttered. It urged the clergy to remain in close association with the bishops, and made some acrid comparisons between Nazi and Communist attitudes toward the Church; and it declared any pastor influenced by a political power rather than by the leadership of the Church was a disloyal shepherd of his flock. His criticism evoked a response, but one more moderate than had been foreseen. Communist spokesmen declared that there was no conflict between Church and State in the Eastern Zone, and that none was desired. They added that the Bishop had permitted himself to become a mouthpiece for Western Imperialism.

That is the story of 1953.

# III

# ON POLITICS

Reared in a strong German-American home in rural Wisconsin, Shuster imbibed a lasting empathy for his parents' homeland and its rich cultural legacy. He learned to speak German at home and mastered it at prep school where he also spanned its literature "from Goethe at one end of the spectrum to Karl May on the other."[1] Proficiency in the language earned him an intelligence assignment in occupied Germany during World War I and later led him to translate several German religious and literary works.

Shuster became a keen student of German political affairs, and several trips to Germany in the early 1930's sharpened his observations about its political developments, even if they were not always accurate. It was during this period that he first met Heinrich Bruning, the leader of the German Center Party and head of the government which collapsed in 1932, paving the way for Hitler's ascent to the chancellorship the following year. Bruning was an implacable foe of Nazism who eventually escaped to the United States. He was a frequent guest in the Shuster home and both men engaged in friendly, if sometimes spirited, conversation. Their close friendship did not mitigate political differences and Shuster never shared Bruning's fiery zeal against persons he considered to be enemies of Germany. Pope Pius XII was one of them. Bruning believed that he had pursued an anti-German policy as apos-

[1] George N. Shuster, "An Autobiography," in *Leaders in American Education: The Seventieth Yearbook of the National Society for the Study of Education* (Chicago: University of Chicago Press, 1971), p. 280.

tolic nuncio to Berlin and continued it as pope. Shuster notes that any "attempt to canonize [Pius XII] will encounter a formidable obstacle in Bruning's recollections; and although some hypothetical Papal Commission may ignore these as prejudiced, it is not likely that the objective historian can do so."[2]

Shuster's several trips to Germany and his later efforts in World War II resulted in a series of books dealing with German questions. In *The Germans: An Inquiry and an Estimate* (1932), Shuster investigated German life and politics (especially since World War I) and sketched a forecast for the years ahead.[3] His earliest estimate about Hitler proved to be more optimistic than realistic. He was convinced that Hitler would never achieve power in Germany and said so forthrightly. Yet it is easy to snipe at a book written in the midst of an enormously complex period and fault it for inaccuracies of perception which are in reality only a human lack of clairvoyance.

On the other hand, the book's astute observations make it a valuable source in the study of American reaction to the rise of Hitlerism. Shuster assumed that the Germans were characteristically concerned about the plight of less fortunate people and seems to attribute to them the gift of instinctive altruism. If there was anti-semitism at times, he notes that it was directed against Jewish monopolists or raucous politicians. Surely he felt in 1932 that the German people were incapable of standing by and watching six million people deliberately exterminated in concentration camps throughout Europe. Rather than attribute notable characteristics to people as a national group, it seems wiser to adhere to the old German dictum that "the German people are just like people everywhere" with the same noble and ignoble tendencies that bless or afflict humanity as a whole.

From the outset Shuster regarded Hitler as a menace at best. He believed that Hitler was employing American political models in his quest for power. "Personally, I have a feeling that Germany's first campaigner, in the American sense of the word, is Herr Hitler. This gentleman's ideas are no more commendable for wisdom and practicableness than are the notions of the average United States Senator. But he knows how to get out the vote, how to sway an audience, and how to swim with inconstant public opinion. What will

[2] George N. Shuster, "Dr. Brüning's Sojourn in the United States (1935-1945)," in Ferdinand A. Hermens and Theodor Schieder (eds.), *Staat, Wirtschaft und Politik in der Weimarer Republik* (Berlin: Duncker and Humblot, 1967), p. 458.

[3] George N. Shuster, *The Germans: An Inquiry and an Estimate* (New York: Dial Press, 1932.)

Germany be like once it has produced a dozen Hitlers?"[4] In perspective, it is horrible enough to contemplate one Hitler—never mind conjuring up a dozen!

And yet Shuster's other observations smack of uncanny insight and depth. He judged the rebirth of modern German culture and the aesthetic value of German artistic and architectural experiments during the 1920's; he understood the endurance of the old-fashioned Bavarian quality of *gemutlichkeit*; he rightly saw the direction of the German universities; he recognized the tenuous footing of the Weimar Republic; and he acknowledged that anti-semitism was rampant in Germany. His listing of the German ills of this time is remarkably similar to the causes historians would later employ to account for the speedy Nazi conquest of Germany: the disastrous consequences of the Versailles Treaty; the coming of the great depression; and the ceding of lands with German populations to Poland and Czechoslovakia. Shuster recognized the possibility of a Nazi dominion in Germany, even prophetically entitling one chapter "The Third Kingdom"—*Reich* being translated loosely as "Kingdom." The tragedy is that he discounted such an eventuality, believing that the German people would never sustain Hitler's drive for control.

Events in 1933 witnessed the coming to pass of the improbable and the necessity for Shuster to write a sequel to *The Germans*. In the preface of *Strong Man Rules* (1934), Shuster opens with an admission: "This book ought to begin, no doubt, with an apology. . . . Today it is evident that in several respects I was quite mistaken. Will the present work share that fate? Perhaps it does not greatly matter. . . . We of the present register impressions with the understanding that a world in transition may soon render obsolete what we write. . . ."[5] The remainder of the volume re-examines the conditions which had rendered the improbable a reality and once again plots some sort of vision for the future. He reiterates the vogue of American-style politics in Germany and examines the rhetoric of Nazi oratory and programs. He felt that the Nazi confiscation of Jewish business and property was the policy of only "a clique of blockheads no one even dares mention in public."[6] Yet he was not blind to the rising plight of the German Jews and later in the book details the bloody pogroms taking place throughout the country. Shuster did place some responsibility on Jewish shoulders, though he was not prepared for the horrible fate that awaited these unfortunate people. The book's tone

---

[4] *Ibid.*, p. 71.

[5] George N. Shuster, *Strong Man Rules: An Interpretation of Germany Today* (New York: D. Appleton Century Company, 1934), p. v.

[6] *Ibid.*, p. 19.

is melancholic and it includes a great sense of foreboding for the future. After reading *Strong Man Rules* (and *The Germans*), one has the feeling that perhaps Shuster had intuited, at least in part, the tragic turn of future events.

In a third book, *Germany: A Short History* (1944), written with Arnold Bergstraesser when Allied victory was just a matter of time, Shuster assesses the causes of the war and believes that "the question of the responsibility of the German people for the outbreak of hostilities is likely to be debated for years. Certainly that people cannot be divorced from its government."[7] The shattering effects of Hitlerism were all about him as he viewed Germany on the eve of defeat. Although, in the more reflective *The Ground I Walked On,* Shuster cites the large number of decent Germans who understood Hitler's sinister purposes and resisted them even to death, the Nazi debacle burned deep within his heart. And he pleads with mankind never to forget its evil shadow that put "to death thousands of years of the hopes of mankind."[8]

If Shuster recorded his antagonism to the rise of Nazism in Germany, he was not oblivious to other forms of totalitarianism rampant throughout Europe in the 1930's. He vigorously attacked Communism and Fascism through his columns in *Commonweal* and became involved in an intra-Catholic dispute over his anti-Franco position in the Spanish Civil War. Because the Loyalists were Communist-dominated and played havoc with the Church in Spain, American Catholics generally supported the anti-Communist but equally totalitarian Franco insurgents. Yet Shuster characterized Franco as a Fascist who was no better than Hitler or Mussolini and certainly no "archangel rising to annihilate Satan." Since the Catholic Church was weak in Spain, Shuster thought it would fare no better with Franco than under a red republic. It was not that he preferred Communism to Fascism, but that he hated both with equal intensity. He warned that "every effort to uphold Christian ethics by upholding an anti-Christian social order is bound to fail." Furthermore, not all Loyalists were Communists, and Shuster maintained that the American Catholic pro-Franco position failed to account for Fascist and Nazi influence in its camp. Totalitarian influence in the Spanish struggle was clear in his mind as he set down these thoughts:

> European Catholic journalists have reflected earnestly on the reasons why Mussolini was induced to strike the bargain with Franco which started the Insurgent uprising. What kind of pact was it, and what were the ultimate

[7] George N. Shuster and Arnold Bergstraesser, *Germany: A Short History* (New York: W. W. Norton and Company, 1944), pp. 214-215.

[8] *The Ground I Walked On,* p. 230.

objectives the bargainers had in mind? We do not know. But little by little Germany was drawn into the fray; and fantastic efforts were made to get people used to believing that the Hitler-Mussolini combination was saving Europe from Bolshevism. Perhaps there are people who do not find all this a hoax. But they might at least try to explain why it is that a dictator who places Herr Rosenberg in the saddle in order to destroy the Catholic Church in Germany feels it is his duty to sacrifice men and money in order to save that Church in Spain.[9]

Shuster suffered a nightmarish week following the publication of these sentiments Threats were made on his life. The New York Archdiocesan Chancery callously telephoned his parish priest in Connecticut to inquire whether the *Commonweal* editor fulfilled his Sunday obligation to hear Mass. Hate mail criticized his position and questioned his motives. Certainly too harshly, though understandably at the time, Shuster concluded "that for Catholic New York the world outside the United States was either Communist or Fascist and that therefore they had opted for Fascism."[10]

Many Catholic periodicals supported Franco and denounced Shuster in sharp terms. The ultraconservative *Brooklyn Tablet* called Franco the George Washington of Spain and compared his soldiers to the American patriots of 1776. Since the Spanish Loyalists were truculently anti-Catholic, the Reverend John La Farge, S.J., of *America* reluctantly concluded that Shuster was betraying the Church's heritage in that country. But it was America's editor, the Reverend Francis X. Talbot, S.J., who responded most vociferously to Shuster's position. Both men knew each other personally and respected each other's convictions. Talbot recognized Shuster's intellectual integrity, and Shuster admired Talbot as a poet but never thought that he possessed any special "endowment to discuss political affairs." Men like Shuster, declared Talbot, have successfully "split the corporate influence of Catholicism" and have indeed made a "poor impression" on the Catholic world. Talbot commended Shuster's stand against Nazism and Fascism but believed that "his preoccupation with them is clouding his vision of that other more dangerous form of the totalitarian state, Moscowism. But why does he assume, and rabidly, that General Franco is a Fascist and committed to Fascism? Franco never was a Fascist, and I judge that he never will be." Shuster responded with the basic conviction that very little separated Communism from Fascism

[9] George N. Shuster, "The Spanish Civil War and American Catholics." Speech delivered at a Conference on the Spanish Civil War, Massachusetts Institute of Technology, May 21, 1969, pp. 6-7.

[10] *Ibid.*, p. 7.

and Nazism. Both disregarded basic moral principles and both engendered bitter social antagonisms. "War for war's sake gradually becomes the only reliable recipe. In short, there remains of Christian ethics less than enough to press between the pages of a book."[11]

Shuster remained adamant in his anti-Franco attitude, but he realized that he could no longer remain with *Commonweal.* His position had in large part accounted for the periodical's loss of one quarter of its subscriptions. His righteousness rebelled against such a decision, but his mind knew there was no other choice. And so his resignation was a bitter pill to swallow. "My wife and I had very little of this world's goods. How could we have had on the salary I had earned? But at least I had mustered enough courage to express my convictions."[12]

There was a sequel to the Franco controversy. Shuster's religious faith was now suspect by the more conservative clerical and lay members of his church. He became one of the heroes of the *"Commonweal* Catholics," that is, Catholic liberals who refused to toe the ecclesiastical party line in controversial matters. This designation and Shuster's defense of academic freedom at Hunter lent credence to the suspicion in McCarthyite quarters in the 1950's that he was soft on Communism. Of course he was not. He understood the evils committed by both sides in the Spanish Civil War and said so in no uncertain terms. His basic contention was that every form of totalitarianism deserved condemnation, and it did the Church no good to side with the one against the other since eventually she would suffer under each of them. Evil was evil and the Church could not be morally associated with it—not if she wished to remain a beacon of light in a world of darkness.

A man who hates totalitarianism so intensely because he loves peace even more, Shuster realized that the European conflagration occurred in large measure because of the failure of the League of Nations after World War I. When a new international body, the United Nations, was formed in 1945, Shuster took an active interest in its success as an important means for preserving world peace and preventing future dictatorships. While the United Nations was still in its formative stage, steps were taken to establish an international agency that would be concerned with educational reform and cultural exchange. Two meetings were held, in London in 1945 and in Paris in 1946, out of which the United Nations Educational, Scientific and Cultural

[11] *Ibid.,* pp. 8-9.

[12] *Ibid.,* p. 9.

Organization was born into a world already divided between East and West. Shuster participated in both conferences and became closely associated with the affairs of UNESCO. Unfortunately, UNESCO became the target of considerable criticism in the United States, especially from conservatives and from the McCarthyites.

Shuster received an opportunity to express his views on international cooperation when he delivered the annual Gabriel Richard Lecture at Loyola University in New Orleans in 1952. Out of this address came the small but spirited volume, *Cultural Cooperation and the Peace* (1953), which outlined the case for UNESCO.[13] As his text, Shuster quoted Pope Pius XII, who urged unity in the Church which respected the individual and social customs of the peoples of the world. In other words, unity without uniformity, an idea which did not really infuse the mind of the Church until the Second Vatican Council. Shuster felt from the start that UNESCO was concerned with such ends and argued that, despite cultural differences, humanity must recognize its essential brotherhood if peace were ever to be achieved in a divided world. He supported the UNESCO Constitution's assertion that "peace must ... be founded, if it is not to fail, upon the intellectual and moral solidarity of mankind."[14] He was optimistic as he viewed notable humanitarian advances, but he also warned that the greatest weakness of UNESCO was a recurring and "viciously competitive" nationalism. Peace would be realized, maintained Shuster, only when men recognized a common brotherhood of humanity.

Ten years later Shuster published a progress report on UNESCO. Primarily an apologia rather than a theoretical analysis or a detailed historical study, *UNESCO: Assessment and Promise* (1963) compares the ideals of the organization with its accomplishments and measures its values against criticisms levelled against it.[15] He divides the UNESCO program into five main parts: (1) services to education, science, and culture; (2) indirect educational action; (3) offices of liaison; (4) direct educational action; and (5) operational activities within the United Nations. He analyzes the operations of the organization and concedes that its goals for the future often seem visionary. Much is easier said than done in UNESCO—especially in promoting universal literacy. Yet

[13] George N. Shuster, *Cultural Cooperation and the Peace* (Milwaukee: Bruce Publishing Company, 1953.)

[14] *Ibid.*, p. 28.

[15] George N. Shuster, *UNESCO: Assessment and Promise* (New York: Harper and Row, 1963.)

high aspirations are important in view of ultimate accomplishments. In the long run, Shuster conceives UNESCO as a forum in which all nations, young and old, rich and poor, can discuss problems and solutions in an environment that will enhance their own good and at the same time improve the condition of mankind. Certainly this is no easy task, but Shuster has never offered simplistic solutions for difficult questions. In the final paragraph of *Cultural Cooperation and the Peace,* Shuster emphasizes his belief for the need of cooperation and good will before the world can achieve the peace that so many desire but which is still a dream:

> I am profoundly convinced that if scientist and saint could somehow join hands for the final conquest of the human spirit, men would in that hour be emancipated from the petty narrowness and the divisive passion which have so often flung them at each other's throats, making the green earth the scene of their grim, revolting, and moral combat. Will they be able to do so? I shall not take upon myself the burden of attempting to answer that fateful question. All of us remember the words which were spoken by our Lord Jesus as he gazed upon the fair city of Jerusalem. But we likewise know that he addressed speech of momentous optimism to those who were of good will.[16]

Shuster remains confident that UNESCO is the pre-eminent organization in this quest for peace within a spirit of good will.

[16] *Cultural Cooperation and the Peace,* p. 59.

# Dr. Brüning's Sojourn in the United States (1935 - 1945)

The pages which follow are not designed to provide an exhaustive study of the years in the career of Heinrich Brüning which extend from the *Machtergreifung* to the defeat of Germany in 1945. These are, rather, a digest of my own recollections of him during that period. These have, however, been supplemented with what some friends at Harvard University were kind enough to provide about his activities there. A biographer would have to probe more deeply and use materials to which I do not have access. Perhaps when one does set to work he may find this memoir somewhat useful.

The most important event of the period was Brüning's coming to the United States after his successful escape from Germany just prior to the assassinations of June, 1934. It is already now difficult to reconstruct the attitude of the people of the United States toward him and his country at that time. The years 1930-32 saw a high-water mark of understanding and indeed of affection for the Weimar Republic. Itself stricken grievously by the impact of the great economic depression, the United States nevertheless hoped sincerely that German statesmen would master the difficulties which rose menacingly with each new day. There was a widespread expectation that reparations would cease to be a factor of any real importance, that some further revision of the Treaty of Versailles could be effected, and that an agreement concerning armaments might be reached.

From George N. Shuster, "Dr. Brüning's Sojourn in the United States (1935-1945)," in Ferdinand A. Hermens and Theodor Schieder, eds., *Staat, Wirtschaft und Politik in der Weimarer Republik* (Berlin: Duncker & Humblot, 1967), pp. 449-466. Reprinted by permission of the publisher.

The major reasons why this favorable situation existed—and it must be remembered that only twelve years had passed since the close of the First World War, during which a passionate hatred for all things German had been stirred up—were unquestionably three. First, was the measure of economic cooperation which had been effected. Vast private and public loans had been made; German efficiency was held in high regard; and German commerce had earned a merited respect for integrity and imaginativeness. Indeed, as later events were to demonstrate, the basic economy was sound, so that it might be assumed that when banking and credit problems had been solved, Germany could look forward to being one of the greatest economies of the world. The second reason was cultural. The German language, German literature, German music, and to a lesser extent German art were once more greatly esteemed; and seen in retrospect, tragically enough all these were affectionately treasured by a cultivated Jewish minority which considered them part of its own cultural heritage. The third reason was Dr. Brüning himself. He was rightly held to be a strong and intelligent man. But what the American people believed above all was that he possessed the qualities of honor and moral repute.

Events which followed his dismissal from office were naturally observed with dismay. But the agreements he had so skilfully laid the ground work for came to maturity under the Chancellorship of Franz von Papen; and it was not until during that tarnished aristocrat's second tour of duty that Adolf Hitler came to exercise what at first seemed to be limited authority over the German people. British public opinion as voiced by such eloquent spokesmen as David Lloyd George was so vocal in its belief that the Führer should be considered a reputable spokesman for legitimate grievances that on the other side of the Atlantic hesitant optimism was likewise in vogue. The British Government, dedicated to what in ordinary circumstances would have been a commendable desire to avoid a war for which it was quite unprepared, believed that making concessions to the Nazis might perhaps mitigate rabid nationalist sentiment or, if the worst came, deflect the conflict to the East. Therefore opinion in the United States, even among some Jewish minorities outside New York, was not unalterably opposed to the new regime in Germany. Few really believed that the German people, long held in such great respect, should be identified with Storm Troopers.

Nothing in this rather surprising sequence of events lessened the profound esteem in which Brüning was held. I had met him during a study tour (1930), the chief object of which was to look at the report on what were then the eastern boundaries of Germany. When I returned during the summer of 1933 he was already a hunted man. As we conversed in the room he occupied in a Berlin Catholic hospital, secret police were always stationed outside. I have never known whether in the rendezvous we arranged at a variety of places for members of the now disbanded Center Party, we were carefully watched or not. But at long last a remarkable German-American, Gustav Oberländer, assured Brüning that if he wished to come to the United States the cost of the journey would be underwritten. Oberländer, a successful manufacturer, who had migrated to the United States from Germany, had made notable contributions to cultural causes in Germany. He also accepted during the fall of 1933 an invitation to the "Berghof" and bluntly told Hitler that his anti-Semitic campaign was deplorable and that any military adventures he might undertake were doomed to failure. Undoubtedly he was the most unpopular visitor of the season. Other Americans, notably professors, had applauded the Führer.

At any rate, having by some sort of miracle escaped from Germany, and having spent some time with friends in Great Britain, Brüning arrived in this country as "Henry Anderson." The family name was that of dear friends he had made in London, and the reason for the disguise was the obvious fact that if he had appeared in the United States as a spokesman for German opposition to Nazism, the oppressor's hand might have fallen heavily on still more victims. So far had the might and prestige of the *Reichswehr* and of its then commander-in-chief, President von Hindenburg, fallen. When Brüning arrived in the harbor of New York, Mayor LaGuardia sent a police boat to welcome the guest, who was thereupon escorted to his temporary destination, the Hague Club, a private club to which he was introduced by a friend, H. George Murhane. Then he went to live for some months at Immaculate Conception Seminary, situated in almost monastic seclusion at Huntington, Long Island.

The Bishop of Brooklyn, under whose jurisdiction the Seminary stood, was a man of marked liberality of views and notable generosity. During ten years refugee priests and laymen could be sheltered in his diocese, even though the gates of the neighboring Archdiocese of New York were locked against them. At any rate here Brüning was lodged in a simple though comfortable room, taking his meals with the Rector, the Rev. Patrick Barry, an able and genial church historian who had studied in Munich. It was not an isolated life he led, but rather a gregarious one. He went to New York and to the homes of friends outside it. At the Seminary, he also lectured to the students with great frankness and wisdom. The transcript of one of his addresses has been preserved, and this reveals the kind of historical reflection to which he was then turning more and more. It has many interesting passages, among them this:

In Germany, unlike England, and the other Anglo-Saxon countries, liberalism stood for absolute freedom for the State alone, for the economic life of the nation. Even as early as 1840 the idea of the Totalitarian State was conceived, the radical effects of which may now be observed. Liberalism was in some ways a concealed attempt to get back to older times when the phrase *cujus regio, ejus religio* was the law. Whoever ruled the country determined the religion which the people were obliged to follow.

Perhaps not all the seminarians, or their professors for that matter, understood everything he said, but they could form an impression of the man and his career, and gain some insight in the world forces which had brought him to their midst. It is quite remarkable that no one in the Seminary or indeed in the circles outside which Brüning then visited revealed his identity. All scrupulously kept the secret. Once in New York we dined at the Player's Club, a very friendly and congenial place. A drama critic stopped at our table and I introduced my guest as Mr. Henry Anderson. "Has anyone ever told you," the critic asked, "how much you look like Heinrich Brüning;" "Yes," replied Mr. Anderson, "people have sometimes pointed that out."

At the Seminary, where I was then giving two lectures weekly in English Literature, we became friends and indeed collaborators. Week after week I listened to his comments on the Center Party, of which I then planned to write a history insofar as the years after 1918 were concerned. All that actually came of this project is my section of Germany: *A Short History*, written in collaboration with Arnold Bergstraesser. But I accumulated voluminous notes based on conversations with him. Among them is an account of the making of his career as he himself saw it; and since nothing comparable is as yet available elsewhere, I shall now summarize this. Returning from the Front, where he had served as captain of a machine-gun company, Brüning first explored, in conversations with a revered professor of the University of Bonn, Heinrich Dietzel, the possibility of appointment as a *Privatdozent*. But by reason of the French occupation of the Rhineland, he decided instead to embark on a political career. He heard Adam Stegerwald, with whom he was later to collaborate intimately, speak in Muenster and decided to throw in his lot with the Center Party. Stegerwald headed the Christian Trade Unions, which were interconfessional; and it was Hermann Platz who pleaded with Brüning to focus his attention on that organization, then in some danger of losing its ideological identity. But nothing came of this temporarily because the available post, that of acting as secretary to Johannes Guisberts at the Versailles Peace Conference, was given instead to the younger Fritz Thyssen. Brüning then went to Berlin and joined forces with the famed Catholic social reformer, Dr. Carl Sonnenschein. Sonnenschein's office was described by Brüning as a "huge room lined with filing cases into which information considered pertinent was dumped pell-mell." Sonnenschein was an indefatigable debater, always ready for an argument but courteous to his opponents. In this atmosphere Brüning constituted, in his own words, "a kind of conservative minority." He toured the country, reading speeches he had previously written, having an interesting time.

He was already then deeply concerned with the fact that if the Center Party was to grow it would have to attract non-Catholic voters. The loss of Alsace, the Saar and part of Eastern Silesia had reduced the percentage of the Catholic population in Germany from one third to one fourth. Nor could the Party hope to attract more than 65 to 75% of the Catholic voters. Therefore Brüning was bent on reviving the tradition of Windhorst and seeking to make of the Center a Christian rather than a Catholic Party. One modest effort in this direction was made under the aegis of Sonnenschein. The *Akademischer Arbeiterverband,* an organization for academicians, notably veterans, regardless of their political affiliations was one of Brüning's creations. During August, 1919, Brüning joined forces with Stegerwald, and also became a Referent in the Ministry of Welfare. Soon he was knee-deep in the affairs of the *Christliche Gewerkschaften,* at Stegerwald's request. The first post-War conference of the organization was convened in Essen during September, 1920, and Stegerwald delivered a since famous "enlarging of scope" address, written by Brüning, which may be considered the first plea for a Christian Democratic Party. The idea attracted attention in Protestant circles, but there was strong opposition within the Center Party itself, voiced primarily by Matthias Erzberger.

Then, in 1921, Brüning rather reluctantly agreed to serve as adviser to the *Deutscher Gewerkschaftsbund* (German Federation of Trade Unions), combining this with efforts to strengthen German groups in the plebiscites ordered by the Allies in several sectors of the Eastern boundaries, in accordance with President Wilson's policy of self-determination. Since virtually all political parties were represented in the Federation, it was possible to continue to seek ways to increase the influence of the Center Party. But it was through the foundation of the Union daily, *Der Deutsche,* for which he subsequently wrote a great deal, that the formation of Brüning's political life was accomplished. The point of view to which he gave expression in those years (as well as in conversations and conferences during the period of his stay in the United States) was that of the "ideal of a Christian democracy." That this ideal was cultural and ethical as well as political was one of his basic convictions. In a remarkable essay on German anti-Semitism which appeared after the death of Walter Rathenau, he counseled Jews to follow Rathenau's example and to avoid, while they sought assimilation, imitating the worst faults of the Germans. These, he said, were:

> Always wanting to be right, inability voluntarily to subordinate one's own ego to the quest of larger goals, a shunting aside of the convictions of others, the belief that with theories one can fashion the world schematical-

ly, narrowness of outlook, lack of courtesy, intellectual calcification, fondness for intrigues which because they are not carried out in silence can be seen through forthwith, a habit of trying to squelch an opponent not only as a political person but also as man through attacks on his moral integrity.

Nevertheless the man who wrote these lines was a German patriot ready to seek with every ounce of his strength the restoration of German society and of German honor. It is in all truth one of the greatest ironies of history that the man who amidst the ruins of post-Hitlerian Germany, was to attain these goals was not Brüning but Konrad Adenauer. Almost every earmark of Adenauer's policy and position is to be found clearly outlined in *Der Deutsche*. And the reason for the irony is doubtless that during the years spent in the United States Brüning somehow lost confidence in his ability to lead.

Those who came to know him well in this period were often surprised, first of all, by the insubstantiality of a myth which had grown about him. Was he not a stern ascetic? It is true that he had never married and that every form of profligacy was alien to his nature. He never made any money other than his salary nor did he seek to do so. But in all the places where he stayed and all the homes which he visited he proved himself a man of such charm, good humor and sociability that a week-end on which he came was looked forward to by everyone, young and old alike. In our house he played with our children, joined fully in whatever merriment there was, drank the wine we offered—it was never as good as what he had left behind in Germany—and then welcomed and talked with our guests far into the night. We cherished him not merely as a statesman and an intellectual of genuine distinction but as a human being so courteous of spirit that even his one eccentricity, namely his profound affection for the life of the soldier and his admiration for German feats of arms, seemed engrossing. Brüning as we knew him was a deeply religious person, but he detested any sort of "professionalism" in the expression of his Catholic beliefs. I think that an anecdote he loved to tell about a small Westphalian town is applicable here. Some farmers, he reported, had a *Stammtisch* in a tavern. A young man who was just taking over his father's acres was invited to join them. He entered and said "Good evening" cordially. No one returned the greeting and after a while the young man left. "Comes of good stock," growled one farmer, "but he talks too much."

The range of his thought and reading was very wide. During his university days he had read Walter Pater's *Marius the Epicurean,* which remains an extraordinary evocation of a young Roman lover of beauty who discovered in his own way the beauty of early Christianity. T. S. Eliot had called the book second-rate, but Brüning's comment was that Mr. Eliot seemed to lack good judgment. Of earlier German poets he particularly liked Annette von Droste, as might perhaps have been anticipated, but of the moderns Rilke was a special favorite. But it was his indefatigable study of economic developments which astonished us. Not only did he amass a formidable quantity of clippings, from newspapers and journals, but he seemed always to know just how one fitted on to another.

His health, however, left much to be desired. A physical weakness, dating back to early childhood, was when properly diagnosed found to be without fatal implications; but it did often sap his strength and raise doubts in his mind concerning his ability to be active during his later years. Indeed the coming of his sixtieth birthday persuaded him that he was now "an old man." Equally distressing was the breaking of a leg due to a fall in a New York hotel. It took a long while to recover from the accident and indeed he was thereafter usually compelled to walk with a cane. Meanwhile the Seminary was doubtless a godsend. It gave him an opportunity to calm his nerves, to relax and to muster his strength. But he was never again really a well man, though the fact did not prevent him from doing prodigious amounts of work, conducting a vast correspondence, and traveling a good deal.

The visit of "Henry Anderson" to the United States ended of course in discovery, probably because of a "leak" in Canada, to which country he repaired prior to taking off for London again. During twenty-four hours the press hounded both the Seminary and my house, but although the fact of his having been here could no longer be concealed, everyone kept faith, so that nothing more in the way of information became available. Though it would have been easy for someone to gain fleeting public attention by reporting on conversations with the guest, not a single person did so. In reality this restraint was a quite moving tribute to Brüning, regarded by all who knew him as the standardbearer of the cause of decency and justice.

Letters from London indicated first that a long bout with rheumatism had been overcome and second that the outlook for the future seemed to become bleaker with each new day. For the sake of gathering further information he took the first of several trips to Nijmegen to stay with friends who at the time still had close associations with leading men and women in Germany. There he had the experience of being sought after by Gestapo agents. But even though the spirit among German workers had clearly deteriorated, so that audiences had to be herded together to listen to Ley, the hopelessness of any effective opposition seemed to increase steadily. Still more ominous were the military and religious situations. Whereas in 1933 there was a time when Pilsudski's Poland had actually thought of a preventive war, the only possibility open to it now was an alliance, in concert with Czechoslovakia, with Russia. But instead the Poles were still playing a dangerous game with the

Nazis, while Austria dreamed that it had been given a providential mission to effect a spiritual triumph over Nazism.

The really shattering event was of course the occupation of the Rhineland by German troops, during March, 1936, in violation of the Treaty of Locarno. This was one eventuality with which neither Brüning nor the German General Staff had reckoned. I, too, had taken it for granted that this was just the kind of surrender to fate which France could not possibly make. It had at the time a quite overwhelming military superiority—one so great that the German generals had forced Hitler to undertake the venture on his own responsibility. The consequences were now unavoidable, though not all could be foreseen at the time. If the French and the British were not prepared to defend their vital interests in the West, at a time when they still could do so with virtually little risk, what would they willingly undertake in the East, in support of Austria, Czechoslovakia or Poland?

Brüning returned to the United States during September, 1936, this time without disguise, and began to give a series of talks which were terminated only with the declaration of war between Germany and the United States. Among the most wonderful memories of the subsequent months of that year were two periods spent with my family, one on the occasion of his birthday (November 11) and the other at Christmas time. He lived for a while during this period with Father George B. Ford at Corpus Christi Rectory in New York, and began those relationships with Boston which were to prove so fruitful in the years ahead. Of his numerous associations with leading personalities in Washington and London, nothing will be said here since they lie outside the scope of this memoir. No doubt everything needful will be reported in his own memoirs, so eagerly awaited but not yet published. An initial copy of these memoirs, still in an early stage of writing, was deposited with the Columbia University Library by Professor Carlton Hayes. This was, however, later on withdrawn when Brüning decided to undertake a revision for publication.

During 1937 I went to Europe for the purpose of continuing studies in modern German history, with the help of a grant from the Social Science Research Council. Brüning had accepted a temporary appointment as Supernumerary Fellow and Lecturer in Political Theory at Queen's College, Oxford, and I had the pleasure of visiting him in his rooms there. It was his introduction to university instruction and he doubtless found it both trying and interesting. But more important were associations on the Continent after the *Anschluss*. He had introduced me to a number of his friends and associates who were then either in exile from Germany or able to travel— Joos, Foehr, Wirth, Treviranus, Brauns, Hoegner, Hilferding, and even on one occasion Krupp the elder (who was, however, not a friend). We met in Switzerland for, among other things, an unforgettable visit to Fribourg, where

Friedrich Dessauer was then teaching. The most impressive meeting, however, took place in Nijmegen, Holland, during a conference on social work organized by the great moral theologian, Monsignor Poels, and the Rev. Pieter Memmersteeg. I was very much incognito, in order to screen the fact that the German participants were conferring with an American.

There the conversation went on for days. Among those in attendance were the Jesuit anti-Nazi Friedrich Muckermann, of whom Brüning never fully approved, and a number of good friends from inside Germany. Of these Brüning's special favorite was Bernhard Letterhaus, one of the most effective and far-sighted younger Germans I have ever met. It was upon him that Brüning then relied heavily for service to Germany after what now appeared to be a long and undefinable Hitlerian adventure. Alas that he became involved in the venture which lead to the attempted assassination of Hitler during July, 1944, which doubtless miscarried because Count Stauffenburg placed the briefcase containing the bomb on the wrong side of the table support. His execution filled us with grief, but for Brüning it was a bitter loss. I sometimes thought in those days that Brüning was too critical of Goerdeler, leader of the German opposition and the man he had once suggested to President von Hindenburg as his successor. But in retrospect, having read and thought a good deal, I agree that he was right. It may be that Brüning sometimes allowed his pessimism free rein, and overestimated the power of the Gestapo. Goerdeler for his part badly misjudged their efficiency and placed too blue a tag on the Army High Command.

Especially dear in recollection is the time when my wife, acting as chauffeur drove us to Laon, where Brüning was to catch a train for London. We drove through the then sunny French countryside, stopping at Chaumont for a luncheon during the course of which we drank several wines of his choice. It was an unforgettable journey, both because of shared sadness about Germany—we had taken a long and affectionate look at the Badenese country from the terrace of a restaurant in Basel—and a kind of awed feeling that we were going to Paris along the road of St. Bernard. In Laon the hotel-keeper was in a terrible predicament because the government of Léon Blum had introduced a two-day week-end holiday for all workers. As a result the fare we enjoyed was sparse, and the room-service non-existent, but we made up for that with a long visit to the cathedral which he specially appreciated. It was characteristic that on the next morning we arrived at the railroad station nearly two hours before the train was scheduled to depart for London. But those were rare days of intimate talk and great courtesy, every moment of which I cherish because the man with whom I spent the time was one of the noblest citizens, from every intellectual, spiritual and political point of view, his country and perhaps the world have ever known.

It is true that he sometimes had doubts as to the wisdom of having adopted so drastic a policy of deflation in 1931. The choice was however a difficult one to make or avoid. Kaisen, a Social-Democrat who later on became the beloved and successful mayor of Bremen, told me over and over that had Brüning not waited so long in introducing a program of public spending, which would have eased unemployment, the Nazi tide would have receded. But Brüning, relying on the constancy of President von Hindenburg and the Reichswehr, took a chance and, in his own language, came within a few inches of reaching the goal. He had healed the economic wounds of his country, but the hale body was to serve Papen and Hitler well. He knew that the "welfare state" could not expand its activities unless money to support them was available. Nevertheless as Social Democrats of ability often pointed out, the welfare payments made in Germany during the depression were more substantial in terms of real wages than were the wages of East Prussian industrial or agricultural workers during the heyday of the Emperor Wilhelm II.

Leaving the aberrations of the "Hindenburg circle" and the Nazis aside—the second were originally a kind of "bonus army" displaced by the defeat of 1918,—the trouble was that, despite the favorable balance of trade which German industry still maintained in 1932, a segment of the old aristocracy and of industry were fooling around with restorationist ideas. Brüning, whose sympathy lay with labor, and who on principle lived almost as simply as he had while an officer in the field, did not lack sympathy with industrialists. Indeed a segment of them remained friendly to the bitter end. But everything implied by the criticism of the German character he had spelled out in the *Arbeiter* applied especially to them. It is true that such strictures were not deserved by all. Many of them were sorely troubled, nauseated by Nazism. But in the end their record of resistance, as compared with that of the Civil Service, the army and the intelligentsia, was pitiful indeed.

Equally questionable in Brüning's eyes was the record of the Church. He retained throughout these years a profound respect and affection for Cardinal Bertram, Archbishop of Breslau, and an equally deep suspicion of the motives of the Papal Nuncio, later Cardinal Paccelli and eventually Pope Pius XII. Any attempt to canonize the second will encounter a formidable obstacle in Brüning's recollections; and although some hypothetical Papal Commission may ignore these as prejudiced, it is not likely that the objective historian can do so. Perhaps his criticism of the German Church in general found its most severe moment in the belief that when the Archbishop of Osnabrück visited a concentration camp and reported that it was a necessary institution conducted with genuine humanitarian solicitude a nadir in the history of Christianity had been achieved.

He had always to reckon psychologically with the certain fact that if a friend in the Gestapo had not spirited him out of Germany he would have perished, but on the other hand with the opposite fact, namely that those who remained were in growing peril both of body and of soul. I can give ample testimony to the fact that the resulting burden was often heavy. He tried to bear it by doing nothing to endanger those who had been left behind, by helping whomsoever he could, and by offering such counsel to governments as they wished. What he had to give, in addition to his amazingly detailed knowledge of the economic situation, was his insight into German methods of organization, which Hitler took over and used for his purposes. But the world was full of refugees and others who quite understandably felt the need for words that give vent to their feelings and for projecting some kind of "action" against the Nazis. The "silence" of Brüning and his situation about publishing his memoirs became a favorite target of Waldemar Gurian, who edited the anti-Nazi *Deutsche Briefe* in Switzerland.

The attitude is very well illustrated by an account written by Klaus Mann during December, 1937, of a Brüning lecture given in New York. He said in part:

> Der Erzkanzler sprach beinahe anderthalb Stunden lang in fließendem, korrektem, elegantem Englisch. Er benutzt kein Manuskript, keine Notizen. Seine nachdenklichen, gescheiten, etwas müden Augen, hinter den runden, spiegelnden Brillengläsern, halten das Publikum fest. Es ist sehr stille im Saal. Brünings Botschaft wird mit der gleichen Andacht, der gleichen Feierlichkeit empfangen, die in seiner ruhigen aber untergründig bewegten Stimme spürbar sind.

> Aber ist es eine „Botschaft" mit der Brüning vor diesen gewählten Kreis von Interessierten tritt? Der Begriff der „Botschaft" hat etwas Leuchtendes, Positives. Dieser feine ältere Herr am Rednerpult scheint nichts mehr bieten zu wollen als wehmütige—freilich sehr fesselnde Erinnerungen. Sein Blick ist noch in die Vergangenheit gerichtet; nicht auf die Zukunft. Hat er überhaupt noch einen Willen zur Zukunft? Hat er Hoffnungen, Vorstellungen, Visionen? Wenn er dergleichen in seinem Kopfe und in seinem Herzen trägt, so hält er es doch für klug und angebracht, mit keiner Silbe darauf anzuspielen ... Es fand sich in seinem langen Vortrag nicht einmal der Ansatz zu einer konstruktiven Idee. Er gab nicht den flüchtigen Hinweis auf Kräfte, die vielleicht, innerhalb des Reiches oder im Ausland, gegen Hitler zu mobilisieren wären.

It was his fate not to believe that any such strengths were present, except those which would be assembled for the dread arbitrament of war. Inside Germany? No one knew better than did he that there existed a "decent" Germany. But around what could it rally? The army and the captive old Fieldmarshal had sanctioned the bloodbath of 1934. Labor was caught in the vise of bitter unorganized resentment. The Church had been deluded and was now powerless except for the Vatican's flirtation with the belief that a menace to Communism was present. For Brüning the final proof of its delusion was the Spanish Civil War. In concert with him and Jacques Maritain I wrote at the time for the *Commonweal* the only disapproval of Franco's action to appear in any significant Catholic journal of opinion in the United States. It aroused fierce dissent. What should he have said to people in terms of some kind of "vision"? All that he knew was that holocausts were in the offing and that no one could foresee what the outcome might prove to be.

But it is true that he sometimes gave the impression that for him Germany and Nazism were two wholly different entities—that the second could use the strength of the first, but that it was solely accountable for the results. Occasionally he seemed to believe that Hitler could be defeated without bringing the conflict close to what was beautiful and treasurable in Germany. And in the end he found it quite impossible to credit reports concerning the extermination of the Jews. He did not of course condone what had been done, but that Germans—even when they were Nazis—could actually pile millions of men, women and children into gas-ovens was a fact that he came eventually to accept, but it left a wound in his spirit which could never again be healed. That Hitler's war was first of all a "biological" war made it so alien, so horrible, so sure to leave a stigma on the German name, that it seemed to Brüning, the patriotic German who, though he had himself been an excellent soldier and, admittedly, thought he had profited by the "war experience," was a great humanitarian, not only in theory, but in daily life, something so ghastly, unthinkable, that he could not accept it without losing some of his grip on the world. It was very saddening to observe this, knowing that there was nothing anyone could do to help him recover from the wound. But since these reflections lie outside the scope of this essay, they may be broken off here.

During 1937 Brüning began his work at Harvard University, serving for two years as Lecturer on Government and Tutor in Government and Economics, and then (1939-1952) as Lucius N. Littauer Professor of Public Administration, Harvard Graduate School of Public Administration. I cannot offer a detailed analysis or even a complete description of these years of service at Harvard. But I have conferred with a number of men who were his colleagues there, and the company was an illustrious one—Professors William Y. Elliot, Bruce Hopper and Carl Friedrich were among them. Dean Reginald H. Phelps, who already knew Brüning during the Berlin days, kindly consented to write an account which is, I think, commendable for succinctness, lucidity and candor. It is therefore being reproduced here. Professor Bruce Hopper, whose first-hand knowledge of foreign affairs Brüning deeply appreciated and in whose university office he conducted a seminar, has been good enough to provide papers concerning one seminar, and reference will be made to this later on. The greatest boon conferred on Brüning by Harvard was the appointment of a brilliant and devoted secretary, Miss Claire Nix. She has not been invited to contribute to this account because no one should try to diminish the opportunity which will some time be hers to write the story more fully.

Dean Phelps's memorandum follows:

Dr. Brüning first came to Harvard, as far as I recall, during 1935-36, and his first appointment was as the Godkin Lecturer in 1936—a distinguished title, but one applying only to the delivery of three lectures on "The Essentials of Free Government, and the Duties of the Citizen." He spoke in New Lecture Hall (now Lowell Lecture Hall) to a good-sized audience; but, as will be further discussed below, the quiet presentation of the long view of constitutional history was perhaps a disappointment to many who came seeking revelations. They indeed did learn in the last lecture something of Brüning's strategy in the presidential elections of 1932, which he hoped would lead to a plebiscite, the regency of Hindenburg, and the restoration of a constitutional monarchy under a younger member of the Hohenzollern line. The report of this project for a legal restoration, a desperate attempt to contain the revolutionary force of National Socialism before it was too late, might indeed have been regarded by some as sensational, but not in comparison with inside stories of the Third Reich. Very professorial, one might say, was his approach in the lectures—very cool and judicious, and auguring well for a rôle in the contemplative life of a university.

In 1937 Brüning was named Lecturer on Government and Tutor, and in September 1938 became Littauer Professor of Government in the Graduate School of Public Administration. His teaching of course crossed the official lines between Public Administration and Arts and Sciences. He worked entirely in graduate seminars—five of them, with slight variations in some of the titles—starting with "International Economic Policies" in 1937, and an abnormally large enrollment of sixteen, followed in 1938 by "Government Regulation of Industry: Some Post-War European Experiments in Industrial Control." Both of these he taught in association with Professor William Y. Elliott. In 1939 he installed Government 146: "Topics in Post-War Diplomacy," also with Professor Elliott. He presented "Topics in Comparative Public Administration" in 1940, and repeated this course, sometimes with Professor Arthur Holcombe, almost every year until his retirement. A fifth seminar subject, "Topics in International Organization," replaced the diplomatic seminars in 1943, and remained, with the seminar on public administration, his staple offering. The enrollment was a mixed one, with the largest groups naturally from the School of Public Administration or the Graduate School, but an occasional undergraduate signed up also, and, somewhat surprisingly, one Freshman had the temerity to enroll in the Seminar on International Organization in 1943, and one (presumably not the same man) in Comparative Public

Administration in 1945. The seminars often—perhaps generally—met in a small common room in Lowell House, in the evening. There were frequent visitors: John Wheeler-Bennett, for example, came regularly in one semester, and faculty members occasionally dropped in. As examples of the art of teaching, they were highly interesting—Brüning tended to use many of them as opportunities for informal lectures to small groups, probably his most effective method of teaching.

From 1937 on he lived in a comfortable suite on the ground floor of Lowell House. My impression is that he was no active social lion at any time, but that he of course had many visitors from outside as well as among faculty and students. One does not forget the quiet courtesy with which they were greeted, or the pleasant warmth of the fireplace in his big study on dark Sunday afternoons. He seemed wholly at home in this scholar's milieu, like another Erasmus in another Cambridge, and it is not surprising to note that he had been thought of in the days before 1914 as a probable professor of economics at Bonn.

He was in the public eye chiefly through several series of lectures. I suppose the most notable among those he delivered in this country—though perhaps this is because he let me use the manuscripts of them when I was writing my doctoral thesis—were the Godkin Lectures at Harvard, four lectures given at Dartmouth in 1937, and the Lowell Lectures in Boston in 1935-36. None of these were any more "sensational" than the Godkin Lectures mentioned earlier. People expecting exciting disclosures came to the first lecture, and when they found they were faced with a scholarly discussion of constitutional and economic problems, such persons generally stayed away. Not that exciting incidents were omitted from the lectures—but even such wonderful phrases as that describing the aging Hindenburg in 1931—"Suddenly he grew older in mind"—were delivered with the unimpassioned calm of the scholar. The personality and presentation, the avoidance of "exposures"—it added up to a historian's, or a political scientist's view, a Rankean *,,bloß zeigen, wie es eigentlich gewesen.* "The Dartmouth lectures, it is true, sometimes breathed a more ardent fire, a fine, if subdued, presentation of the weaknesses of German democracy in the Weimar Republic, and a firm defense of the *Rechtsstaat*. In the other series, too, as well as at Dartmouth, he undertook to make the case for his chancellorship, that his use of the emergency clause of the constitution, Article 48, had followed a rigorously constitutional line, and that the evil advisers of Hindenburg—typically, he left them unnamed and omitted details of their activities—brought about the first deviation from the constitutional path under Papen in 1932, after Brüning's forced resignation.

Looking back on Brüning as a professor, one thinks of him as perhaps somewhat secluded from the main tide of university life. He certainly was not active in faculty affairs—doubtless his own decision—and perhaps he was a somewhat baffling figure to undergraduates, who in those days would have expected the last really constitutional Chancellor of the

German Republic to speak out constantly and emphatically about the end of Weimar and the Third Reich. But this was not in his nature. What *do* you do when you have been driven, a hair's breadth from death, out of your own country—if you are a person of Brüning's burning patriotism and intense religious-ethical conviction? He gave his answer at the start of the first Lowell Lecture: he stated his unwillingness to speak then of foreign policy or the rise of National Socialism: 'rather to suffer from any form of calumny, than to speak out facts and truths which . . . may do harm to my own country, for which I feel the most filial devotion.' So he spoke, and so he acted.

Though he published relatively little, his scholarship was of remarkably high quality. The essay on "Wartime Administration in Great Britain and Germany," which he wrote for the volume, *The British Commonwealth at War,* edited by William Yandell Elliott and H. Duncan Hall (N.Y., 1943) is a masterly comparison of the two administrative systems and procedures. Problems of administration always interested him—sometimes, his friends thought, inordinately. This essay also retains of the flavor of his seminars. All who attended these saw excellent study of government being done quietly and effectively. The record of one seminar, based on notes taken by an efficient secretary, which Professor Bruce Hopper was kind enough to permit me to see, shows that it dealt with the problem of Nationalities in Eastern and Central Europe and in so doing discussed expansionism, frontiers, economic resources and political organization. It could easily have been expanded into a book and that would have been notable for its breadth of view. Doubtless, however, one can see Brüning's own views on German and general European history reflected in the publications of his friend, John W. Wheeler-Bennett. This historian's most substantial book, *The Nemesis of Power* (New York, 1954), a study of the German Army in Politics, contains one of the most searching and affirmative evaluations of Brüning's activities as Chancellor to have seen the light of day.

Brüning's interest in and insight into military questions is well illustrated by a profoundly interesting paper on *German Strategy: 1914 and 1940* contributed to the leading periodical *Foreign Affairs* under the pseudonym of "X" (Vol. 19, Nr. 2, January, 1941). This is a substantial comparison of the campaign which ground to a halt in 1914 with that which proved so spectacularly successful in 1940. In it he contends that whereas Germany had lost the pre-war diplomatic battle by the summer of 1914, the French had in turn lost it irretrievably by 1936. Concerning the German invasion of the Rhineland and the abrogation of the Treaty of Locarno, he writes of the French government: "The mere order for total mobilization would have been sufficient at that time to bring about the collapse of the Hitler regime." The military debacle is analyzed on the basis of a comparison between the

Schlieffen Plan as it was conducted during the First World War, when Holland was not invaded, and during the Second World War. It is a masterly paper, still very much worthwhile.

Sometime a qualified student will prepare for publication the significant articles and addresses of a man so well-prepared by training, experience and reflection for the study of government and history. And if he can then assemble and add the significant letters of the period, we shall have not only a chronicle but also an interpretation of the sombre events through which Brüning and so many others have perforce lived.

During all his Harvard days but particularly after the fall of France Brüning was busy at a task which does him great honor but which few at the time knew about. The number of those who after fleeing from Germany were surprised in France by the sudden military collapse was very considerable. The Emergency Rescue Committee was set up in the United States and it had in Varian Fry an extra-ordinarily gifted and industrious representative. With this group Brüning was in almost constant communication. His correspondence must have been a crushing burden at the time. I myself have a whole sheaf of letters from him concerned with efforts to assist people of varied political parties and in all walks of life. In addition he sought and personally gave financial help (he could scarcely afford to do so) to wives whose husbands were now in concentration camps or had disappeared.

No single instance involved him more deeply than did the fate of Rudolf Hilferding and Rudolf Breitscheid, Social Democrats whom he had come to esteem highly. Both were in Southern France; and due to Brüning's constant prodding Fry made a valiant effort to get them across the border into Spain, from which they could have reached Portugal and eventually the United States. But Breitscheid proved to be a stickler for the legality of his emigrant papers. The delay was fatal. Both were seized by the Gestapo. Breitscheid is reported to have died in Buchenwald, after having been sent there, but Hilferding did not leave France alive. The circumstances surrounding his death are unknown. One of my most moving recollections of Brüning is that of the great courtesy he afterward showed to Rose Hilferding, the widow. He held these and many others, foes once upon a time, in rarely affectionate memory.

It is also far from true that he did not take an interest in what was to happen in Germany after the war was over. Following the entry of the United States into the conflict, the Council on Foreign Relations established a group to advise the Department of State concerning the outlines of the peace to follow. This group conversed with representatives of all governments in exile, and Brüning was the principal representative of what it was then hoped would be a revived democratic Germany. The memorandum prepared by the group was written by me, but it reflects in the main, Brüning's hopes and appraisals of the situation. At the time he was also a firm believer in the possibility of a coalition between a revived Center Party—which again he believed should be a Christian Democratic Party—and the Social Democrats. Yet all such hopes were destined to fail.

The last period of the War was of course bitterly disappointing. Mounting antipathy to all things German, naturally fed by news about the horrible treatment accorded the Jews, led eventually to President Roosevelt's policy of "Unconditional Surrender" and to the Yalta Agreement. Brüning was also haunted by the feeling that the atmosphere at Harvard had become hostile. There was a strong anti-German group, true enough, but his friends remained constant and, though his freedom of movement was somewhat hampered by war-time travel regulations, the work he was doing could proceed as smoothly as always to the time of his retirement from the University. He came to see us in Stamford on a number of occasions during this period and I shall take the liberty of citing just one letter, dated May 6, 1943:

Dear Mrs. Shuster:

I wish to tell you how much I enjoyed the weekend spent with you and your family. I was so happy by being able to talk about a number of problems which one cannot discuss by letter. In addition it was a real rest for me and I enjoyed playing with Bobby. He is really a fine boy.

Give my love to George, Bobby and the little girl.

With many thanks for your kindness.                    H. Brüning

Such was the Brüning we remember with affection from those years. The problems were there and they would take on a new and sombre intensity. But he could find some peace at a fireside, with children about him. When the War was over and I had gone to Germany for the War Department, I could help him in a small way by traveling to a farmhouse in Westphalia to see his sister, who was staying there because of the destruction which had reduced Münster to rubble. It was a somewhat venturesome journey because my friend Colonel Orin J. Hale and I were in uniform and not supposed to be on any such mission in the British Zone. When we finally found the farmhouse, we discovered that even the tiny bridge across the creek in front of it had been destroyed at Hitler's orders. We crossed by a plank only to face a tall, determined young Westphalian armed with a pitchfork which he seemed quite ready to use. But after I had explained our mission we were received cordially and I could give the sister news of her brother. It was perhaps as odd a task as any performed in Westphalia during those days.

I shall end these recollections with as sincere a tribute as I could pay to anyone I have known long and intimately. However dark and often bitter the years which followed may have proved to be—years which also separated us,

for reasons which I regret and which were not of my making—I shall say of
Heinrich Brüning that he has been a man whom the world and in particular
Germany should cherish by reason of a singular combination of greatness of
intellectual endowment, untarnished probity and luminous humaneness of
character. Perhaps he loved Germany with too great an intensity. He loved it
because he had fought not only for its existence as a nation but for the sake
of its honor. When the first was sorely imperilled and the second tarnished,
he was undoubtedly unnerved. But it is well to remember him as he was when
he lived in our midst. For he has been a great gentlemen . . . and Germany has
produced far too few of them.

# The Third Kingdom

Definite relationships have been traced between Stahlhelm and Reichswehr personalities and Hitlerites. The National-Socialistic German Workers' Party is a comprehensive title for a political movement set in motion by Adolph Hitler. In accordance with the organization principle to bring everything within the range of the people's minds, this label has been shortened first to Nazi-Sozi, and then to simple Nazi, which we shall accept gratefully. Imagine a nation accustomed to elect its representatives in accordance with the almost impersonal customs previously described, suddenly developing campaign stunts which remind Americans of good old days when a steam calliope went down the street, followed by some such celebrity as Joe Cannon. The Berlin Sportpalast is a huge indoor gymnasium of Madison Square Garden proportions, normally destined for running and frenzied bicycle pedalling. But on a given night a strong cordon of police is thrown about the place, and inside that are groups of men in brown shirts who collect a mark, usher you in and generally help to maintain a variety of awesome hush. The place fills up rapidly—there is not a seat left. People crowd into the aisles, droop over banisters. Then suddenly there is music, a parade of more brown shirted men in rigid military formation, and a speaker. Or perhaps, if you are lucky, three speakers—maybe even the great Hitler himself. The crowd—or nearly all of it—is electrified, distilling that weird current which the spectator knows will sooner or later prove to him, too, that political action is essentially very primitive—and possibly dangerous.

From *The Germans: An Inquiry and an Estimate* by George N. Shuster (New York: Dial Press, 1932), pp. 260-279.

The speaking begins. It is demagoguery of the Jacksonian epoch, though not much worse really than we Americans got from very eminent gentlemen during the War. The orator is not expected to say much—he is simply a machine which generates shocks. Wheels move, contacts are made. The sparks click and flash, as the man on the platform hurls adjectives at the government, the Young Plan, unemployment, socialistic ideals. Then suddenly he takes a fling, usually humorous at first, at the Jew. Immediately the crowd is in a frenzy. Bryan accusing the Republicans of wholesale executions on a cross of gold cannot have made anything like this impression. The word "Jew" is a red rag; wave it correctly and the bull dances to your satisfaction. After this it is merely necessary to pile up the denunciation to a frenzied peak. Everything these people have suffered, all the curses they have heaped on the reputed authors of their sufferings, are expressed vicariously here. It is a mounting torrent of rage which begins by thrilling you and then slowly, steadily saddens you. So much of what the man on the platform is saying is literally, horribly true. Many of these people do live in the shadow of economic despair. Many of them watch the successful combinations of modern business undermine their own little shops, banks, endeavors. Whole masses of them live on a petty dole, even restricted in hard times.

A man like Goebbels, the Berlin drummer for the movement, is a masterly agitator combining aspects of Bill Heywood, Mayor Thompson and Jimmie Walker. He may be described as a Menckenian with a fondness for practical jokes, or as Bryan turned Chicago gangster. In the Reichstag he staged a veritable tumult, adorned with white mice. When *All Quiet on the Western Front* appeared in Nollendorfplatz as a movie, he broke up the show by ordering his worthy followers to strategic points from the tribune of an automobile. He runs a newspaper—*Der Angriff*—which has all the journalistic virtues coveted by Mr. Franklin Ford, plus a modicum of real intelligence. This man has run Berlin ragged. But of course he is only a play-boy, an organizer, a measure of substitute for Barnum. The power behind the throne is Adolph Hitler, no doubt the strangest figure in world politics today.

To declare that Hitler's rise is utterly inexplicable is merely to say that German politics have begun to develop American traits. Who can explain the rise of any one of two dozen eminences picked at random from Washington's great? Let us go back to a previous statement—that the moment inevitably came in Germany when those who had nothing to lose, nothing to jeopardize, asked for a new deal. Herr Hitler appeared with the answer. The man is personally rather unprepossessing until you hear him speak, and even then it is difficult for an American familiar with the electoral methods of yore to see how he does it. But there is no doubting his efficiency. Or his bravery. Or, in spite of inconsistencies, his integrity. The man is possibly so much of a puzzle because he is so simple.

Born in Austria, in 1889, Adolph Hitler became an interior decorator who dodged military service in his native country, moved to Germany, and "signed up" when the War came. He distinguished himself in no way, but emerged during those curious times in Bavaria when a people which had unwillingly to do without its ruling house saw one agitator after another clutch for the reigns of authority. General Ludendorff, who had developed curious notions about the sinister natures of Jews and Jesuits, was in the background, and more or less against that still formidable setting Hitler staged his famous "Putsch"—after a speech in which he declared that on the morrow he and his followers would be either successful or dead. Some of the followers perished, but the leader was tucked in jail safely enough. He emerged the author of a book which countless people have ransacked in vain for a clue to the man's reputation.

We can find in it and in his subsequent remarks only traces of the ideas which have swept him onward to international notoriety. First of all, he brought from Austria the "racial" philosophy in vogue there among a group of patriots who felt that Semitic and Slavic influences inside the old Austro-Hungarian monarchy were depriving Germans of their rightful places in the world. After the War the example of Mussolini, who proceeded to establish a new economic order by means of nationalistic sentiment, appealed very strongly to Hitler's circle. He himself was conscious of unusual gifts as a popular speaker, and gradually began to dream of being Germany's Il Duce. Ideas sponsored by the reactionary wing within the Stahlhelm blended in his mind with the doctrine of race advocated by followers of Houston Stewart Chamberlain, and with certain conceptions of social reform long since current in this or that branch of the Youth Movement. It was not, however, until [Alfred] Hugenberg and some of the interests he represented came into the foreground that Hitler acquired genuine significance. How much money the Nazis have received by way of slush funds is not known, but cash flowed into the party coffers even from abroad. It is likewise asserted that quantities of Italian lire found their way to Hitler's Munich headquarters.

At any rate the party waxed so strong during 1930 that it pooled a sufficient vote to send 107 men to the Reichstag—and it takes 60,000 votes to send one man. Germany and the world were alarmed; France succumbed to a veritable attack of fear, so that really excellent Parisians went to bed convinced that a German army would be nearby next morning. Something like a panic developed in Wall Street, where rumors that the Bruening government had been overthrown passed muster. And it is true that the event was serious enough. If the Nazis had been sufficiently adroit to use their newly-acquired power to genuine advantage, there is no telling what might have happened. But they weren't. In all probability the remarkable fact that the vote supporting them was pretty evenly distributed throughout Germany, and that therefore they controlled no state completely and Thuringia only in a measure, kept them from developing a solid center of activity. At all events, they contented themselves with a bizarre campaign of agitation, which ranged from window-breaking in Berlin (Jewish shops) to bombastic speeches and intellectual incompetence. Very soon it was Hugenberg who really controlled the situation. He engineered the famous march of the opposition parties—including the abhorred Communists—out of the Reichstag and more or less in the direction of Weimar. This march absolved the Right from responsibility in the financial crisis which soon developed, but it hamstrung Nazi politics for months. What the future is, no man knows. That depends upon what happens to the forces which have really bred Hitlerism.

First of all, let us see something of the ideology upon which the party reposes. To a considerable extent this is not the leader's own creation. He clings to a relative handful of slogans which express German desires rather than immediate German possibilities. But the movement has a plethora of theorists who are by no means in constant agreement but who tend to come out at more or less the same places. First and possibly foremost is the concept of organization, into which the Nazis have infused a bit of Fascist color though they have in all essentials clung to a thoroughly German pattern. The ground work is laid by a never-ending series of meetings or rallies. These have for their purpose keeping the enthusiasm of the party cenacles alive *and* displaying to the public specially trained disciples or "shock divisions," as they are called. Officers of the old army act as drill masters; military insignia, flags and brown shirts create the illusion of soldierly discipline. "Groups" of thirteen men are arranged in "troops" which merge into other units and eventually into "brigades." These are supposed to profess unquestioning obedience to the leader, but this is to date something of a myth. Even so the whole has a decidedly martial aspect, and tends to make an onlooker profoundly serious. In addition the party has made earnest efforts to organize student associations, workers' and parents' societies, and "professional corporations."

The ideas which dominate must be sought chiefly in the press. Some books exist, but none of them is more than an elongated pamphlet. Why should NSDAP leaders write tomes, when their chief stress is consciously laid on emotions? It is the newspaper upon which they rely chiefly, and which they have developed into an extraordinary instrument of propaganda. I have mentioned the *Völkische Beobachter,* Hitler's organ, in another connection, but it must be stressed here again as one of the most curious throw-backs in modern journalism. From end to end—and there is often quite a bit of it—the sheet quivers with invective, sputters with critical dynamite, expands with a strangely coagulated idealism. Other editors of moment are Goebbels (who is the most Nietzschean, or Sorelian, of the group and whose diction has left Baltimore miles behind), Otto Strasse (whose doctrine inclines toward Socialism but whose credo of action is ultra-nationalistic) and Count Reventlow (a vitriolic enemy of France and international capitalism in the name of Wotan). Sometimes marked differences of opinion flourish in the various editorial sanctums, and clashes between leading articles have been reflected in the party organization itself.

Enter the "brains" of the NSDAP. (I) Alfred Rosenberg, editor-in-chief of the *Völkische Beobachter* and author of *The Myth of the Twentieth Century*. Not a man to mince words, Dr. Rosenberg is the chief exponent of the Ku-Klux-Klan idea in modern Germany. Racial ties are the sole cement upon which national unity can rely; Christianity "owes its lasting values to Germanic character." What happens to the Jews or even to the Catholics, according to this theory, is perfectly evident. It should be noted however, that Nazi doctrine does not identify German virtue with any established form of worship. On the contrary, this virtue is counted upon to produce a new religious unity inside the "third empire" which will dawn as soon as the NSDAP comes into its own. (2) Gottfried Feder, likewise of the *Völkische Beobachter,* is an engineer who is looked to for authoritative pronouncements on industrial and social problems. He is perhaps the most systematic mind, and certainly the ablest pamphleteer, among the Nazis. We shall examine his ideas in some detail later on. (3) Dr. Wilhelm Frick, for a time Minister for Cultural Affairs in Thuringia, is the renowned educator of the movement. A fanatic of the fieriest sort, who regularly threatens his foes with the gallows and the guillotine, Frick is nevertheless a reformer with many right ideas formulated without poise. During the period of his incumbency, he made war not only on obscene literature and art (which needed some attention, no doubt) but on modern aesthetics, root and branch. Anything later than Richard Wagner was automatically voted "degenerate" and "anti-Nordic," while the right of the state to root out all spiritual effort not subordinate to its ends was endorsed unqualifiedly.

Generally speaking, these men and their associates are agreed upon the Fascist principle of government, but they differ (often very noticeably) upon the means which that principle should adopt in practice. Twenty-five points have been laid down as binding upon the party conscience. They may be summed up under a few headings. First come demands for the revision of the Versailles Treaty, most of which are the standard nationalist aims—union of all Germany into one nation in accordance with the right of self-determination; annulment of the Treaties of Versailles and St. Germain; restoration of the colonies. Second in order are the racial ipse-dixits—only persons of

German blood can be citizens (Jews are expressly outlawed), all non-citizens are to live in Germany subject to laws governing strangers, immigration of non-Germans is to cease at once. Third come the economic and social doctrines, chief glories of the NSDAP—the curbing of interest, the acquisition of all trusts (corporate enterprises) by the state, far-reaching old age pension laws, abolition of department stores. Finally, the cultural mandates appear in serried array—universal military service, fostering of sports, censorship of the press, unqualified central governmental authority.

That is, as the boy remarked who was bidden to take a swallow of codliver oil, several mouthfuls. Why should such a program have cast such a spell over millions of voters? A month before the elections of September, 1930, Arthur Dix had predicted that 6,000,000 votes would be cast for the NSDAP, simply because that many voters had reached maturity since the War. Of course not all of these voted for Hitler's ticket, but it was largely the young women who did not. Their places were filled in by older men. In other words: *the Nazi movement is the creation of people directly affected by the War and not inured to any previous social order.* If we put ourselves into the German's boots, we shall see: (a) that some of us, mostly older people, have struggled to save over into the new order the advantages and forms of the old order, primarily because life seemed impossible or inconceivable to us on any other basis; (b) that others of us had nothing to save, either because of our losses or because we had never known what had gone before. Naturally it has been the members of group (a) who have, during the past twelve years, managed the affairs of the German government. The dominant parties in particular have been, as was noted, maintained by savers. And it follows as night does day that when group (b) grows, as it almost inevitably must, creative action rather than rescue will be demanded. Likewise, by a strange but natural corollary, conservative ideas will accompany the appeal to action. Why did Mussolini talk of Roman tradition, and why do the Hitlerites applaud the old-fashioned cultural ideas of Schulze-Naumburg or the no less antiquated doctrine of militarism? Simply because the clash between new trends of thought or culture complicates the community formula and disrupts the unity of authority.

Post-war Germany is the era of a steadily-increasing Teutonic proletariat. This is first of all the result of economic and financial conditions, chiefly the fact that whereas the Hohenzollern Empire was characterized by a steadily growing capital surplus, the new Reich is best defined as a community burdened with a constantly mounting indebtedness. Secondly, it is the consequence of a radical change in the social order. Thousands of families which formerly stood within class boundaries shut off from the proletariat by tradition and status, have now joined the ranks of the have-nots and the hopeless; thousands of other families have, under the new system of massed mechanized production, lost every shred of their quondam independence as tradesmen, shop owners, small manufacturers. Credit restriction and central- ization of all forms of enterprise have made nearly one-half of all living Germans wage dependents, and the percentage is bound to increase—unless something happens.

What do the apostles of the NSDAP say will happen? First, Germany will get rid of people whom the new proletariat doesn't like. The Jews head the list, as they do in every European country East of the Rhine. This is partly due to sheer envy among the unemployed intellectual groups, who dislike the ascendancy which the brilliant Semite obtains by reason of gifts peculiarly fitted to an age of capitalistic control. On the other hand, however, racial consciousness, even when not pushed to the absurd extremes set up by men like Rosenberg, is (I) inevitable in a world which decreed that nations should exist where racial groups exist (i.e., a world which gave even legitimate nationalism a racial foundation), and (2) necessary to a people for whom culture is conveyed by a vernacular, as distinguished from a universal language like Latin. It would hardly make so definite a target of the Jews, however, if the Jew were more folk-conscious in his activity. Where the Semitic mind is folk-conscious—and to a marked extent it is in Germany—trouble does not easily arise. But the individual Hebrews too frequently identify themselves with movements to which a given nationalistic mood is hostile. German Jews have been prominent in ultra-capitalism; they have likewise been leading protagonists of Marxian doctrine. There comes a time when such sorties will meet resistance, and the unfortunate thing is that a people never thinks of Jews as individuals but always as another people.

Personally, of course, I find this NSDAP swashbuckling absurd and despic- able. Germany would be considerably worse off without its Jews, though of course it might profitably choke some of them as an annex to a raid on not a few Christians. The same observations apply to the Hitlerite revisionist program. Naturally a nation which had eaten dust and ashes for twelve years may be pardoned for wondering irately when a few vegetables will begin to appear. Six million young Germans will hardly walk about perennially with penitential faces because an Allied Commission, inspired by diverse hungers and thirsts, decided in 1919 that the Kaiser had started all the shooting out of sheer murderous ambition. To expect them to look at the contour of contemporary Europe with a beaming smile of satisfaction is to conduct oneself with considerable naïveté. But how do the Hitlerites hope to remedy matters? Their recipe is Mussolini's. A strong, conclusively centralized govern- ment backed up with a hugh standing army, allied with the forces of Italy, will show the French where to get off at. M. Poincaré is to get a few bottles of his own medicine.

Yes, absurd and deplorable! It is true that a German army is a political instrument which may eventually be created if the French persist in maintaining an armed camp. The true psychological reason why this statement is correct happens, however, to be generally missed. No nation will in the long run submit inactively either to invasion or the threat of invasion. Germans who are in their right minds do not believe that the French maintain huge forces solely in order to repel invasions from across the Rhine, and it is time we all stopped thinking so. To be sure there are groups in Gaul—clergymen, professors, simple bourgeois—whose days are passed in dread of potential Uhlans. But (and I hate to say this, because it does a fine old man no honor) Briand's speeches anent the *Anschulss* debate made the issue perfectly clear. The armies of Maginot exist to prevent any action in Europe of which the leaders of France disapprove.

On the other hand the mirage of a possible military victory, doubtless entertained by some Germans, will not mislead any balanced mind. There is no German army excepting the Reichswehr, which is an excellently trained force, just about large enough to quell uprisings and to maintain the neutrality of the nation in case of a European conflict. The Reichswehr has none of the modern weapons of offense—no fortresses to fall back upon, no heavy artillery, no armed planes, no chemical equipment. Most of the old drill grounds have become parks or stadiums; the barracks are used as hospitals. These deficiencies, however, are less important than the fact that a military Germany would be without the political support required. So long as a Communist vote of more than four million exists, and so long as the aims of this vote are what they are, any conceivable war would be lost in advance by sabotage. Of course Germany could unite with Russia in a revolutionary attack upon the rest of Europe. That, however, would be not a nationalistic but a social war, the prelude to which would be the disappearance of Germany as a world power.

Few even among the extreme Nazis are, however, actually counting on a war. Everybody realizes very well that to take this way out would simply mean plunging the country still deeper into misery and helplessness. A victory over France would not help the suffering millions of Central Europe; it would merely destroy the wealth and stability of the vanquished. What the NSDAP really wants is an army, and very many Germans share that wish. Why? Because of the effect on international opinion, for one thing—the expected resultant restoration of diplomatic equality to the Reich. Even more important, however, is the hope that a standing army might restore economic and political balance. The garrisons would absorb vast numbers of the unemployed, and at relatively small cost; and a year of military training would develop now unused human energies. Finally, the proper distribution of cantonments would create markets for agricultural products and textiles in regions which have lost ground since the coming of peace. It is easy to object and say that armies are dangerous playthings. Huge hordes of jobless men are perilous, too; and the damage they may do to society is surely important enough to justify the statement that social sanitation is an important part of any disarmament program.

The industrial economics sponsored, under Hitler's patronage, by such a man as Dr. Feder, varies the Fascist formula in some respects but apes it on all questions of basic importance. Note for example the two most practical points in the NSDAP program: nationalization of corporate enterprises, organization of groups on the basis of position and profession (podesta system). Since the party does not believe in confiscation of private property, the first principle can only mean in practice about what it does in Italy. Where Hitlerism differs from Fascism is in its somewhat fantastic two-sided war against capitalism and socialism. On the one hand it demands a reform of the banking system by emancipating Germany from "slavery to interest," by which is meant the necessity for paying dividends to international capital. "The task of the nation's industry is to supply demands," says Dr. Feder, "and not to earn the highest possible rate of interest on borrowed capital." On the other hand, it believes in certain forms of distributivism, holding, for instance, that the large department stores should be reorganized so that each department would be placed in the possession of an individual merchant. It was a French observer of intelligence, M. Edouard Trogan of the *Correspondant,* who first pointed out to me how both sides of this fight are conceived as of anti-Semitic. In recent German practice, Social Democracy (theoretically but not actually led by Jews) has borrowed heavily from the bankers (likewise supposedly owned and managed by Jews).

Leaving this last detail aside, one may well believe that National Socialism advocates certain desirable reforms, which Christian economists in particular have demanded for many years. Indeed the party program is, from this standpoint, a hodgepodge of remedies borrowed from various sources mixed and put into a single bottle. Besides the measures outlined above, one meets some of the theories of Henry George (as reconstructed in Germany by A. Damaschke), certain conclusions of the pension critics (especially old age allowances), and modifications of "Distributivism" as advocated by Mr. G. K. Chesterton (for example, Dr. Feder argues that though such enterprises as ship-building wharves must be conducted on a large scale, 500 independent shoemakers are better than one shoe factory employing 500 men). If we now ask ourselves how all this managed to get into one bottle, we must again take a clue from anti-Semitism. Perhaps the primary source of every such program is to be sought in France of Drumont's time (Dreyfus epoch), when a campaign against the Jews was conducted on much the same basis.

If one now wonders how these things are expected to come to pass, the reply is simply that the government to be established by the NSDAP will be strong enough to enforce what it wants. To those who can accept such reasoning, everything is clear. The rest of us are necessarily put to wondering first if a nationalistic economics of this kind can be put into effect by the Germans, and secondly if a nationalistic economics can endure at all. It would be easy to tout Socialism in Europe, if the problems which the Socialists have vainly tried to solve in their way could be disposed of differently. But certainly the years have not proved that Signor Mussolini could borrow money any more cheaply, or spend it any more efficiently, than the German government which antedated Dr. Bruening. Above all a nation like that which Herr Hitler hopes to govern with an iron hand—a nation constrained to live by its foreign trade—cannot well plan to isolate itself from world economic trends. The French can afford to do so because the French make money by lending it, Jews or no Jews. Even so it is not a socially minded man who will dismiss as idle talk what the NSDAP has assembled in the name of social reform.

Nor must one overlook the fact that a movement of this character challenges a great amount of political routine. German party lines on the whole antedate the post-war epoch. Social Democracy, Center and the Right groups all rely upon a mechanism evolved under older conditions and now expected to function in the same old way. The men who come to the fore in the government are men produced by the parties, and men who normally belong to the War period. A movement like that inaugurated by Hitler affords an opportunity to many who have perforce resided in the political suburbs. Orators who would otherwise never have been listened to have addressed large audiences and even the Reichstag; relative youngsters who have looked in vain for employment see a chance to figure on the pay-roll. Such matters are of great importance in a country like Germany, which as we have seen still moves on the hub of its old bureaucracy. Spokesmen for a large, hungry crowd of academically trained young men and women feel that an hour has struck when their talents may be put into circulation.

The ultimate significance of Hitlerism is a matter of conjecture. We can only come back to the same important figures:

35,000,000 Germans work for a living.

26,000,000 Germans depend on some one else for their work.

2,000,000 Germans are normally out of work.

5,000,000 Germans have been thrown out of work by the depression.

60,000,000 Germans have pocket-books which are affected by the Young Plan, by the industrial unsettlement caused by territorial losses, by the mechanization and centralization of industry, and by the indebtedness incurred as a result of the nation's *Sozialpolitik*.

It requires no extraordinary equipment of brains or information to realize that every change for the worse in these figures means an increase in the number of those who approve a program of protest against what are felt to be intolerable conditions.

On the other hand, it is by no means obvious either that Hitlerism could come even relatively close to a successful application of its policies, or that the movement itself will cohere. Critique of the party's purposes has made sufficiently clear that, regardless of all appeals to Fascist doctrine, it is essentially a restoration of Prussian methods effective in a bye-gone age. Careful students—for instance Dr. Ludwig Stahl—have shown that the "principle of action" essential to the NSDAP movement is standard German idealism "which in its purest form was unfortunately mostly the will to throw one's life away during a moment of greatness," and that what really made the reign of Mussolini conceivable was the deep-rooted Italian admiration for Prussian efficiency and order. But these ideas can in the future be no more creative of German advancement than was the idea of restoring the Holy Roman Empire in the early nineteenth century. History obviously does not repeat itself that way.

Secondly, a country as committed to the principle of disparity as Germany is will never assent to the kind of dictatorship which a Fascist movement proposes. Hitler's 7,000,000 voters congregated almost over night; many of them have disbanded almost as rapidly. Witness, for instance, the manner in which party representation marched away from the Reichstag without Hitler's consent or even knowledge. They were manoeuvered out by an astute politician who belongs to another group—Herr Hugenberg. Similarly, sharp conflicts have raged between Hitler and Goebbels, between Goebbels and his lieutenants, between the various lieutenants. Again and again the organization has quarrelled with the Stahlhelm, though this is by all odds the strongest reactionary force in the nation. An army so divided against itself will never "march on Rome." In my opinion, the only conceivable German dictatorship will be exerted by the man who can get control of the *Reichswehr* and use it as an instrument of power. That man is, however, far more likely to be a brilliant general or a scion of old nobility than an oratorical interior decorator. Often, indeed, the observer has a feeling that Hitler is really being used by someone—or some group—for ends which have hardly been formulated consciously.

That is why the growth of Hitlerism among the proletariat is a grave social danger. Sooner or later, one of two things must become apparent: first, either that the leaders of the NSDAP are powerless to effect what they propose to accomplish, or that they are the instruments of some other power. In both cases the resultant disillusionment of devotees will probably lead to a more definitely proletarian form of action. So far Communism in Germany has not gained overwhelmingly for three reasons: first, it is not a German movement but a Russian one, and the intelligentsia know too much about Russia; second, it has no broad cultural structure, even its atheism running counter to profound currents of religious revival, especially in academic circles; third, it offers no chance for political advancement or for traditional social relationships. Germany, I think, will not be communistic unless it fails to see any other way out. That means a way out for a *steadily increasing proletariat.* And here is, then, the final conundrum proposed by the War.

Bearing these things in mind, one is prepared to consider more effectively the actual task confronted by the Bruening government. Ostensibly that government has relied upon a measure of dictatorship. It has ruled by a slender parliamentary majority, by the principle that the powers of the President could be used to the full during a crisis. And with what end in view? To save, but to save other things than had concerned the governments which ruled from 1920 to 1930. Bruening came to the fore as one who believed that Germany must rescue its credit; he had gradually become one who wished to conserve what Germany has gained *since* the War. Thus, in spite of the rising tide or reactionary nationalism, he has tried to glue his government to the position in the European balance which has fallen to it as the result of events. He did not break with France, but quite apart from credit considerations realized that there was something to be had for not breaking with France. And almost at the same time he moved closer to England, closer to Italy, closer to the United States than any of his successors had ventured. If this new policy of *rapprochement,* which has certain fortunate possibilities not open to [Gustav] Stresemann, can be continued, the German will eventually capitalize upon the bequests of political time. On the other hand, Bruening has clung resolutely to the national productive structure. To keep this intact and to improve it he has tried all the recipes—carefully manipulated tariffs, wage reduction, price curtailments, modification of the social insurance laws, taxes. If this productive structure can be harnessed to new demands in a revived market, improvement will be automatic. Such improvement in turn will be—it is hoped—an instrument in the workshop of international economics with which a lock in the door to German financial betterment can be picked.

That this program is hazardous, that nationalistic and proletarian restlessness (note again that the two go hand in hand) impair its chances for success, that mistakes have been made—all this may be granted. But the route now followed, regardless of whether the Bruening government continues in office or not, affords a hope. Everybody who has looked beneath the German surface knows, of course, by how thin a thread that hope is suspended. In all human probability, the coming year will see Hitlerites entrusted with a measure of authority. What form this will take remains to be seen. Perhaps (as some think) the Center Party will manage to effect a new "labor synthesis," thus separating the NSDAP from the reactionary "Harzburg Front" (Hugenbergists and rightward moving People's Party). Others believe there will be a definite swing to conservative nationalism, utilizing the advantages gained under the Bruening regime to curb violent radical tendencies. Of course some unforeseeable, miraculous victory over odds may still save the present coalition.

I think that the issue depends less upon the sacrifices now imposed upon a sorely tried people than upon whether a new resolve to draw a deeper breath from the fountains of cultural tradition stirs and animates millions. Germany's willingness to do what the generation of the *Freiheitskriege* achieved is now a matter of doing without pennies rather than of dying on battlefields. Social Democracy failed because it was materialistic—because it supposed that the nation could survive by working, by getting better houses, by *Sozialpolitik* and loans of foreign money. Bruening's idea will triumph if the light of sacrifice and heroic renouncement written on his remarkable face enkindles the hearts of his countrymen.

# What I Saw in Germany

## I

The examination of Nazi policies . . . may be easier to digest if I attempt to give some impression of what Nazi Germany seemed like to me recently. To me! It would be farcical to claim omniscience, or to deny a certain amount of bias. The underlying conditions were these: I was, had long been and still am deeply interested in what may be termed the experience of the German people. On two previous occasions, I had made tours of inquiry through the country for the purpose of learning all I could, so that the directions I wished to follow this time were relatively clear. In short, what follows are the observations of a friendly observer of the German people, who hopes to visit them again in the future . . . but not the immediate future.

Germany after the burning of the books (May 1, 1933) was a great deal like a pot of jam simmering over a fire. People were still speculating as to what was likely to happen—wondering if the apparent desire of the government to dampen the ardor of hotheads would be sufficiently strengthened by foreign protests to win out, if the new and moderate Minister of Industry (Dr. Schmitt) would maintain the upper hand over a variety of rabid prophets of new economic orders, if all other parties save National-Socialism were to disappear (they soon did), and if Hitler would succeed in making his peace with the Churches. It was a time when many still felt that the age of reason had not ended after all, and when pessimists believed it necessary to argue. There was an extraordinary hustle and bustle everywhere. Even the least

From *Strong Man Rules: An Interpretation of Germany Today* by George N. Shuster (New York: D. Appleton Century Co., 1934), pp. 225-252. Reprinted by permission of Hawthorn Books Inc.

among officials appeared to be working overtime. The leaders of defeated groups were still looking for an opening here and there, and everybody with a taint of suspicion was refusing to commit himself.

The amazing tempo of the so-called "revolution" set in motion by the burning of the Reichstag had slowed down. This tempo was doubtless the principal phenomenon of Hitler Germany. It was very like the swiftness of an earthquake:—the nation was dumped out of bed, dazed, paralyzed with fear, sent scurrying for safety. During the impoverished years which followed the War, virtually nine-tenths of German existences had been utterly dependent on the daily wage or salary. These in turn were, for increasingly large numbers, the reward of service as employees of the state. Many had also begun to save a little, slowly and laboriously, so that very considerable sums had been invested with organizations more or less directly affiliated with groups, political and semi-political, which the upheaval endangered. The coming of the Nazis was, therefore, a challenge to life itself. What if—if the job, the savings account, were suddenly engulfed in a catastrophe more horrible than inflation itself? During almost four years, the employed had struggled with might and main to keep from tumbling into the abyss of joblessness. They now felt as if they were walking a tight-rope above this abyss, and that any false move might send them toppling down.

When a nation has these sensations, it offers little resistance to any wave of political change. Indeed the majority strove to become optimistic—to feel that, after all, it was not the Communist who was knocking at the door. Thus a gasp of terror mingled with a sigh of relief as Hermann Goering held Prussia in his grip. The sigh grew more audible when the first Hitler speeches proved more moderate than had been expected. In the Rhineland of those days, at least a million people (the figure is, I think, based on accurate estimates) lived afraid of a French invasion; and the pacific utterances of the great Adolf sent countless humble folk to bed happier on both sides of the boundary line. The workingman's coöperatives were still doing business, too—he persuaded himself that his meals and his savings were safe. We have all felt that way during a lull in some terrific storm. Well, we have said, here we are still, and it can't get any worse. I remember talking to a little Jewish haberdasher woman in west Berlin. She spoke like a creature sentenced to death and then reprieved.

In those days, Hitlerism made a good deal of progress. I went, for example, to see one of the most prominent Catholic dignitaries in Germany. He informed me that if we met again in November, I should be obliged to admit that National-Socialism would prove advantageous to Christianity. The best authorities had assured him of their most beneficent intentions! A Lutheran clergyman friend was almost equally sanguine. As for the Jews, lunch time at Rubinstein's was then the proper moment to bolster up one's jaded hopes for the human race. The leading Hebraic journal had even grown a bit pert and

issued a number of demands. Various sensible members of the Nazi party—
most of them, to be sure, had acquired their swastikas fairly late—were
honestly convinced that the anti-Semitic wave had been checked and that the
ultimate result would be no Jews in public office. Only this and nothing
more! Even more roseate views were expressed in confidence by eminent
personages. An old monarchist acquaintance assured me that the date of the
restoration of *Seiner Majestät* had already been fixed. And Herr Franz von
Papen, a clever man who lost his way among ultimate simplicities, was
convinced that the French would fall in line with his pet scheme for a great
crusade against Russia, thus burying the Franco-German hatchet forevermore
in the snows southeast of Moscow. Of course there were also some very wise
men, who smiled grimly and in despair. One of these invited me to his home
of an evening, introduced me to his family and then sketched a picture of
what was going to happen. He is the most accurate prophet I have ever
met—and before I had left Germany two of his children were suicides.

Tempo! I come back to that word and fact. There has never been anything
like it. A nation hollowed out economically and spiritually by decades of
privation and seething emotion crumpled together in the twinkling of an eye,
and a new nation—perhaps the most primitive seen in Europe during a
thousand years—came into being. What was the guiding ideological force? I
went to listen to Hitler again, but Hitler is a windbag and a wire-puller—a
politician who knows how to capitalize his own emotions and those of others.
Just prior to leaving New York, I chanced to witness a gathering of some
thousand Negroes hearkening to a spellbinder. His booming voice came
through a megaphone, he painted the old colored Utopia gold and silver, the
crowd was riveted to the soil of Battery Park, there was a chill in the air as of
cold steel passing. To me that Negro spellbinder (whoever he is) has the edge
over Hitler; and doubtless if he got into office we should discover in him the
same magnetism and "genius" which a lot of sentimentalists, who still believe
that the history of these days is made by personalities and not by advertising,
have discerned in the champion ward boss of Germany.

No, it wasn't the great Adolf I wanted. Thereupon a friend took me to
meet a group of strapping young fellows, all of them well educated, some of
them really very charming. We discussed the collapse of capitalism, the limbo
to which liberalism had been consigned, the vigor of the younger generation.
And what do you suppose was really on their minds? They were preparing for
death—death on some battlefield as yet unknown, possibly against Poland, for
the liberation of German soil. It was exactly like what Ireland must have been
in 1916, with Pearse and MacDonagh writing sonnets in honor of their
coming patriotic demises. Two of these youngsters were ardent Catholic
aristocrats. They were making monthly retreats so as to be ready to die
worthily when the great crash came! *This is the real thing*—the thing which

dozens of meetings, endless conversations, were to impress upon me as the core of the religion which in those days was struggling to find expression. Part of the creed was set down years ago by Moeller van den Bruck; some of it has never found, never will find, utterance. One has to think of everything Germany has been for more than a thousand years, one must not evaluate the age of Wilhelm II as more than a tawdry episode, one must go to meditate understandingly in the cathedrals of Bamberg, Speyer and Aachen, where the great emperors and their queens have already waited long hundreds of years for the stir of judgment day. Then one must think of what Germany is now, under the burden of ignominy and discrimination, trying hard to comprehend the pull of sacrificial heroism which was tugging these youngsters away from the prosaic here-and-now toward some crusade such as the Irish patriots saw in their dreams.

Nationalism can be a poison fostering the flush of beauty. If one swallows it while one is still young and ardent, it will prove stronger than hashish and more seductive than the glass before which Dr. Faustus lost his soul. What did these German youngsters have against Jews, or Lutherans, or Catholics? Some of them may have gone on a rampage against literature adjudged anti-national or pornographic. Some of them detested the writings of Alfred Kerr and Emil Ludwig—and so, for my part, do I. But all such matters were trifles to them, were incidents born of political agitation, were sores which would heal. What they had in mind was so much purer, nobler, grander, that one almost felt it criminal to refer, at these gatherings, to such earthly occurrences as the brutal floggings which were then daily events in (let us say) the Papestrasse, Berlin. Yes, it was this surge of youth to welcome the embrace of the national ideal which decked out the harlot Hitlerism in a bridal gown of sentiment to which even tired Germany bowed the knee. It is after all an English poet who has said the thing needful:

> Now, God be thanked Who has matched us with His hour,
> And caught our youth, and wakened us from sleeping,
> With hand made sure, clear eye, and sharpened power,
> To turn, as swimmers into cleanness leaping,
> Glad from a world grown old and cold and weary,
> Leave the sick hearts that honour could not move,
> And half-men, and their dirty songs and dreary,
> And all the little emptiness of love!

That is Rupert Brooke, of course, and Rupert Brooke is dead. But if he could have come back to life in 1933, he would have found congenial spirits in that ardent, clean, poisoned young crowd. . . .

Of course for them literally everything was on the verge of transfiguration. Gone forever were the old days of endless partisan wrangling, when fat-bellied defenders of groups and interests bargained in the corridors of the Reichstag for some concession. Rooted out was all special privilege, every form of dishonest juggling with the economic and moral substance of Germany. The nation went arm in arm, nothing was to be thought of any longer save the common good, a comradeship like unto that of heroes on the eve of battle would make the lowly follow the masterful not by reason of any compulsion but because the goal of both was the same. Such were the moods which dozens upon dozens of bright-eyed but exceedingly serious young people tried to convey to you in bookshops, at meetings lasting far into the night, during hours of chance acquaintance. There was nothing specifically German about the content of all this—some of us have met it in Poland, the Ukraine, Ireland or Italy. To me it sounded singularly like a panorama of the future which a pretty English war nurse outlined one afternoon, as the cannon of a month before the armistice were roaring round about Verdun. But there was a German essence in the philosophy distilled from these moods, and in moments of practical reflection one might have fancied it curiously like the perfume hidden in the music of Schubert and the lyrics of Hölderlin.

## II

The harlot Hitlerism. Prior to the time I am describing, ghastly things had happened. We have all of us read enough about them, and if they alone were to be chronicled we might chalk them up to the frenzy of revolution—revolution such as we ourselves are bound to face in the United States some day. Mankind has done worse a thousand times and forgotten about it. How many have a clear impression of what occurred in Russia during 1919? A few months after bloody massacres had been reported in Spain, an editorial writer for the New York *Times* refused to be concerned about them. But unfortunately it was the destiny of German National-Socialism to go on and on until it would seem to the outside world an endless, monstrous nightmare.

Not that one really noticed much as the summer approached. This summer was extraordinarily beautiful. After weeks of rain, a spell of the clearest thinkable weather bathed in cool, pellucid sunshine the long rows of castled towns which extend from Dresden to the Bavarian Alps, through the Schwarzwald and Suabia up the Tauber to the red and yellow mazes of Frankfurt's miraculous streets. I saw places lovely enough to make one fondly count the chances of staying on forever; I looked out at villages through the edges of cool forests and believed they must be fringes of lost Paradise. There is nothing more tragically beautiful in all the world than is Germany from Hildesheim to where the Danube rises between tall cliffs. Nor is there anywhere a people upon whom the lone traveler can count for so much honesty and hospitable kindliness. Hitler was at a mountain resort, surrounded by henchmen, photographers and fools. Somehow it seemed for a time that the land was rid of him—that there were only the people and the ghost of Albrecht Dürer, listening to the horn of some dead Emperor, jovial and solemn both like Charlemagne.

Yet all the while one was oddly conscious of uniforms, now massed and then scattered again. Even when they were not present, they were still somehow part of the scene. The S.A. was always said by journalists to be composed of lads in their teens. But as more and more brown shirts and leather belts passed by in ubiquitous files, singularly intent upon themselves, one's vision became a blur of bloated paunches, bald heads, scarred cheeks, iron crosses and ribands straggling across chests, heavy thighs. Then of course there were also the very young—the *Hitlerjugend*—not swarming everywhere as they would once school began, but in goodly numbers even so and pertly smothered in brown usually too big for them and oddly offensive. Ugly? Yes, but the trouble was not quite that. They degraded something. . . . When morning came, like as not the clatter of shoes on cobble-stones, mingled with staves of harsh songs, would rouse you from sleep; and late at night, if you came in after a day's journey and a meal, some parade of children would rush past you at mad speed. In a certain museum there is a marvelous collection of German faces, painted in the sixteenth and seventeenth centuries; and here or there, in some street of some city, you are sure to meet most of these faces in real life. How was it possible that countenances invariably so grave, almost unworldly, should suddenly throng together in a gross caricature of what one had always felt was the true Germany?

Observing carefully, you began to notice something. It was a fierce desire to be strong—strong through boorishness and violence. Not that one often saw the desire flaring into action. I have been asked for a light by S.A. men, fingering three-pfennig cigarettes; have turned to others for help in finding my way; and have now and then sat with a group of them in a train compartment. But none ever deviated an inch from the shy courtesy which the average German shows to people he doesn't know. Only in the mass did they become something else. They could be and were rude, coarse, barbarous, insulting, cruel. You had glimpses of them, for example, training in city courtyards or out in open country fields. It was not the drill of recruits. It was a kind of rhythmic stripping-off of good nature, and a putting-on of indifference to what has long been called "civilization." The phenomenon is difficult to describe, but it is there. Assembled these people were horrible. They had been trained to listen to nothing save the jargon of soldierly and "mystical" phrases, redolent of leadership, dying, hatred, self-importance, hardness. But when the individual emerged, it was almost as if a woman had suddenly recovered from hysteria.

To come back to the jargon. The anti-Semitism of S.A. and *Hitlerjugend* meetings originated, as I have said and will probably say again, in a skilfully planned attack upon the pacifism of various Jewish writers many of whom were also Marxists. But to-day it has far outstripped its first phase. It is, for the average man who follows Hitler, a mnemonic key. It reminds him of tumultuous, catastrophic, humiliating, bitter, hungry times—times of war and of inflation, of Germany's degradation while Senegambians had brothels in the Rhineland and French poilus quickstepped into the Ruhr Valley—times when the word "Jew" first began to circulate widely among the common people as a designation of the forces, economic and ideological, which cynically wrought destruction and then profited by it. Years ago Ernst Troeltsch expressed somewhere his hope that the stupid anti-Semitism of the inflation era would demonstrate to politicians the need for reason and caution. But the Hitlerites, shrewdly able to divine what slumbered in the breast of *homo civilis,* were not interested in reason or caution. They aroused the beast, and they have not been able to put him to sleep again. The nearer one comes in Germany to the "average man," the closer one is to the pogrom.

The trouble with Jew-baiting in northern Europe (or the United States) is its naturalness. It is the satisfaction of a deep-rooted animal craving. Here again many decades of "civilization" have usually emancipated the individual. People say to you: "I have many Jewish friends, and H____ is a splendid fellow. But . . ." It is the Jew in the mass who offends—the herd which is different from (in an unfathomably strange but real way) our herd. The ordinary German has no Jewish friends. Anti-Semitism is strongest in districts where Hebrews are hardly known excepting as phenomena which appear in the press, on the stage, in the vague contours of banking and "big business." And that is why Hitlerism, creating its own masses, inevitably also stigmatized the misunderstood and hated Jewish mass.

At last, toward the early days of September, the greatest assemblage in the history of the new Germany was gathered together. The *"Parteitag"* at Nuremberg is the most fantastic spectacle which modern Europe has witnessed. This it was not merely by reason of externals, the prodigal expenditure of lumber, bunting, flowers, fireworks, music, oratory which changed the quaint old city into a grotesquely exaggerated county fair of 1905, with a revivalist and William Jennings Bryan come to town. The genuinely extraordinary thing was the emergence of the "vision." It was suddenly learned and believed that National-Socialism had been the fruit of lofty mystical intuitions granted various of its leaders more or less at the same time. Hitler reëmphasized the declaration that Germany's whole future had been revealed to him in a kind of open book first while he was near the trenches and again while he languished in jail. Walther Darré informed a hundred thousand peasants that a number of years ago, as he sat under an apple tree, he was shown in a dream how German rural life was to be transformed. An eminent

Nazi pedagogue revealed to his students that the new educational ideal burst upon him one night as he was awakened by a clap of thunder. There were minor visions just as extraordinary and perhaps even a little more bizarre. All this came to a kind of climax at the time of the Nuremberg meeting, and it was there that Hitler for the first time spoke like a transcendentalist visionary, outlining a doctrine of racial election and fated leadership which sounded exactly like a class essay by a sophomoric Fichte. After that, we all knew there was no hope.

Essentially—let us not forget—there was reason to expect some good from the victory of Hitler. It had catered to the German people's hunger for assertive nationalism not by putting into office a cordon of bushy-browed conservatives but by giving the power to the vastly more democratic, manageable and human "bonus army." It had likewise given form to a social upheaval impossible to postpone much longer—the upheaval of the honest individual "citizen" of traditional Europe against the Marxist system. That system was during many years a genuinely necessary construction. It organized the helots of modern industrialism, made them willing and able to fight against oppression and so saved Europe from the catastrophe of a slave populace so gravely affected by disease and privation as to undermine the stability of the western world. Yet there inevitably came a time when this advance carried the laboring class as such—i.e., the "struggling class" of the Marxists—farther along the road to comfort than the bourgeoisie, ruined by war and other calamities, was able to go. The solid, enterprising person who had saved his money, undertaken some business or pursuit and given thought to his "cultural life," found himself at a grave disadvantage. When a worker or his wife became ill, there was a public hospital and a public doctor. The labor union fought stubbornly against wage decreases. Coöperative stores, banks, insurance companies and housing projects served those who bore the label "worker." But when the professional man, the merchant or the entrepreneur was sick, lost clients, noticed a decrease of earnings or needed money, he found himself alone against the world. Besides he was forever being taxed, through levies or wages, for the upkeep of the worker. Was all this just or necessary? A sullen rage smouldered in the breasts of thousands of such men. But they could not, being individuals, seek redress through collectivism. Their revolution would consist in taking advantage of their innate superiority over the worker—the kind of superiority which finds in political action its natural weapon.

These things were inevitable. Brüning realized them—many other Germans talked of them constantly. But the weakness of the older German reformists was their attachment to now historical ideas and forms of organization. Anchored firmly to the bedrock of precedent, they were not to be shaken loose for agile deployment in a great modern struggle for readjustment.

Hitler, therefore, was the representative of a new force—wild, chaotic but nevertheless rich in energy. He was the man who tapped the gusher. The oil, however, could not be put to use. There was no adequate motor, and apparently nobody to design one. Month after month went by without anything taking place excepting idiotic experiments in political organization and foreign policy. A sane and classical-minded minister of industry applied the brakes every time the ramshackle Nazi car headed straight over an economic cliff, and Hitler himself urged caution as the driver speeded through the traffic snarls of religious and social ideology. But who had either a map or a destination? The visionaries sped on and on, their heads full of schemes as idle as Ernst Hanfstaengel's pseudo-Wagnerian tunes. Hitler's primary concern was race, his favorite instrument still the anti-Semitic drum. Dr. Rosenberg was craftily "fooling" the Poles with a plan for exchanging the Ukraine for the Polish Corridor in advance, while every day brought more news of Polish actions against the German minorities. General Goering continued to wave the baton of Richthofen, dreaming of 100,000 young Nordic "aces." And so forth and so forth. The climax was doubtless reached when Herr Darré, after months of patient research, discovered that behind the Mosaic prohibition of pork there lies a natural incompatibility between this meat and the Jew, who is thereby labeled unfit for the "nobility" which is to rise from the soil. Rarely in the world's history has a minister of agriculture found time to make so remarkable a contribution to anthropology.

The end was more repression—repression which this time expressed itself in law rather than in massacre or wholesale arrest. Germany was too awed and cowed to resist. "Law" is perhaps not the correct word. The Reichstag Fire trial was, as we have seen, an effort on the part of the Nazis to create a bit of confidence in the honesty of the courts; and yet even that trial ended with the conviction of an idiot under an ex-post-facto law. But at all events, a long series of grandiose proclamations were issued by the Cabinet—"laws" concerning the S.A. and the Arbeitdienst; laws effecting the sterilization of the unfit; laws altering the status and activities of labor; laws curtailing the jurisdiction of the states; and laws regulating the conduct of those engaged in agriculture or just plain culture. With every new *Erlass,* the hopes of all who still believed Germany would pull herself together grew fainter. Nor was this all. The various forms of collective endeavor began to reflect the vogue for standardization and terrorism. Student organizations, youth groups, women's associations, press and social clubs—all began to shrivel up in the glare of the hot Nazi fire and turn brown.

Strangest of all was the circumstance that many Germans did not see what was happening. They read morning newspapers with far less of a shock than an interested foreigner experienced. Among my friends was a professor who has several times visited the United States and who is an honest and very intelligent man. During the earlier months of 1933, he had lived in a state of constant alarm, not for personal motives (bravery is a virtue in which he is not lacking) but for nearly every other reason imaginable. But as autumn drew to a close and the corpus of German social tradition was being flayed to the bone, he found it rather odd that an American should be so deeply disturbed. No doubt he was right. I should have been at home minding my own business instead of acquiring a heartache as a result of my fondness for Germany. He himself was proceeding with his lectures, finding S.A. students rather more docile than he had anticipated. Even the pulse of his patriotism seemed to be beating more regularly. In short, his normal personal routine was obliterating most of the social panorama; and the professional rut left him worrying chiefly because a little daughter had to have her tonsils out. So it must have been with literally thousands. They had swallowed so much excitement that they were immune to it.

Possibly the women were least affected, in the sense that under the stress of an enthusiasm blown into Germany each day from a central heating plant each lady could remain her normal self rather better than each gentleman could. Many young ones docilely became veritable storage batteries of patriotic fervor, just as a few years previous they had been obediently pacifistic. They assembled with admirable patience whenever the Nazi muezzin call was sounded; they hoofed up and down streets with passionate zeal; and doubtless the highwater-mark of feminism was reached by a late summer parade in the Rhineland—girls in their early teens chanting vigorously: "*Wir sind deutsche Mädels—wir wollen Kinder kriegen!*" My friend, the Countess X, who has long been generosity itself to me, viewed the whole development with angry amusement. There came to her house one afternoon two advocates of the "new woman." One was the wife of an industrialist, who doted on the peace and quiet which now reigned among wives of factory hands— wives who listened with rapt attention to lectures about Frederick the Great, couldn't get enough of expositions of old peasant gear and positively yearned for information about the Third Reich. The other was the Munich type of feminine Hitlerite, an enormous and explosive creature who leaped from Wagnerian overtures to the degeneracy of the French to the extirpation (*Gott sei Dank!*) of Communism in ecstatic gutturals. It was on that afternoon that I first saw the Countess on the verge of tears. She had lost a husband and a son at the front, her fortune had all but disappeared, she had fended for herself with smiling fortitude, but she had doubtless never felt worse in all her life as she did on this September day. Now the Countess has many peers in Germany, humble and proud. They have kept their presence of mind and their reason far better than the men. But they have watched the German women's movement, once perhaps a model for this kind of thing, dwindle into the primmest conceivable female chauvinism.

At the end of all there was, of course, the religious conflict. Smouldering throughout most of the summer, it developed into a Protestant free-for-all during the last months of the year. I shall never forget the day when Professor Karl Barth delivered his famous challenge to the theological presumption of the state. Countless thousands had been awaiting some word, other thousands had despaired. The older theologians were too tired and cynical to be of much use. They felt certain that any attempt of theirs to address the public would create less impression than the crash of an apple blossom on a lawn. Indeed there were not a few who saw for Christianity no future save a resumption of the hidden life, the state of being hunted and of retreating from the hunter, which had been the lot of believers under the dominion of ancient Rome. Barth could not, it is true, tell these prophets they were mistaken. His was only the refusal to burn incense or to surrender the tables of the law. And after him there came a vast congregation of protesters, difficult to organize but impossible to ignore. But the god of unreason, who after a hundred and fifty years followed the goddess of reason (each the ultimate typical idol of a people), has not dragged his foes by the cartload to the guillotine. He does not confer upon his victims the dreadful liberation which is death, but the long slavery of silence, suffering, hunger and ridicule of the mob.

# III

The decision to leave Geneva and to arrange for a plebiscite of the German people came as a surprise not merely to diplomats but to the public also. It is as certain as anything can be that such a step was not premeditated. Up until the very day of the news, even persons exceptionally well informed took it for granted that Hitler would bombard the League with orators, arguments and threats until he got some concession with which to justify his policies as the dictator of Germany's foreign relations. There is, indeed, excellent reason to believe that plans had been made to play up a "victory" for domestic consumption. Precisely what caused the sudden shift in the weather is known only to those who belong to the inner council of Nazidom. Perhaps the defection of Mussolini may have been in part responsible. Perhaps it was—as I have remarked previously—disappointment at the attitude taken by the British.

At any rate, the decision unquestionably did reckon with the state of German psychology during October. There was noticeable something like a vague drift toward a monarchist *putsch*. Economic dissatisfaction had grown; the rift between orthodox conservative Lutheranism and the government was wide; there was sharp criticism of various policies in important army circles; and the virtual suppression of the Stahlhelm had caused a good deal of bitterness. Old guard nationalists, when a little befuddled, would tell you that they were shocked at the way things were going. Professor Spengler had published a review of the Hitler "revolution" which sold well over a hundred thousand copies, despite any number of remarks uncomplimentary to the great Adolf. Other and less famous authors had continued the investigation, under thicker veils, so that plenty of critical literature was on hand well in advance of Christmas.

Whatever else the departure from Geneva may have done, it certainly scotched the monarchists. Hitler now opened a whooping electoral campaign and served up piping hot the favorite nationalist theme—"Down with the Treaty of Versailles, away with the League of Nations!" Every leather-lung and every available brown-shirt was called out of billets and sent to the oratorical front. The billboards were festooned with more posters than there are spots on a dowdy restaurant window; the radio turned out appeals as if they were sausages, steaming and peppery; every voyager entering the country was searched for literature of a subversive nature; and the air was charged with something like the fumes of vodka in a room stifling full. Orders were given that when Hitler delivered the final message all good citizens would be found listening. It was great theatre. To an American hailing from the Middle West, it was of course a bit reminiscent of thundery stock shows. Not all the Germans ate it up. Many in all ranks and classes of society made wry faces; not a few snarled. But there is no doubt that the great middle class, which is now thumping up and down most of Europe with a sabre pinned to its trousers, was immensely stirred and edified. The vote which followed was to some extent merely the electorate's way of taking out one form of insurance policy. But the typical burgher voted and did not vomit afterward.

From that day to this the opposition in Germany has, so far as I can see, been crushed. Many of the nation's most competent minds ask themselves: Is this what the people really want? Or do they know either what they want or what they are getting? One experienced person said to me that Germany so seldom had a civic idea that when it found one, good or evil, it clung to it for dear life. There is something in that. The Germans, whose achievements make them one of the great peoples, do not know how to think or feel collectively. A notion which gets into general circulation plays the devil with them. There was the War, for instance, which they could not stop. And after the War there was (for example) neo-Malthusianism which swept like a plague through the world but was in Germany a fit of madness. Women literally stood in line waiting to be relieved of the fearful possibility that they might have children. Some years later, apocalyptic fancies swept the country, so that Pastor Russell's forecasts of the millennium corrupted even orthodox Christian neighborhoods. To-day it is the cult of race which evokes frenzy and fear. If it were not for the tenacious, stubborn, hard-headed toil of numerous individuals, who blow the bellows of criticism all the harder because the wind is against them, the intellectual climate of Germany—which has never been, in the true sense, a land of inner unity—would be just an everlasting tornado.

To-day National-Socialism is the form of irrationalism which passes from hand to hand. Nobody can stop it now, or even successfully oppose it. The only possible hope lies with the quiet band of those who, like their predecessors in all generations, watch the mob go by and still seek after truth. The genuine German is not always, like Dr. Faustus, persuaded to go out and join the crowd. For hundreds of years he has maintained a reputation for stubbornly clinging to his own personality, and I do not think he will abandon the task now. Above all we must remember that his position is not singular. It is now the status of the civilized man in virtually the whole of Europe. A storm is sweeping across the western world, we can do no more than hope that there are cellars where the light of the mind of man is kept aglow. . . .

The lowlands north of Bremen receded from view under a wintry sky. What was one to say of the whole that had been witnessed? I thought of tales told by men who had sat during long weeks in concentration camps, of brutal deeds the evidence for which was undeniable, of the enormous lusts which the Hitler movement as a whole represents. Would any just cause be served strangely by all this rampage of horror and idiocy? Or was the cause of mankind a lost cause? It was then that I remembered the law of compensations. If the tragedy which stalks all our endeavor is somehow engrained in the very structure of our world, it may be that our common history is more an affair of seasons than we customarily suppose. Perhaps humanity slays its best because these no longer live intensely enough. The civilization which Europe is now eradicating, slowly but surely, was full of tares and imperfections but it was, no doubt, primarily too rich in relative perfection. The man and woman who constituted the types of tolerance, wisdom, cultivated taste and sense of duty had—compared with the status of the race as a whole—reached a point where they were like ears of wheat in late autumn. No longer quite aware of their social function, they existed for the contemplation of their own selves. Therefore, as so often in the past, the primitive slays the aristocrat. But in so doing this primitive sentences himself to a long, slow, infinitely sacrificial climb. It may take hundreds of years. That doesn't matter.

# Adolf Hitler
# and the Second World War

It is still too early to record the events that followed the nazi seizure of the government. One may, however, attempt to chronicle the more obvious happenings and to adjudge the significant changes in German life. The story develops, first of all, out of a marked difference between the objectives of Hitlerism and the setting in which it rose to power. While the movement was violently revolutionary, it captured the government legally, with the help of conservative groups that were in revolt against the international order established by the Treaty of Versailles and the League of Nations, but that were, in so far as Germany itself was concerned, counter-revolutionary. The abolition of parliamentary rule through the Enabling Act meant that prodemocratic forces no longer counted, and that the sole political struggle of consequence would have to take place between nazis and conservatives inside the government.

During the first period of the Hitler dictatorship, which lasted until June 6, 1936, when the German police were unified under the command of Heinrich Himmler, the nazi bid for absolute control was still opposed by powerful German influences. Indeed, the early months of the regime bore a conservative stamp. The Foreign Office was in a position to dictate the relatively moderate pronouncements of Hitler on the subject of German relations with other countries. Conservatives in the economic ministries initiated and carried out a program of expansion, thus reducing unemploy-

From *Germany: A Short History* by George N. Shuster and Arnold Bergstraesser (New York: W. W. Norton & Co., 1944), pp. 201-215. Reprinted by permission of the publisher.

ment and getting the labor market under a measure of control. Economic autarchy was to some extent achieved with the help of drastic financial methods. Even the special moral concerns of the Hugenberg group seemed to be reflected in efforts to stamp out prostitution, to cleanse the stage, and to censor literary production.

Nevertheless the nazi goal clearly was the removal of opponents inside Germany and the utilization, for rearmament purposes, of unrest and dissension in other countries. The principal weapon was the Versailles Treaty, referred to at home as an indictment of the Republic that had signed it, and quoted abroad as a basis for appealing to consciences made uneasy by years of historical and economic criticism of the peace. German political groups that had contested the rise of nazism were systematically destroyed. The Social Democratic party and the trade unions affiliated with it could offer no resistance other than the propagandist efforts financed with funds transferred to neighboring countries. Communists were ferreted out, and even to some extent absorbed into nazi organizations. The Center party was dissolved. The Vatican signed a concordat with Hitler upon the advice of German bishops and prelates who deemed resistance imprudent. Even the German National party broke up under pressure, despite Hugenberg's appeal to the president for support. On July 14, 1933, attempts to organize political parties were outlawed. Two months earlier, the offices and funds of the labor unions had been seized by the Nazi party.

Meanwhile the Reichswehr, under the command of the enigmatic Blomberg, professed its neutrality. Former officers, assigned to new government bureaus, were drawing up plans, many of them wholly unorthodox from the official military point of view, for training the Third Reich in the arts of total war. The first steps were taken toward building up an air force. Laws that subordinated the federal states to the central government enabled the nazi dictatorship to control and militarize the police. The Labor Service, gradually extended and finally made compulsory on June 26, 1935, was an auxiliary military organization. Concentration camps, at first erected to detain enemies of the regime, were expanded and developed into stern, even barbarous instruments of repression. The Hitler Youth, embracing both boys and girls, offered physical training preparatory to military and government service, but served primarily as a means for the indoctrination and surveillance of youth. Most important of all, possibly, was the new secret police—the Gestapo— which was organized during 1934 on the model of the Russian Ogpu.

All cultural and propagandist agencies were subordinated to government control. Under the leadership of Joseph Goebbels, an opportunistic intellectual who had helped to make possible the rise of Hitler to power, the press and the radio blotted out every trace of the German democratic tradition. Books by dissident authors were burned and banned. Newspapers were controlled with an iron hand. It slowly became impossible for writers, thinkers and teachers not in sympathy with the party to express their views. Nevertheless, though the record of the great papers and of the universities is deplorable, a large number of dauntless spirits did display extraordinary bravery and persistence. They were listened to in religious and labor circles particularly. Even after years of oppression, men like the scientist Max Planck and the writer Ernst Wiechert spoke fearlessly and at the risk of their lives.

## Public Opinion and the Nazis

That these somber attacks upon the basic freedom of the people were so successful can be accounted for in part by the complete dependence of nearly all Germans upon a daily wage, and indeed upon employment, directly or indirectly, by the state. Men rescued from the maw of inflation years previously could not face the threat of abject poverty which haunted every dissenter. And when they did stand their ground, they did so conscious of what might be their fate in a concentration camp. Conditions inside those camps were horrible. Yet it is also true that the German nation had lost its soul, not only by reason of enervating philosophic and political doctrine, though that abounded, but also because of the indescribable weariness that affected particularly many of those who for years had stood in the vanguard of the republican cause. Leaders had lost faith in the people, and these in turn had listened to so much argument and oratorical noise that they craved to be left alone. The average German had no desire to prepare for war, and his spirit froze when he thought of 1918. Therefore he blindly hoped that things would not turn out so badly as the pessimists predicted, and that nazism was intended for domestic consumption only.

It should be noted that as a whole the civil service was immune to the nazi ideology. The great majority of the career officials wanted no adventures and were prone to be critical or even somewhat ostentatiously hostile. The reservoirs of nazism, apart from the discontented war veterans and the unemployed, were the white-collar groups and women of the middle classes. Here resentment, opportunism and emotion were prevalent. Support was skillfully solicited by fostering loves and hates. Young families, for example, were encouraged by grants of aid, and on the other hand illegitimate children were, at first timidly and then openly, declared welcome additions to the population. Anti-Semitism as well as antipathy to all foreigners, including Americans, made many Germans swallow hard. Relatively few wished to indulge in orgies of detestation. Religious passions were excited, but with the strange result that Protestants and Catholics began to have a deep regard for one another, while internecine strife inside both confessions assumed formidable proportions. The first of many nazi "plebiscites" was staged (November, 1933) and huge majorities were reported in favor of the government's foreign policy.

And yet the nazis unquestionably did not win the support of German public opinion as a whole. They were applauded and feared, but they were not believed by many. Since open opposition was impossible under laws that suppressed freedom of speech and assembly, recourse was had to the fiction that whereas Hitler had acquired the virtues hitherto attributed to Hindenburg, his followers were conducting themselves, without his knowledge, in scoundrelly fashion. Many induced themselves to believe this Hitlerian legend. By the spring of 1934, the German right was thoroughly sick of the nazis. Papen delivered at Marburg a fighting speech, written by Edgar Jung, demanding the end of outrages. On June 30, Hitler replied with a "purge." Many prospective victims were warned and fled the country. Others, certainly more than a thousand in number, were shot without trial. The massacre clearly reflected the origins and character of the nazi mentality. The sincere revolutionists in the party, Roehm, Gregor Strasser, Heydebreck and others, were callously murdered. The conservative opposition was dealt a savage blow. Schleicher and Bredow, Klausener and Kahr, were among the victims. Vengeance was also taken on almost forgotten enemies. Thus, prior to the murder of Rathenau, a priest came to see Chancellor Wirth on behalf of a young penitent who had shared in the plot. That penitent was Arnold Probst, who later became a Catholic youth leader. On June 30, the long arm of nazi retribution struck him down, thus revealing clearly the pathology of a movement rooted in frustration. When Hindenburg, near death, did not act to empower army leaders to prevent or punish this mass murder, opposition in Germany was dealt a mortal blow. The "revolution of nihilism" now went on uninhibited, corroding and perverting the substance of German society.

Meanwhile other nations, undermined by the depression and acrimonious class conflict, by scandal and political ineptitude, did not take the menace of nazism at its face value. A "preventive war" urged by Marshal Pilsudski was not even seriously discussed. Russia, where *Mein Kampf* had been read, joined the League of Nations in 1934 in order to foster collective security, and shortly thereafter signed a pact with France. The French and the British were divided by varying concepts of European policy and by alien patterns of social thought. In France a conservative movement strongly fascist in character plotted dictatorship, with the knowledge and perhaps the support of Germany; and in Britain a "businessman's government" assumed that the nazis, if left to their own devices, would provide a strong buffer, or possibly more, against Russia. When a popular-front government was formed in France, and when civil war broke out in Spain, the British became still more "realistic." The League of Nations failed to prevent a Japanese coup in Manchukuo, by reason of a lack of understanding between London and

Washington; and it virtually signed its death warrant when it did not impede Italy's seizure of Ethiopia, restricted as it was by the oscillating policies of France and Great Britain.

The democratic idea was facing as severe a test as that endured by feudalism in the eighteenth century. One after another of its bastions and its pseudo-democratic supports fell. Chancellor Engelbert Dollfuss of Austria strove to ward off the menace of Hitlerism. But before long—the fault was by no means his alone—he had suppressed the socialists, abolished the parliament, and made common cause with profascist groups. King Alexander of Yugoslavia was slain by assassins at Marseilles. Poland attempted to play the Russians against the Germans. Mussolini, at first determined to keep Austria from being forced into the nazi orbit, gradually became economically dependent upon Germany. In France, Léon Blum did not combine badly needed social reforms with a successful appeal to the nation's patriotism. The Spanish war ended with a Franco victory, by reason primarily of "nonintervention." Profascist organizations sprang up even in England and the United States. Meanwhile Russia witnessed a series of trials which doomed veteran fighters for the Soviet cause.

German rearmament could therefore get underway, to the accompaniment of oppression. Attacks on the Protestant and Catholic churches sent hundreds of clergymen to prison. The campaign against the Jew was marked by increasingly destructive legislation. Laws issued (1935) at Nuremberg separated the Jewish group from the German people, and threatened a large "non-Aryan" population with economic extinction. For all oppressed minorities the courts, which at first were still impartial except when extreme leftists were on trial, slowly ceased to be places of defense against injustice. But although the task of rebuilding the armed forces was facilitated first by a decree that re-established universal military service and then by a treaty with Great Britain which permitted expansion of the German navy, there were manifest weaknesses both of equipment and of organization. It was conservative Britain that aided the nazis to overcome some of these handicaps, by extending credits for the purchase of such vital raw materials as nickel and copper, and by actually sharing in the erection of armament plants. Bankers and others believed that only the munitions industry could solve the riddle of unemployment, and fancied that if Germans got jobs, sanity would return. French conservatives shared in this delusion, though they may have been motivated primarily by a dread of leftism at home.

By 1936, the disarray was so complete that Hitler was ready to gamble. His own people had now endowed him with absolute power. One day prior to the death of President von Hindenburg (August 2, 1934), the offices of chancellor and president were united in Hitler's person. This legislation was confirmed by a plebiscite on August 19. Therewith all vestiges of German constitutional tradition and principle were removed, and the "leadership" of the *Führer* could be delegated to absolutistic subordinates in every government agency throughout the country. The end had almost come even for the still somewhat independent Foreign Office, for the star of Joachim von Ribbentrop was rising. Hitler began by proclaiming his ardent desire for peace. Then he suddenly ordered German troops to occupy the Rhineland, despite the express caveat of the Versailles Treaty. Fewer than thirty thousand troops marched in, much against the wishes of the high command, which gave orders that the soldiers were to retreat if resistance was offered. But the French, unable to secure a British promise of support, took no action. Hitler obtained a stupendous victory. He formally renounced the Treaty of Versailles and also the Locarno Pact. Now he was free to fortify the western boundaries of Germany and to erect the so-called Westwall, which would effectively prevent France from going speedily to the aid of her allies in the east of Europe.

The general political situation thus created was promptly reflected in events of great significance. The Rome-Berlin axis was formed on October 27, 1936, indicating that Mussolini had definitely broken the ties that had bound Italy to the Western Powers during so many years. Two weeks previous, Belgium had disavowed her military alliance with France, in view of the German threat, and received in exchange Hitler's guarantee of the inviolability of Belgian neutrality. Then, on November 17, Germany and Japan signed an agreement known as the Anti-Comintern Pact. In three months the *Führer* had wrested the initiative from the French and had obtained a relatively free hand in the east. Only his intentions toward Russia remained uncertain. And it was perhaps for this reason that some French and British observers were still inclined to be lackadaisical, if not optimistic. Even yet the democracies did not undertake the task of rearmament with the requisite earnestness.

Hitler did turn east. A previous abortive nazi uprising in Austria had been put down, so that to this small country goes the honor of having been the first to resist the Germans. Even so the nazis considered Austria to be part and parcel of the Third Reich. Dollfuss was murdered shortly after the "purge" in Germany. HIs successor, Kurt von Schuschnigg, may fairly be said to have lacked energy, but at least he was not, like so many of his associates in the government of his unhappy country, a traitor to its best interests. Having assured himself that Mussolini would not intervene a second time, Hitler summoned the Austrian chancellor to a conference at mountain-fringed Berchtesgaden; and a few days later, on March 12, 1938, Austria was invaded and annexed, after Schuschnigg had resorted to the desperate expedient of a plebiscite on the subject of Austrian independence. It is to the chancellor's lasting credit that he did not flee but remained to submit to nazi vengeance. The banks of the country were looted, and it itself made a province of Greater Germany. The Gestapo and its Austrian affiliates, aided by local sympathizers of the nazi cause, organized a violent purge and pogrom. Thousands were sent to Dachau and other notorious concentration camps. Jewish property was confiscated. This consciously fomented wave of anti-Jewish terrorism, the worst Europe had seen since the Middle Ages, was followed during November of the same year by a bloody pogrom inside Germany itself. Catholicism in Austria suffered almost as severely.

Meanwhile Czechoslovakia had been threatened. It was alleged that the inhabitants of the German portion (Sudetenland) of the little Republic desired the protection of the Third Reich. Konrad Henlein, leader of the German minority, presented a number of demands at Hitler's request. In view of the changed international situation, these demands constituted a kind of ultimatum. The British government dispatched a commission, headed by Lord Runciman, to study the question; and the mere fact that it was sent was enough to indicate that the prime minister, Neville Chamberlain, had decided further to appease Hitler. The Czechs, however, endeavored to hold France to her pledge of support. By late summer of 1938 the danger of war was great. At the height of the crisis Chamberlain, after telling the British people that Czechoslovakia was remote from the sphere of their vital interests, went to see Hitler at Godesberg. There and at a conference held in Munich (September 29) the *Führer* was given what he desired. The Sudeten territories were ceded to Germany, and few doubted that despite a nazi promise to respect the boundaries of what remained of the little Czech republic, Hitler would soon be in Prague. Great Britain and France guaranteed the integrity of the new border, but President Benes resigned on October 5, and the next day Slovakia seceded and proclaimed its autonomy. During the next month of March, Hitler annexed Czechia and declared Slovakia a German protectorate.

The surrender of Austria and Czechoslovakia was effected without loss to the Germans of enormous military and economic advantages. A substantial reserve of gold and foreign exchange remained in the banks of Austria until the nazis confiscated them. And the Czechs, victims of attacks, desertion and utopian political ideas, permitted the Skoda Works, doubtless Europe's greatest arsenal, to fall into Hitler's hands intact, together with great stores of rubber and large fleets of tanks. That neither the French nor the British made any serious attempt to prevent these disasters is clear evidence of the weakness and blindness with which the democracies were stricken. But in the case of Britain, the malady was only superficial. When on October 9, 1938, Hitler spoke at Saarbrücken, gloating over his victories and deriding Chamberlain, the tide began slowly to turn. His ruthless march to Prague and his annexation of the Skoda Works were still ruder shocks.

Then during March, 1939, the German government settled down to even more important business. A note to Warsaw suggested that significant problems were in need of solution; and when the Poles took alarm, strong language was used in Berlin. But this time the British, it may be quixotically, took a firm stand. On April 6, 1939, the text of a promise given to the Poles by Chamberlain was published. Obviously the British were not yet averse to appeasement, but they were determined that they could have no share in the destruction of another free nation. But the nazi leaders would offer no concessions. Firmly persuaded that the "decadent English" could not fight, they prepared to force the issue with Poland. It was, of course, to their great advantage that the Russians, angered and disturbed by the obvious implications of the Munich Conference, now sought to reach an understanding with the Germans. On May 3, Maxim Litvinov, advocate of collective security, was replaced by V. M. Molotov; on August 19, a commercial treaty was signed by Germany and Russia; and four days later a fateful nonaggression pact was announced. This last was the stroke of lightning which brought war to the world. A few belated efforts to save the peace failed, and for propagandist reasons the German Foreign Office announced a post-mortem compromise solution of the dispute with Poland. On September 1, Hitler's army attacked without a declaration of war.

Thus there was referred to the judgment of arms an issue deeply embedded in the recent history of Europe. The borders of the new Russian state had been fixed by Germany. Ludendorff had compelled the bolsheviki to accept a peace that deprived the empire of the Czars of Baltic territory once to some extent colonized by Germans, of a broad strip of the Ukraine, and of Finland. But although the victorious Allies did not undo the work of Brest-Litovsk they established a new Poland on a basis as unacceptable to the Germans as to the Russians. A "corridor" was opened to the Baltic across the territory of the Reich; the ancient Hanseatic city of Danzig was made a "free city," administered by the League of Nations; and after bloody fighting subsequent to acrimonious plebiscites, large portions of Silesia were ceded to Poland. Thus there came into being a state that could not be maintained except by force either against dissolution from within or against pressure from without. The world was on the side of a free Poland, but the problems of that Poland had not been solved.

During the years after 1918, the initiative lay with the Russians. They attempted first of all to sovietize Germany, in the hope of then being able to squeeze Poland and the succession states between two Marxist powers. This attempt was not abandoned until Hitler came to power. The history of the Communist party under the Weimar Republic reflects the determination of the Russians to make this party an instrument of Soviet policy. German "comrades" who tried to adapt the program to the German scene were systematically removed from party offices, and instead men wholly subordinate to the will of Moscow received the blessing of the Comintern. In the end the lack of realism that characterized German communism shocked even its own intelligent exponents. What could they make of an order to strike in association with nazi labor groups, for example? The party became the "grave digger of the German Republic" primarily because it was compelled to act as if the triumph of Hitler would lead automatically to a proletarian dictatorship. This delusion was the principal characteristic of Stalin's early years in the Kremlin.

On the other hand, the Russians had also sought the friendship of Germany on a realistic basis. That the two countries could collaborate politically as well as economically became perhaps the principal doctrine of the German Foreign Office after 1918, and it did everything it could to establish a durable and profitable alliance. Relationships between the army leaders in both countries were also for a long time cordial. Nevertheless after the death of Lenin disillusionment became widespread in German circles, and by 1930 many had come to believe that the imperialism of Stalin differed from that of the Czars only in ideological coloring. The initiative then passed slowly to the Germans, and the idea of a continental bloc against the Russians became a popular concept in Western Europe. It was this idea that proved of such value to Hitler, who created an illusion of conservatism which died slowly.

Poland was the unfortunate victim of this situation. She had once had a choice between two courses of action. And when in 1932 her statesmen sought an agreement with the Weimar Republic, which was even then eager to establish cordial relations, they were too late to prevent what later happened. No doubt the Poles had suffered too intensely. National feeling, which often rose to fever heat, could not countenance the concessions that would have been necessary after 1918. The boundary that ran from Gydnia, the newly created seaport, to Kattowice was, therefore, a long open sore. A million Germans were ejected from their homes in territories ceded to Poland. Mistreatment of the German minority became a cause for League intervention. On the other hand, Polish relations with Russia were equally troubled. An early postwar invasion by bolshevist armies, instigated, it may be, by Polish designs on the Ukraine, was repelled with French help. But the victory was followed only by what must be termed a long truce. The second course of action was the creation of an army powerful enough to defend the country. This was attempted; and by a superhuman effort Poland made herself a military state whose position was not hopeless so long as the Germans remained weak.

Yet it was precisely this militarization that kindled German desire for rearmament and sapped the strength of pacifism. If Poland could rely on armed might, why should Germany, it was argued, expect to get what she considered justice and security with any other means? The support that Hitler received no doubt derived, in so far as it was genuinely patriotic, from those

who resented what was happening in the east. And therefore it was inevitable
that Germany and Russia should some time agree to seek redress for what
they deemed common grievances. That when the moment came it brought a
fantastic agreement between Hitler and Stalin is surely ironical. Neither
dictator looked upon the pact as being more than a ruse. The Russians were
enabled to push their zone of defense westward. Hitler was merely biding his
time. In this cynical fashion, by depriving revolutionary ideologies of every
vestige of their original significance, did the tragedy of the Second World War
begin.

## Hitler's Responsibility for the War

An hour before the fearful attack that would lay Poland waste was set in
motion, Hitler called a learned aide and asked the question, "Who was
Genghis Khan?" In all truth memories associated with a famous ancient
scourge of mankind pale into insignificance when one tries to estimate the
blood and tears which in these our days an unsuccessful Austrian painter,
become dictator of Germany, has exacted of mankind. History will, one
thinks, hold him and some of his henchmen solely and fully responsible for
the outbreak of the greatest war in human annals. It may be that he did not
envisage a worldwide conflict, even though his diplomats and officers had
reached a kind of agreement with Japan and were busily fomenting trouble in
India. The purpose of these and kindred maneuvers may have been to keep
Great Britain and the United States occupied until the Third Reich should
have grown strong enough to control for a century or more the destinies of
mankind. Humanity may never possess the information on which to base an
accurate and realistic appraisal of Hitler's true purpose. But it will remain
forever evident that the democracies, for all their faults and failures, wanted
no new holocaust of the peoples and were therefore ready to make costly
sacrifices. Hitler, on the other hand, plotted a war of vengeance and of
conquest. He was the conscious builder of the world's doom.

The question of the responsibility of the German people for the outbreak
of hostilities is likely to be debated for many years. Certainly that people
cannot be divorced from its government. Had there not been many millions
who cast their ballots for nazism, the events of the year 1933 could not have
taken place. And if there had existed any widespread conviction that war
would spell the doom of European civilization, even the Gestapo would have
found it difficult to get the military machine into even and successful motion.
All trustworthy evidence indicates, however, that the discernible trend of
public opinion was overwhelmingly in favor of peace. The steps by which the
Hitler government led Germany into war were so gradual and so well masked
by a controlled press and a propagandist radio that very few had any insight

into the dire import of what was happening. At the time of the Munich Conference (1938) a wave of fear was so strong that every foreign observer on the spot referred to it. The Germans, even the military leadership itself, greatly overestimated the military strength of France, and were restrained by anxiety if not by ardent antipathy to militarism. Hitler's unqualified victory over Chamberlain and Daladier therefore had a moral effect comparable to that which resulted from President von Hindenburg's inability to exact an accounting of those who carried out the blood purge of 1934. The old world of ethics seemed to have gone together with the once stable world of the balance of power. The German who was not deluded no longer had a place in the realm of reality on which to stand. Later on, when the fact that a new world war was in progress had become evident, he and all he had and hoped to be was caught up in the struggle for his country. That, it would appear, is all one can at present report of this somber and incredibly tragic story.

# Some Reflections on Spain

I know very little about Spain. This is apparently not a circumstance which need deter one from writing about that country, if the majority of those now vocal are any criterion. The remarks which follow will endeavor to answer some recent criticisms of *The Commonweal*, particularly those which have been directed at the publication of "European Catholics and Spain" in a recent issue. They are not to be interpreted as an apology either for ourselves or for Barbara Barclay Carter. She needs none, having a long and brilliant record for disinterested service in the Catholic cause. Our policy has always tried to be one of courtesy toward the truth—which means that we have striven to place facts first and interpretations second, even when the interpretations are our own.

It would be deplorable if the unutterably tragic conflict which has decimated Spain and the Church in Spain should lead in this country to a kind of literary civil war serving no other purpose than to emphasize anew certain deep-seated and calamitous partizanships. During several years we here have tried to familiarize Americans with the perilous unsettlement of Europe. In times when it was fashionable to regard our attitude as "too somber" or "too remote from normal interests" we were predicting a number of things which have since happened. That record speaks for itself, and I am quite willing that it be compared with the achievement of any periodical in our field. Why, then, should it be assumed rather arbitrarily that on the subject of Spain *The Commonweal* is following some kind of will-o'-the-wisp?

George N. Shuster, "Some Reflections on Spain," *The Commonweal*, April 2, 1937, pp. 625-627. Reprinted by permission of *The Commonweal*.

I feel that many, whose motives are of the highest, have taken the Spanish tragedy (and beyond that the European tragedy) far too lightly. The picture as painted is: a republican government fell under the sway of Communists who began to perform every kind of injustice; and thereupon some fine old soldiers rallied all stanch Catholics to safeguard religious and national rights against tyranny. This act of rebellion was legitimate, since the government overthrown was elected through fraud and was later guilty of violating the Constitution. If General Franco had waited another month, all the priests and religious in Spain would have been shot. Proof of this is found in the fact that hundreds have been massacred wherever the Reds have gained control. Catholics everywhere ought, therefore, to support the Insurgent cause and to hope for the speedy destruction of all Marxists. Of course a few benighted persons have ventured to differ from these conclusions. But it can easily be shown that they are tainted with "liberalism," or guilty of French patriotic emotions, or singularly unfamiliar with logic and moral theology.

This analysis is of course in part correct but has three major faults; and I shall try to show what I think they are. First, a great many unimpeachable Catholics do not believe all of it. The European press has been impressively reluctant to commit itself to any such thesis. I wish we had either in this country or in England a journal as free of chauvinism in every form as is *Esprit*. To accuse it of "natural" French sympathies with a Popular Front government in Spain is to demonstrate that one has not read it. During 1933, I made a special trip to London in the hope of inducing some Catholic papers to make a fuss about the laws against non-Aryan Christians then about to be promulgated in Germany. Had such a protest come from England at that time, much might have been accomplished. But to my amazement I found that these gentlemen looked upon every adverse reference to Hitler as "French propaganda." Perhaps there is an unregenerate streak in me, but ever since then I have found it difficult to believe that the palm for objective visualization of major Catholic problems was to be hung on certain quasi-official door-posts in London. And when it so happens that the *Esprit* point of view, which is very critical of the Franco movement as a champion of religion and culture, finds support in leading, veteran journals in France, Austria, Switzerland and Germany, one cannot help avoiding the obvious conclusion.

These journals all point out that no authoritative verdict on the situation is available. It has been suggested that Miss Carter is hardly a moral theologian. I answer, who in this case is? If he be available, he ought to emerge at once and put us all at our ease. Until then it is probably safe to assume that the Holy Father is best qualified to speak. If his allocutions mean anything, it is this: the Church, fully aware that the background of the Spanish conflict is the assumption that religion must be saved by Fascism, warns the faithful against falling into this trap. The Pope wanted Catholic neutrality in Spain. He made the magnificent but immemorially Christian suggestion that it is better to suffer than to do evil.

That evil has been done on both sides is the unanimous contention of the journals referred to. Perhaps only in America are there many naive enough to believe that the present Valencia government is anything much better than an aggregation of oratorical mortals trying to get the bull populace to see something besides a red rag. It is shocking to think that ninety-two writers—no matter how idealistic and intelligent—could be found in and about New York to underwrite what honest French radicals have repudiated in their journals. But shall we also be obliged to record the equally shocking fact that Catholics are ready to ignore the manifest brutality, reactionary political method and intellectual simplicity of the Francoites? No detailed history of the outrages and the blunders of the Insurgents need be written. It must suffice to declare that the person who set the wheels to grinding out propaganda for Franco as the saviour of religion and culture was that eminent defender of the faith, Dr. Goebbels, while the person who has done most to undermine that illusion is the great, dead Miguel de Unamuno. When Unamuno said first of all that he favored the Right against the Left, he spoke for all of us. If one must have a dictator, let it be the best available. But after he had seen too, too many things, there was only one step Unamuno could take—resign from the university, go into seclusion and die there of a broken heart.

European Catholics know and say in addition that no one can ignore what is doubtless the most poignant aspect of the whole civil war—the struggle of the Basques to escape from the clutches of an iron totalitarianism that would automatically destroy their age-old culture. The three Basque provinces are the Ireland of the Iberias. Nowhere else in the world is Catholicism more autochthonous, and nowhere else is it more social-minded. This region is not merely devastated by war. Its priests have been torn from their churches by Insurgent troops and shot down in cemeteries and prison yards. Its schools and its places of meeting have been closed. Its visions of a measure of independence have been threatened with extinction. The emissaries it has sent to other countries have been ignored. Some of us may be pardoned for a weakness that is doubtless sentimental, atavistic—a weakness which suggests to us that if we elected to stand anywhere in this terrible struggle it would be with the people who have defended Bilbao and Irun. For somehow we cannot forget that our fathers loved freedom.

The second fault with the analysis quoted cuts deeper. Spain is a terribly sad example of a country the people of which have in great part lost their faith. Why should this have happened, and how can the evil be overcome? During 1933, a visitor to one of the great cathedral towns of southern Spain saw that besides himself only two old women heard Mass in the minster on Sunday morning. The fact startled him, even as the more bloody fact that priests and religious are tortured and murdered by warring mobs startles us now. In 1931, Father Ludwig Veit wrote, for Kirsch's "Kirchengeschichte," his two volumes on the story of the Church in the nineteenth century. He has been criticized for a too conservative attitude, so that no defense is necessary. Father Veit showed how the whole period, especially the time of Espartero, has forced the Spanish Church into dependence upon a State hostile to even elementary demands of social justice; and he indicated that unless the problems confronting peasant and worker were somehow solved, the blows that would some day be struck at religion might be like those of the French Revolution.

For this inability to exercise leadership in the practical realization of fundamental moral principles, the Church is only relatively to blame. It was tied hand and foot to a régime against which papal complaints were powerless; and so, no doubt, one must beware of criticism that saddles the major responsibility upon the clergy. It is very true, of course, that—as the German observer, Cramer von Bessel, says—no real advantage was taken of opportunities afforded by the revolution of 1931. Now the Church was free, and brilliant leaders like Father Palau were available. But too many were sound asleep, and the despair of a Catholic proletariat was the beginning of a triumphant Marxism and Anarchism.

The present dilemma is therefore a dreadful one. Shall the Church again live under the thumb of a reactionary, militarist régime, which has sent Moors to smash the organizations of workingmen and peasants? Is such a policy, historically responsible for the decline of faith, to be relied upon now as a missionary enterprise? To those who believe that General Franco will inaugurate a beneficent and progressive social order I shall reply very simply that yesterday was not my natal morn. Shall we then say that the Church is to seek, through years of martyrdom, a new contact with the people, snatching wherever it can brands from the fire of a Bolshevist dictatorship? That is something about which heroic poetry can be written, but from the thought of which every man shrinks in horror. It means being hunted down and despised, while one sees hatred squeeze life out of the souls of even the elect.

It is a heartrending prospect, but it must be confronted honestly if one hopes to grasp the import of what is happening. In Wordsworth's "Prelude," a passage describes the poet's sensations as he went into the Grande Chartreuse just as revolutionary troops were driving out the monks; and the agony with which he weighed in his own mind the conflict between aspirations to lawful freedom and addiction to traditional faith must be repeated now in many a heart. But surely this can be said. Was the kind of freedom the Church enjoyed in the France of Louis XIV a greater treasure than the brunt of persecution under Robespierre? The consequence of that "freedom" was that France almost lost the Faith—lost it to such an extent that even most of the religious orders could not withstand the impact of Revolution and apostatized. But to one Sisterhood that remained steadfast and went to the guillotine singing, there was later given as a reward the most beloved saint of the nineteenth century; and if there were no other evidence than that, one might almost say that the horrors of the Revolution restored the "Eldest Daughter" to the Church.

Of course this is dangerous ground, and none of us may feel like staying on it too long. It is not unlike, though it does transcend, the position of those who feel that the commoner values of civilization must wither inside the cages of a kind of nationalist botanical garden. Dante's exile is once more a symbol. We may concede that it is the ultimate norm, even though we feel incapable of adopting it. But are those Spaniards so utterly quixotic who feel some stir of hope that in the end a sufficient peace might be made with the republic to ensure at least a modicum of religious and cultural freedom? It is not, so far as I can see, unethical to cherish such a wish. On the other hand one cannot well deny either that much is to be said for those who feel that a Fascist state in Spain might be induced to give a number of guarantees and liberties. Both views have a clear right to exist. We here have thought it proper that one should be presented as fairly as the other.

The third fault in the current picture of Spain is that it fails to take into account all the shadows which fall upon the scene from without. European Catholic journalists have reflected earnestly on the reasons why Mussolini was induced to strike the bargain with Franco which started the Insurgent uprising. What kind of pact was it, and what were the ultimate objectives the bargainers had in mind? We do not know. But little by little Germany was drawn into the fray; and fantastic efforts were made to get people used to believing that the Hitler-Mussolini combination was saving Europe from Bolshevism. Perhaps there are people who do not find all this a hoax. But they ought at least to explain why it is that a dictator who places Herr Rosenberg in the saddle in order to destroy the Catholic Church in Germany feels it his duty to sacrifice men and money in order to save that Church in Spain.

There are some who possess so little faith in this argument that risk of life has seemed as nothing to them. To assert that the "international brigade" fighting with the Loyalists is composed entirely of Russian and French Communists is simply not true. I know too many of those who have gone. They are victims of concentration camps, oppression and torture. They wear on their hearts the brand which tyranny alone can burn. True enough, all of them are exiles whom life has made a trifle fanatical, as it can when strange people adopt strange ways to save the world from Bolshevism. One may say of them that they have chosen evil bed-fellows. I find myself wishing, too, that they might find a greater glory in death. But Americans generally have too little experience of despotism and the despair it enkindles to warrant their feeling anything save awe in the presence of such tragedy.

These are men whom millions of the oppressed—millions of workers who are in slavery, and millions of freemen who have lost freedom—look upon as their representatives. To all of them the Spanish war is the test of humanity's ability to escape from bondage. Grant that they are mistaken. Concede that the Loyalists are in reality only a mob of ruthless Bolsheviki. The fact remains that the masses, especially in the dictator-ruled countries, do not think so, as anyone can find out if he takes the trouble. Do many of us really want to bar the route to Christ in all those hearts for generations to come by identifying His Church with the apostles of violence?

That is the most difficult question of all. One can pile up ever so much evidence for either answer. But one should at least look at that mound of facts and beliefs, of prejudices and suffering, before rushing to some kind of easy formula. Europe today really seems something man alone is no longer able to save. It is ravaged by maladies of heart and soul. The spectator is reminded of that somber passage in Newman's "Apologia" which sets forth a vision "to dizzy and appal." The mere omens of things since come to pass once maddened Nietzsche and Léon Bloy. We live in the time of their maturity . . . and must sometime realize more is happening than that "Spanish patriots" are putting down Bolshevism!

Thank God that this terrible time has the splendor of a Sovereign Pontiff unafraid—unafraid especially of the power and the peace of the Christian Gospel. To visit the sick. To feed those who starve and are thirsty. To make room for those in exile. To bind up wounds. Yes, to kiss even the leper. That is the message which has come from the Rock of Peter and the Shepherd of the Fold.

# Some Further Reflections
# on Spain

My good friend Father Talbot has wasted an article on me in *America* for April 10, and what he wrote he wrote like a gentleman. It seems expedient to reply on a few points, and I shall try to do so *non in furore,* thus concluding what I have to say on the subject of the Spanish war.

On one point we are agreed—I know very little about Spain. But no harm is done by adding that neither does Father Talbot. What can we really know? When one has read the press and the propagandists, one is certain only that for months a savage massacre has been in progress, doing nobody any good. And if one talks privately with those who have returned from the scene, the conversation becomes a long dribble of horror stories. Nothing in the whole dreadful business makes sense excepting the simple fact that Spain is being destroyed with the help of imported fanaticisms. Under these circumstances the part of wisdom would seem to lie in every decent effort to sift the evidence, or, if that cannot be done, to weigh the conclusions which relatively competent Europeans have formulated. But when *The Commonweal* published an article summarizing Catholic views critical of Franco, not a few persons seemed to feel called upon to exhaust the less attractive portions of our common vocabulary. My paper was an attempt to defend Miss Carter's right to say what she thought; and in a more general sense it intimated that the more one listened the more certain it was bound to become that Spain is the scene of a great tragedy rather than of any victorious crusade.

George N. Shuster, "Some Further Reflections," *The Commonweal,* April 23, 1937, pp. 716-717. Reprinted by permission of *The Commonweal.*

I can't help believing that the English language is sufficiently flexible to permit the relatively clear exposition of such views. But somehow my remarks led Father Talbot to say: "I rather believe that Mr. Shuster's preoccupation with them [i.e., the Nazis] is clouding his vision of that other more dangerous form of the totalitarian state, Moscowism." He was nice about it but he really meant what a very irate lady declared—that I had turned Communist. I can't help finding this rather amusing. Father Talbot must surely know that since 1933 a great deal of "joint effort" has been made to "demonstrate" against the Hitlerites. Has he ever seen me on any of those programs? I can assure him that it was not for lack of opportunity! Whenever any organization has approached Nazism from against a partly Communist background, I have made myself conspicuous by retiring from the scene. And if what I have written on the subject cannot be read without too much trouble, it is after all easy enough to find out what the radical Marxists have issued by way of an indictment. This policy is, I know, subject to criticism. But at least I have adopted it, and may add rather proudly that it has cost me a good deal more opportunity and popularity than have been sacrificed by those who venture to suspect me—a Borah Republican and, I hope, a Catholic—of secret flirtations with Herr Stalin.

Father Talbot has asked me this question in particular: granted a dictatorship by General Franco and one by Senor Caballero, which would I choose? I can only repeat emphatically that I want neither. And I shall add quite candidly: one's human affection for embattled priests and religious lead one to side with Franco; but one's love for the timeless mission of the Church leads one to believe that he may, after all, prove to be the greater of two evils. It is a dreadful dilemma. Now let me ask Father Talbot this: were Caballero a devoted Catholic, on which side would the outlook for social justice lie? There is no doubt of what the answer would have to be, for Caballero (not the individual but the representative) is the scourge that follows upon certain sins. And so let us ask ourselves the final and the only important question: why is Caballero not a devoted Catholic?

When we put that fateful query, which lays bare what we modern men have done in nearly every country to the poor and to their love for our holy Church, we have found the key to comtemporary Europe. It is not a matter for dialectic. It is simply the horrifying contrast between the ethics of the Christian Gospel and the conduct of modern society. And every effort to uphold Christian ethics by upholding an anti-Christian social order is bound to fail, while, conversely, our social order can only be supported by a restoration of Christian ethics.

That may sound remote and even banal. But one can be very specific. Father Talbot has forgotten to mention that although antagonistic to Fascism

I have often expressed admiration for the gifts and achievements of Mussolini. And it seems to me that if we observe the position in which this skilful statesman now finds himself, we shall discover a highly important truth. Inherent in Fascism is the assumption that safety is to be found in a purely nationalistic economy which can subordinate both labor and capital to a martial state purpose while allowing a measure of freedom to both. But: since this economy is necessarily costly in itself, primarily by reason of the martial state purpose, a heavy burden is created which must be passed on to the toiling masses. Therefore in times of stress the political and social responsibility of the government becomes enormous. It cannot shift part of the blame to other shoulders, for it alone exists. Consequently the Fascist state must proceed to use more and more violent means. Inside the country, private energies are increasingly liquidated. Outside, acts of violence become more and more necessary. The working out of this process in Italy can be observed with the naked eye. It means that both at home and abroad the masses of the people must be victimized (e.g., the "volunteers" in Spain), so that antipathy to the régime cannot help but grow. That it is growing seems quite certain, nor are the reasons why either hard to find or hidden from view.

If Mussolini and Italy present this spectacle, what shall we find elsewhere? One has only to look around and see that Fascism is rapidly being converted into what has been termed "National Bolshevism." In Germany, for example, a system is coming into being which differs so little from "Moscowism" that the eventual alliance of the two states is no longer the fear of just a few dreamy mortals. The fourth partition of Poland has ceased to be a mirage. Very probably a large number of Nazis wish no such development. It is merely the inevitable finale of their system. The most elemental moral principles are discarded. A deep and bitter social antagonism is engendered. War for war's sake gradually becomes the only viable recipe. In short, there remains of Christian ethics less than enough to press between the pages of a book.

This is the one reason why any identification of the Church with Fascism, however denominated, is so exceedingly dangerous. The concessions made in the name of "patriotic tradition" are of course tempting. But I do not see how anybody can read the writings of Pope Pius, from the decision concerning l'Action Française to the latest encyclical to the Mexican Church, without feeling that they constitute a long warning against that temptation. This point I do not wish to stress, knowing full well that it lies outside my competence. But let me say this: conservative people often fail to see what they are doing when they ignore the evident perils of the Fascist state on the ground that it is after all preferable to Communism. They do not stop to think that this state by no means stamps out the things that make Communism and must therefore eventually absorb Communism or perish. (We shall see, I think, that

Mussolini will either restore a measure of parliamentary government, and therewith of freedom, or give way to a Leftist revolution.) It is not widely enough realized that under modern conditions a conservative ethos is impossible unless two things are done: the rights of the worker must be made an integral concern of society, and those rights must be freely and creatively exercised. There will be a condition of permanent revolution in the world until a sound conservatism has been reestablished, and it is not to be reestablished in any other way. Communism and Fascism are simply twin forms of this revolution.

The situation in Spain is in two respects particularly dangerous. It is not important, whether General Franco calls himself a Fascist, just as it was inconsequential whether Franz von Papen was behind Hitler, or Hitler behind Franz von Papen. With the help of swarms of Moors, 150,000 Italians and as many Germans as can be packed into Bremen, the "march on Madrid" is being carried on. But: the condition of labor is worse in Spain than it is anywhere else in Europe, and it is assumed that Catholicism (for the first time) is backing the other side. These things mean that if the Fascist state wins out, the cleavages will be extraordinarily great, and (automatically) that antipathy to the Church will grow.

I cannot help facing that probability with the deepest alarm, because I am both a Catholic and a conservative. If my fears prove unfounded, I shall be very happy indeed. Meanwhile the other way—the course of action recommended in the encyclical to the Mexican Church—seems fearfully hard. But the centuries before us often took it, and there is no record of failure. Hugenberg's Lutherans believed that if they put Hitler into power, they could restore the vigor of their Church. We now see that wherever that Church has compromised with Nazism it has been infected with death, and that Protestant Christianity has been kept alive by men who risked all. One able critic has reminded me that I am living at ease in a peaceful country. And very glad of it! Nevertheless many of my German friends have learned what bearing witness to the Faith means. I have had the privilege of suffering with them in spirit as they bore up under months of brutal treatment in concentration camps, or years of exile in poverty and loneliness. I have known men who have given their lives; and there are those among them in whose name the whole Church will some time assuredly pray.

We have no right to suppose that to us has been given the privilege of saving Cleanness with unclean hands. In so far as poor unhappy Spain is concerned, I find myself wishing only that Christians in this country were sufficiently strong and united to support their government in an endeavor to bring about a cessation of the conflict. For however our opinions may differ on this or that, Father Talbot and I are surely in agreement that Christ is the Prince of Peace.

# The Spanish Civil War
# and American Catholics

This paper will be concerned, of course, with old, unhappy, far-off things and battles long ago. Still there may be some value in it for this reason: it will help, we shall hope, to present the social thinking of many Americans, notably Catholic Americans, during the very trying period which preceded the Second World War. The picture it provides is not wholly new since the part I personally played in it has been reviewed in master's theses and doctoral dissertations, sometimes with too much approval. Nor is the documentation as complete as it might be, since the accumulated correspondence coming to the *Commonweal* was not preserved after the magazine changed hands in 1938. Some letters were, to be sure, reprinted in the correspondence columns.

The *Commonweal* of the early thirties was not the same kind of periodical as that which appears today. It was then strongly committed to presenting both points of view about any given problem, rather than proclaiming a commitment to a position, and it was doubtless more Catholic in the "classical" sense of the term. To be sure it was a bastion, often a beleaguered one, of what is now called Ecumenism; and when it said that it was conservative it meant that it walked in the light of the Papal Social Encyclicals and not in that of Marxism or *laissez faire*. For the most part, excepting for a few minor bits of backsliding, it also was anti-totalitarian in every sense of the term.

Speech delivered at a conference on the Spanish Civil War, Massachusetts Institute of Technology, May 21, 1969.

For my part, I had completed two periods of study abroad, both concerned with Germany; and since the second (1933-34) coincided with the rise of Hitler to power, I wrote the first critical review of Nazism in action to be published in this country as well as the earliest account of Hitler's war on Religion to see the light of day. I also read widely in French and German journalism and literature. At the time this was a rather rare occupation inside the American Catholic Church, almost all the official ties of which ran to Rome and back again. There was a good deal of anti-Semitism about, largely the result of economic conflict, but in part also fomented by Father Charles Coughlin and a few other people. Everybody was against the Communists, and possibly as a result there was here and there, notably in New York, active sympathy with Fascism.

Such was the situation when the Spanish Civil War erupted. Meanwhile a little group of Catholic observers of the European situation had come together informally. Among the best known of its members were Heinrich Bruening, exiled former Chancellor of Germany, who had managed to escape from his country just prior to the purges of 1934 and was staying for a time (prior to his coming to Harvard) with friends on Long Island, and Carlton J. H. Hayes, then professor of History at Columbia, who would later on become Ambassador to Spain. We had unusually good ties with persons abroad, including the famed Jesuit opponent of Nazism, Father Friedrick Muckermann, who was then doing some public relations chores for the Vatican and could keep us informed of what was happening in the citadel of Catholicism.

The Civil War started with a military mutiny in July, 1936, and by the end of the month was raging violently. It was by no means clear at first what the outcome would be. Insurgent officers did not carry the day in Barcelona, and on the other hand Nazi aviators helped to subdue the Basque country, one of the most solidly Catholic areas in Europe. But it became evident that the angry attack in many parts of Spain on Catholic priests and religious, resulting in great slaughter and brutality, was the consequence of deep-seated Anarchist and Syndicalist aversion to the Church.

Matters came to a head in the United States in March, 1937, when a large group of writers signed a statement supporting the Loyalist Valencia Government and condemning Franco.

This statement was opposed in the *Commonweal* by Michael Williams, its editor-in-chief, in an editorial written on March 12, and in an article published on April 8. Williams accused the Loyalists of being directed from Moscow; and, having described briefly the attacks on the Church, he urged support of Franco, despite some doubts about the wisdom of his views on the topic of government. No doubt I should indicate very briefly my attitude toward the editor of the magazine of which I was then the managing editor.

Michael Williams was a good journalist who had recovered his faith in the Catholic Church and ardently supported it. I still cherish his memory and am happy to say that after both of us had severed our relations with the *Commonweal,* we corresponded in very friendly fashion until the day he died. All during the years of his editorship he had suffered from frequent spells of illness, one of which occurred during the early months of 1937. By reason of the state of his health, commmunication with him was difficult and often impossible.

The writers' letter referred to gave unusual significance to two happenings in which I was involved. First there had appeared in the *Commonweal* an article entitled "European Catholics and Spain," by Barbara Barclay Carter, who was closely identified with Catholic lay leadership in Great Britain. The author revealed what we already in part knew, namely that many Catholics did not consider Franco an archangel rising to annihilate Satan. It aroused a considerable furore in this country and the attacks on it were numerous and vociferous. The second happening was a meeting of New York's Catholic journalists arranged by Father Francis X. Talbot, S.J., editor of *America,* to determine what common position, if any, could be taken.

At this meeting I suggested that Señor Gil Robles, who had headed the Catholic (as we would now say Christian Democratic) Party in Spain, and who had sought a haven in Portugal, be invited to confer with us as to what we ought to think, say and do. It seemed to me that this suggestion had been endorsed, but it soon became obvious that it had not. Many were far beyond needing any advice.

Shortly after this meeting, on April 2, 1937, I published an article in the *Commonweal* entitled "Some Reflections on Spain." It was prefaced by a brief comment by Michael Williams which said that he wished to "express my agreement with Mr. Shuster's views concerning the Spanish situation, after making one reservation, namely, that I believe facts are producible which prove that Communism and Anarchism played a far greater part in provoking the revolt led by General Franco than his article shows." This amiable pat on the back was to cause him a lot of grief in the days that ensued.

My article was in essence a summary of pro-Franco sentiment in this country and a critique of it. The summary said in essence:

> Catholics everywhere ought . . . to support the Insurgent cause and to hope for the speedy destruction of all Marxists. Of course a few benighted persons have ventured to differ from these conclusions. But it can readily be shown that they are tainted with "liberalism" or guilty of French patriotic emotions, or singularly unfamiliar with logic and moral theology.

My critique made three points. The first was that a great many unimpeachable Catholics did not believe all of this. I tried to dispel the charge that they were victims of "French patriotic emotions," by which was meant at the time support of the *Front populaire*. The second point was that great evil had been done by both parties in the Spanish conflict. I said:

> Perhaps only in America are there many naive enough to believe that the present Valencia government is anything much better than an aggregation of oratorical mortals trying to get the bull populace to see something besides a red flag. It is shocking to think that ninety-two writers—no matter how idealistic and intelligent—could be found in and about New York to underwrite what honest French radicals have repudiated in their journals. But shall we also be obliged to witness the equally shocking fact that Catholics are ready to ignore the manifest brutality, reactionary political method and intellectual simplicity of the Francoites? No history of the blunders of the Insurgents need be written. It must suffice to declare that the person who set the wheels in motion to grind out propaganda for Franco as the saviour of religion and culture was that eminent defender of the faith, Herr Goebbels.

Let me say parenthetically that these remarks did not fail to make an impact on some of those who signed the writers' statement. In particular I received a very moving letter from Van Wyck Brooks saying that he wished he had waited about signing anything in order to endorse my view of the situation. This was one of the very few pleasant things that came my way in the aftermath of "Some Reflections."

The third point, and this is the one which the committee to which I have alluded would have wished to emphasize especially, was that the "shadows which fall upon the scene from without" had not been taken sufficiently into account in the assumed Catholic consensus. The members of our Committee knew though my piece did not say so, that there had been a real possibility that the French armies in North Africa would invade the homeland in order to destroy the *Front populaire* and make common cause with Fascism. What I said on the subject was this:

> European Catholic journalists have reflected earnestly on the reasons why Mussolini was induced to strike the bargain with Franco which started the Insurgent uprising. What kind of pact was it, and what were the ultimate objectives the bargainers had in mind? We do not know. But little by little Germany was drawn into the fray; and fantastic efforts were made to get people used to believing that the Hitler-Mussolini combination was saving Europe from Bolshevism. Perhaps there are people who do not find all this a hoax. But they might at least try to explain why it is that a dictator who places Herr Rosenberg in the saddle in order to destroy the Catholic Church in Germany feels it his duty to sacrifice men and money in order to save that Church in Spain.

The week which followed was one of the most nightmarish ones a man like myself could easily imagine. Some time earlier I had opposed United States participation in the Olympic Games of 1936, to be held in Berlin, and as a result had received three threats of assassination. My secretary was a very good-looking, buxom girl of Sicilian origin who insisted in walking in front of me to ward off bullets; and perhaps the look in her flashing eyes did scare off a potential assailant. But the onslaught which followed my "Reflections," was a different kind of thing. My good friend, our parish priest in Glenbrook, Connecticut, called me in amazement to say that New York's Chancery Office had telephoned to inquire whether I went to Mass on Sunday. The denunciatory mail poured in. I recollect with pleasure, however, that it included letters from priest subscribers, especially in New England, saying that although in the main they disagreed with my position they supported my right to take it. Unfortunately all of these letters have disappeared. It now dawned on me that for Catholic New York the world outside the United States was either Communist or Fascist and that therefore they had opted for Fascism.

In many ways the unkindest blow of all was Father Francis X. Talbot's "Answer" to my "Reflections" which appeared as the main article in *America*'s issue of April 10, 1937. I had assumed that until we had our conference with Gil Robles, which of course was never held, we were pretty much on our own. I liked Father Talbot very much as a poet and an abettor of poets, but had never seen a trace of an endowment to discuss political affairs. Doubtless the "Answer" was a collective effort and doubtless also Father Talbot expressed the solidly united opinion of the Archdiocese of New York. It was a well designed attack.

The article began by saying that the "propagandists"—by which term was meant the writers who signed the manifesto against France—had striven to "split the corporate influence of Catholicism" and that now, by reason of the stand I had taken, a regrettable cleavage had been revealed. Indeed, the "corporate influence" was worldwide, said Father Talbot. Even Catholic periodicals in France, except for a "few terrorized by the Hitler fear" said that if a choice had to be made in Spain they would opt for the Insurgents. It is amusing in retrospect to note that I made a "poor impression" on Father Talbot by saying "the person who set the wheels to grinding out propaganda for Franco as the saviour of religion and culture was that eminent defender of the Faith, Dr. Goebbels" because that phrase was quoted from a letter written by one of his fellow Jesuits at the Vatican.

But the telling core of Father Talbot's piece came in the following paragraph:

> I believe that Mr. Shuster's stand against Nazism and Fascism is to be commended. But I rather believe that his preoccupation with them is clouding his vision of that other more dangerous form of the totalitarian

state, Moscowism. But why does he assume, and rabidly, that General Franco is a Fascist and committed to Fascism? Franco never was a Fascist, and I judge that he never will be.

My "Some Further Reflections" which appeared in the *Commonweal* on April 23, 1937, was of course my swansong. It was now clearly evident that the work which I had been doing for twelve years in the area of Catholic journalism was ended—I thought at the time, forever. The pill was a bitter one to swallow. My wife and I had very little of this world's goods. How could we have had on the salary I had earned? But at least I had mustered enough courage to express my convictions. Fortunately as things turned out it became clear that I still had friends.

I shall quote only one passage from "Some Further Reflections" because it has a sombre prophetic ring:

> One has only to look around and see that Fascism is rapidly being converted into what has been termed National Bolshevism. In Germany, for example, a system is coming into being which differs so little from "Moscowism" that the eventual alliance between the two states is no longer the fear of just a few dreamy mortals. The fourth partition of Poland had ceased to be a mirage. Very probably a large number of Nazis wish no such development. It is merely the inevitable finale of their system. The most elemental moral principles are discarded. A deep and bitter social antagonism is engendered. War for war's sake gradually becomes the only reliable recipe. In short, there remains of Christian ethics less than enough to press between the pages of a book.

Indeed it was the Stalin-Hitler Pact and the partition of Poland which opened the eyes of many, many Catholics. That Pact of course sent American Communists and their supporters reeling, but it had just as marked an impact on the thinking of American Catholics who had preferred one system of totalitarianism to the other. Meanwhile Spain gradually became little more than a blur on the consciousness of the United States. Franco skillfully managed to keep himself pretty well out of the war-time embrace of Hitler and Mussolini. After the fighting was over our military bases helped bolster the economy. But all the while Spain has been seething, and fortunately, very fortunately, young Catholics, priests and laymen, have joined in the seething. I have absolutely no idea of what will happen henceforth. Not another Civil War, let us hope, but the kind of social change which will enable the Spanish people to live in freedom and justice.

I shall close with a few comments on events subsequent to those which I have described. The ownership and management of the *Commonweal* passed during 1938 into new hands, primarily those of Philip Burnham and Edward Skillin, Jr., who had been members of the staff and were fortunately able to do their own financing of the journal. The first issue presenting them to the world contained a statement of purpose signed by them and a number of their friends. I shall quote one passage:

> We oppose the totalitarian state, dictatorships and violent revolution. Except to those who believe *a priori* that any paper which does not fight for the socialist revolution and the ownership of productive property by society is by that very fact fascist, we will prove in action our opposition to fascism and to other imperialisms, in America, in Germany, in Italy, in Spain, in Japan, or wherever else they threaten. No less equally emphatic is our repudiation of revolutionary Marxian communism, which clearly and directly infringes on Christian belief and which merits condemnation on many other grounds. But there will be no red-baiting on the Left, nor any goblin-hunting on the Right. We shall try to deal impartially and charitably with all systems and believers in anything. We want to see incorporated the good of opposed systems in our own, and to steal the truth even from the pocket of the devil.

This was more youthfully put (God be praised for youth) than anything I could have managed, though the departure from the *Commonweal*'s previous outlook was in reality very slight. Nevertheless the inclusion of Spain in the indictment tied a ball and chain on the new management's leg. The surly phrase "*Commonweal Catholic*" began to circulate. This meant that those associated with so open-ended a program had sundered themselves from the Establishment. I suppose that this kind of name-calling went on until the shock of Vatican II sent its tremors throughout the land.

Meanwhile, I, who had exited with a handsome fellowship for study in Europe from Columbia University and the Social Science Research council, had the good fortune somewhat incidentally of coming to know in France many in what would later on be called the *Mouvement Populaire Republicaine,* whose leader was Maurice Schumann. This was "Christian Democracy" at its best in terms of imagination and commitment. One of its ideological fathers was Jacques Maritain, whom I had previously known only slightly. His attitude towards what was happening in Spain was almost identical with mine. We did not associate ourselves with the hardfisted pamphleteering of George Bernanos whose book, translated as *A Diary of My Times,* was the most sweeping attack on the Franco uprising to have been written by any Catholic or indeed I think by anybody. The few Catholics in this country who read it turned all the most undesirable colors in the rainbow. Maritain himself had to face a good deal of unpleasantness when he returned to the United States.

It will do no harm to add that he and I have grown far too conservative in the eyes of our younger colleagues to amount to much. That is doubtless as it should be. Of late years I have received so many Catholic honors that they almost make any triumphal entry into kingdom come seem doubtful. I mention this only in order to indicate that there are immense reservoirs of tolerance and understanding in Catholic America.

# Cultural Cooperation
# and the Peace

... When the Charter of the United Nations was adopted, in an hour when many people believed that only Hitler had hampered progress toward what Wendell Willkie optimistically termed "One World," provision was made for the establishment of an international agency concerned with the reformation of education—that is, with the weaning of schoolmen and scholars away from an all too parochial view of language, history, and citizenship. Steps were then taken to set up such an agency, and UNESCO was organized at conferences held in London and Paris during the winters of 1945 and 1946. It may be well to begin our review of the purposes and history of this agency by calling to mind the simple truth that every collective endeavor naturally looks very different to those entrusted with its operation than it does to those who observe it from the outside. Nothing would, from a purely theoretical point of view, seem simpler than inducing scholarly men of good will to agree upon ways and means of substituting reasonable and friendly cooperation for bellicosity . And nothing is from a practical point of view more difficult.

As one who participated not merely in both the conferences alluded to and also in the preliminary attempt to rally American public opinion in support of the idea, I think I may say that the great majority who took part were genuinely eager to enlist every person of good will in the cause of peace. Thus from the very beginning persons as diverse in many respects as James

From *Cultural Cooperation and the Peace* by George N. Shuster (Milwaukee: Bruce Publishing Co., 1952), pp. 20-59. Reprinted by permission of the publisher.

228

Marshall and Stephen Duggan constantly stressed the importance of the contribution which religious institutions in particular could make to the success of the enterprise. But it is quite clear that the effort was undertaken under three persistent and important delusions. First, many of us had formed relatively unrealistic notions of education and of what it can accomplish. Second, we were so aware of the manner in which Nazism had threatened to destroy the foundations of Western civilization that we were inclined to believe that all would be well once this menace had been removed. Third, not a few of us made the quite natural mistake of assuming that after so vast and fearful a holocaust, symbolized by the ghastly rain of death which had fallen upon Hiroshima, nobody would again think seriously that war could be aught else than the ultimate calamity, to be avoided by every means possible. I shall say a word about each of these errors of observation and sound judgment.

The word "education" can be defined in a number of different ways. We can, for example, use it to allude to the formal schooling which associates young people with selected elders in the hope that the fledglings will be prepared for life thereby. This process is obviously of the very greatest importance. We are accustomed to assume that the moral, intellectual, and social weaknesses of human beings are due to their lack of the "proper education." And of late we have been heard to say again and again that faulty school training is one reason why peace has not been secured. Is it not true, for example, that chauvinist teachers inoculated German youth with the germs of the Hitlerite disease? Nevertheless, suppose it were admitted that improperly motivated schooling is one of the principal sources of defection from high ideals, it does not follow either that all teachers can suddenly be rendered immune to every undesirable impulse, or that if they were immune they could then in a short time make paragons of virtue of their charges. Alas, teachers are very limited human beings; even if viewed by and large they do constitute an elite. Their opportunities are also circumscribed. Whenever and wherever they teach the values of pacifism, as they often did precisely in Germany, they will be ostracized as soon as the nation to which they belong decides that military preparedness is the order of the day. And if on the other hand they bristle with patriotic fervor, they will be ridiculed as soon as the public decides that all wars are created by the "merchants of death."

Teachers know these things very well. In addition they realize, better than other persons can, that the chasm of age which sunders them from youth is not easily crossed. The young, anxious to try their wings, will come to pride themselves less on what somebody has taught them than on what they have been able to persuade themselves are insights arrived at by use of their own imaginations and intellects. Youth is the time of metaphor, and this in turn is the symbol spark ignited within the spirit for the illumination of the outside world. Age is the period during which metaphors are viewed with a measure of critical disillusionment or even of irony. Youth does not wish to compromise; age is aware that compromise is inevitable. These tensions, which develop at the very core of the teaching process, are, if rightly dealt with, good. Because they exist, men do not grow up to be identical peas. But they also clearly establish limits to the amount of uniformity which academic life can produce. All this does not of course mean that the schools cannot prove to be powerful forces of divisive nationalism, or agencies to promote a healthy internationalism of outlook. But it is, I believe, true that they will in large measure be reflections of what the public mind in any time happens to desire.

And therefore many have concluded that education in our time is above all a process for the exchange of information—a sort of cultural product manufactured by the great mass media (the press, the radio, the motion picture, television), which the individual is usually powerless to withstand or influence. It is contended that if these media were employed throughout the world in order to break down prejudice and promote understanding, nationalistic hysteria would soon become a thing of the past. All this may no doubt be true. Yet we unfortunately know that even where these media are quite free—as by and large they are in the Western World—they do not uniformly serve the cause of interhuman conciliation or even of virtue in the traditional sense.

For instance, there are many good and beautiful motion pictures. But Hollywood has—to cite just one instance—conveyed to the outside world an impression of manners and mores inside the United States which may well have alienated millions of people. That the concepts of free access to sources of information and the honest dissemination of it are sound concepts need hardly be stressed. People will never really know what is really happening until some qualified observer can find out and make his report. Yet even if we omit from consideration the censorship imposed by the Russians on all dispatches from within the Soviet orbit, it is unfortunately a fact that restrictions on the gathering and distribution of news are at least as numerous and hampering as they have ever previously been. On the other hand, the quantity of news now available is potentially so great that only selection and evaluation can help to make it usable by the masses of mankind; and no proper standards for such selection and evaluation exist. Once more all this does not justify the conclusion that the mass media are not important instrumentalities for the shaping of human conduct. But they are not devices which will prove automatically benevolent. Even if such a thing as a world-wide radio network existed, everything would depend upon what was said over it and how it was said.

Now let me say something about the second delusion. Nazism was a very evil thing; and though it sprang from a variety of sources, some of them obscure, it was above all the creation of fanatical imperialism, which appealed to the German's pride in his language and "race." As the peoples of the world listened to the utterances of Hitler and his henchmen, and as they took cognizance of the brutal and cynical recourse to wars of conquest which were the stock-in-trade of these fanatics, the conviction was formed in their minds that, as Mr. Clement Atlee said at the London Educational Conference of 1945, "wars begin in the minds of men," and that accordingly the defense of peace could best be sought in making it impossible for nations to acquire the intellectual disease with which Hitler infected his people. It was no doubt inevitable that such a conviction should have dominated so large a part of the reflection of mankind. But it was nevertheless a tragic delusion. Was all that there remained to do holding out a hand to the Russian people? It was forgotten that no one had been able to enter into such a relationship since 1917, when the Communist Revolution began, and that Russia was firmly in the grip of a dictator concerning whose purposes little was known save that he had pledged his vast domain and all who lived therein to the spread of Leninism-Stalinism. Few of those who misjudged the situation were evil or traitorous men. But it may well be that they were naive, and their lack of insight had its effect on the early history of UNESCO, even as it did on so much else that happened after the war had ended.

The third delusion was the most plausible. Just as veterans of the battle-fields of Verdun and Flanders did not think it possible in 1918 that during their lifetimes any nation would again willfully resort to war, so also were the peoples who had survived the incredible torture of the years after 1945 persuaded that the discovery of the atomic bomb had left mankind no choice save that between destruction and peace. It was widely felt that accordingly the race was being driven, perhaps against its will but nonetheless irresistibly, toward world government. That the nations were soon to face instead a number of limited but nonetheless bloody and costly conflicts, in the Near East, Korea, and Indo-China, to name the most important only, was a tragic eventuality which not even the pessimistic conjured up at that time. It is true that fear of atomic weapons may be the principal reason why none of these lesser wars grew into a new Armageddon. But as soon as they broke out it was apparent that the road to peace would have to be traveled for a grim and bitter period with tanks and battle planes rather than in those wagons which Emerson said can be hitched to stars.

At any rate, the good ship UNESCO left the keel, amid the plaudits of many eminent philosophers, scientists, teachers, artists, and spokesmen for the masses. It had a constitution and a program, both devoid of any tendency to vest cultural dictatorship in the new organization. The Preamble of the Constitution, drafted by Etienne Gilson and Archibald MacLeish, reflected very clearly the temper of reflection at the time. It said in part:

> ... that a peace based exclusively upon the political and economic arrangements of governments would not be a peace which could secure the unanimous, lasting, and sincere support of the peoples of the world, and that the peace must therefore be founded, if it is not to fail, upon the intellectual and moral solidarity of mankind.

The program, too, was derivative from current moods. Everything UNESCO undertook was to be based upon an appraisal of its usefulness in promoting world peace. The modest goals of the Office of International Cultural Co-operation were held to be quite unworthy of the far-reaching ambitions of the new organization. While the Paris Conference did not frown forbiddingly upon all forms of cultural activity (for instance, it even endorsed Professor Gilson's suggestion that an international card catalogue of publications in the field of philosophy be maintained), it initiated projects such as these: the establishment of a world-wide radio network and the formulation of conventions assuring free access to and dissemination of news; the development of a program of "fundamental education," by which was meant the fostering in each country of that basic training which it most needed in order to make its contribution to peace; and the study of the tensions which arise between nations, with a view to suggesting what might be done in time to reduce those tensions. I list only these because it is desirable to restore in broad outline the feeling prevalent at the time. This feeling can perhaps also be indicated negatively, by pointing out that the most obvious educational tasks which were the legacy of the war, those of helping to rebuild schools and other educational establishments then in ruins, and of assisting in re-creating a cadre of teachers, were not accepted by UNESCO as properly its own. In this case, however, the decision was based upon an anticipated lack of resources with which to carry on such work.

The waters proved stormy and the route uncertain. I shall always recall with mingled sympathy and dismay how throughout the Paris Conferences the delegation from Czechoslovakia, then not yet a wholly shackled land, tried in every way to follow the leadership of the West, while its counterpart from Yugoslavia inflicted upon the Assembly, in whole and in part, unrestricted outpourings of Marxist doctrine. Through a chance resulting from equally fortuitous circumstances—primarily the coming to power of the Labour Party in Great Britain—Dr. Julian Huxley was made captain of the vessel, which was no sooner out of sight of land than it was headed for the harbor of "scientific humanism." This was a kind of Shangri-la in which, it was blithely assumed, the Russians would be delighted to meet the Western World. Naturally these latter had no intention of embarking at such a port, which from their point of view was a minor and untutored outpost not yet conquered by dialectical materialism; and on the other hand the Christian folk of the West were shocked at being told that they had been invited to go on what was for them a quite unalluring journey. To be sure, UNESCO never got as far as "scientific humanism." The ship turned round in mid-ocean and looked about for a place to land. It finally came back to the point of departure, and its crew began to take inventory of their resources.

These were not inconsiderable. Let us begin a survey of them by venturing a mildly challenging statement. Alexander Pope surmised that a little learning is a dangerous thing. He was right. Still more perilous, however, is no learning at all. Let me illustrate. We may not have been able to teach the young people of the United States a great deal—and as a college president I am often inclined to take a dim view of the proceedings—but we have managed to convey certain things to them with rather commendable success. There exists, for example, far more social security in this country now than there used to even twenty years ago, and this means that not everybody who becomes poor will be stripped of every vestige of human dignity. There is also far less race consciousness among us than existed prior to one generation ago, and race consciousness translated into practical terms means lynching Negroes, starting Ku Klux Klans, and blackballing Irish-Americans from country clubs in New England. The average citizen is moreover able to find out much more about the manner in which his government conducts its business; and it may even be that television, a blessing not without its admixture of curses, will help us to control what goes on at political conventions. There is not one of these advantages which is not in part due to the fact that the American people have been induced—and therefore in at least a small measure taught—to insist that they be acquired.

If the blessings of education as we have known them are not inconsiderable, it may well be that "fundamental education," so interpreted as to include the most vital instruction required by peoples currently in great distress, can be a great boon. Let us look, for example, to the impoverished millions of India who are now wondering why national independence, achieved after so long and arduous an effort, has not raised them above the worst kind of poverty. They, like their fellow human beings in many parts of China, have become targets for Communist propaganda, which preys dishonestly on their emotions. It has now been convincingly demonstrated that even a minimal increase in literacy can not only change the political and social outlook of India but can also help to improve its health and economic status.

The peasant who is told in simple language he can understand how to raise chickens and how to shield his children from disease-bearing insects is a man who has found out how to do something very useful through his own efforts and has therewith acquired an endowment of hope and of desire for freedom. The task of bringing this kind of "fundamental education" to him is one form of intellectual exchange across national boundaries which it is the business of UNESCO to foster. Yet it is not India merely which has received assistance. Latin America and Africa as well have been the recipients of aid. And at the same time, through its endeavors to afford information concerning the varied activities of the United Nations, and through its close association with the National Commission which represents it in this country, UNESCO tries to foster legitimate pride in all the activities which bind the peoples of the world together in amity.

What has been said—and it could be supplemented with much beside—merely indicates that this relatively new international organization can and is assisting in bringing about a better distribution of the world's intellectual goods. To be sure, it has also made mistakes. Who has not? Perhaps the most serious problem it confronts is not that of finding worth-while things to do (our world is filled with them), or that of keeping out of blind alleys and dead-end streets, but that of defining in a way which will be both intelligible and appealing the central aims of intercultural cooperation. You will remember that Dr. Johnson said that patriotism is the last refuge of a scoundrel. Unfortunately international cooperation sometimes appears to be the ultimate enterprise of those who are not merely clean of heart but simple of mind as well. And no doubt this simplicity is most clearly discernible when one encounters it among highly literate exponents of recondite panaceas for the world's ills. They may be devotees of the social sciences, of anthropology, or, in particular, of psychology. It is characteristic of them that they should have implicit faith in some intellectual or emotional gadget into which historic time is assumed to have poured all its acquired wisdom.

By way of illustration let us summon to mind much of a sizable literature written during the recent world conflict to comment on the proposition that the German people were an aggregation of paranoids. A cure could be effected (it was asserted) if an army of psychiatrists were engaged, as soon as peace had come, to undertake the manipulation of each separate German soul. Now one can entertain a deep respect for the psychiatric profession and still find the suggestion more amusing than reassuring. When I try to visualize a fairly stout Bavarian ex-Nazi in *Lederhosen* and with the scent of beer upon his mustaches, forcibly ensconced on a couch over which a young analyst from Johns Hopkins leans in an attitude of hopeful ministration, I can think only of how well such a scene would consort with burlesque. We may grant that psychology, with its carefully devised batteries of tests and its knowledge of reflexes, conditioned and otherwise, might succeed in preparing the national psyche for the reception of almost anything. This was the possibility that haunted George Orwell. The Russians use methods of Pavlovian indoctrination relentlessly but on the whole rather crudely. Those methods are certainly capable of further refinement. The difficulty is, however, that the process permits of varied use by various people.

No one can deny that within limits, and granted at least a measure of social coercion, constantly reiterated assertions within a circumscribed group from which escape is relatively difficult do produce a measure of conformity. Thus in Tudor England, despite strong popular allegiance to Rome, tireless repetition of accusations against the Papacy eroded the convictions of the people. We know also that in our own times complete control of the agencies of propaganda during war periods will result, particularly if penalties for nonconformism are introduced, in a notable volume of patriotic fervor. When, however, a free market of ideas is maintained, the best one can hope for is competitive conditioning, and sometimes even that remains out of reach. We Americans have latterly been served with a beguiling illustration. Corruption in government offices had led to public discussions of it which had certainly "conditioned" Americans not otherwise addicted to thievery to judging harshly defections from political honesty. A candidate for the vice-presidency of the United States was thereupon accused of having been given a secret fund from which he paid bills for publicity and similar services. The conditioning had been so effective that, if one credits the newspapers and random samplings of public opinion taken at the time, this candidate's usefulness was wholly at an end. And yet, in less than one hour of television time, Senator Nixon, employing his own version of how to make friends and influence people, had "conditioned" most of his hearers to look upon himself, his wife, his children, and his puppy as incarnations of probity who had collectively been kept out of the poorhouse and the dog pound by the unselfish charity of friends. Indeed, if one can further credit what one saw and heard during the following days, our fellow citizens were inclined to rank those who contributed to the Senator's subsidiary exchequer among the great philanthropists of mankind.

As for the anthropologists, who profess a most useful discipline about which I know far less than I should, one may perhaps not unreasonably accuse many of them of having become so deeply convinced that since everything human is different, everything human must be the same. In other words: since moral and aesthetic standards show discernible variations, if one observes how differently they have been formulated in the various cultures, there is no point in arguing about them because science can attribute to none a superior value. Of course not all anthropologists have argued in this wise, but a sufficient number of them assuredly did. The ancients sagely declared that there was no use arguing about tastes. If we moderns were to add a dictum that there is also no use arguing about morals, there would in all truth be little left to get into a dither about. A major difficulty, however, is that then Hitler must have been quite all right, too, save that possibly he failed to include a chapter about anthropology in *Mein Kampf.* He did write a rather canny essay about mob psychology, and what is more he proved that minds of a certain inferior quality can be invoked to absorb almost anything.

What I have written by way of criticism should not be taken to imply that the social sciences are incapable of making a very great contribution to a practical program of intercultural cooperation. We know, for instance, that the teaching of citizenship in schools and colleges does provide young people with a far clearer understanding of their responsibilities for good government. There is much information concerning wages and housing, business cycles and government control, which is not merely available to the average person but which serves to make his own views less immediately selfish and more directly concerned with the common good. But I think we might well concern ourselves with one aspect of this question: how much light can the study of the social sciences cast upon the proper conduct of international affairs, granted the circumstances in which we now live?

Many of us have during recent months been interested in the ideas which George Kennan has expressed. He has challenged what he terms the established habit of American statesmen of approaching political problems which must be solved by nations acting in unison from the "moralistic" or "legalistic" point of view. Is it not true, he wondered, that power determines the outcome, and that therefore the basic inquiry is whether the balance of power is in your favor? There is not a little to be said in support of this point of view. But if you stress the argument too vigorously, you will clearly be put into the position of saying in effect that the outcome of a football game depends upon how much strength you can put into your eleven, regardless of whether they play according to the rules. In a trenchant commentary of this thesis (which has been endorsed by a number of American social scientists) Frank Tannenbaum has stoutly maintained that the American people will never approve of the Kennan position both because they consider it untenable from a moral point of view and because their own experience has proved that it is not correct. And indeed we Americans have made the counterconcept of "coordinate states" work within our own Republic, and we have at least tentatively applied the same principle, though in a more limited way, to both the American hemispheres. By "coordinate states" we mean those which have been willing, in greater or lesser ways, to merge their sovereignties in a larger unity. We may add that contemporary efforts to establish "coordinate states" in western Europe are to a not negligible extent the result of a confluence of American experience and that gained both by the old Austro-Hungarian Empire and the British Commonwealth. It is apparent that if these efforts succeed the power factor as it affects relationships between East and West will assuredly in large measure be determined.

In short, there are social and political conceptions which have proved their validity not merely because they can be put into practice but because they serve the peace. And so it is unquestionably the primary objective of the United Nations to establish not "world government" but a system of cooperating national sovereignties; and if UNESCO can propagate insight into the true character and possibilities of this system, it will at the same time be in complete consonance with what appear to be wholly commendable findings of the social sciences. To be sure, the merger of coordinated states necessarily encounters difficulties which do not affect a monolithic social structure, such as the Roman Empire was or as Russia now is; and so the need for constant patient explication of those difficulties and for the development of shared experience is very great, indeed. What Reinhold Niebuhr has called "the sense of community" is, I surmise, attainable, if it is viewed as the eventual outgrowth of awareness that each nation is primarily itself, but secondarily also part of a cooperating family of peoples carrying on within a framework of laws and forms of cultural cooperation. True enough, the danger of secession from a unification of coordinated states remains constant. But if the bonds are not unduly taut, the risk of partial disruption can always be faced calmly, in the sure knowledge that the advantages of union will soon become apparent once more. Such a system of states is not merely suggested by the best of modern philosophic thought—notably that of Immanuel Kant—but is clearly adumbrated by the teaching of the popes. Pope Benedict XV, for example, speaking in many encyclicals and allocutions about the family of the nations, did not hesitate to say that in the last analysis this was a reflection of the highest unity, namely that of men in the Mystical Communion of Christ. The Church, he declared, does not desire the death of individual nations. It seeks rather the survival of their individualities inside a larger unity.

Accordingly it is difficult to comprehend why a number of recent emotional attacks on the United Nations and in particular on UNESCO have sought in obvious ways to appeal to Christians and also Catholics. Both have been accused of trying to establish world government at the price of destroying the citizen's allegiance to his own country. Very probably a few rash spokesmen for both organizations have unwisely employed phrases which can, when quoted in isolation, give the impression that only monolithic world control will help us. Nevertheless the constitutions of both organizations are as clear as anything could well be. UNESCO, for instance, does not have the right to interfere in the educational and cultural affairs of the countries which support it. Its officers can act only in concert with the authorities of a given nation on their invitation. The objective must always be assistance and joint

effort to promote the free flow of information. If something of the sort be
not what the Popes have had in mind, their clear words become wholly
incomprehensible.

At all events, as soon as we accept the principle of coordinated states as
that which has been posited to determine the framework within which the
collective and therefore peacemaking decisions of the several nations are to be
arrived at, we can at last begin to wrestle with some of the grave difficulties
which the problem of language, which may also be termed the problem of
communications, presents to us. There is first of all the eminently practical
matter of being able to communicate at all. The Roman Empire and the
Middle Ages had a common language, used at least by educated men. Indeed,
the value of such a tongue seemed so self-evident that well into the seventeenth century—that is, three hundred years ago—many still believed that
only the Latin tongue would be proof against the erosive influences of time.
Today it is entirely conceivable that the adoption of a relatively simple
international language—say, Basic English or Esperanto—would be of inesti-
mable advantage not merely because it would help us all to converse but
because it would demonstrate the willingness of the world's peoples to
establish contact with one another. However you may view the matter, I
think you will agree with me that the mastery of at least one other tongue by
every reasonably well educated person is a possibly indispensable prerequisite
to the creation of international understanding.

If these things be true, there is need in the United States for considerable
revision of our educational thinking. We have assumed, on pragmatic or
quasi-pragmatic grounds, that since interest and utility were the twin faces of
the scholastic medallion, the academic ideal must be to dignify the two by
giving to the school the high collective purpose of citizenship. In other words,
we have said to the young, study what interests you and what you believe will
be of use to you in later life, but remember you ought to do so in constant
awareness of your obligation to the community. And since the young have
not been addicted to finding language study interesting, and since their elders
have hardly been able to persuade them of its social usefulness, familiarity
with the ancient tongues has become a lost art in this country, while the
acquisition of a knowledge of even the Germanic or the Romance languages is
considered by the great majority a dreary business. Now we have suddenly
discovered that we are living not in a national community merely but verily in
one that is as wide and vast as the world. Our consciences are beginning to
trouble us. It seems likely that even if we do not revise the prevalent
educational philosophy, we shall have to find out what can be done to give
our citizens the linguistic skills which are so desperately needed. For all over
the world the story about us is the same. I myself have seen it being told in
Germany, where the dreary helplessness of countless thousands of Americans,

chained to uncommunicativeness, is comical when it is, indeed, not grimly tragic in every moral and cultural sense.

But for my part I believe that the philosophy itself is badly in need of revision. No one would, to be sure, wish to question the basic function of interest in the learning process; and by carrying out exhaustive studies of that function modern psychology has made a highly important contribution to education. It is also self-evident that neither the duties nor the values of citizenship are to be denied. But there is something else to be considered, namely the careful training of the individual for cultural insight and moral responsibility. I wish to say a word about language study in terms of such training. Through the effort to master another tongue, one crawls as a young man or woman out of one's parochial and nationalistic chrysalis. For not a few of my generation this was achieved above all through the study of Latin and Greek, which are still perhaps uniquely excellent keys to a world of universal truth and beauty and constant quest beyond the special urgencies of the time in which any individual of necessity lives. Yet the language need not be a classical one. If within the years which lie immediately ahead, a million young Americans can get out of their shells of American English and learn to move about inside the world inhabited by some other people, we shall be vastly better prepared than we are now for our role in history.

So much for language. Next we must realize, and do so with the requisite humility, that there are certain lines of cultural demarcation which we cannot easily cross. It has been said that the truly educated man feels at home in every century. But I do not believe that there are many, except men of the stamp of St. Francis, who could be quite at ease even with the Sultan, who will feel responsive to every cultural environment, even when in terms of civilization it is highly developed. We may not be like the soldier who at the end of a visit to the great park at Fontainbleau remarked that it was "nice" but not as nice as the one in Kansas City, but it will on many occasions be difficult to do any better. There are Europeans whom the United States impresses and enchants. There are other Europeans whom it rebuffs and appalls. Some Americans do not like southern France (which to me is a veritable paradise), and others can see nothing that is good in Germany. Very well. But as Matthew Arnold's immortal phrase reminds us, some things are the best that have been known and thought in the world. They have not come out of one nation alone, or of one time. If we are unable to recognize and assimilate them, the fault is ours. And it is a grievous one.

Then it must also be noted that living in a culture as technological as ours we often tend to be more impressed by the fact that the bathtubs in a hotel are constructed of tinted porcelain into which hot water runs efficiently than by the intellectual temper of the community around about. It will, of course, do the American no harm to recall that Homer, Dante, Shakespeare, Pascal,

and Goethe owned neither shower baths nor automobiles, neither refriger-
ators nor radios. On the other hand, many of us can be jolted out of our
complacency even in this respect, when we discover, for example, that some
modern European homes are better designed and more comfortable than our
own. Or we may find that up-to-date school buildings, in such countries as
Switzerland, Sweden, and Germany, have more teaching aids and timesaving
devices than do our own. Though we correctly maintain that our competitive
economy produces more and therefore insures a higher standard of living than
does any other, there are some technical tasks which Europeans perform
more efficiently than do we.

The difficulties which any of us must face when crossing national boundaries in the cultural sense grow more challenging when the gulf between
humanistic and technological achievement is very wide. It is utterly improbable that the average American will find life among the Bedouins or the
Sudanese exciting or stimulating. In all likelihood the frequently reported
decay of white men in the tropics is due far less to climate than to the
psychological depression which results from cultural isolation. I am convinced
that only love can surmount those barriers—love as it shines from the lives
and writings of such men as Père Foucauld, Ernest Psichari, and Albert
Schweitzer. You may recall that it was by reason of his experience among the
Moslems of Morocco that Psichari was led back to the Catholic faith,
wellspring of his own culture. There is a great deal of missionary literature to
tell us how frequently the apostles of religion in far-off lands were not mere
exiled Church functionaries but men and women who spanned the cultural
chasm with buoyant hearts and sensitive minds. We should, however, delude
ourselves if we believed that in the foreseeable future the great majority of
men will be brave and good enough to make that leap with success.

Critics are not lacking who urge caution and restraint; and in all truth
naive talk about "one world" and "world community" is fearfully reminiscent of certain glib assumptions that all a parent has to do in order to rear his
offspring well is to read a popular handbook about child psychology. Unless a
man is really open of mind, to some extent trained, and willing to try to love
his neighbor as he loves himself (and how many of us in particular are
sufficiently disciplined, intellectually or spiritually, to observe the onerous
commandment of affection), he may better serve the cause of peace by
staying at home, except for infrequent ventures into the Riviera, where the
tourist profession has been trained to deal with his ilk. If all one had to do
was to get acquainted and sit down at the same table, as the phrase goes,
there would be no unhappy marriages, no divorces, and no juvenile delin-
quency. If I may make an observation based on my own experience, it is far
more likely that an American (or anyone else, for that matter) who goes to a
foreign country with very little of his own to offer will get extremely little in

return, excepting souvenirs of buildings at which he has stared. The enterprise of exchange is one in which your partner will invest no more than do you.

This astringent comment is rendered the more pertinent by the fact that even if one excludes Russia and its impermeable psychology of hatred, the world in which we moderns perforce live is not a courteous world. The grace of God, says Belloc, is in courtesy; and it is only too true that the lack of both is manifest. We must remember that as a result of two holocausts millions of people have lived through trials almost beyond endurance. Most of them have survived a quite elementary scramble for their very lives. One notices the results most clearly, of course, in Europe and Asia. The continuing smoldering feud between the *Resistance* and the collaborators in France; the tense rift between natives and expellees in Germany; the dramatic struggle between Right and Left in Italy—these are some jets from the secret source of historically engendered hostility which coarsen manners and intensify suspicion.

Above and beyond this is the stark truth that large numbers even in the so-called Christian world have utterly lost faith. God has gone out of their lives except as a convention. He may still be Someone mother used to talk about—Someone indifferent to the fate of human flotsam, or at any rate powerless to help it. Derouted by prophets for errant philosophies, unable to find peace among the machines, not knowing how to sublimate any of their instincts and urges, they have become people without poetry in their lives; and poetry, as Wordsworth long ago observed, makes the universe habitable. Yet it is out of this brittle human substance that civilization must be molded anew. One day in Munich I called to see a priest who had in his care a kindergarten. Above his desk hung a beautiful crucifix. He said to me: "One day after a heavy raid, I walked down a badly damaged street. A man stood at a shattered window and threw this crucifix out with the remark, 'Pick it up. I don't believe in Him any more.'" And perhaps by being transferred to a place where little children are daily trained with loving care, the symbol of the Saviour of mankind became also the symbol of the mighty task of rebuilding civilization which confronts us all. No doubt what can really help is a quite simple, personal kindness, which asks no reward or any semblance of gratitude. This kindness can, to be sure, be only one aspect of holiness, and we cannot attain to its practice save through a dark night of the spirit. This night may well have the form, I think, of one's own penitential insight into how lacking in fidelity one has been to those plain things which are so easy to say and so hard to do—judge not and you will not be judged; unless you be like a little child, the Kingdom of Heaven will not let you in. Charity, says St. Paul in the passage which perhaps finds him closest in spirit to the Master he encountered on the way to Damascus, endureth all things.

Yet I do not by any means wish to imply that the Christian's approach to the problem of international cultural understanding can lead down the path of individual effort alone. The institutional organization by means of which society is enabled to carry on is the creation of the human intelligence and is therefore in some measure necessary and good. UNESCO is to be seen, then, as an official international agency of cultural exchange, which should desirably endeavor to be less an initiating body than one which sustains and abets the many efforts which are being made by a great variety of public and private bodies to counteract the divisive influences which foster hatred rather than cooperation. It is very easy to be critical of such an organization, but it is also difficult to indicate what any of us would do if we were in charge of its activities. Thus one often hears that because UNESCO does not open and close its meetings with prayer it must be an atheistic establishment. We need only to bear in mind that the peoples of the world profess various faiths in order to see how absurd this observation is. As a matter of fact, UNESCO more than any other existing organization has the allegiance of a large number of devotedly religious persons—larger than does any other international body.

Cooperating with UNESCO is a varied congregation of groups which try hard to bring about international cultural cooperation. The great caritative organizations—Catholic, Protestant, and Jewish—work together despite denominational differences to alleviate human distress. Associations of scholars and businessmen, of civic organizations and labor unions, of artists and journalists, do as much as they conceivably can to promote better relations. Perhaps the exchange of students is the most notable of these endeavors, and the one which has elicited the greatest amount of generosity. We in the United States have welcomed innumerable thousands of young people to our colleges and universities; and in turn large numbers of our young people have studied abroad. Nevertheless, viewed in the light of the existing international situation, the need is so much greater than what has been done to meet it that one's breath stops. For if we compare the inevitable hit-and-miss of our efforts with the fanatical, pile-hammer drive of the Communists for world domination, we shall hardly avoid upon occasion the sensation which must be that of men and women on a ship buffeted by hurricane winds and so threatened by the waters of the great sea. I think that in such moments one can really be comforted only by the recollection that our Saviour once walked upon the waves.

Therewith I come, in conclusion, to the great enigma of our day. Is there any way in which we can win through to the submerged and enslaved peoples of Russia and its satellites and establish some kind of cultural community with them? It is not easy for us who are the peoples of a Western society still relatively free to surmount the barriers which separate us. Is, then, communication with the Russians at all conceivable? Surely if there be any likelihood whatever that the query can be answered affirmatively we should, not merely out of a sense of ethical obligation but by reason of our own hopes of survival, be bound to weigh it with all possible earnestness. A number of suggestions have been made. For a time some American business-men thought that through the orderly development of trade it might come to pass that Moscow could be induced to manifest interest if not amity. But the Russian economists upon whose cooperation this hope depended were speed-ily liquidated by Stalin. Scientists, too, have believed that the sharing of the products of research might prove a common bond; and unfortunately it is now wholly evident that scientific inquiry likely to have any economic or military consequences is merely a target for Soviet espionage. Russians cannot freely discuss with others even so harmless a matter as the latest findings in genetics.

Religious fraternity remains. One cannot help recalling that in another and also troubled time the sons of St. Ignatius came into the territory of the Czars and made friends there. Ironically enough, had it not been for the support mustered in what was then St. Petersburg, the Society of Jesus might no longer exist. I do not believe that we can reckon with anything comparable in our time. Five or six years ago, a vigorous effort to find a new religious approach to the East might have met with some success. Not all hope of doing so should be abandoned now. But it must be borne in mind that the turbulence of evil has waxed far mightier in the intervening period. Often it seems impossible to pit anything against it save hope and prayer. It rests in the hands of God whether we shall live in the twilight hours of Christian civilization, or whether there is to be a change of fortune. Even so, I shall venture to offer a few suggestions for your consideration.

The great weakness in the armor of the West, at least insofar as Europe is concerned, is still viciously competitive nationalism. Therefore it is possible for Communist Russia to play one subject satellite country against another, as well as to sponsor the cause of any such national entity against the rest of the free world. Let me adduce by way of illustration: Moscow can fan the flames which separate Czechs from Slovaks, Hungarians from Roumanians, Ukrain-ians from Poles, and all East Europeans from Germany. In none of these situations can practical American statesmanship do much more than adopt an attitude of neutrality. Were an American diplomat to express, for example, a measure of sympathy with the Slovaks, he would immediately expose his country to attack from Czech quarters, and vice versa.

But I am persuaded that it is quite possible for a strong, well-organized, and adequately financed Catholic Association for International Peace to sponsor a series of fruitful conferences designed to evolve through amicable and charitable discussion compromise solutions of the questions at issue, so that these proposed solutions—supported by strong groups in the free world—

could in turn be advocated in a spirit of unity and utilized for what are often termed propaganda purposes behind the Iron curtain. If it could be shown that Catholic and Christian—for if at all possible Protestants must be drawn into the debate—solidarity can triumph over explosive differences rooted in the past, we shall undoubtedly be in a position to bless the peacemakers once more. Naturally it will not be easy to build up and utilize such an Association, for the one we now have is pitifully poor and limited in scope, or to find the answers desired. But it is far less improbable that this can be done than that we shall be able to oppose successfully the onslaught of Russian Communism with forces which are perennially at odds with one another.

Second, we very badly need a Catholic Institute of Russian Studies for service to which we can enlist both competent and experienced refugees as well as devoted young Americans. Such an institute should be concerned not only with theological problems such as that of Church Union but also with the exceedingly complex and difficult issues which are presented by the economic and social programs sponsored by the Soviet Union. We are, thank God, witnessing the formation of an ardent and well-trained young American Catholic cultural elite; and I very much wish that it were possible, through a generous grant of scholarships and the establishment of an institute faculty such as I have proposed, to prepare to meet in a wholly adequate way the intellectual challenge of Communism. Our approach to this challenge is, if you will permit me to say so on the basis of such information as I have gathered, far too negative in character. Almost any American can tell you why he does not like Communism. But he is usually unable to give any indication of what he proposes to do about it, apart from the quite obvious prescription that devotees of Stalin ought not to be working for the Department of State. This will not do. It is really quite unimportant whether a file clerk in that sedate department can smuggle out a memorandum of the flora and fauna of Australia. But it is of the utmost consequence to develop the intellectual and moral ability to cope with the Communist attack.

Third, I am convinced that we should assist in establishing, preferably on German soil, a School of Advanced Intercultural studies, designed to bring together students of the problems we have been considering. Attempts to establish such a school have already been made. If it is argued that such an establishment would be too academic and remote from practical life, I shall say in reply that no one can hope to win the contest for the minds of men unless he is willing to concern himself with what absorbs, engrosses, and disturbs those minds. Phrases will not help at all. For example, during the summer of 1952 a Catholic conference in Berlin listened to a number of young people from the Russian Zone comment on the Russian contention that scientific thought buttressed the Communist position. The manner in which these young men and women dealt with this favored item on the Soviet propaganda menu was so impressive that one could not help wishing there were some way in which what they had to say could be summarized and systematically developed.

Finally, it seems to me that there might well be organized, on a nationwide scale, courses dealing with the present world-wide situation for the benefit of young men who await enlistment in the armed forces. Unless we can give them something better than sporadic doses of what is currently termed McCarthyism, they will have no insight into the causes of the conflict which may demand of them the supreme sacrifice. I can only say that our soldiers abroad, fine young men though they are, often seem immersed in an intellectual fog. It is deplorable that this should be the case.

To be sure these recommendations would not, even if perchance they were adopted, suffice to insure a peaceful and permanent solution of the bitter debate in which mankind is now involved. Freedom can be maintained only if we will utilize to the uttermost every resource which is available to us. Not the least of these certainly is the intense desire of men and women in all the countries of the earth not to have comfort or tranquillity or satiety only, but finally to possess that brotherhood which is the natural presupposition on which the Church of God can build. It is scarcely possible not to hear the mighty murmur in which this desire finds expression, whether it be from the midst of the poor and relatively uneducated, or from the company of those who have some small measure of learning.

To be sure, the issue will depend ultimately less upon what we do than upon what we are. And so I should like to adduce as evidence a few words of Cardinal Newman's:

> Let us turn from shadows of all kinds—shadows of sense, shadows of argument and disputation, or shadows addressed to our imagination and tastes. Let us attempt, through God's grace, to advance and sanctify the inward man. We cannot be wrong here. Whatever is right, whatever is wrong, in this perplexing world, we must be right in "doing justly, in loving mercy, in walking humbly with God": in denying our wills, in ruling our tongues, in softening and sweetening our tempers, in mortifying our lusts; in learning patience, meekness, purity, forgiveness of injuries, and continuation in well-doing.

This has been the task of man since the dawn of his awareness that he possessed responsibilities as well as instincts. Today, in a century of unparalleled discoveries, there are above all two kinds of responsibility. The first, because the most elementary and obvious, is to the facts in the case. The scientist who in so large a measure determines the character of our age is bound with a rigidity surpassing that of ancient serfdom to respect with unremitting meticulousness whatever conclusions are dictated by the outcome of his experiments. He cannot say that the formula which emerges from his research is other than it is; for if he were to do so, not only would science have lost its meaning but he would soon be exposed to the common gaze as a charlatan and a deceiver. And in all truth the honesty and persistence of the scientist is one of the supreme phenomena of the time. Even Hitler and Stalin have not been able in the long run to tie him ideologically to any conclusion not dictated by the test tube and the mathematical calculation.

But the logic of the saint is no less inflexible. For he, too, is engaged in august research. His task is not merely to discover what the laws of God are, but to follow to the last jot and tittle whatever conclusions result from awareness of those laws. And I suppose that the collective demonstration of the saints is nothing less than whatever mankind has been able to discern to date of the justice and the love of God. We see through a glass darkly. Even St. Paul did so. But I have no doubt that before the fullness of time has come, mankind will have the opportunity to know (though it may lack the interest and faith to take advantage of its knowledge) whatever in this life can be discerned of immortal verity and bliss. Human beings will still stand shivering on the fringe land of eternity. Nevertheless the light of the Holy Spirit will be upon them.

I am profoundly convinced that if scientist and saint could somehow join hands for the final conquest of the human spirit, men would in that hour be emancipated from the petty narrowness and the divisive passion which have so often flung them at each other's throats, making the green earth the scene of their grim, revolting, and mortal combat. Will they be able to do so? I shall not take upon myself the burden of attempting to answer that fateful question. All of us remember the words which were spoken by our Lord Jesus as he gazed upon the fair city of Jerusalem. But we likewise know that he addressed speech of momentous optimism to those who were of good will.

# What Is UNESCO?
# Basic Programs and Services

## *The Program*

... Since UNESCO is an international agency concerned with the exchange of cultural goods, it must of course work side by side with, and in an effective way complement, a great variety of national agencies serving the same purpose while also seeking to advance the interests of their respective countries. Learning to know what can be done with more success through *multilateral* than through *bilateral* efforts has been and continues to be a very difficult task. For a number of years the far-flung assistance and exchange programs of the United States, for example, have dwarfed UNESCO efforts by comparison. In addition, it is not possible to strain political implications out of multi-lateral activities altogether, try though one may. These and other obstacles have not, however, prevented the organization from obtaining a measure of success no one could have anticipated. The achievement is due to the persistent efforts of men, for the most part wholly unknown to the general public, who worked in the shadow of almost constant criticism and under stringent budgetary limitations.

The program consists of five main parts:

1. Services to education, science, and culture
2. Indirect educational action
3. Offices of liaison

From George N. Shuster, *UNESCO – Assessment and Promise* (New York: Harper & Row for the Council on Foreign Relations, 1963).

4. Direct educational action
5. Operational activities within the United Nations

Although this nomenclature is somewhat arbitrary, it serves fairly well to highlight groups of activities with which all, or virtually all, the departments of UNESCO are concerned. They are listed in an ascending order of their relative dynamic character. That is, the first two groups, which form the older segments of the program, were developed while the organization was in general restricted to tasks having an "informative" or a "stimulating" character. The last two groups reflect the responses to a constantly changing world scene which UNESCO has since been authorized to make; but it should be noted that while they probably generate more excitement and require more imagination and leadership, they are not necessarily more important. There are excellent reasons for thinking that if the older program had not been devised, the newer one could hardly have come into being.

The "fragmentation" of the UNESCO program has become a grim refrain to almost any discussion of that program. Probably no other issue so differentiates official from unofficial comment in the United States. If one looks at international cultural relations from the standpoint of the struggle between communism and freedom or of the relations between the advanced and the underdeveloped countries, it may well seem that the only task which really matters is bringing the resources of education to bear on meeting the needs of peoples struggling to throw off the shackles of poverty and ignorance. Since finding money to do this job is so difficult, why waste it on undertakings of marginal utility? But if one then proceeds to ask what education is, apart from literacy and machine shop skills, the answer given by the arts and the sciences is sure to range over the gamut of the human mind. Consequently, professors of the humanities as well as natural scientists are sure to oppose making the training of man's mind a purely technical process; and so the members of the U.S. National Commission have steadfastly demanded a strengthening of the "basic" or "continuing" program. Still there can be no doubt that, particularly during the earlier years, the Secretariat was literally shoved into some pleasant blind alleys by enthusiastic General Conferences, and that by now life in some is so agreeable that those who benefit from that life resist moving out into more turbulent roads. Some tasks UNESCO has assumed ought unquestionably to be lopped off. But they are not as numerous as is sometimes supposed, nor do they affect either the budget or management in any very appreciable sense.

## The Provision of Services

The first and second parts—the service activities and the indirect educational action—constitute what is called the "basic" or "continuing" program of UNESCO. They cannot properly be isolated from the other parts though attempts have sometimes been made to do so. UNESCO's provision of services carries on and has significantly enlarged the work of the International Institute of Intellectual Co-operation. It is a multiform endeavor, which employs in the main these methods: the gathering, analysis, and reporting of information in the fields of UNESCO's interests; other publications; and conferences. Although in the category of other publications the Department of Mass Communication accounts for many journals, books, and pamphlets, all departments or divisions are involved—Education (which is the largest), Natural Sciences, Social Sciences, Cultural Activities, and International Exchange Service. In addition, there is a sort of "Department *ad interim*" (destined eventually to lose its separate status), concerned with a "Major Project" designed to promote cultural understanding between Orient and Occident. The administrative services required to support these activities are considerable and complex. Since UNESCO is a multilanguage organization, using English, French, Russian and Spanish as official tongues, the arts of translation, far from easy to master, are also a major responsibility.

The statistical documentation being provided seems gradually to be acquiring the quality and status that will make UNESCO a great center for this kind of service, which may lack glamour but is very badly needed. Indeed, if fully developed it would constitute a good reason, were there no other, why the organization should exist. At present, statistics are provided in a number of fields—among them, education (enrollments, teacher training data, opportunities for study abroad, etc.), the social sciences, library services, and mass communication. In view of the almost unsurmountable difficulties which attend the gathering of statistical data in many parts of the world, the results obtained reflect credit on the UNESCO staff. But a great deal would have to be done in terms of modernization of the equipment and of additions to personnel if UNESCO were to attempt to achieve its manifest destiny in this important area. To a marked extent the ground is being prepared by sending experts to member states to help them develop or refine their statistical methods.

Other informational and exploratory services are in many ways more problematical in character and may be described as a blend of some activities which have become traditional with others which have largely been improvised. Sometimes, as in the case of the *Index Translationum,* an heirloom from the past that records as correctly as possible whatever has been translated from one language into another throughout the world, the result is a bibliographical product which, however often applauded by librarians, probably costs more in time and effort than it is worth. At the other end of the spectrum are film strips now available in a wide range of subjects from arid-zone research to practical education in such matters as building a stove. Sometimes the dimensions of a task contemplated may be titanic. Thus, at the request of another U.N. agency, UNESCO undertook to collate reports of scientific work being done all over the world. The information was found to be so broad in scope, and the task of arriving at precise descriptions and definitions proved so baffling, that it seemed unwise to seek an immediate solution of the problem. Nevertheless, the assignment was manifestly important; the fact that entrusting it to UNESCO was thought eminently natural affords a good indication of the reputation its reporting services have earned over the years.

At the close of 1962 recommendations were being formulated for effecting further progress in scientific documentation. For it is clear that the peoples who must achieve a measure of success in coping with modern technology cannot succeed unless some way is provided for gaining insight into both the philosophy and the ever-continuing progress of the natural sciences. It is now proposed that the whole of the present bewildering area of publication, abstracting, translating, and coding be subjected to careful scrutiny; that less advanced regions be assisted by setting up centers designed to deal with the very difficult problem of keeping abreast of scientific advance; and that new technical means—notably machine translation—be developed in order to speed up improvement. If the matter is pursued with adequate vigor (which will to a large extent depend on the amount of financial support made available), there is little doubt that within a relatively short time science and technology will have taken another hurdle in stride.

The sheer bulk of what UNESCO publishes, under the rubric of "documentation" and otherwise, is almost overwhelming. *A General Catalogue of UNESCO and UNESCO Sponsored Publications* (Paris, 1962) lists 2,681 titles as having appeared by the close of 1959; and even if some entries are duplicated by reason of publication in various languages, the number is still impressive. Anyone who goes on to consider what is issued by the several departments might begin to feel that nothing is done except to see publications through the press—a quite erroneous assumption, since perhaps department heads should have more time to read and criticize manuscripts before they see the light of day in print. Just to scan publications in the field of the social sciences, for example, one would discover that what was originally the *International Social Science Bulletin* was expanded tremendously and became in 1959 the *International Social Science Journal.* Nearly everything else has developed comparably; *Basic Facts and Figures,* a yearbook reporting events in fields of interest to UNESCO, has now become the *UNESCO Statistical Yearbook.* There is an *International Bibliography of Political Science,* and comparable attention is given to sociology. One would also have to consider— the enumeration here is much briefer than the subject warrants—*Reports and Papers in the Social Sciences* as well as a veritable host of major and minor publications of a comparable kind. UNESCO pioneered, for instance, in publishing a series of books on the question of race. These were perhaps more hortatory than scientific, it is true. Not all the other departments assail the reading public with equally formidable barrages, but each does have its program, which is usually diverse and broad in scope.

Then there are more general journals of information, designed for a wider reading public even when the subject matter is somewhat specialized. First there is the UNESCO *Courier,* a lively illustrated magazine which now has a paid circulation of about 300,000 copies and a vastly larger free circulation. It discusses appropriate themes and certain organizational concerns such as observing the anniversaries of distinguished men and women. The UNESCO *Bulletin,* on the other hand, provides a running commentary on the organization's activities—is, in short, a kind of house organ. Published directly or through contract are such periodicals as *Diogenes* in the field of the humanities, *Impact,* which is a scientific journal, and *Museum,* which as its title indicates has to do with an institution important in the annals of the organization. The circulation of most of these publications is small, the quality normally good. There is a persistent temptation to increase the number of UNESCO-sponsored periodicals. . . .

## Indirect Action for Education

We come then to the second major part of UNESCO's program, its "indirect" services to education. Initially nearly everything UNESCO was instructed to undertake in the area of teaching fitted quite naturally into this classification. It was proscribed from "operating" any project—indeed, its budget was so designed as to make this kind of activity virtually impossible. To all intents and purposes it was limited to "stimulating" educational endeavor, though the term was left comparatively vague. Much of what was accomplished could also be described as the results of liaison activities. Yet there is a good deal more, often undertaken with meager resources or seemingly subject to curious inhibitions. Upon occasion there was, however, success and even drama.

Thus, although the plan to establish a world-wide network of centers dedicated to "Fundamental Education," approved at the 1951 General Conference, did not materialize in full, UNESCO established at Patzcuaro, Mexico, a most interesting "pilot" institution which combined teacher training, the production of educational materials, and work experience. In this effort, which has been known as CREFAL (from the French initials of the Regional Fundamental Education Center for Latin America), UNESCO profited from the collaboration of the Mexican government, the interest of other Latin American countries, and assistance given by several Specialized Agencies of the United Nations and also by the Organization of American States. In the light of more recent experience, the Patzcuaro experiment resembles a Latin American Cooperative Peace Corps, except that the emphasis was primarily on training rather than service. The students, coming in groups of five from various Latin American countries, were in residence during nineteen months on scholarships provided by their governments. Six months were devoted to the study of a quite practical kind of rural education, which stressed the devising and making of educational materials ranging all the way from primers to pantomine plays. During the following ten months the students applied what they had learned in villages of the surrounding countryside. Then the final three months were dedicated to the evaluation of the work experience.

The hope which inspired Patzcuaro was to stimulate Latin America to repeat on a wide scale this attempt to promote a realistic kind of rural education; and though that hope was not realized, it is generally believed that CREFAL was one of the most imaginative of UNESCO's educational enterprises during the 1950s. The United States sent two groups of students to Patzcuaro, though later its collaboration was nipped in the bud by then prevalent fears of "subversive" orientation. The nation appeared to have little confidence in its own youth.

The Patzcuaro project had a counterpart in the Middle East known as ASFEC (Arab States Fundamental Education Center), established in 1953 at Sirs-el-Layyan, a village in the Nile Delta. The Center resembled that at Patzcuaro, though the orientation was specially adapted to the environment and stressed community building. The students, who came from nine Arab states, were for the most part persons who combined leadership experience with some measure of previous training. A very considerable impact was made on surrounding villages in the sense that a remarkable community cooperative spirit was awakened. Sirs—el-Layyan, the first UNESCO undertaking to make a deep impression on European observers, was commented on appreciatively and at length by correspondents for prominent newspapers and journals. In retrospect, it seems regrettable that this "experiment station" in rural and community education could not have been duplicated many times over throughout the Orient. Regional centers proved impracticable because of intense national feeling. And in 1955 the total annual budget of UNESCO was only $10,314,538—less than the budget of many a municipal college in the United States. Nor was the climate of public opinion, particularly in the United States, very favorable to the development of education at the expense of countries other than those immediately concerned.

Meanwhile, UNESCO had begun and was busily pursuing another of the more creative, if upon occasion troublesome, of its activities in the area of indirect education. This was liaison with international organizations dedicated to education, science and culture and the provision of an increasing measure of support for them. Some organizations were closely affiliated with it, many others had consultative status, and still more were cast in the role of observers. Quite elaborate rules were established governing inclusion in any of these categories. Organizations applying for recognition were required to be truly international in character, to refrain from serving a political cause, and to entertain goals consonant with UNESCO's purposes. These rules, it may be noted, have for the most part so far prevented recognition of propaganda organizations created by the Soviet Union or its satellites, although recently the Director-General has admitted some of these to a group (Category C) over which he has control.

The number of those in all approved categories has grown steadily. The list is today a quite formidable array which includes almost all the genuinely international groups in the free world. What is the total value of this system of affiliations to UNESCO? The question is debatable, and it is to be regretted that no careful study has been made. Financial assistance given to some of the organizations is considerable. To cite two examples, the biennial subsidy proposed for the International Council of Scientific Unions in 1962 was $410,000, while that pledged to the International Council for Philosophy and Humanistic Studies was $273,000. There are many more grants-in-aid, though not in comparable amounts. In addition, contracts have been signed with a number of organizations for special services. Many others require no subsidies, though they receive UNESCO documentation and probably compensate for that favor by assisting in promoting UNESCO objectives.

One may conclude that although the nongovernmental organization program has not developed with the logic and clarity desirable, it is assuredly one very important method for accomplishing, however indirectly, the purposes of UNESCO. Possibly in the future there will be more emphasis on contracts for specific tasks and less on direct subsidies. Though exceptions unquestionably can be cited, it is almost a rule of thumb that granting subsidies year after year freezes bureaucracies to their chairs. Contracts seem more likely to keep organizations alert and alive. This is particularly true in UNESCO, which has acquired so many interests with the passing of time that some unquestionably may escape the scrutiny of the Director-General and his major assistants as completely as do the migraines of the janitor's wife. . . .

## *Liaison*

Since service to education is often the product of liaison, this third major group of activities will be considered now, before discussing in the next chapter UNESCO's direct services. . . . It should be noted here that in many of the more sensitive areas of education as it is concerned with cultural values UNESCO has opportunities which are not open to countries operating bilaterally. Few people attribute to it any propagandistic intent; and since those whom it sends as experts or counselors must be approved by the host country, its mission is accepted as disinterested. Nevertheless, one must immediately add, many states in need of help prefer bilateral assistance because of the greater volume of support likely to be forthcoming. National attitudes are as always complex and far more predictable.

The most significant of UNESCO's liaison services in the area of education, science, and culture are no doubt those which have been developed in the Department of the Natural Sciences. Soon after the close of the Second World War, it became apparent to thoughtful scientists that a large measure of international cooperation would be required if genuine progress was to be brought about in certain important fields, both of inquiry and application. This cooperation would insure the exchange of knowledge and endeavor across national boundaries otherwise virtually closed to traffic, and might also make possible in some instances the pooling of resources. As was to be expected, UNESCO would be considered the international agency potentially best qualified to effect the collaboration needed; and in 1950 a formal request was addressed by the U.N. Economic and Social Council to the organization, as an associated member of the U.N. family, for leadership in determining the need for international scientific research institutes and in evaluating ways and means of establishing them. During the same year the General Conference, meeting in Florence, instructed the Director-General to proceed with the request for liaison services.

The first such center was an international laboratory erected in Geneva by a Council of European Member States to provide for collaboration "in nuclear research of a pure scientific and fundamental character." CERN (the name derives indirectly from the French equivalent for European Organization for Nuclear Research) arose from an intergovernmental preparatory conference convened by the Director-General of UNESCO at the close of 1951, but almost immediately thereafter began to lead an autonomous existence. Nor was the situation different insofar as other studies associated with nuclear energy—e.g., the effects of radioactivity on living organisms and the use of radioisotopes for medicinal and other purposes—were concerned. Although UNESCO might take this initiative and stimulate efforts, it did not yet possess the strength, nor perhaps did it inspire sufficient confidence, to take the lead in scientific research of such obviously vital importance.

Still another venture in international scientific organization dates from the early 1950s. This is the Major Project on Scientific Research on Arid Lands. In this case UNESCO's participation and leadership have been more direct and persistent. During 1951 it created an Advisory Committee on Arid Zone Research, which has since then convened annually to consider studies conducted throughout the world on some aspect of aridity control. The reports prepared by the Committee are then published by UNESCO. This program is still being carried on. Continuing efforts are made by the Secretariat to enlist the interest of competent scientists and also to insure consideration for problems faced by those member states which are particularly affected by soil aridity.

But it was doubtless the effectiveness of UNESCO as an instrumentality of international liaison during the period of preparation for the International Geophysical Year (1957-58) which first earned for it the respect of scientists. It could open doors which otherwise would have remained closed, and in particular it made possible Soviet participation on a scale which seemed the precursor of an era less afflicted with international tensions. The value of UNESCO was again demonstrated when international cooperation in oceanography was being planned during the late 1950s. But something new had now been added. Scientists placed a high estimate on UNESCO's ability to sponsor educational action designed to conjoin research and teaching, particularly insofar as countries likely to benefit from oceanographic inquiry were concerned. The financial share in the costs of the enterprise borne by UNESCO has been a modest one. As a result of the experience gained, the area of interest has been expanded to include other sciences, notably hydrology and seismology. The latter took on special human interest because of the plea for help made by Morocco after the catastrophic effects of earthquakes suffered there. Once again a country not yet in command of modern scientific knowledge turned to UNESCO for assistance, which in turn was able to tap the resources of the U.N. Technical Assistance Program.

Other departments likewise exercise a liaison function. Of particular moment during recent years has been the study of the problems arising from social and economic development, particularly in Asia, Latin America, and Africa. We may allude here to one problem, that of coordinating progress in education with economic development. If the higher schools of a given country or region educate young men and women in relatively large numbers without any regard for what they are to do later on, the result will be an "academic proletariat" which may highlight the fate of the unemployed with notable venom. Cuba has had too many lawyers. The slums of Calcutta are doubtless teeming with philosophers having nothing to do except learn to revel in dialectical materialism. Meanwhile the real manpower needs for teachers, engineers, doctors, nurses, and technicians may not have been met. Practical international work in this field depends to a considerable extent on the proper coordination of the various interested agencies of the United Nations. Faithful to what is now one of its traditions, UNESCO has established two centers, one at Calcutta to deal with conditions in South Asia, and another at Rio de Janeiro which it is hoped will minister to Latin America. Such success as these may have must depend on the ability of the Director-General to enlist the interest and support of the member states involved, and of course also upon how well the appropriate agencies in the United Nations can work together in developing experience in this complex field.

## The Free Flow of Information

One area in which UNESCO's liaison efforts have been persistent, but unfortunately only in part successful, is that of the free flow of information. In the early years great stress was laid on this task because international understanding can develop organically only when it is possible to create an uninhibited traffic in information, considering the barriers of ignorance, fear, prejudice, and sheer surfeit of materials. But the nature of the time in which we live has not been favorable for the application of this principle. In several respects the situation has undoubtedly deteriorated. Armed conflict in parts of the world, the cold war, intensified nationalist sentiment in some areas, animosities between peoples, and sometimes a failure of technical organization have all led to censorship and, more regrettably still, to waves of propaganda designed for the most part to obscure the truth. It was quite impossible for any international body, no matter how widely supported, to remove all these deleterious factors from the scene.

UNESCO has therefore worked, and upon occasion effectively, to improve the mechanics of exchange. As early as 1950, the General Conference approved an international agreement designed to eliminate import duties on books, periodicals, and certain educational materials. The Director-General likewise urged the GATT Conference of 1956 to propose a reduction of duties in the same categories. In both cases a measure of success was achieved. Help of a different kind was effectively provided through the UNESCO Book Coupon Scheme, authorized in 1948 when the purchase of books needed by scholars in war-devastated countries was a matter of vital necessity. Since UNESCO was operating in Paris and to some extent at least in "soft currency" areas, it could manage to pay publishers in the United States, for example, in hard currencies and accept the equivalent in other kinds. By 1956, when the scheme was modified, coupons in the amount of nearly $9 million had been redeemed. The service was not abandoned, but a reorganization of the procedures eliminated the drain on UNESCO's budgetary resources. In retrospect, the Book Coupon Scheme can surely be characterized as an effective means of aiding in educational reconstruction.

Efforts to remove financial obstacles to the free flow of information continue. The GATT agreement is to be reviewed presently, and UNESCO has taken steps to help safeguard the gains so far made, as well as to seek the cooperation of states not yet involved. More recently three conventions, proposed by UNESCO and the Customs Co-operation Council to facilitate the import of mass communication equipment and material designed for exhibitions, have been drawn up and wide acceptance of the provisions is anticipated. Another convention dealing with scientific instruments and equipment is under consideration. These constitute additional useful instrumentalities for removing barriers in the interest of education. While these achievements do not come near accomplishing what is desirable, they are nevertheless very much worth while.

## The Nubian Monuments

An unusual venture in liaison was begun in 1960 when the Director-General of UNESCO, responding to a request from the governments of the United Arab Republic and the Sudan, launched an appeal for contributions to rescue the monuments of Pharaonic culture in the Nubian Valley from inundation as a result of the building of the Aswan High Dam. For decades British officials stationed in Egypt had known how to use the three months of the year when Nubia is almost as close to being paradise, insofar as climate is concerned, as it is possible to come on this woeful earth. Nor had they lacked skill to advertise it. But that art works of priceless value were to be submerged under the pent-up waters of the Nile was news for most people. (If the United States had chosen to build the High Dam, the major temples would doubtless have been preserved as a matter of course, but it did not so elect.) The appeal which the Director-General thereupon addressed to the world was in accord with one of the responsibilities which have been entrusted to UNESCO, namely the preservation of cultural monuments as parts of the precious legacy of mankind. But what was to be done? The language used in the Director-General's Report of 1960 says in part:

> An organizational structure has been set up, commensurate with the importance of this project. It comprises: a Committee of Patrons, under the chairmanship of His Majesty, Gustav VI Adolf of Sweden, bringing together some forty persons of world-wide renown; an International Action Committee, consisting of 15 leading figures in the world of culture; a special consultant to the Director-General, Prince Sadruddin Aga Khan; advisory panels of experts attached to the two governments directly concerned; National committees in more than 20 Member States. . . .

In short, all the secular icons had been aligned, and it remained only to be seen whether the response would be adequate to make available the huge sum required, estimated as high as $100 million. The project was divisible into four parts: first, archaeological research on sites which would be inaccessible once the waters of the Nile had been artificially raised—research which was in fact rather widely undertaken as a result of the appeal; second, the removal of several smaller temples, stone by stone, and their transfer to new sites—a task which several European countries undertook and which the United States has in part subsidized; third, the building of a protecting wall round the Temple of Philae, gem of the Nubian Valley, which the United States agreed to sponsor; and finally the rescue of the Temple of Abu Simbel from the waters, an enterprise which has not yet been underwritten. In order to save Abu Simbel it was thought necessary to cut sections into the rock out of which the twin temples of Rameses and Nefertari have been carved, two vertical sections and one horizontal one, and then to raise the huge severed mass two hundred feet. Doubtless the Pharaonic builders would have considered this a feat worthy of their best tradition.

The Director-General tried in vain to induce the General Conference which convened during 1963 to accept responsibility for salvaging Abu Simbel and to allocate funds for the purpose. Orators indicated that there were monuments elsewhere that badly needed rescuing, and so the unfolding vista was one to rouse fear in even the staunchest fiscal officers. All eyes have therefore naturally turned again to the United States. Could sufficient money from the funds accruing in Egyptian currency as a result of shipments of surplus wheat and other commodities be diverted to saving the great temple? A number of practical problems arose. Did the Egyptian government itself attach sufficient priority to Abu Simbel? Was the method proposed for lifting it above the anticipated water level the only possible one, or were there other less costly possibilities? And, more generally, could the expenditure be justified?

It might be argued, and sometimes was, that since the Russians had undertaken to build the dam, it was properly their affair. For were they not vehemently contending that their engineering skills would serve the masses? As a matter of fact, there was no lack of feeling that a sum so large should rather be expended on education or some similarly beneficent purpose. After all, is there not a surfeit of Pharaonic memorials, at Luxor and elsewhere? But when all has been said and done, every lover of mankind's cultural heritage must deeply regret the possibility that Abu Simbel, jewel of the Nubian Valley, may disappear from view. Even from a strictly utilitarian standpoint, it might add sufficiently to the charm of the landscape to make the Valley, assuming a normal amount of tourist energy, a magnet which would bring a measure of life during several months of the year into the desert world through which the Nile flows like a lost ribbon of silver.

In any event, this is the story of what no doubt can be characterized as UNESCO's most romantic enterprise. Whether it was wise to undertake it, in view of the bewildering complexity of the tasks assigned to the organization, is a moot question. But beyond any doubt it stirred the admiration of many throughout the world and proved that an international organization need not be merely a bureaucracy. The plan required daring, imagination, and a large measure of optimism.

# IV

## ON EDUCATION

Active in national and international affairs, Shuster has remained primarily an educator and is most at home in a university setting. He has always loved the classroom but has spent most of his years administering one college and advising another. It is not surprising, therefore, that he should have strong views about the nature and functions of a college president.

In 1968 Shuster delivered the "Founder's Day Address" at the installation of Robert D. Cross as president of Hunter College. Reminiscing about the old Hunter and encouraging the new president, Shuster presented his perception of an effective academic administrator. He thought no better description existed than that penned by St. Benedict for his monastic community fifteen hundred years ago:

> Let one of the community be chosen; . . . who is wise, mature in character, temperate, not a great eater, nor arrogant nor quarrelsome, not insolent, and not a dawdler, nor wasteful, but one who fears God and is a father to the community. Let him have charge of everything . . . and not make the brethren sad. If any of them shall perchance ask something unreasonable, he must not vex him by contemptuously rejecting his argument, but humbly and reasonably refuse what he wrongly asks. . . . Above all, let him . . . give a gentle answer to those to whom he can give nothing else, for it is written that a good word is above the best gift. . . . [I]f the community be

Adapted from the article by Vincent P. Lannie in *Leaders in American Education,* Seventieth Yearbook of the National Society for the Study of Education, Part II (Chicago: University of Chicago Press, 1971), pp. 306-320.

large, let him be given helpers, by whose aid he may without worry perform the office committed to him. What is given let it be given, and what is asked for let it be asked at suitable times, so that no one is troubled or distressed.[1]

Although some of these Benedictine admonitions must be refined and seen within a contemporary context, Shuster believes that they summarize the functions of a top administrator and enable him to be "courageous and forward-looking, resourceful and wise."[2]

Even before he addressed Benedict's maxims to the young Robert Cross, Shuster had categorized the qualities necessary for an effective college president. Such a person must be able to speak with large groups persuasively, meet countless and diverse people with equanimity, possess an iron stomach for public dinners, be a good public relations man and an excellent fund raiser, and "be in tune with the traditions of a given campus . . . without being hidebound about his allegiance to them." He must be accessible to students, genuinely fond of them, and aware of their problems and hopes. He must learn to delegate authority but be prepared to shoulder responsibility for decisions which are his alone. In the last analysis Shuster, looking back over his many years as an administrator, contends that a college president must have "a stout heart, a tough skin, a sense of humor, and . . . a core of unflinching and indestructible honor."[3]

Yet Shuster has never been interested primarily in administrative theory and practice. In discussions of educational values his priorities have been goals and ideals. Nor has he been oblivious to the fact that any educational ideal depends upon its underlying concept of human nature. Such an ideal becomes even more difficult to fashion in a philosophically and religiously pluralistic country such as the United States.

Shuster has always related religious thought to human behavior and educational philosophy. A deeply religious person with an abiding conviction in man's moral integrity, he has affirmed, as another commentator has declared, "the spiritual roots and moral overtones of all American education with its historic democratic convictions and purposes."[4] His creed that learning and wisdom are of little significance without moral purpose emerges

[1] George N. Shuster, "Founder's Day Address." Speech delivered at Hunter College of the City University of New York, February 14, 1968, pp. 1-2.

[2] Ibid., p. 2.

[3] The Ground I Walked On, p. 30; George N. Shuster, Education and Moral Wisdom (New York: Harper and Brothers, 1960), p. 13.

[4] Education and Moral Wisdom, p. v.

clearly in a group of essays published in 1960 under the title *Education and Moral Wisdom.* Knowledge is important, but moral wisdom is indispensable to man's most noble and ultimate values. As a result, human virtue always takes precedence over the acquisition of human knowledge. Above all, the seeking after truth is more important than its discovery because the search itself is a "heartening, cleansing, [and] ennobling experience." The quest for truth and beauty is not affected by a particular environment nor is it lost simply because "the world in which one happens to be living is false and tawdry." Shuster happened upon this insight one evening while lying in a "louse-infested" trench in Lorraine during World War I. Next to him lay an old French soldier who nightly read a battered volume of Aeschylus before he slumbered into a few hours of restless sleep. It was as if this Frenchman were telling him that Greek poetry is as impervious to war "as the sunset is to a man's desire for day." Shuster had studied Greek literature for many years in school, but it was on the Lorraine battlefield that he discovered its rich dimensions. In the final analysis, declares Shuster in language reminiscent of Platonic thought, "the sole thing that matters is that a boy or girl go away from college with an unfettered mind, knowing that the only treasure which will not trickle away is the small change of beauty and truth he keeps in his soul." This is why he defines education as "human nature trying to become more human, in the best sense of the term." With regularity he has stressed the belief that moral decision is indispensable to man's intellectual life. "One cannot honestly or successfully live the life of the mind," he once reminded incoming students as they were about to begin their college career at Hunter, "unless one is committed wholeheartedly to what is true and what is free."[5]

These views about the general nature of education are consistent with Shuster's understanding of the liberal arts, which he places at the core of the college experience. And yet he is quite candid about certain "myths" which he insists are associated with the meaning of a liberal education. The first myth is that "merely taking a program in the liberal arts" will prepare people to earn a livelihood. For a knowledge of all the great ideas of the world and a familiarity with the leading figures of history will not equip students to cope with the world in which they find themselves. Thus, at Hunter Shuster urged students to take such courses as typing and stenography and advised his girls to understand the psychology of the male and the problems encountered in raising a family. He has always thought it incredible that a college should

[5] *The Ground I Walked On,* pp. 1-3, 100; *Education and Moral Wisdom,* p. 43.

"help young people fail in everything else than their classes."[6] The second myth is that colleges can offer a complete education for the professions or specific vocations. Certainly they can offer preparatory instruction and some training, but no more. The other ingredients are obtained on the job and depend in good measure upon the moral integrity and determination of the practitioner. The good physician, for instance, has knowledge, character, insight, and magnanimity, while the bad doctor is an imposter "who sells patients his wholly worthless degree."[7] Shuster reflects that students are harmed when a college conveys the impression that competency in a pre-scribed course or program will prepare them for a lifetime of work.

In this connection, Shuster has recorded his observations about the educational views of John Dewey and Robert Hutchins—both of whom he came to know personally. A reformer of education whose prose style often clouded his thought, Dewey persuaded the American public that youthful participation was an important dimension in education. But Shuster contends that Dewey's followers overestimated "the prowess of the junior members of the firm" and that the master was romantically naive in thinking that "making democracy interesting in school would also make it work outside of school." More important, however, Dewey's philosophy of pragmatic relativism has always been alien to Shuster's religious absolutism. He has never been able to understand Dewey's proposal "to bridge the gap between the 'liberal' class-room and his new way of looking at the world, in which Relativism had become the only Absolute and so made the past obsolete." Although many of Dewey's strictures of traditional pedagogical methods were valid, and some of his ideas on the teaching process are still relevant, Shuster believes that the Columbia professor's grand mistake was to see "the enemy in caricature rather than in the round."[8] At the same time, Shuster argues that Hutchins' thought is really understood only within the context of Dewey's *Democracy and Education*, which stresses "the fostering of community, and the forma-tion of character." For Hutchins learning means the mastering of a "common language" of the mind, that is, familiarity with the basic literature of mankind (hence his emphasis on the great books) and the ability to use this language in reasonable dialectic. The true end of education is the formation of a community of persons competent in these abilities which would then

[6] *Education and Moral Wisdom*, pp. 6-8.

[7] *Ibid.*, p. 8.

[8] *Ibid.*, pp. 88-91.

establish a democratic society—one, it might be added, envisioned both by Dewey and Hutchins.[9]

Shuster finds it almost impossible to define a liberal education. It seems to be "an experience to be lived through, a banquet that is served, a journey entered upon and only in a certain sense completed." At another time and in a less poetic mood, he characterized the liberal arts as "a course of study designed to encourage tentatively integrated learning about man's most fruitful insights into himself and the reality about him, so that a student may feel the texture of the known in order to be able to realize, sooner or later, that this is only the garment of the unknown."[10] When he talks about the pursuit of truth, therefore, he is referring to a person who comes to grasp at least a part of reality regardless of where he finds it. As a result, he feels that the real value of Hutchins' program of the great books lies not so much in the books themselves as in the methods proposed to discuss them, namely, the *disputatio* and the *colloquium*. Thus, influenced by "Dewey's idea of the community, Hutchins' practice of dialectic, and Martin Buber's philosophy of the dialogue," Shuster maintains that the "great conversation" is indispensable in the college experience. However, this emphasis on dialogue leaves room in the curriculum for vocational subjects or as Shuster labels them, "vocational inlays" which he describes as "modest essays in the art of preparing for life."[11] Although knowledge can be systematized and organized, Shuster concludes that it can never finally be synthesized, even if all the encyclopedias of the world were added to the hundred or thousand great books. For each human being is on his own. In its ultimate sense, integration is something quite different. "It is silence." Or to put it in the thought of St. Paul, to whom Shuster pays devotion, one sees in part now and in full only later. And so in a utopian stance, Shuster offers a dream of a new world:

> . . . [a world] in which anyone who desists after his fiftieth year from gainful employment, in order to devote time and energy to the task of thinking through his experience for the benefit of himself and his fellows, will be exempt from all taxes. Such men will not write a great deal. But from time to time, I trust, they may say something in which humor, caution, and learning are blended with a deep concern for everlasting values. Perhaps in that blessed era one or two of them will receive

[9] *Ibid.*, pp. 91-94.

[10] *Education and Moral Wisdom*, pp. 42, 113, 110, 62-63; *The Ground I Walked On*, pp. 110-111, 108.

[11] *The Ground I Walked On*, p. 106; *Education and Moral Wisdom*, p. 9.

honorary degrees, even though they cannot endow the university with a chair for the study of Belgian marbles and Egyptian miniatures. It may even be that someone will be honored for having suggested that prayer is an intellectual exercise.[12]

Interest in higher education kept Shuster at Hunter for over two decades. Concern for Catholic education returned him to Notre Dame thirty years after he had left his alma mater. Just as he has expressed beliefs about higher education in general, he has presented strong views about its Catholic dimension. A Catholic college must be primarily a good college which at the same time is Catholic in religious orientation. He has little sympathy with Catholic colleges which confuse their intellectual responsibilities with their religious commitment. In this respect he quotes John Henry Newman: "Knowledge is one thing, virtue another; good sense is not conscience, refinement is not humility, nor is largeness and justice of view faith." The personal holiness of a cleric, nun, or lay person can never substitute for effective teaching and sound scholarship. Shuster first recorded these thoughts in an essay "On Catholic Education" written in 1958. Nine years later, after the Second Vatican Council, he wrote *Catholic Education in a Changing World,* which offers fresh insights into the present state and future progress of Catholic higher education. In this volume Shuster argues that the Catholic college, like any first-rate institution of higher learning, must alert students to new problems and solutions facing contemporary man, must be staffed by competent teachers who will be given freedom to pursue scholarship, must be concerned with the aesthetic as well as the intellectual life of man and, as a specifically Catholic institution, must foster man's social responsibilities within the spirit of Vatican Council II. No longer can a Catholic college justify its existence on the nineteenth-century immigrant rationale of preserving students' religious faith in a hostile and secularistic society. Shuster believes that these colleges must demonstrate their capability of providing a "first-rate education within the context of a Catholic community."[13] Otherwise they will simply dry up and fade into a happy but justified oblivion. This means that such colleges emphasize not only the past but the present, not only the heavenly city but the earthly one as well.

In some ways Shuster's ideas about a Catholic university have remained unchanged, but in other ways his thinking has been altered by the intellectual

---

[12] *Education and Moral Wisdom,* pp. 62-63.

[13] George N. Shuster, *Catholic Education in a Changing World* (New York: Holt, Rinehard and Winston, 1967), p. 182. (See also paper edition University of Notre Dame Press, 1969.)

currents of post-Vatican II days. Whereas formerly he subscribed to New-man's contention that the primary justification for a Catholic university was an unfettered school of theology, in *Catholic Education in a Changing World* Shuster concedes that this rationale is no longer adequate. For theology offers ways to study the family of man and the life of God, but only some of the ways. The social sciences have their own methods; the physical sciences offer other alternatives; and the arts, still other avenues. As far as he can understand the present and glimpse into the future, Shuster would place the following sentiments upon the lips of faculty members and students:

> We are men and women who have resolved to lead the life of the mind in a way which only a genuine university, combining rigor with courtesy, can provide in every dimension of scholarly venture and worth. At the same time, we have accepted with all our hearts Pascal's wager that God is and has spoken. We have done this for a variety of reasons, so that in our diversity we offer, as does life itself, testimony which is one through man.[14]

Nevertheless, this change of focus has not altered Shuster's other basic contentions about a Catholic university. All points of view must be present and yet be justified before the exacting demands of their respective disciplines. Such diversity alone can "provide the breadth of association with the whole human family which is the proper mode of the life of the Church. Indeed, it is not too much to say that a Catholic university without such a leaven would be stale bread."[15] In this environment, the freedom to explore and challenge is indisputable, and the new function of the Catholic university is to "replace censorship with criticism." A competent scholar must proceed where his evidence seems to lead him regardless of his conclusions and despite their real or apparent antagonism to official Catholic doctrine. Within such an intellectual milieu, administrators must come to accept this freedom of inquiry the more they realize that "only the unfettered mind can be unimpeachable."[16]

Shuster insists that this freedom is essential if Catholics are to comprehend the diversity of experiences, disciplines, and aspirations in the life of man. Picking up Pascal's reference to the human-divine wager, Shuster judges that "it makes all the difference which side of the wager a man is on, but, above everything, all are members of the human family, guided by conscience and

---

[14] *Ibid.*, pp. 198-199.
[15] *Ibid.*, p. 202.
[16] *Ibid.*, pp. 203-204.

the laws of evidence."[17] Thus, the university must be open to those who are qualified to enter and must give ear to all who have something to say. Moreover, the university must never prostitute its intellectual or moral position for financial gain, though it "must do many things which are in the public interest" even when the "work may be distracting and sometimes disappointing."[18] Here Shuster seems to reflect Dewey's concern that an educational institution become part of the total community in which it finds itself.

For nearly half a century Shuster has argued that Catholics have traditionally lived in social and intellectual isolation and have had little inclination to enter into the nation's total life. But the university's environment has now changed, just as church and country are in the agonizing process of change. American Catholics must now take their place on the national intellectual scene—not with any chauvinistic pride that they alone possess *the* truth, but rather as partners engaged with their fellows in the human pursuit of truth and light. Hopefully, the new Catholic university will help them "sense more acutely the blessing which lies on all Being, all truth about Being, because it is of God."[19]

Does such a Catholic university exist anywhere in the United States? In 1958 Shuster evidenced pessimism in response to this question. "We have as yet no such university, and unless there is a change in the way things are going we never will have one."[20] But that was before the Second Vatican Council opened wide the gates and allowed fresh air to come into the many doors of the Church. Shuster arrived at Notre Dame before the sessions of the Council had begun. Since then he has tasted of its substance and has feasted upon its possibilities. He came to Notre Dame to contribute toward the transformation of a college into a great Catholic university. And although the academic millennium has not yet arrived, Notre Dame is at least moving in the right direction. For this Shuster is pleased and has youthful confidence in the work ahead.

[17] *Ibid.*, pp. 202-203.
[18] *Ibid.*, p. 204.
[19] *Ibid.*, p. 207.
[20] *Education and Moral Wisdom*, pp. 78-79.

# What Is Education?

"Truth," said Pestalozzi the optimist, indicating therewith his approach to education, "is a medicine which takes hold." This metaphor appears to find wide endorsement. The pragmatist may have his version of "truth," and the Thomist another, but they seem to agree here, even if (to venture a debatable generalization) the first judges by the value of the medicine and the second by the value of the truth. Pessimists also appear not to dissent, save when they are devotees of total negation; and it is to them one naturally turns for comment on the ills of our time. "There is in man," George Bernanos wrote, "a secret and incomprehensible hatred, not only of his fellowman but of himself." This hatred, thought to be more than a mere absence of love, is thus viewed as the hidden malignant malady of the human will, and truth flowering in affection alone can cure it. For H. G. Wells, on the other hand, as his final treatise reveals, man's tragic difficulty lies in his mind's inability to adapt itself to the constantly changing conditions that result from its own inventiveness. He has gone into the cellars of nature and come up with its headiest wine. But he cannot cope with the power intoxication that this induces. This view, if correct, would seem to suggest that one kind of truth at least is a fateful poison. The medicine has taken hold, but it is evil. Therefore, unless there be another kind of truth no antidote can be found.

Should we not then say, somewhat tritely, that the schools must seek what man tries to find? And if we discuss education in such a context, should we

Reprinted by permission of *Daedalus,* Journal of the American Academy of Arts and Sciences, Boston, Mass. Winter 1959, *Education in the Age of Science.*

not consider what it is as a process before we attempt to define its concern
with truth? At any rate, this is what we shall proceed to do. The schools
constitute a kind of arc, the extremities of which are rooted in wholly
disparate functions. At the outset, the teacher is a person who tells children
what it is considered desirable they should know—verbal symbols, the multiplication table, the names of rivers and seas, and phrases expressing civic,
ethical, and religious beliefs. A little later there will be consideration of what
Paul Weiss calls "the mastery of techniques"—of diction and reckoning, of
accuracy, of the progression of thought from data to conclusions. At the
other end of the academic span there is, however, in principle no concern
with the imparting of knowledge. The scholar in his study, the monk in his
cell, the scientist in his laboratory—if you will, the poet under his tree—for all
of these the dialogue is starkly between the self and Reality. Moses is on his
mountain, Pascal in his room. To make such conversation possible in terms of
scholarship may well be the central assignment of the university. And if one
would see what the cost is, inside or outside of academic walls, one has only
to study the lives of four men who perhaps best represent the aspirations of
modernity—van Gogh, Kierkegaard, Einstein, and Planck. Only gradually,
sometimes with agonizing slowness, will the thrill and the terror of discovery,
or pseudo-discovery, be communicated and begin to travel back over the line
of the arc. Some discovered values never disappear from education, and
others do not enter into its purview at all.

Between the grade school and the research institute lie the reaches of
education in which there takes place a sort of fusion between exploration
shared and knowledge imparted. The reputable college, for example, must at
least upon occasion be akin to Augustine's *Cassiciacum,* where in goodly
fellowship problems like that of "the happy life" were discussed in the give
and take of dialogue. Yet even the best of such institutions will normally be
busy with things thought rather than with man thinking. Carlyle held that
one must be content with enough happiness to get one's work done. Manifestly, education in its intermediate stage keeps busy giving young people
sufficient knowledge (and it may be insufficient wisdom) to perform useful
service in the world. Catering to utility, as a matter of fact, may tempt the
fully academic mind to derisory or even ribald comment. But if all of us on
campuses are quite honest, will we not admit that a great deal of what we do
is cognate in character and purpose?

At any rate, scrutiny will reveal how closely the three concerns—knowledge, inquiry, and usefulness—are intertwined. A great many young women,
for instance, are trained to teach in nursery and grade schools. I think it quite
probable that my own college, while little more than a secondary school, was
graduating teachers fully as able to impart the kind of instruction needed as it

is now doing when it has become a sedate and rather exacting college of liberal arts. Why not? If your task is to teach addition and subtraction, you need to know about these and not about the calculus, which is in the course of study only because it is believed to give the student as a person insight into an aspect of Reality that she will then know about but not use. Even more notable is the fact that we have added to the training program a great deal of information about theoretical and applied psychology. Obviously this, whatever its value, is not supposed to be taught in turn. It is part of the course of study because of our hope that when the teacher has learned something of what research workers have found out about children, she will see these in a broader and clearer perspective than would otherwise be the case.

Nor is the situation fundamentally very different with college teaching, though at first sight it may seem otherwise. No one has as yet proved, or is likely to do so, that there is any genuine relationship between earning a doctorate by writing a treatise on the sources of *Samson Agonistes* and teaching a course in Milton to juniors. Granted a reasonable amount of aesthetic intelligence, one no doubt could manage a wholly satisfactory semester with only the text and a convenient manual. The academic accessories probably do little more than befog the student's mind. But the fact that the instructor has the long trek to the doctorate behind him does, unless he be a dolt, enable him and his students to see each other in a wholly different and more invigorating light than either would otherwise manage, for through this companionship a young man at a desk will gain some insight into the processes of the exploration of the knowable. Fichte thus instructed the scholar: He "is to forget what he has accomplished as soon as it is accomplished, and is to think constantly of what he must still do." To have lived for some time in communion with such a scholar will be for many a young person as exhilarating, and one must immediately add as humbling, as standing on a Darien peak.

It appears unlikely that the situation is wholly different insofar as other callings are concerned. A candidate for appointment to the foreign service will have to know whatever that service at the time deems important, including how to write and speak a foreign language. But having painfully mastered Spanish, he will normally find himself in Timbuktu or Saigon as a vice-consul, dutifully writing out visa prescriptions or practicing minor roles in the eternal drama of commerce. The average chemist will become a member of some chain gang of scientists marshaled like a posse for ferreting out a new explosive or antibiotic. And the political scientist, fresh from the study of the arcana of government, will be fortunate if he can pass a civil service examination and proceed daily to chores with the Housing Authority or the Bureau of the Budget. But if somewhere along the road such a student has caught a glimpse of the "city" as seen by a man for whom the span between Plato and Quincy Wright does not exhaust the vision of that "city" as it has been or may be, he will not sleep without dreams.

I believe we may therefore conclude that as education proceeds it does not lose sight of the purposiveness implicit in its beginnings—namely the imparting of knowledge—but will, when it is wisely conceived, also reckon constantly with the ultimate objective, which is sharing the life of the scholar, poet, and saint. As a matter of fact, it will be driven to do so by the passion of the best students it serves. These will question the knowledge of their teachers but never the awe of them as they stand on the brink of discovery. Thoreau in his time asked whether Concord could not "hire some Abelard to lecture us." The query seems to be universal, save possibly when men have become uninhibitedly utilitarian. It seeks wisdom for the many through the contemplation of the one. And whether the answer be given in terms of experimental science, or in those of the speculative intellect as with the Greeks, or in those of the prophecy embedded in the Hebraic tradition, or in those of mysticism either Christian or Oriental, it will be in the final analysis the celestial fruit of a wedding between the "I" and the "Thou," to use Martin Buber's pertinent phrasing. We begin with the communication to others of the easily known in order that at long last we may find ourselves closeted with the unknown. Only if we are so placed, at least waveringly, hesitatingly, fleetingly, can we mortal beings acquire the sense of comedy and tragedy, of the holy and the profane, that gives us the stature to which it is our destiny to aspire.

Perhaps we may now venture to define the liberal arts as follows: a course of study designed to encourage tentatively integrated learning about man's most fruitful insights into himself and the reality about him, so that a student may feel the texture of the known in order to be able to realize, sooner or later, that this is only the garment of the unknown. If the known were the whole of being, we should have no answer to Newman's question about Scaliger: How could so much learning have passed through the mind of one man—and why did it pass? Aquinas in his day held that the ultimate properties of being must remain unknown, just as the potential existence of a human creature cannot cease to be enigmatical. To think of molecular movement going on constantly inside a baseball thrown to a hitter is merely to tease oneself out of thought. If the psychiatrist could map out his patient's psyche, the therapeutic task would be less impossible. He cannot do so. In the final analysis there is relatively little we can really know of other men, save that we aspire to the truth about them.

Let me add a few comments that regrettably are more addicted to the vice of generalization than could be wished. First, the educator must realize that what the storerooms of the past contain is indispensable treasure. Of necessity he will challenge the accusation of pedantry constantly leveled against him, but he cannot function unless this charge is in some measure justified. He must have books about him that few other men read. The genesis and progression of ideas he will observe with a reverence other men do not feel. Indeed, one may go so far as to say that the great teacher has a genuine affection for the past, which makes the sharp lighting up of any of its moods or features a memorable experience. But he must avoid like the plague every form of dotage leading to the assumption that he or any other human being exists for the sake of knowing what is already known. How often, indeed, does research undertaken by the fraternity of educators seem a tedious adding up of figures in old ledgers!

One need not assert that it is valueless even so, but the teaching scholar will not live for his students if he be merely afraid of becoming an unwise virgin with no oil in the lamp. Yesterday must be for him the coast line on which he can stand before plunging into the unplummeted and perilous sea of tomorrow. Therefore, secondly, education must accept as a kind of law that even the rediscovery of the past must have relevance for the present. A man will be worth his salt if he sees quite clearly that his life will be worth while only if at some moment at least he is visited by a creative and illuminating intuition of reality, personal and not mimicked. This, I think, can be seen occurring again and again in the experience of Whitehead or Hocking, but it is no doubt the fire that brings wisdom into being wherever it is enkindled. At any rate, age is meaningless if this virility be present in the teacher, and that youth knows instinctively. Thus gifted, the scholar will realize that Kierkegaard's grasp of the meaning of Hegel, or Einstein's insight into the principles of relativity, came to them as young men. He will not disparage what is called the "creative," though he will cling to his role of critic. Because he himself has passed through the open door of the mind, he will respect pioneer intellectual effort, no matter how seemingly revolutionary or unexpected the forward thrust may be.

It follows that education is in part the preservation not merely of what has been learned but also of the traditions, the methods, of learning. These are several, not singular. No doubt a major educational mishap has been the assumption that the always salutary debate about what should be selected for the classroom from the vast accumulation of the known involves agreement as to a certain formula for learning to know it. There are educators whose pedagogical dogmas brook no criticism. But as a matter of fact one individual's best way of learning may be quite different from another's. One nation, to some extent conditioned by historical environment, will not learn most adequately in the same way another nation does. We may note in passing that this is probably the principal discovery made by the Soviets in their satellite areas. Why should anybody take it for granted that all teachers must subscribe, for their souls' salvation, to a single formula? But if any teacher be a canny person, he will certainly weigh methods that have proved useful for other teachers, and he will be as objective in evaluating them as a purchasing agent is when examining samples of leather. He will consider the advice of Comenius and Kirchensteiner, Loyola and Dewey, Ulich and Livingstone. It will not occur to him that all sound educating is contained in an approximation to a full comprehension of one aspect of education.

Therewith we come to the meaning of the terms in Pestalozzi's maxim. What shall we say about truth? And what about the medicine that takes hold? In other words, how shall education conceive of the real and the good? What then is truth? You will not expect me to put the questions in terms of philosophical inquiry, as if perchance I felt able to improve upon Spinoza. What will be under discussion here is this: When education declares that its function is to find and to teach truth, to what is it committing itself? The completely frank answer in terms of the actual existing situation is: to not very much. There are vast numbers of students and teachers, at all academic levels, for whom the task assigned is merely to absorb and emit a specified quantity of information, in the hope that a sufficient amount will be retained by the student to make possible his academic survival after examination. Of course it is expected that the data imparted will be reasonably accurate from the giver's and the receiver's point of view—that the class will not say *le escargots* or assert that Shakespeare began his career by writing *The Tempest*. Therewith truth has become accuracy in the mnemonic reproduction of determinable data. It is of considerable interest to note that the majority of the vocal critics of our schools are like most of those schools' supporters in seeming not to want more of education than this. The difference between them is merely one of emphasis on certain facts as being more valuable than others.

It is probably evident from what has been said that this version of "truth" seems inadequate to me, though I should not wish to be thought ignoring the kernel of realism that is in it. Nor does it seem less injudicious to isolate, as some have, what Pestalozzi may have meant by "medicine." To assume that "good citizens" can be made to emerge from the schools as hot cross buns do from a bakery is to take a benign view indeed of human nature and the teaching profession. This happens to be what never happens. To be sure, good schools are often effective conditioning devices. If youngsters can be induced to absorb moral maxims into their blood streams at a sufficiently early age, the effect may be relatively lasting. But in this realm it is especially pertinent to bear in mind Heidegger's phrase, *das im Sagen Ungesagte*—that which the sayer has not said. The moral *paideia* of the schools will congeal in the psyches of young scholars like a lump of indigestible fat in the pottage unless it can be fused with the drift of the intellect and the genuine drive of the will. Character is never formed as aught save conscience; and this is not a recipe book but a living commitment to sublimation of the self. That most reason-ably gifted men and women wish to make that commitment is, I think, fortunately true. Yet all experience seems to indicate that what can be done from without to intensify this desire and direct it to good ends—that is, by the family, the school, and the church—is to awaken joy and pride in belonging. A youngster who is jubilantly confident of the stature of his preparatory school will wish to be worthy of it, and this longing may endure through life. And it seems indubitable that the influence of the church is proportionate to its ability to evoke affectionate trust in its practice of the holy life. This may seem as if man were here being doomed to becoming "organization man." Aristotle long since so doomed him, as the evidence required. What alone matters is the quality of his gregariousness.

"Truth" as education must conceive of it is, then, primarily awareness of the vital activity of the receptive, creative human mind face to face with reality in the whole of its illusory overtness and its revealing concealment. It is on the one hand "man thinking" and on the other that which can be seized and held in thought. "Truth" therefore cannot be for any wise teacher merely "what he troweth," to borrow Newman's words, because while awareness must be vividly personal it is nevertheless bound to the whole with hoops firmer than steel. Here is a brief comment on a characteristic, though not always recognized, trait of Aquinas taken from a recent book by Josef Pieper:*

> The same intrepidity made him ask, in his *Commentary on the Book of Job,* whether Job's conversation with the Lord God did not violate reverence—to which he gave the almost outrageous answer that truth does not change according to the standing of the person to whom it is ad-dressed. He who speaks truthfully is invulnerable, no matter who may be his adversary.

What is here meant by "truth" is a firm grip on some part of reality. The earth does spin round; there was a process of evolution, though we may never fully know how it operated. The right to discover and report such truths is the most inviolable of rights. But if a man proceeds to assert that any part of the true is the whole, if he construes his article as being the encyclopedia, he is as gravely in error as would be the planner who believed that if he built a city of skyscrapers there would be no traffic problem.

Accordingly, here are the poles between which education moves in prac-tice: the scholar's free, creative, but rigorously controlled awareness of the cosmic or human verity that he holds with awe in his hands, and his humble,

---

*Josef Pieper, *The Silence of St. Thomas,* translated by John Murray, s. j., Daniel O'Connor (New York: Pantheon Books, Inc., 1957), pp. 20-21.

submissive realization that this little, precious though it be, is only like one of the diamonds on Cecil Rhodes' plain. This is why, to think in contemporary terms, it is utterly senseless and life-destroying to hold that education can be either purely scientific or not concerned with science. In the wake of the eerie excitement caused by Russia's ability to push a satellite into outer space, we seemed for a time wholly to forget that for years education in the United States has been veering strongly to a one-sided concern with engineering and other forms of applied science, and that we were in grave danger of losing our collective dedication to the deeper forms of contemplation, whether they were· concerned with mathematics or psychoanalysis, metaphysics or pure poetry. Having been told over and over again that the United States could have sent a rocket to the moon years ago had it been so minded and willing to foot the bill, why should we now imagine that safety can be found only in thicker dabs of science on the schoolboy's bread?

The reason why the veering alluded to has taken place is of course this: The impact of scientific discovery on our modes of living is so great that we are all caught up into a Heraclitean world. Cellulose fiber makes growing cotton on sun-parched fields a dubiously profitable venture, and vegetable oils deprive the cow of a major reason for being. Indeed, one by one the animals become superfluous save when dead. I can think of no statement that more vividly indicates the change that has already taken place in the human environment. It would be incredibly stupid of the educator not to do what he can to make young scholars aware of the steps by which the mind of man has moved thus far. Yet who can doubt that a stern appraisal of our people's ability to live in the world that is now its companion, day in and out, will reveal equally glaring weaknesses—widespread inability to cope with the leisure that is the by-product of technology, and a resulting softness of mind, heart, and hand; the lack of impulse to enter into the cultural worlds of other peoples, past and present, that has so often led to manifestations of puerile gullibility or assumed superiority, or (what is even worse) to the isolation of the American in environments that he has been expected to influence or indeed improve; and above all a hankering after spurious kinds of "peace of mind," as if these might not prove to be the ultimate enfeebling narcotics.

If what has been said is in a measure. correct, a number of conclusions are suggested, some few of which will be advanced here with the requisite intrepidity.

First, it must be obvious that education can proceed in its full glory and significance only insofar as it is concerned with those for whom it is not merely an obligation, to be met by trudging more or less wearily to school, but also primarily and increasingly an adventure. Young scholars must be chosen and not simply endured. While Maritain and the Harvard report on *General Education in a Free Society* are right in holding that some measure of liberal education is the privilege of all citizens, it remains as certain as anything can well be that even in the most democratic of societies many will fail to move beyond the stage at which knowledge is communicated fact, either because they are unable to do so or because the journey does not interest them. Those who are eager and able to embark on the *adventure* of education should be singled out as soon as possible, freed of crippling economic handicaps, and made to realize that the training of the mind is at least as rigorous as the training of the body. To continue to accept the lowest common pupil denominator as the norm is to doom the potential intellectual power of the nation to turning somersaults around the statue of Huckleberry Finn.

One happy result of emphasis on pupil selectivity would be that at long last we should be able to train teachers in a relatively rational manner. These are candidates for the profession able and willing to go with unquenchable enthusiasm to the task of guiding the unfolding creative mind. Others will be more at home with the larger numbers for whom awakened interest is the only lure. And there will be some who, sensing perhaps a vocation akin to that of nursing, will concern themselves with young people who are in a sense abnormal, because of either handicaps or some lesion of the will. As things are now, exception having duly been made for the most fortunate of colleges and preparatory schools, no teacher working at a level below that of the university can tell what it is he is expected to accomplish. He will know only that his work is with youth and he usually will find himself in as impossible a situation as is the driver of a twenty-four-mule team some of whose charges are halt and lame while others are eager for the road. It is no wonder that problems of teacher morale exist, particularly in schools compelled to assemble in the same rooms youngsters who should no doubt be in jail and the sons and daughters of parents who have long been devotedly interested in the progress of the human intelligence.

Some clarification of what is meant by the freedom of the teacher seems highly desirable at this point. What Aquinas and many others have said about the inviolability of the mind when it is aware of truth must be supported, even when the cost is as tragically heavy as it has been in Hungary. This freedom is the inner radiance of every free society. It is the "single string," to use Donne's phrase, that cements scholar and teacher in comradeship and mutual respect. But one cannot conclude that the same freedom should be claimed for the imparting of information *unless this is actually the communication of truth in the sense defined.* The assertion may need a word of comment. For instance, the historian who might contend that the Roman *limes* was a deposit of quicklime should be free to say so only until somebody finds him out. Or again, a mathematician who has not in a measure kept abreast of developments in his field can hardly claim a natural right to remain in a state of ignorance. But a student of the Roman past who advances a new hypothesis concerning the nature and functions of the *limes* based on evidence fresh or old must have complete freedom to publish it, no matter how startling the contentions or how inconclusive the argument may seem. Failure to make this distinction, admittedly difficult to arrive at though it be in concrete instances, is responsible for a widespread reputable skepticism about academic freedom. This failure is no doubt rooted in a too uncritical readiness to apply standards indispensable for research to the lower schools. One may argue that this is the less dangerous course. Yet the fact remains that the maxim, "Once a teacher, always a teacher," regardless of quality, performance, or vigorous elation, is unquestionably a reason why the profession of teaching has fallen into some disrepute. Is it not more injurious than the difference between the salary paid to the president of Amherst College and that of the chairman of General Motors?

Conversely, the proper freedom of a pupil does not consist in doing what he wishes. I am persuaded that, once young people have progressed beyond the years with which Madame Montessori was concerned, they rather wistfully expect someone to tell them what to do and how. This does not mean, to be sure, that they will wear hair shirts with pleasure. But few statements can be made with greater assurance (or have so been made) than that pupil satisfaction and response are far greater in exacting high schools like Hunter or Brooklyn Technical than they are in makeshift mental factories for which the football season is the major academic event. But there is a kind of freedom at higher levels to which the fledgling young scholar has every right to lay claim. This is on the one hand freedom to respect as a person, regardless of his ancestry or the affiliations of his family. The right to gross discourtesy is not one of the attributes of the teaching profession. On the other hand, the student should have the feeling that his own dawning awareness of part of reality will be accorded mature critical respect. Who has really learned to teach who has not at some time realized that a young mind can light up a scene that has hitherto been dark? When I dealt with a class concerned with some aspects of English verse, it was not a commentary by a distinguished critic that I used to clarify a stanza by Marvell but an essay written by a Harvard senior.

It is at this point that the marvelous utility of student discussion should be adduced. Young people do not suffer one another's foolishness gladly. Indeed, they are loath to accept the mutual exchange of wisdom. Very rarely can a college student talk as an equal with a teacher. He can speak at, back to, about, around a revered instructor; but the generations dig their moats and lower only certain drawbridges. Each young person dealing with others, however, under the aegis of education, has in the company of his fellows a priceless abrasiveness, a hugging and pushing aside, an abrupt and vigorous way of proceeding from enmity to affection and back again, which are all like sprouting combative antlers of the mind. How good and fruitful the college campus is (as Newman indicated a century ago) on which thought etches itself out in jagged contour during student debate! Can we not all look back gratefully and see ourselves limping by reason of the bruises earned in such struggles and the depths that had to be leaped over, but still having in the end weary but exhilarated companionship? Alas that we should lose this skill later on! I am sadly reminded that in the days of yore Henry Mencken and Stuart Sherman, the first a stout brew of Nietzsche and *Simplicissimus,* the second a glass of pure humanistic port, were wont to assail each other with uninhibited vehemence. It was not a pleasant spectacle for anyone who liked them both, for neither was any longer young. But if I had my way no student would graduate who had not had a similar glorious row at some time.

Finally there is the harassing but unavoidable ground on which "truth" and "medicine" meet. The educated person will not always be driven by inherited impulses or find himself unable to get away from the screen on which are flashed pictures of his subconscious mind. Virtues, whether of the practical or speculative life, are disciplines. The Latin-speaking students of Aristotle referred to each of these as *habitudo,* as a form of thought and action to which one voluntarily has grown accustomed. For the great Greek, even as for Confucius, wisdom could never be synonymous with knowledge. The knower might be all else than wise in his knowing. There is no graver peril to which modern man can be exposed than surmising that *phronesis* is automatically built into his practical application of the insights that he has acquired. As he succumbs to this error, he becomes a thing that can be used rather than a man deciding of what use he can be. This we have seen with implacable clarity in the moral callousness of the gifted—scientists and engineers, jurists and writers—who have served tyrants. We shall see it even more plainly in the manipulation of minds by new and subtler forms of propaganda.

On what basic convictions the commitment to virtue is to rest becomes therewith the query that must be put, even though the answers given may prove so stormily different that many will turn aside persuaded that life is too brief to justify the quest of a decision. I shall say no more here than to remind you that Max Planck, under the torment of nazism, joined Newman in believing education without theology incomplete. Assuredly this affords one gateway to the final dialogue between oneself and reality. That dialogue will have for its theme where the last boundary is, what foundation lies below the deepest cellar into which we can look. Perhaps a man will decide that there is neither boundary nor fundament. A large number have so concluded. The "disinherited mind," of which Erich Heller speaks, indeed seems, oddly enough, the response of the intellectual West to the great Christians of the

Russian East, alive in the days before a sinister form of dialectic made its successful bid for power. The conviction that we are of the warp and woof of the here and now, and have no wedding garment for a feast elsewhere, has been freely arrived at by men of genius. The university must respect their testimony. It must have full liberty to attest to that respect.

But if education is to be what I have said it is, namely "awareness of the vital activity of the receptive, creative mind face to face with reality in the whole of its illusory overtness and its revealing concealment," how can it complete its assignment unless it throws light from every available source on the questions asked by Albert Einstein eight years ago about modern scientific man: "Has he not in an effort characterized by being intellectual only forgotten his responsibility and his dignity? A man who is inwardly free and loyal to his conscience can, it is true, be destroyed, but he cannot be turned into a slave or a blind tool." These things Max Horkheimer had in mind when, returning to Germany from exile to become rector of the bombed-out University of Frankfurt, he established chairs of Protestant and Catholic theology without being personally a devotee of either. He believed that some light might be cast on the queries of Einstein by a disciple that has played and still plays a mighty role in the drama of the West. Most assuredly he was not thinking of an acrimonious debating society, nor did he acquire one. The European university seems to realize, far better than our truncated experience will permit, that a theological faculty consists of educated men and not of self-appointed functionaries either in a kind of hypothetical Office of the Inquisition or in a club of intellectuals the primary activity of which is to blackball the parson.

It is not too much to say that the immaturity, or it might be better to say the incompleteness, of American culture manifests itself at no point so clearly as it does when religious issues are under discussion. There are many reasons why this is so, but the principal one undoubtedly is that theology has been studied so far away from the main stream of university life. Quite without knowing it, we have agreed with Tito and Rákosi in banning religion to the rectory. Therefore Catholic theologians are widely and falsely identified in the public mind with rigorous censorship, while Protestants, with comparable absurdity, are deemed to be a dwindling hortatory minority who have not made up their minds whether God exists or not. As for the antitheologians, need one refrain from saying that their inability to span the gulfs that stretch between themselves is no less scandalous than is the scandal of religious divisiveness? The statement that a faculty of theology must include representatives of every form of theology—thus identifying the proposed venture with absurdity—is admittedly difficult to confute. But it is perhaps in reality no more arresting than would be the contention that an antitheological faculty of philosophy must include every kind of antitheologian.

The fact of the matter is that thinking in theological terms, even amidst the turmoil of recent social tragedy, has attained heights of pertinence and influence that cannot be whisked out of being. It is at least probable that the books of Père Teilhard de Chardin will outlive those of Sartre. I shall say no more than that I find myself wishing American education could face the ultimate questions concerning the nature of human existence with the same willingness to discuss the whole of the evidence that I find elsewhere in the world. The numerous deep-rooted atavistic impulses with which many American scholars embark on life do not seem a replica of the Great Wall. I shall confess that to me it appears rather odd that we may all be blown to kingdom come because of some resolve to end the debate about power powerfully, before the American university has a fair chance to talk about whether man is immortal. Not that a faculty resolution on the subject would be particularly reassuring. But at least if I were a young, inquisitive person, I should prefer to be slain on such a tremendous scene after having weighed all the evidence concerning my survival. It seems a pity to deprive the fledgling American intellectual of that opportunity.

# Education and Wisdom

The subject that this modest essay will deal with has as many branches as a tall tree. I shall treat a few of them. First of all, contemporary America fosters a great deal of scholarly inquiry, and likewise supports a tremendous educational enterprise. Our learned societies have become mass movements. Chemists meeting in conclave can fill Atlantic City to the brim. The modern languages are served by an association of more than six thousand members, who annually produce a program of addresses so complex in character that no one can absorb more than a small part of it. Even musicology and aesthetics, relatively new disciplines in this country, are already evoking so many scholarly papers and monographs that it would be difficult for hard-working specialists to evaluate what is being written. On the teaching side, the major groups of educators resemble vast and powerful unions. They have made the business of tests and measurements a big business, indeed, and when they discuss pedagogical methods they revel in a professional jargon of which the average citizen can make neither head nor tail.

Here then are two mastodons, and one cannot say that much love is lost between them. Merely to suggest to a scholar who teaches at a college or in a university that possibly the specialist in educational arts might tell him something interesting about how to give instruction is to run the risk of assassination. I have tried it. On the other hand, the American schoolteacher is, when measured by the norms of contemporary scholarship, endowed with what might be termed a mid-nineteenth century mentality. He doesn't see

From George N. Shuster, "Education and Wisdom," *The Commonweal* 50 (1949), 36-45. Reprinted by permission of *The Commonweal*.

scholarly publications in his field, his general reading habits are depressing, and his genuine idealism may be coated with lavender and old lace. It seems to me that he does a better job of teaching than his university colleague (exceptions having been duly noted), but there is reason to fear that what he teaches may be thin and seriously out of date.

Much of all this is human and unavoidable. The mere thought that elementary schoolteachers might ask for time off in order to do research sends shivers up and down the spine, and I shall confess that I cannot think of the Harvard graduate faculty taking instruction in pedagogy without a chuckle. Nevertheless one will hardly escape feeling that the fragmentation of learning and education is one key to the dishevelment of the contemporary mind. If we cannot even put together what we know and what we say inside the school system, how shall we ever transfer what we know to our common life? To be sure, much of what is called research probably isn't of breathtaking importance. The world may well get on even if a dozen texts edited by the Arabic Society are never read, though one can't be too cocksure. But a great deal is vital, indeed. How shall we get it into our veins? The ideological naiveté of the American during the past twenty years has had the most appalling consequences. That naiveté seems to me to spring less from malformation of our moral and intellectual norms than from a most distressing untidiness of mind. We are like children who have been given puzzles so large that we cannot sort out the pieces.

I think it may help us to try for the nonce to stand far enough away from what we are doing to enable us to see it in perspective. It may not be necessary, though it would be desirable, to view the scene against the background of eternity. Surely it will do no harm to use a telephoto lens. I trust therefore that you will forgive my making at this point a bow in the direction of antiquity, by which I mean the culture slowly fashioned by mankind prior to the age of modern nationalism. For this present age has a character peculiarly its own. Nations as we know them have possessed great cultural vitality and initiative, but their protagonists can fairly be accused of having coated the human mind with armor plate—that is of having more or less subtly and imaginatively subjected the quest for truth to the quest for power. Almost every European nation has created a great literature, a very influential philosophy, and a noble art; but in general these things have been used, often most unwisely, for the sake of the "national culture" which produced them. While making a study of Germany's eastern boundary in the year 1930, for example, I was taken first by Germans and then by Poles to view the sites of ancient towns which, each group contended, demonstrated beyond the shadow of a doubt the identity of the "national stock" which had originally settled the region. Whether the minster of Strasbourg (or should one write Strassburg) ought to be looked upon as a French or a German masterpiece is again a problem which has whetted the appetite of many a writer.

It may be argued on the other hand that antiquity, circumscribed though it may have been by the special concerns of regions and empires, was by comparison devoted to matters of universal cultural import. The Old Testament is a book about God and the people He chose. Yet it is certainly no propagandistic essay in behalf of that people, being as much a treatise on Jewish, or human, defection from high principle as it is an account of Jewish knowledge of and obedience to the divine Law. The Romans, for their part, lived in constant awe of the Greek mind. Catullus copied Theocritus and Vergil, Homer. Yet the Greeks in their turn had unflaggingly looked eastward. And of the Christian empire which succeeded that of the Caesars, one may say that Alfred and Charlemagne foreshadowed in their efforts to foster learning the inevitability of Aquinas's restatement of the Aristotelian philosophy.

At all events, I suspect that the principal reason why we are dissatisfied with the present state of learning, as that is dispensed through what we are pleased to call "education," is this: We have now come to the place where we can see the compromises of pragmatism, in particular of nationalistic pragmatism, as clearly as a park patrol can see the vestiges of picnics on a Monday morning. We know that man has compelled truth to serve his practical purpose, and we are as a result distressed. Matters may not have been too bad while there was an Italian point of view, or an English way of doing things, or even a Russian Messianism. Now, however, with a fatefulness that would be farcical if it were not so alarming, the nations themselves have in many instances been cut up into partisan, mutually destructive bands of pragmatists, and it is apparent that "we moderns"—whoever we may be—are no longer talking the same language or going to the same places. And when the confusion of tongues becomes so loud that no one can hear what is being said, we cease, of course, to have learning or education as we desire to have them.

Accordingly no great harm will be done by positing, for consideration if not emulation, the relative unity of antique civilization. The man of antiquity seems to have conceived of education in several ways. For one thing, he dealt with the practical arts in a quite nonacademic manner. Despite the fact that the Romans were magnificent engineers who built viaducts and roads, towns and fortresses, with a skill which still earns our unstinted admiration, and despite the circumstance that such natural sciences as mathematics, physics and even chemistry were pretty far advanced in their time, it is impossible to discover traces of any school to which Roman engineers were sent. Quite as remarkable is the fact that such gifted architects as he who drew the plans for the amphitheater of Trier apparently never earned any sort of degree. We can only conclude that the great empire relied on a system of apprenticeship as difficult to reconstruct as it must have been efficient. On the other hand, a slight acquaintance with Cicero will indicate that the pursuit of the highest art, namely wisdom, was, though begun early in the schools of rhetoric, really the concern of men who had profited by wide experience. Cicero's greatest heir, Augustine, tells us that he began his quest for wisdom at the "age of nineteen," but it is not an anomaly that he really got down to it when he was a mature man. What the schools of rhetoric accomplished was to start young men on their way. It was only when some of the best among them had a chance to do what Cicero did, and settle down to the task of reconciling their experience among men with their reflections on the meaning of life, that something solid and substantial was accomplished.

Education of the formal sort, therefore, had precious little to do with the unity of antique civilization. The majority of the teachers appear to have been rather adept at starting discussion, commenting on texts, and propounding scintillating theories of their own. But there seems to have been little solidarity among them. The greatest revolution which occurred in Greek educational history started when a veteran named Socrates came home from the wars. The kind of question he asked was highly disturbing to classroom routine because it was really based on a deep and vital concern with truth. He would not be put off with stock phrases or rule-of-thumb evasions. He gave some of his fellow students an inkling of the meaning life might have for them by appealing to the moral sense, or conscience, of man. And though he ran afoul of prevailing Greek opinion, he prepared the way for Plato and Aristotle, and therewith for all those for whom Greek culture holds deep meaning today.

The unity of the ancient world, therefore, was the result of other forces than those engendered by the schools. It was based in part upon an assumed universality of religious belief, so widely taken for granted that one need hardly be surprised that attacks on dissenters were as vigorous and outrageous as those chronicled in the history of Christian persecutions. It is instructive to note that when Julian strove to re-establish the glory of ancient Rome he did not subsidize education but tried instead to revive the pagan creed. In part also unity was the result of the remarkable efficiency of governmental agencies, which relied upon services having little or no association with education. As long as these two bases of the established order remained firm, the fringes of society were guaranteed against crumbling. But when they gave way, there was nothing upon which the ancient world could any longer stand.

I believe, as a result of weighing this evidence with such care as I have been able to expend on it (and it is evidence which a study of the Christian empire of Europe would reinforce), that we are making a grave error if we assume that education in our time can contribute much more than it did two thousand years ago toward effecting a working agreement among the minds of men. To be sure, the university has taken over the functions once exercised by the Roman army. Technology is not any longer the affair of apprenticeship but of the scientifically controlled laboratory. And it is also true that since this technology contributes to the well-being of the average man, one reason for confidence in the stability of the prevailing social order remains. The other traditional pillar of society, namely religious belief, has to a great extent ceased to be an effective support. Though there are millions of men and women in the Western world who still subscribe to the faiths which contributed to the building of the West, it is religious dissension rather than unity which characterizes the civilization of the present.

A number of measures have been suggested for giving to education the function of religion in the same way as the function of engineering (or science, if you will) has been entrusted to it. Some hold that our whole educational system should be asked to teach "the American way of life," and others have said that controlling the school systems of enemy or conquered peoples would constitute a contribution to world morals. Still others are of the opinion that our school system must itself acquire a set of spiritual objectives, though one cannot discern any marked agreement about the character of these objectives. I gather that there is little likelihood that even philosophy, were it limited to the quest of a social morality meaningful for the youth of our day, could be introduced without extreme difficulty.

For my part, I think that we shall have to accept education as a process limited in efficiency by tendencies implicit in its very nature. It is quite unimpeachable so long as it is concerned with quantities, as was antique engineering. Sulphuric acid simply will not be another kind of acid, regardless of what students and teachers say. But as soon as there is discussion of the qualitative, or value, aspects of life, the scene will be dominated by the kind of logic and the amount of adjudicating experience which the participants possess. Here, no doubt, a rather simple rule of thumb applies. The more highly specialized a teacher is, the smaller the area of his experience with the manifold aspects of life will probably be; and the more emotional the student is, the less probable it becomes that his logic will be above suspicion. Nevertheless, if matters proceed as they have been proceeding, the chances are that on the one hand specialization will be still more sought after, while emotionalism will be intensified by the pressure of the over-all cultural agencies of the modern world—the radio, the motion picture, and the forum. To illustrate: Every year so many thousands of books are issued by American publishers alone that a worker in a given field of inquiry can hope to read only a few of them and will as a consequence be compelled to select those which deal with subjects relatively familiar to him. Similarly it is difficult to believe that the American child, asked daily to make up his mind in a hurry about complex and vital issues by adults whose success is dependent upon ability to evoke surprise and partisanship, will learn the art of noncommittal caution.

I think that at this point we might well go back to Cicero and say that the pursuit of wisdom is not to be carried on through scholarship alone. For the delving intellectual worker must always determine how matters really stood. He is a sort of burglar seeking to decipher the combinations to the safes of the past. Assuredly he must be the most objective of mortals, who cannot dispense with impartiality even for the sake of a flash of insight. It has often been said that the weakness of scholarship is in its inability to exercise the critical faculty, for criticism in the real sense is observation, co-experience, and evaluation. Yet still more obvious is the inability of the scholar to spare time in order to release the creative faculty in himself. Should he do so he would be concerned with his own brain children and not with those of others— he would be engaged in search rather than in research. To say these things is not to belittle scholarship. For what should we do without it? But we do need to remember that criticism and creation are the progenitors of wisdom. Age need wither neither of them, though it may well alter rapture into reflection.

The real difficulty about growing older is that so many of us are not malleable. It was wittily said of Charles Beard that he went from Hegel to Marx, and from Marx to Hegel. But at least he went, if not very far. The noblest report we have about St. Thomas is that when the *Summa* had been completed, he journeyed on to sanctity. Concerning another and lesser philosopher, Schelling, many have said that he taught several kinds of doctrine with the passing of the years. Perhaps the divagations were a little bizarre. And yet? He managed not to be a person who said the same things at seventy that he did when he was nineteen. A student of modern literature can encounter no more stimulating mind than that of Newman secure in the possession of ripe wisdom. Nor is he likely to find a more absorbing book than *Faust.*

I think that the college and the university of the future will be a place in which the limitations of education in the strict sense are recognized. Everybody will understand that in the business of associating youth with age so that both may learn together one must reckon with the inexperience of the young man and the too narrowly channeled learning of the old. The college graduate will still have a great many unanswered questions in his notebook, and the Ph.D. will concede that familiarity with the subjunctive in Apollonius Rhodius would inspire no Sophoclean drama. If, however, both could know that the later years of notable men had been set aside for the pursuit of wisdom, what a difference it would make! We may as well dream of a new world in which anyone who desists after his fiftieth year from gainful employment, in order to devote time and energy to the task of thinking through his experience for the benefit of himself and his fellows, will be exempt from all taxes. Such men will not write a great deal. But from time to time, I trust, they may say something in which humor, caution, and learning are blended with a deep concern for everlasting values. Perhaps in that blessed era one or two of them will receive honorary degrees, even though they cannot endow the university with a chair for the study of Belgian marbles and Egyptian miniatures. It may even be that someone will be signally honored for having suggested that prayer is an intellectual exercise.

# Academic Freedom

A discussion of academic freedom ought to begin, I think, with an expression of confidence. It seems to me that the temper of the American people is, in so far as the great issues of personal liberty are concerned, far better than is often thought. As a nation we seem to have learned, in the aftermath of many turbulent tides of immigration, that Providence intended ours to be a society of many divergent and conflicting commitments, unified by a strong belief in justice for all. That, for example, so many Americans are earnestly concerned that the Negro should at last have a chance to walk upward toward the light is surely a fair sample of the intent of the nation. And so I am persuaded that we need only offer a workable program for the maintenance of academic freedom in order to insure adequate support.

Such a program might perhaps stress these convictions:

First, the nation's basic law should embody a clear recognition of the fact that the Communist party is an aggregation of conspirators and their abettors, so that academic adherents to that party can be dealt with on a basis of clear and well-defined principle rather than of popular sentiment or legal expediency.

Second, the ideological aberrations of "Popular Front" days should be chalked up to the past, in the reasonable assumption that by doing so we shall win time for the performance of important tasks as well as for the reconciliation of Americans with Americans.

From George N. Shuster, "Academic Freedom," *The Commonweal* 58 (1953), 11-13. Reprinted by permission of *The Commonweal*.

Third, every public servant is clearly entitled to do all he can to expose what he assumes to be subversive influences at work in American life. The academic fraternity. on the other hand, is the sovereign custodian of the laws of evidence, as well as of the principle that the search for truth must be scrupulously exact, undeviatingly objective, and free of personal bias. Whenever it has reason to assume that what is being reported to the people from high places is neither completely fair nor unreservedly correct, it has the right and indeed the solemn duty to call attention to deviations from the established norms of inquiry. Reputable scholarship is the principal source from which criticism derives. It should proceed with firmness, candor, and chilly resolution.

Fourth, the sentiment of the nation might well indicate to the Congress with unmistakable definiteness that an investigation by it of what is taught and by whom would constitute a grave departure from well-established tradition, so long as legislation adequate to deal with subversive movements is not ignored by the academic fraternity.

Fifth, every energy must be mustered to repel incursions by pressure groups into the domain of the schools and colleges, and it is to be insisted upon that only duly constituted boards of trustees and faculties have jurisdiction in this area.

Sixth, academic freedom does not mean that inside the academic community itself any individual can divest himself of the social responsibility, ethics and courtesy which the profession demands, so that he is at liberty, for example, to attack with vocal prejudice of a narrow and virulent kind the races and religions to which young people belong. It means only that the academic community shall defend the rights of its own individual citizens to free inquiry, to unhampered teaching of subjects controversial or otherwise, and to their views on matters they are competent to discuss.

Seventh, the great texts in which the tradition of academic freedom is enshrined should be studied painstakingly and disseminated as widely as possible, so that the people as a whole may know and understand what is at stake.

Many who profess to favor an inquiry into the university, in all its branches, believe that the detection and exposure of subversives is a proper function of the government, and that therefore the academic profession ought to welcome investigations which will ferret out the guilty. This contention undoubtedly has validity. Agents of subversion are wholly undesirable crows bent on getting into robins' nests on evil missions. But we may surely ask ourselves whether it is advisable to chop down the tree in order to find the crow. It seems to me that certain arguments currently in favor of dismissing adherents of the Communist doctrine from their posts are open to serious question.

For example, it may well be that the Communist is so strongly committed to a view of life that he has lost freedom to think freely. But some will retort that a philosopher who finds all wisdom in Spinoza, or John Dewey, or St. Thomas is also committed to a doctrine and is therefore likewise not free. If one follows such reasoning far enough, one comes to the conclusion, which some unfortunately already endorse, that the only free person is he, who like the nobleman in Chesterton's *Magic,* believes in everything and nothing at the same time.

But if we say that the Communist is, by means of his readiness to conspire against the government and the people of the United States, a clear and present danger, we can safely proceed against him in the light of our traditions. Therewith one enters the realm of law, which is one of the primary concerns of the university, in both a technical and a philosophic sense. And it often sorely troubles responsible educators that, as matters now stand, the law about Communists is nebulous and inchoate. They do not know how to solve puzzles such as this: a teacher can be dismissed from his post for refusing to say whether he has been a Communist, even though it is entirely legal for him to be one. Or again, while a duly established board of inquiry cannot deprive an individual of the right to seek refuge in the Fifth Amendment, the university, as that individual's employer, is expected to do so by ousting him. To many anti-Stalinists on the campus, such procedures seem indefensible; and it may well be as a result that Communists receive a greater measure of sympathy than most of us realize.

These difficulties could be disposed of if the Communist party were declared illegal. For then an academic institution, presented with evidence that a faculty member was guilty, could act promptly and unhesitatingly. It has been argued that the party would go underground if banned. We may properly ask, "Where is it now?" At best such a contention is based on expediency, and here too the end never justifies the means. Banning a political party is, however, not a step to be taken lightly. We might well follow the example of the West German Federal Republic and write into our basic law a constitutional amendment conferring on the Supreme Court authority to decide whether any political organization normally entitled to freedom of speech and assembly constitutes a clear and present danger.

It may be held that these views are too cautious. But as a citizen who had an almost unprecedented opportunity to observe, with horror and loathing, the rise to power in Europe of brutal totalitarian movements, I have become so deeply attached to American traditions of justice and liberty and so wholly persuaded that free institutions crumble because of concessions erroneously made in the name of expediency, that I think the best way to safeguard the American future is to conserve the American past with rigorous care.

If the Communist problem were disposed of, difficulties would remain but not ones of central importance. I have said that the aberrations of "Popular Front" days should be forgotten. During nearly two decades, from the crash of 1929 to the Blockade of Berlin in 1948, the "Front" mustered a great deal of sympathy and support in this country. On many campuses, as in other walks of life, anyone who opposed not the good causes which the "Front" allegedly supported but any political objective of world communism speedily became a pariah. The faithful respected no one's good name, and shied away from no device of dragooning public opinion. As a result, those who were at some time taken in by it are now on the defensive. It is difficult and no doubt often perilous to admit publicly that one contributed, however unwittingly, to the debacle of our civilization. On the other hand, those who were targets during the heyday of amity for sovietism now sometimes take a human, all too human, delight in taunting or exposing their erstwhile tormentors. Some defend Communists out of a probably unconscious desire to rid themselves of blame. Others devote the silence of the night to thanking heaven for Senator McCarthy. The saddening result is that we are not learning in amity what so badly needs to be learned—that emotions, however reputable, are not substitutes for reason and knowledge in human affairs.

We must close that book. And for this reason Senator McCarthy and those who share his purpose are open to serious criticism. But not blind criticism. It is better that the watchdog on the lookout for subversives in government growl too much than that he bark not at all. It is only that the constant opening and shutting of the Pandora's box of moods, convictions, assumptions and slogans which was America in the days when the rest of the world was being carved up by two opposing and equally vicious tyrannies, is an extremely dangerous business from every educational and psychological point of view. For it points the finger of scorn at people who were certainly as well-intentioned as many of their opponents, however mistaken their conception of political reality may have been. The resulting humiliation, agony of spirit and professional debasement which so frequently result are doing the gravest kind of harm to the substance of American life. And consequently I say let us close the box and the book, once and for all, so that we may at length find a way to stand together in what, if we do not so stand, may well be the twilight hour of history.

There is no text in the history of intellectual freedom which should be cited more frequently than that enshrining the words which, according to Plato, Socrates spoke before he died: "No evil can happen to a good man either in life or after death. Wherefore Socrates will not be angry with his condemners, although they meant him anything but good. He will only ask all of them to do to the sons of Socrates what Socrates has done to them." It is from this faith, held sacrificially and resolutely, that the greater part of what is significant and abiding in the tradition of Western thought takes its origin.

Therefore the last (and really also the first) thing to say about academic freedom is that it will endure only as long as those who profess to have a right to it stand ready to pay for it any price which may be exacted. The scholar, the teacher, is one in whom this freedom is incarnate; and as soon as he indicates that he wishes it were not so, or that he would like to go hide under a convenient bushel, there will no longer be a good reason why others should defend the heritage for him. To be sure, silence and a measure of feigned conformity will be necessary under tyranny. Honest men may have to eat the bitter bread of exile in our day. But compromise with evil they dare not.

If in a nation like ours there should exist widespread fear of criticism and much supine acceptance of gags, it might well indicate that many had fallen so deeply in love with security that their sovereign interest was no longer conscience but conformity. Let us hope that this will never be the case. I am not ready to say, as Carl Friedrich does, that the freedom to seek intellectual truth is akin to freedom to profess a religious faith. But certainly these two freedoms have grown up in the same neighborhood. When one is imperiled or corroded, we can be sure that the other is endangered too.

Editor's Note: A practical example of Dr. Shuster's attitude toward academic freedom is supplied by the following letter, which he addressed to the Hunter College staff on October 20, 1952:

Certain recent happenings which have resulted from inquiries into subversive activities by Government agencies may well give rise to quite unwarranted fears, and therewith to curtailment of educational activities which must be encouraged if public opinion in the United States is to remain vigorous and forthright. I have some reason to believe that these anxieties are not absent from the campus of Hunter College. This letter is an attempt to clarify the situation.

The character of the Communist Party has led to the passage of legislation designed to curtail its potential influence. Hunter College and its sister institutions are affected in particular by the City Charter, Section 903 of which has been held by the courts to mean that failure to answer questions about membership in the Communist Party when those questions are put by a duly constituted investigative body automatically leads to dismissal from employment by the City. All this has been very well known for some time. The Board of Higher Education could not, even if it desired to do so, disregard this mandate.

There are, however, no laws and no rulings by the Board which constitute any sort of limitation on the non-Communist civic and intellectual interests of the faculty, with this exception: attacks on the race or religion of any student are forbidden. This does not mean that a chance remark or an expression of opinion on a controversial subject will be made an issue. Your College administration will defend to the uttermost any member of the staff from suspicion or retaliation except in those instances in which a chronic seizure of vocal prejudice is indicated.

In every other respect the faculty should not only feel entirely free to act as responsible citizens but, indeed, must be convinced that such conduct is indispensable. When I hear that younger members of the staff, particularly those without tenure, are warned not to act as faculty advisers to student clubs having a political character, I am deeply shocked. No victory the Communist Party could possibly win in this country would be more decisive than would be success in depriving younger instructors of an opportunity to give the leadership which only they can provide. After one has reached a certain age, one acquires for students a manifest august dignity which usually consorts poorly with what they look upon as club life. We must therefore rely on our less venerable colleagues for assistance in this vitally important matter.

Far from gazing upon willingness to share in student enthusiasms and even in student mistakes as an indication of brashness, I am hereby insisting to all Chairmen and Administrative Officers of the College that they look with special benevolence on those members of the staff who do not succumb to current fears but who roll up their sleeves and go to work. Suppose the situation does involve certain dangers. If we can ask a Marine to go up a Korean hill with a grenade in each hand, we can surely expect an instructor in Hunter College not to tremble for the safety of his wife and children if he sits down of an evening and listens to students discuss General Eisenhower or the size of the New York City welfare budget.

I came to Hunter in 1939. Since then I have sometimes been troubled and occasionally annoyed. But nothing that has been said about the College in all these years is more disturbing than are the reports alluded to above. I shall hope they are not true. And I shall look forward to receiving evidence to that effect.

# On Catholic Education

I may perhaps be pardoned for beginning these remarks in a reminiscent mood. More than thirty years ago there appeared in *America* an article by a brash young man, asking whether there were any Catholic scholars amongst us, and replying pretty much in the negative. That young man was I; and he still has cause to remember the slings and arrows which beset him from all sides. But what few have realized is that the essay in question was inspired by a distinguished silent collaborator—Father James Burns, then president of Notre Dame. At that time he had a secretary who happened also to be a much beloved student of mine, who subsequently became the Reverend John Cavanaugh, and who in due course was in turn the president of his alma mater. It is, one hopes, not injudicious to remark that in continuity there is strength. Yet continuity does not mean that the world stands still. The problem of effective Catholic scholarship remains, but it would certainly be erroneous to suppose that no progress has been made toward solving it during recent decades.

The remarks which follow will not be primarily another set of reflections of that theme, but will be concerned, perhaps somewhat too ambitiously, with the whole range of Catholic education in the United States and, however perfunctorily, with the social setting in which it has developed. We shall rule out as purely theoretical such questions as what would have happened if the Faribault Plan, sponsored by Archbishop John Ireland, had been adopted.

Speech delivered at a symposium on The Catholic Contribution to American Intellectual Life, Rosary College, River Forest, Illinois, June 14, 1958.

Certainly not a few persons, clerical and lay, still regret that it was not. But we are no more able to go back to it than we can get Lenin out of the train to Russia placed at his disposal in 1918 by General Ludendorff. What alone matters now is to see as clearly as we can how well the structure erected is functioning and then to inquire into the desirability of alterations and improvements. Something similar scholastic America is now everywhere doing, with a vigor which the judicious and their opposites are daily manifesting.

As for the manifesto which will now be offered you, a word of warning is no doubt suggested. You will not hear an acrimonious diatribe nor will a coat of gleaming whitewash be applied to the façade of Catholic education. It so happens that, except for my university training, I am the product of that education. There is no part of it, save for the first years of the elementary school when I happened to be like Huckleberry Finn, which I do not hold in affectionate and grateful memory. It is likewise true that for nearly two decades I have tried to do everything in my power to make a college conducted under public auspices realize all its potential strength. I hold it also in affectionate esteem, and rejoice particularly in the fact that not a few of its graduates have entered religious orders, or have gone into the Protestant mission field, or have become rabbis or wives of rabbis. As a result, I know that people say many things about Catholic education which are not true, and that others say other things about public education which are incorrect and unwise. We shall not be concerned with these. The business before us is to remember that some of us become teachers because a whale of a lot of the rest of us must learn. Upon what is taught and learned the future of the nation depends. There is no way in which we can divorce the well-being of the Church in the United States from the intellectual security of the country. We who are in the business of education must therefore ask ourselves probing questions. But as we do so we need not dangle before our eyes such fairy tales as that everybody in Russia knows as much at sixteen as anybody over here does at forty.

As a sort of text, let me cite some words by Emerson, spoken to the students of Dartmouth College long ago. Having alluded to the tradition of scholarship, he said:

> Meanwhile I know that a very different estimate of the scholar's profession prevails in this country, and the importunity with which society presses its claim upon young men tends to pervert the views of youth in respect to the culture of the intellect. Hence the historical failure on which Europe and America have so freely commented. This country has not fulfilled the reasonable expectation of mankind.

Since that time, to be sure, the university has come of age in our land and there is no dearth of scholarly activity. The present era is, however, reshaping

Emerson's comment in terms of education. Are our schools wasting human resources? Have they set their goals sufficiently high? Above all, has the social "importunity" of which Emerson spoke led us astray?

Now I believe we may say quite earnestly that a wholly different kind of drive and drift have been evident among American Catholics. Certainly there has been a bourgeoning which one cannot look upon without a kind of awe and a sense that a benediction has been upon us. Whose breath is not taken away when at Holy Day noontime in any great city there stream into the streets countless thousands whose goal is the Mass, to be shared in with reverent joy; or when on Ash Wednesdays there appears on the foreheads of stenographers and salesmen, teachers and students, the smudge of mortality; or when having entered into holy wedlock, thought of self is left behind by the girl who hitherto seemed to have no concern save lipstick or a hair-do, and the child is reared by her to that role in the Kingdom of Heaven which was the Saviour's supreme assignment? Out of industrial housing developments, from behind stockyards, not far from pigsties and clearings in the forest most of us have come, not very long ago. But there was a chrism on our poverty and we kept it as an heirloom, not always comprehending what glory was hidden in it, seldom perhaps associating it at all with the intelligence, yet somehow holding it upon our hearts as that which would deflect the bullets of an alien time.

We too had our revolt of the masses in the age of machines. The great growing strength of the labor unions carried most of us up the ladder of the living wage. We could now flex our muscles on picnic grounds, could siphon off the payroll dollars with which to build schools next to churches. The nation became a "social democracy" and what this change has meant to the sociology of Catholics in America staggers the imagination. For with the trend away from farms to industrial centers their initial disadvantage of being workers in textile mills and steel foundries, as compared with the settled older rural population, was overcome almost in the twinkling of the eye of history. Sons and daughters went off to college in ever increasing numbers. The O'Malleys of Salem moved out of a cold-water flat into a Cadillac. The Schulzes of Milwaukee went from the cobbler's last to the management of industry. As for most other folks, the principal grouses became death and taxes. Death helped to keep them close to the confessional; and taxes induced a measure of sobriety and frugality. At any rate, the balance sheet indicates that the American Catholic was groomed for the pursuit of happiness. This would not seldom inundate him, tear him from his moorings, make him more of a Gradgrind and less of a reformed Scrooge, and lead his pastors, anxious about youth, to liken the neighborhood movie house to Gomorrah. But by and large, the lifeline to eternity did not break.

One big reason why it did not break is the Teaching Sister. Another is the Teaching Brother, whose lack of prominence in the discussion which follows is the result of purely rhetorical considerations. Without the generations of nuns who have worked and are working in them, the parochial schools would have remained occasional little academic experiment stations. Let me repeat here what I have said before: This sacrifice of noble and devoted women to the cause of education is no doubt as glorious and moving as anything in the history of the Church in the United States, but it is also from many points of view very costly, indeed. It has with implacable permanence fed into the unending, burdensome process of elementary education, a large number of the morally and intellectually gifted. More than that, whenever there have not been enough Sisters the solution of the problem has been to add steadily to the load carried by them as individuals. Why should one not occasionally reckon with this side of the ledger when educational assets are being considered? Behind the statistics wait flesh and blood and spirit, and these are very precious things.

It is of course true that nobody can understand parochial school education who fails to see that willfully missing Mass on Sunday is far more dire according to the standards of that education than failure to know that two and two are four. And so critics who view the Sister with acrimonious dislike hold that she is shockingly underpaid, priest-ridden, wholly deprived of freedom of thought and expression, carefully insulated from the ways of the world. Contempt for the Catholic school and the women who teach in it is more widespread and bitter than most of us realize. And it is rooted, if Blanshardian fears of Catholic power are left aside, in the inability of a semi-secularist time to understand the stern sweetness of religious discipline; and this opacity in turn has its source in the loss of intimate, concrete conviction that the world is in its innermost core Divinely Personal rather than scientifically impersonal. But who does not wonder upon occasion if Catholics for their part also fail to comprehend? Does not the matter for very many stand so that the child is believed to be safer with the nuns than elsewhere, or that sending it to a parochial school is an act of obedience, often at best reluctant, comparable to putting an envelope into the collection basket or making one's Easter duty? Nor is this perfunctory collaboration, viewed now and then as a tyrannical imposition, greatly altered by coating it with sentimental varnish—by conjuring up blond curls shorn in the days of a Sister's youth, by counting on the value of her prayers in the quest of such commodities as jobs and husbands, or repeating the nonsense that nuns fret not in their narrow rooms.

The true source of a Sister's strength and the very heart of the reward which makes her spirit bloom and flower is the community to which she belongs. This appears to be veiled from our sight. It is singular that whereas the principal forms of the religious life of men—Jesuit, Benedictine, Dominican, for example—emerge as distinct and in some ways even divergent, the communities of nuns appear to be linked in an array which would be uniform were it not for the outward symbol of the habit. Even the best books about them individually seem to tell pretty much the same story, save when the personality of a Foundress or Superior is etched in recognizable contours. Yet anyone who has worked closely with Sisters knows that one community will be radically different in spirit and quality from another. The *Englische Fraeulein* of Austria, for example, are as distinct from the Madames of the Sacred Heart as Boston is from Tyler, Texas. To meet with a community which is presided over by a woman of great qualities reared in the spirit of a noble rule, is to be in a company no salon could rival. But to sit with one held together by nothing save the vows its members have taken is to have another experience entirely.

Therefore the absence of a typology seems highly regrettable. For any essay in constructive criticism of the Catholic educational effort in the lower schools would have to begin with that. Some communities have produced a long line of excellent teachers who have carried on first-rate instruction. Others have manifestly done less well. A given band of Sisters can weather the hurly-burly of urban living with a blend of gusto and serenity. Others thrive only in rural surroundings. Surely one is entitled to say in explanation that in many instances there has been a fortunate combination of rule, tradition, resources and leadership, resulting in service to American education which is beyond all price, but that this has by no means always been the case. Would it not therefore be wise to discern where excellence lies and channel the idealism of young women accordingly? Does it not sometimes seem that the quest for a quantitative attainment of the educational goal appears to involve forgetting that not every Sister everywhere can be placed in a classroom with confidence? I think that among competent educators, regardless of how far removed from the Catholic Church they are, there would be no doubt whatever that many Sisters are among the best teachers the nation knows. They do not like to see them burdened to near the margin of no return. Nor do we relish seeing them lumped with others whom neither aptitude nor training has adequately equipped for the task. Nothing could be further from my mind than to become embroiled in ecclesiastical controversy. But is it not obvious that the maxim "every child in a Catholic school" can be a perilous slogan if only because the Papal Encyclical to which all of us hark back in the discussion of educational matters, that of the great Pope Pius XI, specifically stipulates that the quality of instruction must be of the most admirable texture?

But the major point is that fruitful, mutually satisfactory cooperation between teaching Sisters and Catholic parents, now regrettably more infrequently achieved than is desirable, will come about far less as a result of establishing PTA's and similar organizations, however valuable these may be, than of informed awareness of the goals which a given community of nuns has set for itself, of its history, and of the steps it has sacrificially taken to qualify its members for their tasks. We should know, as parents, that behind every Ursuline nun there stands not only St. Angela herself but also a mighty river into which the rills of many generations have poured their waters. I do not see how, under conditions which now exist, any such knowledge can come to· the average parishioner. Does he hear a reference to it from the pulpit? And certainly, were he to turn to the journals which are edited for parochial schoolteachers, he would find the same pedagogical twaddle which is served by comparable secular periodicals, however heavily sprinkled it might be with holy water.

Admittedly one cannot avoid knowing that teaching has been an anonymous profession in the United States. Public school superintendents are of course in the limelight as beleaguered and sometimes valiant whipping boys for boards of education. But teachers? Miss Daly, having said good-bye to her charges of the fifth grade, sinks into community oblivion as if the ground had swallowed her. Who is told about the deeply religious men and women in the public schools who bring a profound sense of spiritual dedication to their tasks? Who save a few priests of insight and generosity ever remembers them in prayer? Who during the recent almost puerile clamor stopped to think that the situation could not be as dire as it was described with them in the picture? This is the fate of the Teaching Sister, too, and of course we all clearly realize that there must be cloisters in the religious life. But why think always about the dangers of public relations and never of the opportunities? True enough, demons lurk to assail the souls of religious, yet surely the Lord is also their ally. How good it is for the rest of us, and I trust for. her also, when the Sister can emerge from seclusion and join in some collective educational enterprise! I cherish the memory of a dinner of Milton experts which heard a charming and learned nun say that she prayed daily to St. John Milton. This remark quite bowled over some of the nation's most erudite professors. There may have been a bit of cloistral simplicity in it, to be sure, but also great insight and glorious charity. We need both.

For such reasons the value of a good college to any community is very great, dubious though one may be whether all those now established will continue for long to be viable enterprises. The college gives institutional expression to the community's religious and educational ideals; affords opportunity for scholarship and creative writing; and provides a sort of hearth fire round which the hard-pressed and heavily burdened can rally. No one can fail to see that the garnered intellectual fruits are many. Already it is true that, exception having been made for the Society of Jesus, the Sisters of college faculties are making the most notable contributions to scholarship directly fostered by Catholic academic institutions, as well as to creative writing. As one might expect, most of the scholarship is in the field of what we call the humanities—Newman in his time more sensibly used the word literature. And of course, while Americans generally pay lip service to these branches of learning, they have a Hooper rating far below that of either atomic physics or televised comic opera. One can only hope that the major communities of Sisters can keep their colleges going. The trend is against them, primarily it may be because of the lure of coeducation, which might, however, be offset by a well-considered policy of affiliation with nearby colleges for men. There are other adverse factors: the income tax bill, which forces parents against the wall of no economic return; student week ends at home, facilitated by easy transportation; the need for diversified vocational inlays; the imprint left on all youth by the mass media. The situation is therefore not an easy one. For my part, I do not see how our communities of Sisters can maintain the quality of the service they give unless their colleges do survive and prosper. For those I know somewhat, I entertain the deepest respect.

It is all very well to throw an aura of nobility round the Teaching Sister by referring to the reward which awaits her in heaven for having, as a result of the treadmill she often works in, worn the equivalent of stigmata here below. But let us listen carefully to the words of John Henry Cardinal Newman, who assuredly cherished the ascetic life: "Knowledge is one thing, virtue another; good sense is not conscience, refinement is not humility, nor is largeness and justice of view faith." It will forever remain the proper function of education to insure that as large a number of young people as possible will have knowledge, refinement, and largeness of view. How can a teacher inculcate these in others unless she have time and opportunity to acquire them for herself? We should husband our Teaching Sisters as if they were the most priceless of seedlings and ask them to expend themselves only for purposes consonant with the best aspirations of the academic calling.

Little will be said here about the parochial high school. For whatever may be averred in favor of such institutions from the point of view of the moralist and the teacher of religion, the plain fact is that the basic educational problems posed by such schools are not solved under Catholic auspices any more than they are under public ones. When one discovers (as I have) that seniors of a high school bearing proudly its dedication to Aquinas do not have the foggiest notion who he may have been, the prognosis is not less bleak than it is when one finds out that the seniors of Thomas Jefferson High School do not realize that he wrote the Declaration of Independence. The country generally has suffered intellectually from a failure to sense that the age of puberty is not merely the age of puberty. I shall permit myself the dubious luxury of just one further comment. If the reason for assuming the onerous burden of the Catholic high school is primarily pastoral, then possibly one should determine how the best results can be obtained from the effort expended. Now the situation may well be that in good academic public high schools, where the standards are reasonably rigorous and well-established Newman Clubs are in existence, young people suffer no impairment of their faith. Indeed there are such institutions which can even point to a higher incidence of religious vocations among their graduates than that found in Catholic high schools. The situation is different in establishments in urban areas which must admit all and sundry. There the risk of moral infection is serious, indeed, and one must also gravely fear that religious faith and practice will become steadily more tenuous. But is it not the truth that the Catholic high school musters in young people who would in all likelihood fend very well for themselves, and turns over to the public authorities those most in need of religious solicitude?

Here is a problem not easily solved and which is bound to become more perplexing as the era of the great internal migration goes on. As never before the nation is on the move, now not because great immigrant masses seek homes and jobs, but because the shift to the cities of hitherto underprivileged rural populations coincides with the relocation of industry on a prodigious scale. This means not merely the uprooting of old ties for which no substitutes can readily be found, but social conflict as well, with inevitable effects on morals and morale. The demands on education are already heavy and will become increasingly more difficult to meet. In particular guidance and counseling services must be provided, the number of retarded children for whom urban schools will be asked to care will surely increase, and certain groups of maladjusted teen-agers will be more in evidence than they are even at present.

This is neither the time nor the place for a probing discussion of finance, which is as inseparable from education as buying shoes for children is from matrimony. But if Catholic education is to do its share of the work imposed on us by all the great migration now in progress, help must come to it from somewhere. A large number of the parents involved will be able to make little if any contribution to the maintenance of schools for a long time to come. I should think that even a society like ours, which builds a high fence between Church and state (a fence incidentally, it is well to remember, which has often provided Catholics with better neighbors than they would otherwise have had), might well come to realize that the situation with which it is having and will have to cope is one in which religious motivation can be of the greatest social value, and that therefore the community as a whole ought not to deal in a niggardly fashion with the social welfare aspects of religious education conducted under whatever auspices. But having said this, we should quickly add that it will be as out of key to be optimistic on this score as a song from *Oklahoma* would be at a funeral.

At this point one who has no special competence in the teaching of religion but who has had occasion over not a few decades to evaluate some of its fruits may, perhaps, be allowed to make a few comments on one or the other of its aspects. There can be no doubt that in this area children profit by some of the oldest uses of project methods. The boy acolyte comes breathtakingly close to the Mass; the little girl who strews flowers on Holy Thursday identifies herself with service to her Lord; children bless themselves with holy water, St. Francis gave them the Christmas crib, they live in a world of bowed heads, folding hands, genuflections, burning candles. The way to the reality of First Holy Communion thus passes through a field of symbols every flower in which is precious. No one who has walked there can forget—not Renan or James Joyce or Mary McCarthy.

But the times come when questions are asked. These will at first be the interrogation points of innocent rebellion. But later on they will harden into negations. The world of concrete symbol will change into one of intellectual abstractions and emotional fixations. In this last there will loom up as large as the moon the question as to the relationship between freedom and obedience. This is the most fateful of the warning signals that maturity is impending. One can only be candid and admit that the more of ripeness there is, the greater the danger to the religious spirit. There could be no point in denying that Newman wrote the *Grammar of Assent,* and that indeed it was imperative he do so. In the face of a perennial peril he offered, anxiously and painstakingly, a path to salvation. That path is not paved with the symbols we have noted with grateful reverence. It is hewn through the rock of intellectual doubt with the pickaxe of analysis.

It is, in my judgment, during the years identified with the high school that everything will depend, at least for the most gifted and the more turbulent, upon how ably and deftly the young person is led from the land of obedience to the symbol to that other of the freedom to question and to weigh answers. Of course one can go on for a long time saying and doing hallowed things without any longer believing in them. But normally the boy or girl of nineteen will have chosen, often quite unconsciously, to be or not to be in the spiritual sense. How grave the responsibility therefore is! How easily an unwise curb or an injudicious answer can bring a soul to a road which may for some distance seem parallel but which in actuality is veering off! One can only hope that those whom education so heavily burdens will have the strength and the wisdom required. Even when the best is done there will be strange, inexplicable failures. When it is not done, God help us! Men like me have comparable experiences in the teaching of English, writing, history, but these do not mean the same things in terms of life. Should we ever forget that it is the dangerous glory of Catholic education to place in the foreground considerations which if they had never been placed there might not loom so large and challenging? Who could venture to offer advice here? One can only pray, hope, and indeed suffer with those upon whom the burden is laid. At least we should all know that it is being borne and not expect that miracles will be wrought either by sentimentalism or by smart new approximations to a theology for mass consumption.

We come therewith to higher education concerning which, to paraphrase Montaigne, all the needful things have long since been said. It remains for us to put some of them into actual practice. First, there is the vexing business about Catholic scholarship. Obviously there are three seed beds in which such scholarship could grow: the religious orders, the priesthood, and the laity. We can with some assurance say of the first that in accordance with their several traditions they will and have already begun to carry on studies of depth and pertinence in the field of religion. The Jesuits of Woodstock, the Benedictines of Collegeville, fruitfully husbanding the rich legacy of Virgil Michel, the Franciscan Conference—these are estimable achievements by any intellectual standard and one may thank God for them. But it would be unrealistic to assume that the orders can make a very significant contribution to the vast enterprise of secular scholarship. The fact is that in the first instance young people who join them seldom have at the core of their reflection becoming eminent in research. Crashaw said of St. Teresa that she was for the Moors and martyrdom. So it will always be with those who resemble her and it is good so.

The priesthood makes evident the sacrifice which is the other side of one of the special glories of the Church. Many generations of American intellectuals and leaders in all fields of inquiry have a background of family life associated with the rabbinate or the ministry. Indeed, it is probably not too much to say that without the love of learning which has been zealously inculcated in such households, the history of leading American academic institutions would be far less illustrious than is the case. Of necessity such a tradition cannot be fostered among Catholics, which is not an argument against celibacy, dictated as that is by far more transcendent considerations. But there can be no human gain without a compensatory sacrifice. Some secular priests will be first-rate historians, musicologists, sociologists. These will loom up as exceptions to the prevailing rule.

The only way, then, that a tradition of Catholic scholarship—or rather, perhaps, of Catholic participation in scholarly activities—can be firmly established is to use lay men and women as the foundation. This is rather obvious, but when one asks how this is to be done people begin to talk about the weather. We shall venture to refer to other matters. It is the university which constitutes the scholar's smithy. The quality of the work done in it will depend upon the quality of the master smiths and on how well their skill and industry are communicated to apprentices. The college for its part will thrive as its associations with the university do. It so happens that I preside over an institution the scholarly achievements of whose faculty are in several ways quite remarkable. There is no doubt in my mind that this has to a great extent been made possible by the continuing vital relationships between this group and the illustrious universities of the area in which we work. And I am reminded also that in times past it was the tie of mutual respect and admiration which existed between English scholars in the college which is today according us hospitality and the University of Chicago which made for a remarkable flowering of learning here.

If, then, there were a Catholic university in which Catholic lay men and women could live and work on a level of equality with the best scholars in the most reputable non-Catholic institutions, and if such a university had grown to maturity during a hundred years, I am sure the many colleges which have struggled into being under the auspices of religious orders would have a lifeline to a center of intellectual activity which would immensely hearten and strengthen them. We have as yet no such university, and unless there is a change in the way things are going we never will have one. Far too many so-called universities have reared their heads, and we may as well be honest and admit that in none of them do lay men and women have the status, the freedom, or the function of co-building which would as a matter of course be theirs at any distinguished secular center of studies. To some extent the problem is one of relatively meager salaries, but this may well be not the most important thing at all. There are state universities which keep good faculties together despite wage scales below the norm. There are private secular colleges which do likewise. But it is wholly impossible to create a fraternity of scholars unless one first kindles the spark of cooperation. And so we should at long last ask ourselves some really incisive questions, painful and embarrassing though they may be. To what extent is a Catholic university ready to accord to those it has chosen to be its professors full equality of status, whether they be religious or lay folk? Will it give the professor an opportunity to help shape the policies, of all kinds, which are to govern the institution as a whole? Will he be consulted, for example, when a new president is chosen, or when new members of the faculty are to be recruited?

Until such questions (and there are other cognate ones) can be answered affirmatively there can come into being no tradition of Catholic scholarship which rests on a continuing progression of lay men and women through the generations. As things are at present, nothing akin to the solidarity of working Catholic scholars is indicated. Not a few of the best among those who serve Catholic education, clerical and lay, have their closest personal and intellectual ties with the secular universities in which they came to know the meaning and the value of graduate study. I am far from certain that this may be anything less than highly desirable. Anyone who reads the published correspondence of the eminent Jesuit paleontologist, Père de Chardin, will wonder less whether his best work could have been done unless he had been linked with science as a whole, studied under Catholic auspices or not, than whether his quite unusually significant contributions to religious literature would have had their remarkable pertinence and influence unless he had moved with assurance and freedom on the ground of science in his time.

Of one thing I am at any rate certain after many years of association with academic life. The attempt to evaluate higher education from the pastoral point of view is always bound to come round to endorsing what Newman said a hundred years ago. Knowledge will not make people better, just as ignorance will not make them more educated. The sovereign justification of a Catholic university, he held, is that it can and ought to have a school of theology. To be sure such schools have been established at secular universities in Germany, but we are not likely to do anything of the kind in the United States. Newman reasoned thus: "You will break into fragments the whole circle of secular knowledge if you begin with the mutilation of the divine." That remark is profoundly true. It is the severance of theology from the university far, far more than the public school which for a long time was responsible for the rise of secularism. A Catholic student at the University of Munich who knows that on certain days Romano Guardini, to whom the whole world listens, will be lecturing, quite automatically makes room for theology in his view of life. And one may note that the presence of Union Theological Seminary on the campus of Columbia University has altered the academic experience of countless students. May it therefore not be regrettable that only the Catholic University of America has a Catholic faculty of theology?

However one may respond to such a query, the argument that a need for broader opportunities to exercise pastoral care justifies the insistence on more and more Catholic universities will not, I think, hold much water. In the long run the only valid reason for going to a university is to obtain what a university, with its traditions, professors, laboratories, and library has to offer. To assume that because able and sagacious religious pour out their hearts' blood in the effort to keep institutions going, the holiness of their graduates or their ability to move to the forefront of the scholarly procession will be guaranteed, is to run afoul of statistics. It is to be sure true that the temper of the time makes a plea for walled towns plausible. But I often wonder whether the grumbling which goes on in such towns, with their restricted horizons and (figuratively) their antiquated plumbing, may not do more to undermine sincerity of religious conviction than does exposure to the wide and admittedly wicked world.

Let me hope that what has been said will not seem to contain a measure of captiousness or condescension. Perhaps it would help if, as one who has many years of a varied career behind him, I made a quite personal statement at this point. No man could hold the Society of Jesus in greater esteem that do I. There is no other organization of men which has exerted so profound an influence on my life, though I have never studied under its auspices. In Germany, France, and the United States the followers of St. Ignatius have sustained and directed my thought, and it would be impossible to find words in which to express adequately my gratitude to and my affection for them. If I have challenged and in some measure kept the faith, it is to their example and to the grace of God that this is largely due. Nor could anyone be unmindful of all they have done in the United States to improve the institutions of higher learning which are under their auspices. But I shall say frankly that in this matter of the multiplication of universities they are unintelligible to me. They may be right as they are in many other things, but at least I should like to enter a demurrer.

The result of this multiplication is that religious admirably trained in important areas of learning are being tied to backbreaking administrative posts. They wrestle manfully with budgets, stage fund-raising dinners (as do I), cope with faculties perennially underpaid. Meanwhile Catholic enrollments in public and other nonreligious centers of higher education increase by leaps and bounds. Father X is busily computing tuition fees paid in to a School of Law by young men who never have and never will have any interest in Catholic doctrine, while Father Y on the campus of a secular university preaches a streamlined Sunday sermon to thousands of students in a gymnasium. Would it not serve the cause of religion far better if the example of Oxford were followed, as Newman in his day advocated, and foundations were established which the society is uniquely fitted to maintain? I cannot help believing that a hundred Campion Houses serving institutions as diverse as Harvard and Pennsylvania State would not merely take care of the spiritual needs of vast numbers of young men and women destined to occupy positions of leadership, but would bring Catholic learning into a totally different relationship to American intellectual life. In short, why not give the Jesuit Mark Hopkins a log rather than a cabin?

Let me close with a brief comment on the over-all intellectual situation. It is apparent that the social future will be entrusted to the scientist and the engineer. Whether they rule dictatorially, according to an efficiency table on which human resources are listed and evaluated by bureaucratic rule of thumb, or according to patterns which permit of individualistic deviations from the norm, we shall as a race for a long time to come have a queer feeling that we are figures on a logarithmic chart. It will be difficult to gainsay that so many hours of such a kind of work will produce a desired result in terms of human happiness; and at the same time the temptation will arise to consider this result the only thing necessary. Concern with religious ends and values may well become for many quite peripheral.

At work here is a mighty force which has already in many parts of the world torn millions from their spiritual moorings. Its product is the materialism which the Church in Europe has long since identified. Therefore it may well be providential that, just when it almost came to seem that the highest good of the race might well be air conditioners for many and trips to the moon for some, a new way of appraising intellectual endeavor has suggested itself. Already adumbrated by such writers as Von Huegel and Lecomte du Nouy, it has found its most brilliant contemporary expression in the writings of Père de Chardin. Scholarly work is viewed as a form of participating in the realization of God's will, and not as tangential, of this world only, or at best apologetic in some unclear way. It remains as always the quest for truth, to be carried on with sincerity and zeal, but is also a sharing, awesome and sanctifying, with Christ of His world—a world which is coming more and more to seem not a panorama of things fixed in space of time—not for example Mont Blanc or the Justinian Code—but an ever-moving film of the Creator's idea. Reality is for the imaginative scholar a dream, but not one which fades or passes away. It is a phase of the vision which has been held in the Divine Mind eternally. Seeing the structure of the molecule we are at His side. And being there must of necessity be good. If this be so man moving from the shadows of things into their essences at the scholar's behest will gain that awareness of the spirit which no being immured in the illusory material can any longer dispel. At least we may hope that it will be so.

# The New Direction
# of Catholic Education

## Some Realistic Appraisals

What road will Catholic education in the United States take? What is it
likely to come up against on that road? Will it be well and wisely guided?
These are the crucial questions, though one might well add another: Will the
religious instruction and formation provided by the schools provide depth
and intensity of insight? We cannot, of course, answer any of them. Even if
dependable research findings were adequately available, they would provide
little more than clues to what the future holds in store. The major considerations are: what are the probable dimensions of the student body at the four
levels—the elementary school, the secondary school, the college, and the
graduate and professional schools; what financial provisions are likely to be
made to provide for the adequate, or more than adequate, education of those
who enroll; and what can and will be done to provide effective over-all
administration?

In so far as the last consideration is concerned, it is doubtless correct to
say that in general the office of the diocesan school superintendent has now
acquired greater stature than it had some time ago, when it was little more
than an appendage to the chancery office. Even so the Code of Canon Law
was not written to make unique provisions for the system of Catholic

education in the United States, so different in many respects from what can be found elsewhere in the world. The law is concerned primarily with the organization and functioning of parishes and dioceses, so that the bishop and his pastors have carefully defined interrelationships. School superintendents therefore could work successfully only when they could obtain not only hierarchical support but also the good will and cooperation of pastors. In many instances this has been most difficult. But at least it is now known that top administration is important, and the efforts of superintendents to confer together in order to exchange views and consolidate their work are meeting with increasing success. What is unquestionably also needed is a university center where the study of and research in administration can be effectively conducted. It will take time to bring about the improvement needed, but we may hope not too much time.

Concerning the school population to be served, it would seem that the evidence available and the forecasts based on that evidence indicate that recent unprecedented population increases are not likely to recur. That is, while the number of married couples will be larger, the birth rate is declining and presumably will continue to do so. Elementary school enrollments may well tend to "stabilize" some years hence. One may also venture the opinion that although the secondary school population will increase not only for demographic reasons but also because of the results of "Upward Bound" and similar programs, the problem of making provision for expanded numbers should be manageable from the point of view of the Catholic school, if its present character as an "academic" institution is maintained. Matriculation in the four-year college will be more eagerly sought for some time to come, but probably will taper off. The most notable expansion may well take place in the junior college and its companion piece, the technical institute. Since, as has been indicated, very few such institutions are conducted under private auspices, the problem is largely one with which public education must cope. A variety of predictions about graduate and professional schools are available. An arbitrary selection from among these forecasts rising enrollments, with emphasis on the professional schools, though no further mushrooming is anticipated. A great deal depends on whether graduate study fellowships remain obtainable in large numbers. The recent decision by the Ford Foundation to make substantial sums available for the purpose seems to augur well for the future, but only in so far as the more affluent universities are concerned.

Qualitatively speaking, the principal question is whether the training of teachers for all educational levels can continue to improve as it has during the past two decades. We cannot assume that an automatic escalator is in action. As a matter of unpleasant fact, taking care of the "baby bulge" made it necessary to recruit teachers for public and private schools alike, who in more stable times might have been considered marginal. Meanwhile it is true that teacher-training colleges generally have improved, in terms both of method and content courses, and that admission standards have been raised. Institutes for "retraining" teachers in such fields as the "new mathematics" or language instruction have also served a useful purpose, as has a notable improvement in the quality of audio-visual materials. But if we are candid we shall admit that all these were merely steps toward scholastic progress. The numbers problem has not been solved anywhere along the line. Perhaps the elementary and secondary schools have been most hard pressed in confronting that problem, but one has only to read the papers in order to see that the college and the graduate school have also had their troubles. The graduate school has faced problems largely created by the siphoning off of scholars to serve enterprises deemed to be in the national interest. Everyone is aware that the economy is called upon to dig down deep in support of such ventures as putting a man on the moon. But the scooping up of trained scientists and social scientists is doubtless a still more important item in the debit columns of the ledger. Nevertheless, in some respects present-day American education may well have more "quality" than in any previous time.

Let us now take a look at some of the implications for the Catholic educational "system." First, the elementary school. Granted a relatively stable number of vocations to the religious life and some increase in the amount of financial support, it would not seem unreasonable to expect that some manifest faults could be corrected and some well-recognized needs met. The largesse currently provided by the federal government should make possible a measure of modernization, particularly in the area of teaching materials. In addition, it is at least conceivable that even a not-too-impressive increase in the amount contributed by Catholics to the support of their schools would enable them to reduce inordinately heavy teaching loads, provide some salary increases, establish guidance facilities, and set up in-service training for lay teachers. We might even expect that the precarious assumption that the principalship is strictly an extra-curricular activity could be relegated to the past. To be sure, some opinions are currently voiced that teaching religious might best serve the Lord by catechizing the ungodly. If such a policy is followed, it would drain off important resources of both personnel and dedication. At the moment this seems relatively improbable. Does it appear equally unlikely that the financial support given to Catholic schools will increase?

What do we see in actual practice? Notable is a trend, first seriously inaugurated by the archdiocese of Cincinnati, to lop off the earlier grades of the elementary school. Also, we read reports that schools are being closed in a number of smaller towns and cities, presumably because keeping them going is too difficult. Do these things portend a serious effort to curtail, if not indeed to abandon, the elementary school? A realistic answer is difficult to come by. If paying for and maintaining a school were only a local problem, it would soon become apparent (as has already been suggested) that closing parochial schools would benefit no one, Catholic parents included. But as a matter of fact the public schools derive more and more of their support from state budgets. This is an equalization measure, but it tends to make it seem as if the local problem were being eased. Something similar could be done in the Catholic sector if diocesan, or perhaps multi-diocesan, support within a given state could be made available. At the present time the simple truth is that the parish is by all odds the most efficient collector of Catholic revenue. Some experimentation with diocesan collecting for education has, it is true, been in progress, but it is far too early to judge the results. The present situation is clearly indicated by the fact that when the state of Louisiana levied a one per cent tax increase for the support of public education, the resulting rises in teachers' salaries drained some Catholic schools of their lay staffs. The loss was not one of numbers, merely, but of quality.

Therefore, we have come to the point where not only laymen but priests, religious, and even bishops are asking whether it may not be wise and necessary to think of a drastic curtailment of the parochial school effort. Of course, there are many parishes whose revenues can support a school plant in which the twelve grades are closely associated, and it will doubtless take a long time before these abandon the ship. Other parochial schools, one can be pretty sure, will not be closed by the religious communities which operate them. But it certainly looks as if the percentage of Catholic children now in Catholic parochial schools—52 per cent at the time the Notre Dame report was being written—will decrease, perhaps more rapidly than many of us have thought.

It is difficult to discuss an issue like this without pro- or anti-sentimentalism. There is no use crying over heroic effort which has no chance to succeed. But would the Catholic community gain or lose? Perhaps we are currently so interested in the growth of higher, and what is now generally called "continuing," education that we tend to think that the equivalent of the "little red schoolhouse" can be taken for granted, even as are the perambulator and the diaper service. How far from the truth that is! For instance, however desirable it is that more young people from socially disadvantaged groups should enter college, it remains far more important that good elementary schooling be provided for all children in these groups. And how much time must be wasted later on in life by those who find that their first eight school years were practically meaningless!

We shall now concern ourselves with the major purpose of the Catholic school, which is primarily to develop religious knowledge and practice. In a time when religious and ethical assumptions are subject to change, and are being challenged as never before in the United States, what of lasting value can be accomplished by the elementary school? Indeed, may not the simple loyalties which are encouraged in grade-school pupils later come to seem either chains of habit or impediments to sophistication? I have dealt with this problem in another context and will repeat what was said there:

> As one who has no special competence in the teaching of religion but who has had occasion over not a few decades to evaluate some of its fruits, I may, perhaps, be allowed to make a few comments on one or the other of its aspects. There can be no doubt that in this area children profit by some of the oldest uses of project methods. The boy acolyte comes breathtakingly close to the Mass; the little girl who strews flowers on Holy Thursday identifies herself with service to her Lord; children bless themselves with holy water, St. Francis gave them the Christmas crib, they live in a world of bowed heads, folding hands, genuflections, burning candles. The way to the reality of First Holy Communion thus passes through a field of symbols every flower in which is precious. No one who has walked there can forget—not Renan or James Joyce or Mary McCarthy.
>
> But the time comes when questions are asked. These will at first be the interrogation points of innocent rebellion. But later on they will harden into negations. The world of concrete symbol will change into one of intellectual abstractions and emotional fixations. In this last there will loom up large as the moon the question as to the relationship between freedom and obedience. This is the most fateful of the warning signals that maturity is impending. One can only be candid and admit the more of ripeness there is, the greater the danger to the religious spirit. There could be no point in denying that Newman wrote the *Grammar of Assent,* and that indeed it was imperative he do so. In the face of a perennial peril he offered, anxiously and painstakingly, a path to salvation. That path is not paved with the symbols we have noted with grateful reverence. It is hewn through the rock of intellectualized doubt with the pickaxe of analysis.
>
> It is, in my judgment, during the years identified with the high school that everything will depend, at least for the most gifted and restless, upon how ably and deftly the young person is led from the land of obedience to the symbol to the other domain of freedom to question and to weigh answers. Of course one can go on for a long time saying and doing things without any longer believing in them. But normally the boy or girl of nineteen will have chosen, often quite unconsciously, to be or not to be in the spiritual sense. How grave the responsibility therefore is! How easily an unwise curb or an injudicious answer can bring a soul to a road which may for some distance seem parallel but which in actuality is veering off. One

can only hope that those whom education so heavily burdens will have the strength and wisdom required. Even when the best is done there will be strange, inexplicable failures. When it is not done, God help us![1]

A different sort of question is asked by Andrew M. Greeley and Peter H. Rossi. Their valuable study is based on the results of a very elaborate questionnaire designed to secure from a sample of respondents information about whether religious commitment and practice over a long period of time are really affected by attendance in Catholic schools. The authors conclude that, although "further research is necessary before it can be said with any confidence whether one level of education is more influential than another, a hypothesis for further research . . . in so far as religious values are concerned, is: that neither grammar school nor high school is as important as attending both grammar school and high school in a value-oriented system."[2] This may not help much at the moment, but at least it indicates what one would have to look for if one wished to base a decision about the elementary school on a careful inquiry into the facts.

It seems tenable that the development of the high school system would come closest to assuring that *all* Catholic parents who desired to do so could provide Catholic education for their children. This view seems soundly based if one considers either statistical evidence or trends which now seem clearly indicated. As we have seen, the percentage of Catholic children who can be admitted to elementary schools will drop and not rise, at least if all the grades are taken into account. The majority of college- and university-bound young Catholics will not have the slightest chance to obtain higher education under Catholic auspices. Hypothetically, therefore, the high school does hold out a promise of service to the whole Catholic group attending that school, except for certain kinds of vocational education.

Three trends may be signalled which support this opinion. The first is naturally the fact that enrollments at the high-school level still lag behind enrollments in the elementary school. To this one must add the fact that there are only four years of high school and eight of elementary school. The second trend, already referred to, is toward the "upgrading" of teaching religious. More education naturally paves the way to the high-school class-room. But, and this is probably more important, it should, as a result of greater participation by religious, be possible to employ a substantial number of lay teachers on a basis of relative parity with public schools in so far as salaries are concerned. The third trend is doubtless the most significant. Each

---

[1] See above, page 303.

[2] Andrew M. Greeley and Peter H. Rossi, *The Education of Catholic Americans* (Chicago: Aldine Press), p. 164.

new day brings with it the creation of clerical-lay boards concerned with the secondary schools. In many instances these boards include in their membership citizens of substance and influence, both Catholic and non-Catholic. It is already apparent that wherever Catholic school superintendents are willing to work enthusiastically with such boards they can add greatly to the resources of the schools in terms of finance and good will. Admittedly we do not have at present an over-all report on the manner in which such boards function. But on the basis of the samples which we have considered, it seems reasonable to assume that there is solid ground for hoping for success in the future.

Whether it is desirable to concentrate on the high school, in order to provide a measure of Catholic education for all children whose parents wish them to have it, is a query which must be submitted to those in charge of Catholic education as a whole. As has been said, its adoption would not automatically mean the demise of the parochial school, but that school would henceforth be in some measure peripheral. Many—and not merely those who resist the influence of the Council—believe that such a radical change would be a serious mistake. Their argument is necessarily more intuitive than "scientific," but the Notre Dame report does indicate how successful the Catholic elementary school has been in general when it comes to the teaching of religious "values."

The question naturally remains, how effective is religious teaching in the secondary school at the present time? We have already considered some of the evidence gathered during the course of the Notre Dame Study. While these data do not suggest either rejoicing or despair, they clearly indicate that the life of the teacher of religion is not an easy one. A study prepared for the 1966 workshop on the Christian formation of Jesuit high-school students of the Jesuit Educational Association by Father Joseph H. Fichter, S.J., based on "attitudes, impressions and experiences of 7,307 American boys," digests the answers to what we have called a "pupil opinionnaire." It is all the more interesting and valuable because of the long association of the Jesuits with secondary school education, and because of the superior quality of both their student bodies and teaching staffs, which consist of Jesuit priests, scholastics, and laymen. Moreover, the present study is one in a series dating back to 1962, and thus reflects a continuing concern by this group of Catholic educators with the quality of their achievement. In terms of expressed interest, classes in religion declined steadily during the four years spent in high school; the popularity of teachers of religion was similarly affected. On the other hand, the majority of the boys studied had given some consideration as to whether they should decide to follow a religious vocation, even though in the end only a relatively few actually decided to do so.

The Jesuit sociologist realistically accepts two premises. First, the character-building efficacy of the home is greater than that of the school. Father Fichter cites one of his colleagues to the effect that a boy experiences two great influences—the home and the school—of which the first is by far the more important. And he adds, "In dealing with a boy with a good home background, our work is made relatively easy; with a poor one it is made extremely difficult, if not impossible." The second premise is that adolescence is a time for rebellion, and that boys are naturally more likely to kick against the traces than are girls. We have, so far as I know, virtually no information about the boys who drop out of these schools after entering them, for academic or disciplinary reasons. They may represent the outer fringe of rebellion, and it would be of general interest if more could be learned about them.

Among the more puzzling aspects of the over-all high school situation is failure to inculcate personal honesty. Father Fichter's study makes clear that cheating during tests, exams, and similar ordeals remains a problem for Jesuit educators. As in almost all institutions which have reported on the problem, the amount of cheating increases as the student nears graduation and the process of seeking admission to college. There are no easy solutions for those who attempt to bring Catholic educational practice into conformity with the ethical teaching of the Church. Confusion in the home regarding moral values, as well as the pressures encouraging cheating, make clear how difficult secondary education will continue to be, especially if the elementary school is curtailed.

## New Problems for Catholic Colleges

The college is now probably the most widely and intensively discussed of all the divisions of American education. What is even more important, much of what is being said is interesting and helpful, exception having been made for some comment on the teacher-training colleges, which often suffer because their critics are still belaboring conditions which have long since been corrected. The reason for all this attention is the startling growth which has taken place within a comparatively few years. Even the Depression, when jobs were scarce and leisure ample, did not witness a marked increase in the percentages of young people going to colleges, except in those cities which offered free tuition in municipally operated institutions. When the Second World War was declared, about 14 per cent of young people in the appropriate age groups were on college campuses. Demobilization, followed by the "baby boom," which, in terms of children already born, will not taper off until approximately 1980, completely altered the situation. The official estimate is that nearly 16,000,000 young Americans will be of college age in 1975, and that half of them will be seeking admission. In other words, the percentage will have more than tripled during the thirty-five years after 1940. It is an extraordinary phenomenon, which to some extent has a counterpart in a few other countries.

Here our purpose is to place the Catholic college in perspective; comment on the educational situation as a whole is only for the purpose of establishing a relationship. The GI Bill created an appetite not only for college, but for college at a price everybody could afford to pay. Vastly increased public support was called for and is being given in ever expanding measure. Thus the steady development of municipal colleges, offering either a four- (or even five-) year program or a two-year (community college) curriculum, has been vigorous, indeed, and has been followed by a very great increase in the number of branches of the state universities erected in cities other than those where these universities themselves are at home. At some of these colleges no tuition charge is made. In others the fees are moderate. Two results may be noted. The tax-paying parent is likely to feel that since he helps to pay the "bill," his children also have a right to a college education. The community college is a convenient device for meeting this demand because its admission requirements are lower, although it can reward achievement by transferring the best of its graduates to four-year institutions. On the other hand a marked change has taken place in the traditional campus environment. Although something like a college "climate" develops in the municipal institution, strong ties to the home and the neighborhood persist. They are generally not deeply affected by developments which involve the faculty and the adminis-tration of the college. Indeed, many will not have the foggiest notion about how the college is organized and operated. A large number will also have part-time employment, which further restricts their collegiate concern to the classroom and the course work done in connection with it. The quality of the academic performance tends to be high; faculty morale is assured by a frequently affluent salary and fringe-benefit scale; and "democracy" protects faculty status and incumbency. Some Catholic and other private colleges are "competitive" with the public-supported municipal institutions, notably in New York, Chicago, and Detroit. But it seemingly makes very little difference from a religious point of view whether a youngster attends, for example, New York University rather than St. John's University.

The expansion of colleges in the state universities themselves has been rapid and great. Robert Hassenger has observed that in the fall of 1965 the University of Minnesota enrolled 9,614 Freshmen, while the eight "Ivy League" colleges mustered 9,420. No data concerning the total enrollment in all the private colleges of Minnesota, many of which are of very good quality, were available to me at the time this comment was being written, but the likelihood is that the state university surpassed their sum-total. Looking at such trends, a number of veteran observers of American education predict that unless the private colleges can to some extent match the growth of the state-supported colleges their share in forming the outlook of youth will soon be that of a minority stockholder. But how is such growth to be managed? What the student pays in terms of tuition and other charges at the "quality" institutions is less than what it costs to educate him, the difference being made up through interest on endowment funds and through other contributions. Nevertheless the check signed by the parent is a substantial one. In some states scholarship money made available through public bounty is payable to private and public colleges alike. There is also the tuition tax plan sponsored by Dr. Oliver C. Carmichael, which may some day be enacted into law. But as matters stand now any phenomenal relative growth in the number and size of private colleges seems improbable, unless they greatly dilute quality.

It would be erroneous to try to separate Catholic colleges from other private colleges when there is discussion of this kind of development. Of course there are differences of motivation to be considered. The attractiveness of the best institutions in both groups derives from prestige and the loyalty of alumni, but colleges conducted under Catholic, Jewish, or Protestant auspices frequently profit also by religious or group solidarity. If institutions like Brandeis, Vanderbilt, Georgetown, and Notre Dame have both prestige and a religious orientation which commands respect, they can grow slightly without running the risk of impoverishing themselves through expansion. The University of Pittsburgh, which recently faced a giant deficit, has set an example in which there is implicit a warning to all private *universities* which are not amply endowed. The smaller college may, however, be in a relatively advantageous position to expand proportionately, though not ambitiously. Many parents hesitate to send their daughters in particular into the vast mass movement which takes place annually to the public campuses. If they can be sure of the "quality" of the college and of its basic "decency," they will most likely continue to patronize it, at least as long as our society remains comparatively affluent. Henceforth, however, that college must at least try hard to be a reputable academic institution, and not expect that its religious orientation alone will keep it afloat. This is true of course for all denominational or "religiously committed" colleges, and not for Catholic institutions only.

How are these trends reflected in the Catholic college in particular? We estimate that in 1965 approximately 400,000 Catholic students were enrolled in Catholic colleges, while somewhat more than twice that many were attending secular institutions. The 400,000 figure may increase slightly during the years which lie ahead, but the other side of the ledger will show far greater gains. Greeley and Rossi concluded from their study of Catholic youth that Catholics will probably for some time equal if not outdistance other groups in the quest for higher education; and the Notre Dame report corroborates this by pointing to the academic character of Catholic secondary education. Can we determine what this means? The prevailing opinion—at least I think that it is—appears to be that the traditional Catholic state of mind which led to the choice of a Catholic college *primarily* to safeguard the faith can be expected to survive no more than twenty years longer. A very considerable majority of Catholic young people will have attended secular institutions without much more visible impairment of their faith than would have occurred on a Catholic campus. In general, the secular colleges, particularly those associated with state universities, will respect the student's religious commitment or at least ignore it; and the large number of Catholics in attendance will make it seem desirable to college administrators to assist in making provision for religious education and guidance. Indeed, since the recent Supreme Court decision acknowledging the constitutionality of "objective" courses in religion, a profusion of such courses has begun to appear on public campuses. Many of these will be taught by Catholic scholars, a goodly number of whom are now being trained in the divinity schools of the University of Chicago, Yale, and Harvard. This is added reason why the Catholic college may well have no more than twenty years in which to demonstrate that it exists in order to provide first-rate education within the context of a Catholic community.

The first-rate college, besides providing opportunities to acquire needed skills, should observe four "ground rules":

It exists in order to inculcate awareness in depth of problems and situations of concern to modern man, and in order to foster inquiry into whether solutions of such problems can be suggested. In doing so it will fully take into account the history of man and of the ideas by which he has lived.

It is staffed by men and women able to stimulate student thinking to a degree of intelligent intensity which all but a very few could not generate if left to their own devices.

It is concerned not merely with the intelligence but also with fostering a profound regard for the effective and aesthetic life of man.

As a Catholic college, it strives to foster social responsibility in the spirit of the Second Vatican Council.

It is equipped with aids which are now indispensable if these objectives are to be reached. It has libraries, laboratories, opportunities for research, as well as a "climate of opinion" in which the worth and freedom of every individual are recognized.

To be sure, one might list other requisite characteristics. For instance, one could say that the faculty must be relatively harmonious and in the scholarly sense homogeneous, that the presidents and deans must have some visibility on and off the campus, and that the student body must possess the ability to participate with meaningful success in the educational dialogue. Is a "residential atmosphere" desirable? This is a debatable question. The campus on which the student is in residence has advantages, but there are "day colleges" which manage to create a genuinely educational climate.

And so one may legitimately and unabashedly say to Catholic colleges that unless they feel certain of their ability to observe the ground rules they would be well advised to get out of the game. There are relatively painless ways to get out ... at least at present. One way is to exit through amalgamation; another is through transforming the college into a secondary school. But granted that anything like a rash of raw new institutions can be avoided, enough is now known on the basis of sound research done on a variety of campuses or through pertinent committees of the American Council on Education and the American Association of Colleges to enable college administrators to find out what the ground rules involve.

It has often been said that only the student actually knows what a college is like, and that it is quite impossible to find out what that knowledge is. Social psychologists have, however, gone to great pains of late to see what they can discover, and their efforts have been supplemented by fairly courageous "self-studies." The inquiry into its innermost secrets conducted by Mundelein College, Chicago, under the leadership of Sister Mary Ann Ida and Dr. N. J. Hruby is now well known and is being duplicated in part at other institutions. Dr. Hruby did not, to be sure, limit his research to the student body, but nevertheless went to great pains to discover as much as possible what it thought or felt about its "environment" at Mundelein. The development of "instruments" designed to find out whether an institution provides the kind of common life which will engender the good qualities associated with education at the college has been impressive. Thus a given institution may be a very pleasant place in which to live but provide very little genuine intellectual stimulation. Another may offer academic instruction of high quality but fail to provide anything which resembles a rewarding student group life. What we know so far about Catholic colleges in these terms appears to indicate that in general they keep closer to the normal pattern of the secondary school than they do to that of the more "satisfying" collegiate institution in the United States at the present time. This "satisfaction" often fills the European observer with admiration mingled with awe. He has seldom known anything like it. The European student passes from the confinement of the lycée or Gymnasium to the university, unfettered by anything except political movements and fraternities.

It is probable that the "satisfying climate" alluded to results from leisure and affluence, and of course there are people who think we Americans have too much of both and therefore permit our young people to live in an unreal academic world until they are suddenly propelled into the grim here and now. A case can be made for this point of view, and not infrequently a student outlines it for himself. That he never comes to grips with anything outside the make-believe "dream universe" of the campus, that he enjoys liberties which will be unimaginable later on, strikes him with full force somewhere along the academic path. Educators sometimes forget that a "spiritual crisis" is likely to involve a boy or girl during adolescence, just as love may suddenly seem the only important thing in the world. In our time, the "crisis" will probably occur in terms of action. Young people who live with big "brush wars" and underdeveloped countries on one side of them, and the poverty, violence and racism of urban America on the other, may easily come to feel that sitting in classrooms talking with their instructors and fellow students, miles away from the scene of action, is simply being on a kind of vacation. The older Catholic college did not permit its students to wander far from the contemplation of eternity. Through daily Mass and the annual retreat, the spotlight was thrown on the eternal destiny of life with God, and the vocation to the religious life was thought of as the highest and noblest of all callings. Today, although the Council schema on "The Church in the Modern World" does not reduce the hope of eternal union with God, it adds a new *thisworldly* dimension to man's search for salvation. The climate of the Catholic college is changing and will change further; the moment has come for it to develop its own climate of freedom.[3]

The principal difference between the college and the graduate school—

---

[3]At this point a gloss would seem to be in order. The word "freedom" is one of the slippery items in the language. Some years ago Mortimer Adler constructed a gigantic intellectual filtering plant through which he let flow the more or less living waters of the philosophies concerned with the word. Here the purpose is far more modest. In the great classical tradition the word is legal and juridical. It has meant that the individual human person could profess to have rights which the state was bound to respect. When the state agreed to do so, a civil liberty was born. Thus freedom of conscience was recognized, probably because Church and State had so often joined forces to propel that conscience into a desired mold. Caesar and his "church" did so in ancient Rome, making war on Christian and Jew. Later on institutionalized Christendom and a variety of states imitated Caesar to the best of their ability. Anyone who wishes to study the origins of the belief that "this will never do" should read the pertinent documentation concerning the English seventeenth century. Thoughtful Oxford and Cambridge men, looking back over the butcheries of the Tudor and post-Tudor times, decided that something better, or at least more interesting, would have to be devised. John Locke has run away with the laurels, but this is due to the fact that it is easier to read an author than to study a trend. Proceeding from Thomas More to Abraham Cowley is at least as rewarding.

The Constitution of the United States, heir to British experience but sired by men who did not take that of France lightly either, not only protects the which is the heart of the university proper—is to be found in the fact that instruction and inquiry are much more rigorously concentrated on a given segment of knowledge. Training and guiding students in the writing of a dissertation, which should be a detailed statement about something one has studied in depth and with some originality, is the central concern of the graduate school. The course of study as such is designed to provide a comprehensive and probing consideration of the background of knowledge against which the dissertation must be written. This task will be taken seriously by some graduate schools, lightly by others. Implied is the truism that those who teach must themselves be research-minded; they may, therefore, tend to act as if teaching (except in the sense of guiding) were a chore

---

right of the citizen to join and support a religion of his choice (the caveat against the Mormons was rather special, since people did not foresee that having wives in series was really not very different from having them at one time), but also establishes the now traditional deduction that a man's religion shall be outside the pale of government interference, even by the tax collector. We now acknowledge a number of other rights, but doubtless that which transcends all others is that which assures the citizen of a fair trial when he is alleged to have broken a law. This we might almost facetiously, were the matter not genuinely earnest, term the "last right," for then the citizen is pitted against society. No doubt it permits of explication through analogy. Thus integration can be said to be a continuing effort to accord the Negro the right to a fair trial.

During generations he has been tried and found wanting in so far as the use of public and private facilities is concerned, by reason of his color, history, and race. He had long since been accorded freedom of conscience, speech, and assembly, but only if he exercised that right separately from his white neighbors. Negroes in Selma, Alabama, could meet privately in their churches or elsewhere and say whatever they pleased. But they could not appeal to or denounce others in their company. It was a great deal like being a prisoner at the bar who could appeal to a jury only through an attorney who had committed a similar offense. Unfortunately, integration does not mean that the Negro's white neighbors are legally deprived of their freedom to hate, deride, and shun. Negro children in a predominantly white school are often treated abominably, but most of their complaints are without legal redress. White folk have a constitutional right to assemble and demand, if they so desire, that the Chief Justice of the United States be impeached because he has advocated the doctrine that racial discrimination is illegal. In other words, the right to a fair trial does not mean that all citizens must accept the verdict.

The freedom of the Negro, or of any other citizen for that matter, does not imply that he is henceforth to be treated with courtesy, made to feel at home in a neighborhood, listened to with respect, or be invited to attend social functions at which his kind are not wanted. He is at liberty to feel

interfering with the business at hand. And indeed, if the heart of the matter is the dissertation, are not the hours spent in the classroom of peripheral significance? Many an American or European graduate student has been led to accept such a professorial point of view with anguish, annoyance, or relief. At present it would seem that more and more graduate training is being done through participation in research.

The real problem, though, is of a different kind. How is a graduate student, normally likely to dedicate much of his career to college-teaching, to acquire some teaching competence? Several universities, notably Harvard, have exercised leadership in trying to associate teacher-training with graduate study. In some departments of Harvard a fellow may be supported through a five-year period, two years of which are devoted to "supervised" teaching.

---

angry and embittered, but the more vocally he exercises this liberty the more likely he is to come square up against the dichotomy suggested long since by Sidney Hook—that between heresy and conspiracy. In the light of the American tradition, and of course of the Christian tradition as well, discrimination against the Negro as we have known it is heresy. One may deplore or indeed attack it on the basis of a dozen orthodoxies. But if the Negro were to decide that the heretic has no rights, or that something like an inquisitional tribunal (very democratically organized, with guns, Molotov cocktails, and knives) should be set up, he would automatically become a conspirator against the very tradition which has assured him of freedom of conscience and a fair trial.

I wish to draw one rather simple academic conclusion from what has been said. Implicit in the constitutional grant of freedom of conscience is the right to institutionalize it. Any number of people who feel the same way about things, who for example are bound together in respect for a traditional creed, are assured of the right to build a church, a school, or a university. They are not assured of anything else. They may for example find that their neighbors are just as ready to repudiate Catholics in some sections of the country as they are to throw rocks at Negroes (or whites) in another. Some people in the United States hate Catholics so much that they would rather die than contribute a nickel to the support of anything in which Catholics are interested. There are others who feel the same way about Jews or Protestants.

Let us admit that they have a right to do so. But it makes no more sense to grant a right to the Negro, without doing something to clothe that naked right in decent apparel, than it does to acknowledge the civil liberties of Catholics while doing everything in one's power to circumscribe them. The United States has a good many choices to make in this hour. One it does not propose is to limit the defense of the country to this group or that. It would be rather odd if we died together under some rain from the skies before we began to realize the simple fact that sharing death is so much easier than sharing life.

The program has interested some of the best of Harvard's applicants for fellowships, and one may say that the training devised for them is of unusual merit. Other institutions attempt to "structure" the period of graduate study in such a way that recipients of grants can add a year or two of experience as teaching assistants. The faculty of the beleaguered University of California has recently resurrected an idea which I believe originated with Harvard's great humanist Howard Mumford Jones, and hopes to offer a degree preparation for which will demand less of a concentration on the dissertation field, so that the candidate can emerge less "research minded" and more attuned to teaching. I am afraid that I remain skeptical about the practical results likely to follow this effort. The prestige now attached to the straightforward doctorate of ancient Germanic vintage is too great. Nevertheless, many gifted young instructors, graduates of distinguished universities, are quite terrified by their initial classroom experience, and some of them even decide to abandon teaching.

These are other problems which every university, Catholic or not, must face. Can a university deserve the name if in addition to its undergraduate division it operates professional schools only, and not a graduate school in the strict sense? I would say yes, provided that what is meant is not a school so far removed from the undergraduate establishment as to make no impact on it. When they are first rate, the influence of professional schools on undergraduate instruction can be very great and academically significant. An excellent law school, for example, may actually do as much to inculcate social ethics in the general student body as a department of theology. This is a point which existing Catholic universities might well consider. Many of them originated as congeries of professional schools, following in this respect, despite European influence, the pattern of the land-grant college. Perhaps they could serve their student bodies best if they set about making their professional schools truly distinguished, so that when one thought of their law schools or their schools of business administration one would know that they were on a level with similar schools at Yale or Pennsylvania.

At any rate, the question is now sometimes asked whether the very idea of a Catholic university is at all tenable. Rosemary Lauer, in the heat of debate about a special situation, made the somewhat unphilosophical generalization that a juxtaposition of "Catholic" with "university" was a contradiction of terms. There are, of course, others who make the same statement because they hold that the "Truth" which Christian theology attempts to expound is at best a mirage, and perhaps a dangerous and deleterious one. We shall try to discuss the question *contra* and *pro,* with as much candor as possible.

### The Role of the Catholic University

I shall try to present the case *against* the need for a Catholic university—or at least for many Catholic universities—objectively, though with little attention to minor caveats against including religion in education. To begin with, there is no reason to suppose that a contribution to knowledge in any field will be more significant because the investigator has studied or taught in a Catholic university. That would seem to be rather obvious in so far as the natural sciences and the social sciences in particular are concerned, but it may also be true in humanistic studies. Of course, a student will profit greatly through association with a truly creative scholar if such a scholar is present on a Catholic university campus. Normally, however, such scholars will be attracted to secular campuses not so much because of salary differentials, as is often mistakenly thought, but because the most gifted students seek to attend institutions which have prestige, impressive concentration of faculty, and other resources in quantity. At any rate, there is no discernible reason why a dissertation which probes into a chemical compound or analyzes voting habits in a particular city will be any better for being the product of a Catholic university. The only thing that counts is whether or not it is the outcome of sound, honest, and—if possible —imaginative effort. Surely a world as greatly in disarray as ours provides the Church with challenges more significant than maintaining separate institutions in order to sponsor dissertations of this character.

Considered as citizens, Catholics may rightly be expected to carry their fair share of the nation's intellectual burden. It would appear that they have not been doing so, or at least this is the opinion of some of the ablest Catholic scholars themselves. Can it be that their own universities have been too isolated from the mainstream of American higher education? They may be and sometimes are pleasant places, well suited for undergraduate study. But why should they attempt to siphon off a few of the very scarce scholarly fraternity for service in their graduate schools, thus in turn isolating them? It is primarily for this reason that the Germans and the Austrians, by and large, have not favored the establishment of Catholic universities as distinguished from the secondary schools (*Gymnasiums*). German Catholics in particular, so often the victims of discriminatory practices in the past, or suffering by reason of a lack of interest in higher education on the part of some of their bishops, are now trying hard to achieve parity in so far as appointments to the eminent universities of their country are concerned. They will tell you that skimming off any considerable number of their colleagues in order to staff a Catholic university would be highly regrettable, if not indeed deplorable. Cannot a similar case be made for the United States? Might it not be easier to "get a dialogue going" (a horrible phrase but now everywhere in use) against the background of Harvard, Stanford, or Wisconsin rather than that of St. John's University?

The Catholic university maintains that the principal reason for its existence is that philosophy and theology can be taught in it with due regard for what is alive in the tradition of the Church. At any rate this is what was thought not so long ago. The orthodoxy of the teaching theologian was to be assured by exacting an oath of allegiance to the *magisterium;* and it was the Thomistic philosophy which would establish the mode of reason which the theologian could profitably use. But, in the light of the realities all about us, what is the "perennial philosophy" now? The seminary mind used to feel it could wait until the "errors" latent in a given trend of thought had been revealed. After all, many thinkers in Communist-dominated countries have now become skeptical about almost everything in the repertory of Karl Marx. In their views, his theory of the class struggle led only to another such struggle, and his vision of the ultimate state turns out to be an infantile mirage. Why should not the "perennial philosopher" sit back comfortably and say, "I told you so?" It is a pleasant pastime, but unfortunately not very many people want to take it up. They do not simply agree that Marx is passé and that we need only study the *Summa.* Unfortunately, they have got used to wanting much the same things Marx wanted, and are apt to try to reach comparable ends with different means.

Or let us consider Newman's *Idea of a University.* This developed with great subtlety and imaginative power a case for a Catholic institution of higher learning in which the study of science and literature would spin freely round a center of theological studies. But his university turns out on inspection to have been a projection of a Catholic Oxford, with Catholic theologians doing pretty much what the Oxford Movement had done within the framework of Anglicanism. It was certainly not a medieval university in any sense. Professor James J. John has recently clarified the medieval situation:

> It is also common knowledge that there was a hierarchy among the faculties, with Theology at the head and ruling as queen, followed by law and medicine, and then arts in the rear and serving as *ancilla* or hand-maiden. These commonplaces no doubt describe the medieval ideal, but the actual medieval university often fell short, especially in the number of faculties. And strange as it may seem in a Catholic institution the faculty most often absent was that of theology. . . . Formal theological training on the university level was long reserved exclusively to the Universities of Paris, Oxford and Cambridge.[4]

The reason, one surmises, was that it was easier for the Church to keep an eye on a few theological faculties, which in turn found it simpler to exercise an influence on the always changing, scintillating, discoursing philosophers if they did not spread themselves too thin or get too deeply involved in the

[4] *Conditions and Purposes of the Modern University – The Christian Dimension* (Washington, D.C.: Aldine Press, 1966), p. 9.

fracas. In the United States until quite recently we have had a somewhat comparable situation. Just one Catholic institution of the highest quality was dedicated to the study of systematic theology—Woodstock College—though there were several good schools of pastoral theology. And in so far as philosophy is concerned, as long as it was possible to "guide" the teaching of the subject by agreeing that it was to be Thomist, with the modifications based on monastic or university traditions previously indicated, many or most of the perils of the medieval time could be avoided.

But the Second Vatican Council has recognized that it is precisely this kind of control which the modern university man, or woman for that matter, finds unacceptable. Who but the scholar humbly rooted in faith can determine what inferences may be drawn tentatively in philosophical terms from the truth that is in revelation? Nobody, or at least hardly anybody, wants any more inquisitions, religious or secular. Human society is almost fanatically eager to think what it pleases, do what it pleases, read and believe what it pleases. *Only, paradoxically, it wants to believe something.* And so if one asks a Catholic university, moving around a core of theological and philosophical discussion that is itself in a state of flux, what it has to offer to meet this desire for belief, what response can it make?

We do not question the need for centers of theological and philosophical training. They should be of high quality. Above all they should be holy places. But why should it be taken for granted that a university, the contemporary university, should house them, except perhaps in the sense that it has, like Munich or Tübingen, a faculty of theology coequal with other faculties? Was it perhaps providential that the Jesuits in France and Germany were ostracized and frequently restrained from having a corporate domicile, so that they developed a "new theology" by reason of a sense of immersion in and responsibility for the society in which they lived as scattered and secret shepherds? Does not a university make proud claims to knowledge which faith must shun? Not even St. Paul could probe into the mystery of divine Providence. All he could say, magnificently, was:

> How inexhaustible God's resources, wisdom and knowledge are! How unfathomable his decisions are, and how untraceable his ways!
> Who has ever known the Lord's thoughts, or advised him?
> Or who has advanced anything to him, for which he will have to be repaid?
> For from him everything comes; through him everything exists; and in him everything ends! Glory to Him forever! Amen.

Nevertheless it is true that the believing Christian, contemplating the glory and the evil of these days, will not fail to sense with awe that Providence has not ceased in its love for man. And if this be true, is not our principal task to make this evident with insight and humility, patience and affection?

Is it not true that the Catholic university is destined to be a kind of enclave for a few, while the great mass of Catholics in quest of higher education will be found elsewhere? To be sure, the statistical estimate which forecasts that in the not-too-far-distant future 70 percent of all young Catholics seeking higher education will matriculate in non-Catholic institutions is probably subject to some corrective analysis. Many widely patronized forms of collegiate experience in particular lie pretty much outside the Catholic bailiwick—junior colleges, municipal continuing-education programs, technical institutes, and so forth. Even so! If, for example, the state of Illinois puts into effect its almost grandiose plan for creating populous centers of learning, at the college as well as the graduate-school level, the question will immediately arise: Why should I, a parent named John Jones, pay five times as much in tuition costs to send my daughter Ellen to a Catholic college, even though I know that this college is in several important respects a good college? Since I am aware that many of my Catholic friends and neighbors are sending their children to public colleges, can I not assume that the Church, alert to its mission, will provide adequate centers in which religious life can be fostered and strengthened? Is it not already doing so to the best of its ability? Since priests, religious, and well-trained laymen are in short supply, why coop them up to take care of an "elite" while the spiritual needs of very large numbers are so great?

If this argument has any validity with regard to undergraduate education, how much more compelling it must be at the level of the graduate school! It is true that monetary problems of students may play a lesser role, since a Catholic institution with the requisite quality can secure some of the fellowships now available. In so far as higher technological education in particular is concerned, the state universities will inevitably attract the largest number. Religion there is *Privatsache;* in this sense the university is part of what Harvey Cox has called the "secular city," if it is not actually the core. Someday, of course, the worm may turn. Young people may find out that being a skilled craftsman can be a more lucrative and satisfactory calling than teaching English to Freshmen on a sprawling undergraduate campus, provided that reputable opportunities for humanistic education continue to exist. But as of the moment we must assume that the shadow of the multiversity will continue to lengthen and that unless the Church extends a hand, the curtain will drop on repeated scenes of religious innocuousness and irrelevance.

Is not a new dimension of the Church as a teaching and mind-forming society therefore required? We must surely begin to puzzle out the inner and outer boundaries. Call to mind the Puritan William Prynne's seventeenth-century comment on the celebration of Christmas. He found that the connection between Yuletide revels and the Roman Saturnalia were so close—both of them being spent in "revelling, epicurism, wantonness, idleness, dancing, drinking, stage plays, and such other Christmas disorder"—that all pious Christians should abominate them. There have been times when the prevailing Christian attitude toward scholarly inquiry not directed to the study of the sacred texts was likewise that it could only be dangerous folly. It was in conformity with a long Augustinian tradition that Thomas à Kempis wrote: "Never read thou the word in order to appear more learned or wiser. Study the mortification of thy vices; for this will profit thee more than the knowledge of knotty questions." In all truth, it is the folly of the Christian scholar that he must always be ready to say that this counsel is wise. If the pursuit of learning were to mean that we no longer "studied the mortification of our vices," or that in disentangling knotty questions we forgot the Maker of all things, then that pursuit would have to be avoided by individuals committed to the exemplification of Christ in a society which to so great an extent knows him not.

Yet it is precisely the fact that he is not known which, paradoxically, is the reason why the pursuit of knowledge has become the most important Christian missionary activity of our time. In a sense it has been so in all times. Nevertheless if we Christians of the present ask ourselves candidly where our brothers are, we must of necessity answer: they are dwelling within the knowledge of things, in the belief that the kind of knowledge which is science can change and improve all there is, even the psyche and the unborn baby in the test tube. They are living also in a new realm of the spirit, which is that of a humanity freed from physical labor, bondage to ignorance, and to a great extent physical pain. In a sense theirs is a utopian spirit, but never before has Utopia contained so hard a core of realism. The limits of our knowledge are now imposed by the cosmos, not by the human mind.

We cannot do much more than our share in the service of this utopia. But there is something else. The heart of man does not know less of anxiety, even of agony. The "death wish" which Camus found embedded in every human heart is complemented by the death knell which the bomb can sound. How different this is from the "reverent dread" about which Julian of Norwich wrote, saying that this is "the fair courtesy that is in Heaven afore God's face!" Knowing that the infinitude of God is today opposed, as never before, to the quasi-infinitude of the human mind, shall we who are Christ's followers love the men of our time enough to immerse ourselves in the mental and spiritual world which has created them and which in turn they also create? And if we answer affirmatively, do we not belong, as did St. Francis Xavier, in the wide world?

We have now made the argument against the Catholic university. What is the case for it? I should like to write off at the outset any notion that a return to the nineteenth-century conception of such a university is conceivable at the present time. It cannot be a mouthpiece for the *magisterium*, however deeply and sincerely it may respect that *magisterium*. But at the same time neither it nor any contemporary university can be *universitas*—that is, an organization of faculties which purports to provide a synthesis of, or at least a panoramic look (*Ueberblick*) at, everything which is known. It can only be a grouping of specializations. It is now just as difficult for higher education with an overt religious commitment to fathom the mysteries of God's world, the heights and depths of creation, as it would be to map out the "unsearchable ways" of God himself. One can arrive at generalizations about the methods of inquiry used by the natural scientist, but is it really possible to find out much that is basically significant when he himself reports that he has started out with a surmisal, an insight, or an intuition, all of which are beyond definition? Nor are the social sciences easier to integrate in terms of theory. They have attempted to emulate the procedures of the natural scientist; but apart from the previously stated fact that even these are only to a certain extent determinable, it has grown more evident that human conduct is not measurable in qualitative terms unless it is pressed into a mold which makes any other than quantitative responses impossible.

But if these things are true, theology cannot now be the "queen of the sciences" in any meaningful sense. To be sure, one might argue that since it is concerned with God, who is the fullness of being, theology takes precedence over sciences which are necessarily concerned with the contingent. But is even this way of looking at the matter any longer very relevant? If, as the Second Vatican Council has affirmed, the Church as the family of mankind is concerned primarily with salvation and salvation history, then theology is properly the study of some basically significant ways in which God is believed or known to have dealt with man, to have provided a path down which man can come to him, and to have given tangible human expression of his affection. But the perceptive scientist will also be aware of some of God's ways. The conclusion accordingly is that though a Catholic university must be concerned with theological studies—and with philosophical reflection which in some degree buttresses those studies, it will no longer maintain that this is the only reason why it exists. This change of emphasis is radical, but unavoidable.

Those who make up the core of its faculty and its student body may rather say: "We are men and women who have resolved to lead the life of the mind in a way which only a genuine university, combining rigor with courtesy, can provide in every dimension of scholarly venture and worth. At the same time we have accepted with all our hearts Pascal's wager that God is and has spoken. We have done this for a variety of reasons, so that in our diversity we offer, as does life itself, testimony which is one through many."

In listing these reasons, it would be found that some have been deeply moved by the testimony of the ratio, the data-analyzing activity of the intelligence. They are Thomists in one of the many senses which that term now implies, perhaps exploring the validity of a synthesis of the *Summa* and the *Grammar of Assent*. Others have been deeply moved by the testimony of the men and women who are called "mystics," whether of our own time or another, placing Rabindranath Tagore beside Hugh of St. Victor. Still others may have gone down a road similar to that once traveled by Simone Weil and come to the conclusion that "perfection" is "real"—in Augustinian terms, that only the desire for perfection can truly satisfy a human being, and that perfection is in God only. Many will have been bowled over by the person of the Lord Jesus, and have come to agree with Friedrich von Hügel:

> For a Person came, and lived and loved, and did and taught, and died and rose again, and lives on by His Power and His Spirit forever within us and amongst us, so unspeakably rich and yet so simple, so sublime and yet so homely, so divinely above us precisely in being so divinely near,—that His character and teaching require, for an ever fuller and yet never complete understanding, the varying study, and different experiments and applications, embodiments and unrollings of all the races and civilizations, of all the individual and corporate, the simultaneous and successive experiences of the human race to the end of time.[5]

Some, like Lecomte du Noüy, will have felt in their bones the weakness of the reed on which Positivism invited them to lean. They may recall some phenomenon such as that reported by the German philosopher Peter Wust at the close of the first of the two great holocausts. God was never so dead as he was in the early years of the twentieth century! Wust wrote:

> On December 31, 1913, the eminent Berlin jurist, Joseph Kohler, wrote the preface to a book. At the end of this preface he triumphantly spoke of the victory won by the modern mind. With particular pride he pointed out that war, like private revenge, has been, so to speak, left behind, thanks to the great strides made by modern reason which, as Comte had already said, must finally succeed in abolishing all irrational outbursts of violence. The fury of war, in Kohler's opinion, had been banished to the Far East, where it was lingering out its last days. Perhaps the Berlin savant wrote those proud words on the last night of the year, oblivious of the fact that with the stroke of twelve at his back the hands of the great clock of world history had swung forward to the fateful year 1914.[6]

[5] *Readings from Friedrich von Hügel,* Selected by Algar Thorold (London, 1928), p. 41.

[6] "Crisis in the West," *Essays in Order,* ed. Christopher Dawson and T. F. Burns, 3 vols. (New York: Macmillan, 1931), I, ii, 129.

Many—during recent years, very many—have held that a man thinks best about being man when he stops short and asks the mysterious questions, the ones which perhaps cannot be answered. Aristotle's "rational animal" definition is all right as far as it goes, but it excludes too much. Might not the phrase be more satisfactory if it read, "rational-irrational animal"? Then, however, one would have to reason about irrationality, and that is impossible. Is it not far better to say with the Existentialists that one can experience it, and see whether the experience can be shared with others, even God? The anxiety embedded in being human prevents such a thinker from exaggerating the value of humanism. In the case of Kierkegaard the major form of exaggeration was Hegel's. For Dostoevski it was the union of amoral intellect and power. And so on. At any rate the Existentialists are legion and their voices are strong in the concert of Christian and Catholic thought.

Some will cling to what was essential in Romanticism and drink their fill of the beauty of the Catholic cultural tradition. Perhaps this will not happen often to what is now the younger generation. They may not much care whether "The Middle Ages sleep in alabaster, a beautiful long sleep," to quote Wilfred Childe, or even whether the monks once saved the culture of the West. Nevertheless one should not disparage those who respond aesthetically to such a view of cultural history; as a matter of fact, they have effective and persuasive spokesmen.

Then there are those assailed by the doubt which rings itself around their throats like a hangman's cord never drawn tight, often losing the engagement temporarily but nevertheless returning to the struggle. Perhaps they are simply drawing on the memory of a mother who was "like a white candle in a holy place," which pursues them as Monica pursued Augustine's dreams and waking hours. The image we are suggesting is not that of a manufactured phrase ("we must seek truth," or "values are essential"), but rather that of a person—in some sense a saint—through whom the practice of the Christian faith was made so impressive and persuasive, though to the rebellious sometimes so exasperating, that it would be utterly impossible to blot the image out. We shall hope that among those who accept the wager for the sake of their university, there will be not a few such men and women. For they bring to the enterprise the realism of an experience which will build into it a constant struggle for spiritual adventure.

Thus the reason for the Catholic university's being is not a formula, not a philosophical theory or a theological textbook, not a simply defined task such as teaching values because they are not taught elsewhere. The Catholic university is the consequence of a congruence. It is a corporate resolve to achieve the interpenetration of religious and scientific experience. It is like a great farm on which wheat and corn, and woodland and beasts, draw diversified sustenance from the soil. Of course we know that in order to keep the enterprise going we shall need help. There will be places which some can fill whose participation in, and understanding of, the corporate expression of the Christian faith will be conventional, rooted primarily in custom or heritage. No one will toss them aside contemptuously.

In order to meet all the exacting demands of the disciplines we foster we must associate with ourselves men and women not of our faith, not of our group. This is sometimes wrongly held to imply a watering down of the idea of a Catholic university. Precisely the opposite is true. To be sure, if it did not have a constituent body of scholars such as I have described, if the great majority of those teaching were secularists, a given Catholic university should in all candor select another label, even as some universities founded by Protestants have done. But only a leaven of scholars who have different traditions, ranging from Lutheranism to Zen Buddhism, can provide the breadth of association with the whole human family which is the proper mode of the life of the Church. Indeed it is not too much to say that a Catholic university without such a leaven would be stale bread.

At any rate, we who form a Catholic university strive to deepen our realization of what our acceptance of Pascal's wager means. We are a company of gamblers who believe they have a sure thing. Of course, we need freedom. This requirement is often pointed out by friend and enemy alike, but the matter is not simple. Note that if men do not accept the wager, they must live accordingly, and that is deterministic enough. To be sure, they are free to select almost any way of doing so, but this does not in the end lead to much greater freedom of choice than we have. Whether they elect to follow Nietzsche, Santayana, or Marx or any of a wide number of other choices, it is, however, vital that Catholic Christians have comradeship with them, in order to comprehend the great diversity of our experiences, origins, disciplines, and aspirations, and for the sake of the university itself. To a Catholic, it makes all the difference which side of the wager a man is on, but, above everything, all are members of the human family, guided by conscience and the laws of evidence.

The Catholic university of the present, however, has possibilities of freedom which until recently were not accorded it. The ecclesiastical censor who stopped intellectual traffic when that seemed to him the right thing to do is out of date. During an earlier time he could put Antonio Fogazzaro's *Il Santo* on the Index of Forbidden Books; and inside the beleaguered Catholic fortress it required considerable courage even to ask why. Today the traffic in images and ideas is so dense that regulating it through censorship would be like trying to stop the leaves from falling off the trees during November. That in itself is sufficient reason why men need the wonderful courtesy of a genuine university bent on living up to its name. In it people can differ and debate without losing their tempers and phoning for the police.

It is therefore the function of the Catholic university to replace censorship with criticism. For all who are its members the Church is holy, apostolic. By analogy, Catholic scholarship has the task of discerning what in the continuing life of the mind reflects the tradition and the insight of the Church. No illustration is more indicative of this need than the life story of Teilhard de Chardin. That the censor kept on peeping over his shoulder while he was writing, making publication difficult if not impossible, demurring and yet paradoxically being loving and gentle, is one part of the record. The other part is now much, much more important: If the brilliant Jesuit, looking so far back into the past and so far forward into the future, had had the benefit of truly intelligent criticism from within the university, his books might not reveal some of the weaknesses which are now evident. They would have retained their originality and drive, but they would have profited by awareness of the obstacles in the way. It is now too late, tragically too late, for that; and modern Catholicism has too often been too late. Sharp dissent there must be, even repudiation, in religion as in every other field of study and inquiry. It is the duty of a distinguished modern Catholic university to provide them. For the sake of its own well-being, it must also retain a keen penitential conscience. One thinks again of Pascal:

> All that is in the world is the lust of the flesh, or the lust of the eyes, or the pride of life: *libido sentiendi, libido sciendi, libido dominandi.* Wreatched is the cursed land which these three rivers of life inflame rather than water. Happy they who on those rivers, are not overwhelmed nor carried away, but are immovably fixed, not standing but seated on a low and secure base, whence they do not rise before the light, but having rested in peace stretch out their hands to Him, who must lift them up, and make them stand upright and firm in the porches of the New Jerusalem.

Therefore we who in diverse ways have been prepared for the task of building a Catholic university must draw every consequence from our action. We are no longer locked in a house with drawn blinds, behind which—if we push them back a bit—we can smile a little at the assumed folly of others. We are out in the street, with the traffic and the dust, the neon signs, the poking elbows, the spittle dripping off the curb, the girls wearing dresses that cost $9.95, and the prostitutes who get their mink stoles second-hand. There is no significant book in the bookstalls we do not read and think about; there is no tune we do not try to hum; there is no job that promises to amount to anything we will not roll up our sleeves for. Anybody who wishes to stop at our university house will be welcome; we will listen to everyone who wants to talk. And in these days when the university must do many things which are in the public interest we will pitch in though the work may be distracting and sometimes disappointing.

In short, the men who direct the Catholic universities of the future, or teach in them, will take freedom of inquiry and expression for granted, because only the unfettered mind can be unimpeachable. But on another plane they will understand that of necessity a part of their institutional liberty must now be auctioned off. A university can no longer be what in a Platonic or Newmanist sense it should be. It is inevitably part of the contemporary scene, and quite as necessarily in the public domain. If its faculty are research-minded—and how could they be anything else?—it will respond to a recognized public need for studies which may yield some benefit for mankind or again may not. Who can tell in advance? Or who looking back can decide whether the research undertaken to create the atomic bomb opened a door to disaster? Alas, a modern university is like so much else in the modern world. It does not know what it is doing. And so for this reason one must frankly admit that the farther the Catholic university moves into the public domain the less individualized its character will be, and perhaps even the less discernibly spiritual its orientation will become. For the sake of parity with others it will acquire similarity. All it can really say at this point is that it is following the directives of the Church it presumably serves. Pope John XXIII and the Council he summoned into being said nothing more frequently, or with greater zest, than that the order of change, the technological order, is the realm in which the Church's mission must henceforth be conducted. Obviously therefore the Catholic university must live within that order, and train young people to do so with ever increasing skill.

That there are grave risks here may not be as evident as perhaps it should be. Being in the public domain—being chained, where research is concerned, to tasks which are of direct, immediate interest to the body politic—can act as a curb, or even as a stone around the waist. Let us state the problem at a low level of materialistic concern. A private university always needs more money than it has. After having dealt with the student as a tax-collector does with the citizen, it passes the collection-box around to the corporately or individually wealthy. Then, of course, there is always the state. The university which agrees to do things just because money is available may well be venal. Must the galleon always reach port with the gold? Or should one be squeamish about the blood on the gold? No kind of prostitution could be worse than the prostitution of the university, for this is the real treason of the clerks. Accordingly one must say that although the Catholic university should not shirk its duty within the public domain, it must never be for sale. It is a holy place. It must for weal or woe bear witness. I am convinced that the Catholic people sense this deeply, no matter how like other universities institutions those such as Louvain or Notre Dame may become. For this reason, the real, abiding reason why a Catholic university should exist, the university comes alive and stays alive. It grows mysteriously out of the experience, the desire, the affection, and the awe of people who are the Church.

It is often said, and the observation is pertinent and important, that the existence of a Catholic university will depend on whether academically gifted young people continue to want to come to it even though the financial sacrifice involved is necessarily great. Certainly if they did not, if they wished rather to "escape," the Catholic university would be in considerable peril and there would be no point in trying to conceal the fact. But if the question of finance has been deprived of its sting by increased provision for student scholarships, there is no basis for pessimism on this score, if the university vigorously realizes its opportunity. It is true that there is now a conflict between generations which comes closer to the edge of actual combat than any we have previously had to reckon with in this country. The present situation, at least in the eyes of those of us who must look at it from a distance, seems to derive from a very real awareness of the weight of numbers and the babel which has so little room for one voice.

It seems to me that this feeling should prove less bitter on the kind of Catholic campus I have been describing than elsewhere. But it is true that the traditional environment, which was based on a set of rules designed to provide a discipline making holiness possible, cannot long survive. The rules are, in the minds of undergraduates, enforced *in loco parentis;* and it is precisely the parent from whom the young man or woman seeks to break away. To build a university community will therefore not be easy. It never has been, especially when a major part of the job has been bringing the colleges and the graduate or professional schools into some kind of interlocking relationship. But if those, religious and lay, who give the university its scholarly depth and breadth can reach out to young people with respect, hope, and affection, a measure of contagion will be provided. Only this kind of contagion has ever called a Christian community into being.

Just a word in summary of the argument. When one says that an educational institution needs constantly to bear in mind the relationship between its activity and the life of the total community in which it finds itself, one is talking in peculiarly contemporary terms. Probably eighteenth-century Oxford could not have cared less, and a good case could be made in favor of its position. We cannot make that for ourselves. We are modern and therefore mobile, and in this context there is need for centers of higher learning in which Catholics can muster their strength and gradually acquire that measure of casual certainty about their purpose in the nation which is the indispensable complement of maturity. There is no need to make glowing phrases about the matter. It will be quite sufficient if some generations hence the American Catholic scholar can be nonchalant as he walks about the intellectual scene. He will be as little of a prig, we hope, as Colonel Newcombe was, and as much of an adventurer as Daniel Boone. He will wear the hairshirt of his religious commitment but after washing it he will not hang it on the line.

Men will know without being told that there is a place in his heart to which he withdraws, but realizing that will not lead them to think that there is any kind of pride in him. He will understand that his scholarship, however impressive it may be, is only a segment of the total scholarly endeavor, and that its deep purpose is to sense more acutely the blessing which lies on all Being, all truth about Being, because it is of God.

# Christian Culture
# and Education

"I don't want to ride in a car that goes so fast," an elderly African said in response to an invitation. "I'm afraid my spirit might get left behind." Perhaps a comparable anxiety, at a deeper but still cognate level of concern, was in the minds of the Council Fathers who endorsed those sections of the *Pastoral Constitution on the Church in the Modern World* which deal with education and culture. Manifestly the preservation and development of cultural values have been influenced in our time by forces of a magnitude and diversity probably unparalleled in the history of man. "Probably" seems an appropriate word because we are at present so overwhelmed by the rate of change that we may be unable to sense as clearly as the Council did what might be called the condition of permanence in the cultural life. Doubtless this condition of permanence was easier to manage during some previous eras of rapid shifting of the human dimension, for instance the period of mass migration to the United States. The many millions who passed through Ellis Island certainly found their experiences and their circumstances startlingly strange, but at the same time most of them seem to have vowed to preserve what they considered the abiding values of their cultural traditions.

For us the forces of change have come from so many directions with such speed and impact that almost no one has had a chance to list them in anything resembling a rational order, let alone analyze or understand them. In

George N. Shuster, "Christian Culture and Education," in Charles P. O'Donnell, ed., *The Church in the World* (Milwaukee: Bruce Publishing Co., 1967), pp. 86-98. Reprinted by permission of the publisher.

what now follows by way of comment on how Vatican II drew conclusions from its appraisal of them, no reference will be made to discussions which took place formally or informally prior to the endorsement of the document. These were interesting and upon occasion significant. But for better or for worse, only the naked text is before us.

It seems to me that the Council identified five kinds of cultural change:

First, the demonstrated efficiency and range of scientific thinking, which indeed has come to seem to many the only form in which a valid conceptualization of knowledge can take place.

Second, the tremendous social effect of technological management, based on the invention and exploitation of new means of mechanizing labor and movement.

Third, the resulting conflict between "fully developed" and more "primitive" cultures, both of which terms are used in the context of value judgments which may be superficial and time-bound.

Fourth, the growth of an attitude of mind to which the generic adjective "atheistic" may be attached—an attitude which in its simplest formulation takes it for granted that since man has solved problems of almost cosmic magnitude—an achievement which the *Constitution* candidly recognizes—without any discernible help from God or his spokesmen on earth, there is no longer a compelling reason for taking him or them into serious account.

Fifth, vastly increased participation in cultural goods and activities on a worldwide basis indicates that illiteracy and in a wider sense ignorance can be eradicated and replaced by ability to take part in the general cultural life of mankind.

What one is deeply impressed by in the first instance is the Council's ready acceptance of these changes as forming the framework within which the mission of the Church must henceforth be carried on. Some of us might have anticipated a sprinkle of anathemas, perhaps phrased more in the style of the London *Times* than of *Pravda* or even, let us say, *Ramparts* or the *Wanderer*. But there is none of that, though to be sure the *Constitution* does point to certain "dangers" and counsel avoidance of them. If one compares this *Constitution* with the two volumes of the Proceedings of the Eucharistic Congress which convened in Munich during 1960, ecumenical and contemporary in spirit though much of which was said there happened to be, one is quite literally astonished by the change in tone and temper. What had taken place is of course indicated by the following sentence in the Preface:

> ... this Council can provide no more eloquent proof of solidarity with the whole human family with which it is bound up, as well as its respect and love for that family, than by engaging with it in conversation about these various problems.

How shall we picture for ourselves the part to be taken by the Church in the drama of enfolding cultural conversation? It may serve a useful purpose to consider briefly some of the memorable, now historical efforts to surmount what has so often been called the "ghetto mentality" of post-Tridentine Catholics. I believe that these were primarily three in number, although, to be sure, if the theme were broadened to include socio-political discussion major stress would have to be placed on the German experience of the post-Ketteler period. In the order of chronology, the three were these: first, the fruits of the Oxford Movement and of Newman's conversion, to which may be added the impact of the *Rambler* and the *Dublin Review* as well as the·writings of Friedrich von Hügel; second, the growth of the University of Louvain and the coming into being by reason of Cardinal Mercier's initiative of a vigorous, though relatively abortive, ecumenical movement; and third, the *nouvelle théologie,* long associated by men of my generation with the *Nouvelle Revue théologique* which the Jesuits edited at Liége and which, it may be noted in passing, was not wholly without influence in the United States. All of these had their fruition in the *Constitution,* though not unnaturally the presence at the Council of the Cardinal Archbishop of Malines and of the great French theologians who had for so long a time served by standing and waiting most directly affected the outcome. No writing done in the pre-Conciliar period dealt more perceptively with the relationships between humanistic culture and theology than did that of Jacques Maritain. His deeply perceptive comment on human dignity and on pluralism is particularly memorable. But unfortunately there is little to indicate that these writings had any marked influence on those most responsible for the chapter of the *Constitution* under discussion here.

To return to the question just asked. The answers depend on certain assumptions clearly stated. These are that the Church is divinely commissioned to show men the way to salvation through Jesus Christ, that every human person possesses a dignity which is to be considered inviolate, and that each of us can tragically mar that dignity as incarnate in oneself or incarnate in others. These are the basic axioms from which the reasoning proceeds.

The answers given are:

First, the fact that Christians acknowledge that life on this earth is a pilgrimage "in no way decreases but actually increases the weight of their obligation to work with all men in constructing a more human world."

Second, intellectual and ethical civility is (as Newman so stoutly insisted) an aid to the "freedom from bondage" to evil inclinations which is properly the gift of the Holy Spirit.

Third, the scientific component of contemporary culture may so absorb men's attention that they will tend to be disinterested in or "agnostic about everything else." Nevertheless, science fosters important natural virtues, such as "strict fidelity to truth," and is therefore a handmaiden, when properly understood, to the Church's quest for man's salvation.

Fourth, the Church, active in many disparate cultures and showing great ability to accommodate itself to what is best and most distinctive about them, as its liturgy also indicates, has an opportunity to foster a mutual enrichment of cultures.

Fifth, the "two orders of knowledge," which are faith and reason, must not (the Council here reiterated and amplified the language of the first Vatican Council) lead to disregard "of the autonomy of each other." Indeed, in both cases "let it be recognized that all the faithful, clerical and lay, possess a lawful freedom of inquiry and of thought, and the freedom to express their minds humbly and courageously about those matters in which they possess competence."

Sixth, every human being has a right to profit by the fruits of culture and should be assisted in fostering his ability to exercise it. The duty of a Catholic Christian is positive in the sense, for example, that he should help to wipe out as rapidly as possible the scourge of illiteracy, and negative in the sense that he must abhor discrimination "on the grounds of race, sex, nationality, religion, or social conditions."

So ringing and indeed unprecedented is the endorsement of the right of the scholar to seek truth and to present his findings, subject only to criticism of his competence, that not a few have found it relatively astonishing. Although *aggiornamento* certainly was necessary in order to give this teaching its honored place in a Conciliar declaration, it will not seem very strange even to anyone who has, as I do, only a superficial acquaintance with the thought of St. Thomas. Nevertheless, the context in which this freedom is now placed—a context which the *Constitution* describes with remarkable clarity and completeness—is quite different from any that could have suggested itself to the Angelic Doctor; and it is this difference which lies at the root of the perturbation which not a few feel when brought face to face with the fact that even the *nouvelle théologie* of some years ago is now only partially new. We need not blind ourselves to the probability that a measure of anxiety exists particularly in the United States, where until very recently the training provided in seminaries and religious houses generally was conventional, and where conversation even between priests and Catholic layfolk educated differently has been at best no more than sporadic.

Normally, a Catholic of whatever status in religion has had little opportunity to realize how secular the prevailing culture of the West has become. He knows, of course, that there is more laxity in the area of sexual morality, that the movies and the theater are less wholesome and decent, and that there has been some kind of conflict between theology and science. But that there are many prominent intellectuals and makers of public opinion for whom religion has ceased to be in any genuine sense significant is a fact he can have had little opportunity to discover. As a product of Catholic schooling he might often assume that the Thomistic philosophy provided a solid, dependable jointure of reason and faith. But he cannot be expected to realize that in American philosophy as a whole pragmatism virtually ceased to develop just at the point where its concern with theism seemed likely to prove creative and fruitful or that the several varieties of logical positivism—not all of which were, as Warren Weaver has effectively contended, necessarily anti-religious— were rather suddenly merged in forms of analysis for analysis' sake, in order, it appears, belatedly to get rid of Hegel. Nor could he easily realize that when much Protestant thinking, that of John Dewey for example, veered from Hegelianism to determinism something fateful had happened which would leave a mark temporarily indelible on the American mind.

A comparable development had taken place earlier in Europe, and with it important essays as well as the later correspondence of Newman were devoted either in terms of recognition or of prediction. The thoughtful Catholic scholar of the mid-twentieth century could not avoid seeing that he was living in a diaspora—that the older Catholic peoples of Europe had to a very great and tragic extent lost their faith, except sometimes an elementary form of conformism. For this not only social injustice was responsible, or a too long continued identification of the Church with repression. Among the major causes were certainly a sequence of ideologies nearly all of which were rooted in highly individualistic, rebellious philosophies. The variants of determinism have been many and variously destructive—the determinisms of the class struggle, of race, of the survival of the strong. Yet it must be said candidly that all these things could not have decimated Christendom so savagely had it not been for the rise of the conviction that the problem of evil is beyond solution. It was the powerlessness of the individual in the face of tyranny which was so awesome and awful, so shattering and unnerving an experience. Early Christians were unnerved by it too, as the Book of the Apocalypse bears witness. But men of an era contemporary with our own had doubtless lived too comfortably in the green pastures of a Christendom triumphant over its enemies. That this kind of victory, a welcome gift though it doubtless was, could be considered identical with the Savior's vanquishing of the world, as he defined the world, was a delusion. Too many in the Church thought that if they could somehow cling to the trappings of the Constantinian victory, however tattered, peace would come to them in the end. That is probably why there was no ringing protest against Auschwitz. And this is why Hitler could steadily draw a noose round the throat of the Church, which indeed might well have strangled it.

Does it not upon occasion seem that the Church in the United States has been too optimistic in another sense? It may still be too proudly conscious of its strength. This, of course, we should not disparage. The strength has sound roots. But the spiritual landscape is not dotted with regrettable structures like the Shrine of the Immaculate Conception or even of beautiful ones like the Church of St. John's Abbey. It stretches out to life over a bridge of the bones of saints.

Here, then, is the Council, instead of being dizzy and appalled, as Newman sometimes was, by what could be seen in a glance backwards over the totalitarian years, or discerned from what Western culture was currently saying about itself, calling out not from safe towers or embattlements, but from a place in the streets. "Let us talk to a world without a home about its potential everlasting dwelling in God's bosom. We, the little flock, the *pucillis grex,* mindful of our relationship with the early Christian family, will enter into conversation with the whole of humankind. And to what purpose? Because it has been given to us to show the world the way to salvation through Christ Jesus not merely for the sake of the hereafter, but for the sake also of the here and now. Like Paul we know neither bondsmen nor freemen, we are not afraid of the strength of Athens or the forums of Rome." You may answer that a stout heart is called for, but the Council began this *Constitution* with the word, *Gaudium,* which means joy. To leave the walled towns, the barbed wire, and the palisades behind, and go out to share with all the people, talk with each and everyone of them, do with all of them the things which so badly need to be done! What a young Church this must be, and may God grant that the hearts of the young can accept the challenge.

Lest you think that the authors of the *Constitution* went on some kind of binge, bear in mind that something marvelously akin to Pentecost is always taking place—some manifestation of the life of the *Logos* that is in seed when not in flower. One has to look and listen. Of this we have had no more awesome demonstration than that provided by Jewish women in the pre-Hitler time whose intuitions of the fate which evil had in store for the people from whom they were sprung seem upon reflection so breathtakingly startling. There were not a few and I shall name only four—Simone Weil, Elizabeth-Lasker-Schueler, Edith Stein, Raissa Maritain. On the one hand their sense of impending doom was almost as overpowering as Mary's at the moment of surmisal (of what the Germans so wonderfully call *Ahnung*) of what would befall her Son. They were like the woman who bore the veil on which the Lord Jesus dried his face. Nothing is deeper in the mystery of the Incarnation than the fact that whatever proneness to evil stirs in the heart of man cannot rise to greater heights than did the hatred of the Divine Good for patriotic and therefore worldly reasons in the narrow framework of Palestinian civilization. But, quite astonishing this, the women of whom I have spoken came down strange ways to the feet of God. Simone Weil is the most inspiring fashioner of prayers in our time, and Elizabeth Lasker-Schueler one of that time's most haunting religious poets.

Right under our noses another kind of stirring has been taking place.

Young people on campuses or off may get frightfully fed up on courses in theology. Doubtless they should manifest a greater interest in a treatise on the trinity, but they would perversely rather read *The Portrait of the Artist as a Young Man.* But watch them with CILA in the country of poverty-glutted mountains east of Santiago. See them with the Peace Corps in the slums of Lima. Observe them at work in the decaying cities of this country. There the "people of God" come alive for them, the thought of Christ is real, the vision of a young Church is born, in which everyone—priests, religious, laymen and laywomen—find religion relevant.

It is extremely difficult to comment on the implications of this "coming alive." The creative individual can, of course, find his way. He can, like a young North American friend of mine, throw himself fully into the life struggle of slum dwellers in Colombia, or work for the starving people of Kerala, India. But how do all the societies and sodalities, the councils and fraternities, which we have so laboriously established to serve parishes or ward off "secular" influences, suddenly find the key to cooperating with international liberating efforts, for instance, UNESCO and the UN, or discover how to face the world as it would be if delegates from the People's Republic of China suddenly showed up in New York (as they probably will)? What shall these organizations do? Whatever the answer is, they will need a whale of a lot of preparation. We have spent decades conditioning them one way. It is to be doubted that six months will suffice the other way round. The Holy Family Guild of St. Anselm's will not only undertake to supply flowers for the altar but will be encouraged to take a deep, sincere interest in Christian and Catholic activities elsewhere in the world.

When one thinks of these things and many more besides, the almost aggressive affirmations of the *Constitution* seem to become not flags but lanterns. Souls are to be saved, for time and the timelessness beyond it, within the setting of an industrial and technological culture. The fact that this is an age of machines, chemistry, engineering, medical advance, psychiatric care, did not becloud the outlook of the Fathers or unsteady their hands. They seem not to have worried about whether radioactive waste is harder to get rid of than the dung in cow barns. Their eyes were on the changes which will also bring improvement if we know what to do and do it. There is no dismal science in the *Constitution.* Ignorance, disease, undernourishment can be banished.

Nonetheless, at this point I find a sizeable blank page in this *Constitution.* If Catholic Christians are on the one hand to engage in discussion with the whole human family, and on the other hand to exercise leadership in bringing about some sort of equalization of access to cultural goods, they cannot fragmentize their efforts. They must have centers in which they can deepen their awareness of major issues, engage in fruitful conversation among themselves before they take on the rest of the world, and learn not only how to get their feet wet but how to swim under water. Yet it is precisely here that the Council left an almost blank page. Obviously, the list of such centers must include the universities, for they are the primary scenes of modern cultural confrontation.

This one does not have to prove. *Pacem in terris* set an example by taking it for granted. Naturally, we do not mean that henceforth fruitful dialogue between the people of God and the society in which it exists is to take place in academic language only. Even the world's poor will talk to one another about suffering, sacrifice, joy, longing, kindness, need. Their conversation will run the gamut of the beatitudes and the seven capital sins. Still, it is a world of the abstract intelligence which we and they inhabit; and the burning question is, where shall the Christian formation of that intelligence begin? This is a conundrum which the Council seems not to have taken sufficiently into account. To be sure, education must be viewed in a much broader context, and this becomes clear if one reads the *Constitution* as a whole, and does not concentrate only on culture as we are doing here.

*First, there is the Catholic university.* That there are highly important differences between the mold in which it was originally cast, and in which it is still to some extent confined by canonical regulations, and the mode of institutionalized free conversation which the Fathers so confidently proclaimed, seems quite clear. The original intention certainly was to provide in the form of higher education an instrumentality through which the teaching authority of the Church was to manifest itself. Perhaps one may say not unfairly that what had been visualized was instruction and not research. The soundness of the theological doctrine expounded was to be assured by a professional oath of fidelity to the *Magisterium.* Philosophy was to be Thomistic, with minor deviations permitted to religious orders having traditions of their own. Colleges of medicine and law were to foster the Christian ethic pertinent to these professions. And the basic humanistic concern was to be with "Christian culture."

Already in present practice these restrictions have for all practical purposes been removed or curtailed, sometimes perhaps too hastily and headily. Surely, it would be rather odd if a young man desiring to study the Christian cultural tradition would have to matriculate in the University of Chicago, or a young lady, eager to steep herself in Christian Platonism, could do no better than try to worm her way into the male fortress of Princeton. Curiously enough, though this is not yet quite the case, it almost is. Philosophers one consults indicate that the number of distinguished Thomists is small. Personalism, existentialism, and the philosophy of science are almost as unavoidable on Catholic campuses as are glimpses of the clergy. And though I am a rank amateur in theological matters, it appears to be true that the average university theologian would be hard put to answer the question, to precisely what would an oath bind me, apart from basic and inviolate dogma?

Second, the secular university may be seen as an institution in which Catholic scholarship and commitment are to manifest themselves in the general cultural conversation. Several patterns have emerged: that of the German university, with a Catholic faculty of theology; that of Oxford, with its center serving general Catholic intellectual interests and activities; that of the University of Toronto, having a separate and indeed distinctive Catholic college; and that of a secular university in the United States, offering a "pluralistic" solution of the religious "problem" and sometimes even making it possible to take courses in religion for credit. It is apparent that all of these owe their existence to an amalgam of pastoral and academic concern. But though their disparateness is a sign of life, it is certainly not a proof that the spirit which the *Constitution* would infuse into the family of God will necessarily find the given institutional base everything which could be desired. The situation obviously suggests a need for careful study.

The question whether a Catholic university should exist at all unless it has a clearly defined part to play in the kind of world which the Council has mapped out cannot be answered until the reasons for having such a university have been carefully formulated and discussed. Personally I am sure they can be, but they will be quite different from those which would have seemed appropriate a hundred years ago. They will be good reasons if in the broad overall university community they seem liberating and not obscurantist. Thus one thinks that an excellent case for a law school in a Catholic university can be made, on the ground that the social ethic it professes, being that of the Second Vatican Council, will train young men and women for service in the kind of world which must come to be if the world is to exist at all. Insofar as the United States is concerned, the Catholic university has been based on the belief of the Catholic people that every institution committed to Christ and his Church was necessarily a good thing. This belief will persist, but the commitment must be to the Christian mission of the future and not to the Christian mission of the past.

Although the problem just referred to can be summed up as unfinished business, there can be little doubt, thank God, that by reason of the *Constitution* the cultural mission of the Church has been given a charter by which it can live if the language becomes more than static print. The Church, whose missionary effort brought it during many centuries into loving and healing association with many cultures, so that its gift of adaptation far exceeds that of any other form of society, now has a wonderful mission of reconciliation not merely between nation and nation, or between culture and culture, but also and perhaps especially between the older rural social order and the emerging products of technological change. True enough, the people of God have sometimes slept or, what is worse, had bad dreams. But a great stirring seems to be taking place. Only we must not think (and of course you will not) that we now have the solutions for all problems. The *Constitution* wrote the first page in a new book. It will take a long time until the last page has been written.

# Selected Bibliography
# of George N. Shuster

## Books

1. *Catholic Literature: A Reading List* (with Charles L. O'Donnell). Notre Dame: University of Notre Dame Press, 1914.
2. *The Chief Things About Writing: A Syllabus of Freshman English.* Notre Dame: University of Notre Dame Press, 1917 (2d ed., 1920).
3. *English Literature.* New York: Allyn & Bacon, 1926.
4. *The Hill of Happiness.* New York: D. Appleton & Co., 1926.
5. *Catholic Spirit in America.* New York: Dial Press, 1927.
6. *The Catholic Church and Current Literature.* New York: Macmillan Co., 1930.
7. *The Germans: An Inquiry and An Estimate.* New York: Dial Press, 1932.
8. *Strong Man Rules: An Interpretation of Germany Today.* New York: D. Appleton Century Co., 1934.
9. *Like A Mighty Army: Hitler versus Established Religion.* New York: D. Appleton Century Co., 1935.
10. *Brother Flo.* New York: Macmillan Co., 1938.
11. *Look Away!* New York: Macmillan Co., 1939.
12. *The English Ode from Milton to Keats.* New York: Columbia University Press, 1940.
13. *Germany: A Short History* (with Arnold Bergstraesser). New York: W. W. Norton & Co., 1944.
14. *Cultural Cooperation and the Peace.* Milwaukee: Bruce Publishing Co., 1953.

Prepared by Vincent P. Lannie for *Leaders in American Education,* Seventieth Yearbook of the National Society for the Study of Education, Part II (Chicago: University of Chicago Press, 1971), pp. 304-305.

15. *Religion Behind the Iron curtain.* New York: Macmillan Co., 1954.
16. *In Silence I Speak.* New York: Farrar, Straus & Cudahy, 1956.
17. *Education and Moral Wisdom.* New York: Harper & Bros., 1960.
18. *The Ground I Walked On.* New York: Farrar, Straus & Cudahy, 1961. Rev. ed., Notre Dame: University of Notre Dame Press, 1969.
19. *Unesco: Assessment and Promise.* New York: Harper & Row, 1963.
20. *Albert Gregory Cardinal Meyer.* Notre Dame: University of Notre Dame Press, 1964.
21. *Catholic Education in a Changing World.* New York: Rinehart & Winston, 1967. Notre Dame: University of Notre Dame Press, 1969 (paper).

## Editions

22. Newman: *Prose and Poetry.* New York: Allyn & Bacon, 1925.
23. Thomas Walsh. *The Catholic Anthology.* rev. ed. New York: Macmillan Co., 1932.
24. *Pope Pius XI and American Public Opinion* (with Robert J. Cuddihy). New York: Funk & Wagnalls Co., 1939.
25. *The World's Great Catholic Literature.* New York: Macmillan Co., 1942.
26. *Freedom and Authority in the West.* Notre Dame: University of Notre Dame Press, 1967.

## Translations

27. Siegfried Behn. *The Eternal Magnet.* New York: Devin-Adair Co., 1929.
28. Enrica Ludovica Maria Handel-Mazzetti. *Jesse and Maria.* New York: Henry Holt & Co., 1931.
29. Peter Lippert. *Job the Man Speaks with God.* New York: Benziger Bros., 1936.
30. Paul Schulte. *The Flying Missionary.* New York: Benziger Bros., 1936.

## Introductions

31. Introduction to *The Wall,* by John Hersey. New York: Marchbanks Press, 1957.
32. Introduction to *Sieg Heil!* by Morris D. Waldman. New York: Oceana Publications, 1962.
33. Introduction to *The Problem of Population.* Vol. 3. *Educational Considerations,* edited by George N. Shuster. Notre Dame: University of Notre Dame Press, 1956.

## Articles in Books

34. "Spiritual Autobiography." In *American Spiritual Autobiographies,* edited by Louis Finkelstein. New York: Harper & Bros., 1948.

35. "Christian Culture and Education." In *The Church in the World,* edited by Charles O'Donnell. Milwaukee: Bruce Publishing Co., 1967.
36. "Dr. Bruning's Sojourn in the United States (1935-1945)." In *Staat, Wirtschaft und Politik in der Weimarer Republik: Festschrift fuer Heinrich Bruning,* edited by Ferdinand A. Hermens and Theodor Schieder. Berlin: Duncker & Humbolt, 1967.
37. "The Nature and Development of United States Cultural Relations." In *Cultural Affairs and Foreign Relations,* edited by Paul J. Braisted. Washington: Columbia Books, 1968.